Social Enterprise, Health, and Wellbeing

In recent decades, governments have promoted social enterprise as a means to address welfare and tackle disadvantage. Early academic work on social enterprises reflected this development and engaged with their ability to deliver and create jobs, work towards remedial environmental goals, and address a range of societal challenges. More recently, researchers have started to investigate the broader potential of social enterprise for the wellbeing of people and the planet.

In this context, this book aims to answer the question: In what ways can social enterprises improve the health and wellbeing of individuals and communities? The chapters in this edited collection take different perspectives on assessing how social enterprises address disadvantage and deliver health and wellbeing impacts. Drawing on evidence from international research studies, *Social Enterprise, Health, and Wellbeing: Theory, Methods, and Practice* presents the 'first wave' of innovative research on this topic and provides a platform of evidence to inspire the next generation of scholarly and policy interest.

Drawing on the cutting edge of interdisciplinary research in the field, this book will be of interest to researchers, academics, policymakers, and students in the fields of entrepreneurship, public and social policy, community development, public health, human geography, and urban planning.

Michael J. Roy is Professor of Economic Sociology and Social Policy at the Yunus Centre for Social Business and Health at Glasgow Caledonian University, UK.

Jane Farmer is Professor and the Foundation Director of the Social Innovation Research Institute, Swinburne University of Technology, Australia.

Routledge Studies in Social Enterprise & Social Innovation
Series Editors: Jacques Defourny, Lars Hulgård, and Rocío Nogales

Social enterprises seek to combine an entrepreneurial spirit and behaviour with a primacy of social or societal aims. To various extents, their production of goods or services generates market income which they usually combine with other types of resources. A social innovation consists of the implementation of a new idea or initiative to change society in a fairer and more sustainable direction.

Routledge Studies in Social Enterprise & Social Innovation seeks to examine and promote these increasingly important research themes. It particularly looks at participatory governance and social innovation dynamics in social enterprises and more widely in partnerships involving third sector and civil society organizations, conventional businesses and public authorities. In such perspective, this series aims at publishing both breakthrough contributions exploring the new frontiers of the field as well as books defining the state of the art and paving the way to advance the field.

10. People Centered Social Innovation
Global Perspectives on An Emerging Paradigm
Edited by Swati Banerjee, Stephen Carney and Lars Hulgard

11. Social Innovation in Latin America
Maintaining and Restoring Social and Natural Capital
Edited by Sara Calvo and Andrés Morales

12. Social Enterprise in Western Europe
Theory, Models and Practice
Edited by Jacques Defourny and Marthe Nyssens

13. Social Enterprise in Central and Eastern Europe
Theory, Models and Practice
Edited by Jacques Defourny and Marthe Nyssens

14. Social Enterprise, Health, and Wellbeing
Theory, Methods, and Practice
Edited by Michael J. Roy and Jane Farmer

For more information about this series, please visit: https://www.routledge.com/Routledge-Studies-in-Social-Enterprise–Social-Innovation/book-series/RSESI

Social Enterprise, Health, and Wellbeing

Theory, Methods, and Practice

Edited by Michael J. Roy
and Jane Farmer

NEW YORK AND LONDON

First published 2022
by Routledge
605 Third Avenue, New York, NY 10158

and by Routledge
2 Park Square, Milton Park, Abingdon, Oxon, OX14 4RN

*Routledge is an imprint of the Taylor & Francis Group, an
informa business*

Library of Congress Cataloging-in-Publication Data
A catalog record for this book has been requested

ISBN: 978-0-367-64729-2 (hbk)
ISBN: 978-0-367-64731-5 (pbk)
ISBN: 978-1-003-12597-6 (ebk)

DOI: 10.4324/9781003125976

Typeset in Sabon
by Apex CoVantage, LLC

Contents

List of Figures   viii
List of Tables   ix
Acknowledgements   x
About the Contributors   xi

1 Social Enterprise, Health, and Wellbeing: A Timely
   Topic for Uncertain Times?   1
   MICHAEL J. ROY, JANE FARMER, AND JAMES M. MANDIBERG

SECTION 1
Applying Theory for Insights   25

2 Social Enterprises as Spaces of Wellbeing: A Spatial and
   Relational Exploration of Where and How
   Wellbeing Realises   27
   TRACY DE COTTA, JANE FARMER, PETER KAMSTRA, VIKTORIA
   ADLER, CHRIS BRENNAN-HORLEY, AND SARAH-ANNE MUNOZ

3 Transcending Social Enterprise Understandings—
   Wellbeing, Livelihoods, and Interspecies Solidarity
   in Transformation to Postgrowth Societies   49
   EEVA HOUTBECKERS

4 Community Wellbeing and Social Enterprise: Place,
   Visibility, and Social Capital   67
   SUE KILPATRICK AND SHERRIDAN EMERY

5 Community Economies of Wellbeing: How Social
   Enterprises Contribute to 'Surviving Well Together'   85
   KATHARINE MCKINNON AND MELISSA KENNEDY

SECTION 2

Extending Methodological Frontiers 105

6 Spatialising Wellbeing Through Social Enterprise:
Approaches, Representations, and Processes 107
CHRIS BRENNAN-HORLEY, TRACY DE COTTA, PETER KAMSTRA,
AND VIKTORIA ADLER

7 WISE Working Conditions Matter for Health
and Wellbeing 129
AURORA ELMES

8 Designing Work Integration Social Enterprises That
Impact the Health and Wellbeing of People Living
With Serious Mental Illnesses: An Intervention
Mapping Approach 145
TERRY KRUPA, ROSEMARY LYSAGHT, AND MICHAEL J. ROY

9 'They See People in Need and Want to Help': Social
Enterprise and Wellbeing in Rural Communities 170
SARAH-ANNE MUNOZ

SECTION 3

New Insights for Practice 189

10 How Do Social Enterprises Impact Upon Health and
Wellbeing? Some Lessons From *CommonHealth* 191
GILLIAN MURRAY, MICHAEL J. ROY, RACHEL BAKER, AND
CAM DONALDSON

11 How Do Social Enterprises Influence Health Equities?
A Comparative Case Analysis 210
JO BARRAKET, BATOOL MOUSSA, PERRI CAMPBELL, AND
ROKSOLANA SUCHOWERSKA

12 Working With Care: Work Integration Social Enterprise
Practitioner Labour 230
PERRI CAMPBELL, VIKTORIA ADLER, JANE FARMER,
JO BARRAKET, ROKSOLANA SUCHOWERSKA, AND
JOANNE MCNEILL

13 Meeting People Where They're at: Building an Inclusive
Workplace for Disabled People 249
JILLIAN SCOTT AND ROBERT WILTON

14 Beyond the State of the Art: Where Do We Go Next on
the Topic of Social Enterprise, Health, and Wellbeing? 268
MICHAEL J. ROY AND JANE FARMER

Index 291

Figures

1.1 Pathways between engagement with a social enterprise and health and wellbeing impacts   10
2.1 Mapped micro-geographies of wellbeing at Farm   33
4.1 Social capital map for Farm in City 1   71
4.2 Social capital map for AssistAll in City 2   72
6.1 An early sketch of workplace activities, movements, and wellbeing emergence at Farm from participant observation   111
6.2 Identifying spaces of wellbeing with a simplified map of the WISE   112
6.3 3D wellbeing topographies across the three WISE sites   114
6.4 Integration versus Segregation at Farm WISE, incorporating 2D and 3D visualisation strategies   117
6.5 Delivery journeys   119
6.6 Off-site work locations   120
6.7 Farm bonding networks   123
6.8 AssistAll bridging networks   124
9.1 Types of wellbeing facilitated by a rural community transport social enterprise   179
10.1 Pathways to impact—'sense of purpose' example   201
11.1 A theoretical model of how organisational features affect equities and health equity outcomes   212
14.1 Social enterprise, individual wellbeing, and health   270
14.2 Social enterprises and community-level wellbeing   270

Tables

2.1 Aspects helping wellbeing to realise at Catering and AssistAll social enterprises   32

2.2 Typology of spaces contributing to wellbeing and their key characteristics   39

3.1 Grouped leverage points from 'shallow' to 'deep' leverage   53

7.1 Evaluation of participants and attrition rates from 2017 to 2019   131

7.2 Health and wellbeing quantitative findings   134

8.1 Performance objectives   152

11.1 Summary of case study WISEs   216

11.2 Interviewees by case and participant type   217

Acknowledgements

Jane and Michael would like to acknowledge the hard work and dedication of their friends and colleagues in contributing their chapters to this book, particularly during a global pandemic. Jane would especially like to single out Tracy De Cotta, while Michael would like to extend his particular thanks to Simon Teasdale, Cam Donaldson, and Rachel Baker for their unwavering encouragement and support.

Consistent with the themes of this book, both would also like to recognise the vital efforts of everyone who has worked so hard to support and maintain the health and wellbeing of everyone in their community throughout these tough times.

Michael would especially like to thank his wife Philippa for valiantly putting up with being locked down with him for so long and to apologise once again for being constantly under her feet.

About the Contributors

Viktoria Adler is an anthropologist and an experienced qualitative researcher. Her expertise in (ethnographic) field research spans Australia, Latin America, and Europe. Her interdisciplinary research work focuses on social inequality. Viktoria was part of the 'Mapping the impact of social enterprise on regional city disadvantage' project.

Rachel Baker, PhD, is Professor of Health Economics and Director of the Yunus Centre for Social Business and Health at Glasgow Caledonian University. Rachel's research focuses on public values, resource allocation, and distributional justice. She was co-investigator on the CommonHealth research programme and leads Common Health Assets: a mixed methods realist evaluation and economic appraisal of how community-led organisations impact the health and wellbeing of people living in deprived areas (2021–2024 funded by UK National Institutes of Health Research).

Jo Barraket, PhD, is University Distinguished Professor and Director of the Centre for Social Impact Swinburne at Swinburne University of Technology. She is a political sociologist and Australia's premier researcher of social enterprise. She has research interests in the social economy and the interface between state and civil society in policy design and implementation.

Chris Brennan-Horley is a lecturer in Human Geography and former Australian Research Council DECRA Fellow at the University of Wollongong, Australia. The common thread running through his research is deploying Qualitative GIS as a lively technique for transformative ends. He regularly contributes his mapping expertise to interdisciplinary research teams, most recently for revealing geographies of wellbeing and work in social enterprises.

Perri Campbell, PhD, is the author of Rethinking Young People's Marginalisation: Beyond Neo-Liberal Futures? (2019). Perri writes about young people's civic participation and entrepreneurialism, youth-focused social enterprise programs, and digital technology. She works across the fields of critical youth studies and gender studies to explore what it means to 'grow up' post-Global Financial Crisis and participate in social movements, Occupy and Black Lives Matter, and how organisations like social enterprises respond to social inequity and crisis. She has been an Alfred Deakin Postdoctoral Research Fellow at Deakin University and a Visiting Scholar at the Institute for the Study of Societal Issues at the University of California, Berkeley.

Tracy De Cotta is a Senior Research Assistant in Swinburne University's Social innovation Research Institute and Centre for Social Impact. By trade, Tracy is an urban planner and has had both strategic and statutory consultancy roles in Victorian rural and regional local government areas. Her research covers places and spaces (both physical and digital) and their influence on mental health, wellbeing, and community building.

Cam Donaldson holds the Yunus Chair at Glasgow Caledonian University, where he is Pro Vice Chancellor Research and, from 2010 to 2016, directed GCU's Yunus Centre for Social Business and Health. A health economist, Cam previously held the Health Foundation Chair at Newcastle University, the Svare Chair at University of Calgary, and a professorship at the University of Aberdeen. From 2014 to 2019, Cam led the MRC/ESRC-funded research programme on developing methods for evaluating social enterprises as public health programmes ('CommonHealth'). His work has been recognised through senior investigatorships from the Canadian Institutes of Health Research and the UK's National Institute for Health Research.

Dr Aurora Elmes is a Research Fellow at the Centre for Social Impact (CSI) Swinburne. Her PhD research focused on understanding the effects of a social enterprise on employment, social inclusion, health, and wellbeing, through a three-year evaluation of Australian social enterprise, Vanguard Laundry Services. Since joining CSI Swinburne in 2016, Aurora has worked on multiple social enterprise research projects, focused on impact measurement, resilience, and resourcing. Her research interests include social enterprise, inclusive employment, mental health, and the social determinants of health.

Sherridan Emery is an early career researcher exploring intersections between cultural wellbeing, the arts, and sustainability. Her research focuses on journeys towards a more sustainable future, exploring the idea of wellbeing and reconciliation emerging from arts, cultural, and community participation. As a research assistant at the University of Tasmania in the Faculty of Education and the Peter Underwood Centre for Educational Attainment, Sherridan works across a range of projects that focus on wellbeing in education and social enterprise settings.

Jane Farmer, PhD, is Director of the Social Innovation Research Institute at Swinburne Univerity, Melbourne, Australia. She has a distinguished track record of research in rural health services, innovations in health workforce and technology, community participation, co-production, and social enterprise. She led an Australia Research Council Discovery Project examining the impact of social enterprise on regional city disadvantage and has led a number of large international multidiscipli-nary, multi-site research projects on the topic of innovative approaches to healthcare. Professor Farmer previously worked in Scotland as Co-Director of the Centre for Rural Health Research at the University of the Highlands and Islands. She was then Head of the La Trobe University Rural Health School in Bendigo, Victoria, followed by senior research leadership positions at La Trobe. She has led or participated in several studies in rural maternity care, community hospitals, and rural health services that informed Scottish Government policy.

Eeva Houtbeckers (Dr.Sc.Econ.&Buss.Admin.) is presently on a four-year postdoctoral project funded by Finnish research foundations. She is affiliated with the Department of Design at Aalto University and NODUS sustainable design research group. Eeva's postdoctoral research is an institutional ethnography on post-growth work and livelihood in the global North, inspired by ecofeminist philosophy. She studies Finnish initiatives on degrowth, self-sufficiency, and land and forest commons. Her doctoral dissertation 'Mundane social entre-preneurship' focused on Finnish microentrepreneurs' work in sectors that address sustainability challenges.

Peter Kamstra is a Post-Doctoral Research Fellow at the Swinburne University, Social Innovation Research Institute. Peter uses using mixed methods and spatial data analytics in partnership with multiple social purpose organisations to address Australia's contemporary commu-nity health problems. His work produces applied insights that can be used to improve community mental health services, bushfire emergency response, and drowning prevention. His current research adds context and makes hidden mental health challenges and issues of access to mental health services visible within existing GIS architectures.

Melissa Kennedy teaches and researches in community planning and development at La Trobe University. Her interdisciplinary research focuses on community economies and rural regeneration, with a par-ticular interest in cultural and creative economies. Melissa's research, conducted in Australia, explores how communities are experimenting with revitalisation through global cultural networks, with a focus on collective action and commoning.

Professor Sue Kilpatrick is Professor or Education at the University of Tasmania, Australia. Before semi-retiring, she was Pro Vice-Chancellor

(Students), University of Tasmania, Pro Vice-Chancellor (Rural and Regional) at Deakin University, and Director, University Department of Rural Health, Tasmania. Most of her research applies a social capital framework to health, education, learning for work, and/or community development issues in rural areas. Sue combines her research with community-based regional development roles. She holds a PhD in the economics of education.

Terry Krupa, PhD, FCAOT, is Professor Emerita at the School of Rehabilitation Therapy, Queen's University, Kingston, Ontario, Canada. Dr. Krupa's research has focused on community-based initiatives that improve the health, wellbeing, and full community participation of people with mental illnesses. She has been involved in the development and evaluation of work integration social enterprises (WISE) in Canada, Bangladesh, and Kenya. Her work has explored, for example, the impact of WISE on stigma and identity development, best practices in WISE implementation, the transition of traditional vocational rehabilitation programs to WISE, and perceptions of social business by community employers. Dr Krupa was the lead researcher in a study of social businesses for the Mental Health Commission of Canada.

Rosemary Lysaght, PhD, is Associate Director of the School of Rehabilitation Therapy at Queen's University. She is an occupational therapist and has been an educator and researcher for over 20 years. As a practitioner, Dr. Lysaght worked with persons with serious mental illness, intellectual disabilities, and other work-related challenges in programs addressing employment and community living. Her research focuses on work participation and social inclusion of marginalised populations. She has led research and evaluation studies in Canada and the United States and studied social enterprise models in domestic and international settings.

James M. Mandiberg, PhD, is Associate Professor and Chair of the Organizational Management & Leadership Master's degree programme at the Silberman School of Social Work at Hunter College and a faculty member of the CUNY Graduate Center's PhD program in Social Welfare. His joint PhD in Organizational Psychology and Social Work is from the University of Michigan. He held faculty positions at Shikoku Gakuin University in Japan, the University of Wisconsin-Madison, Columbia University, and was a visiting professor at Sophia University in Tokyo prior to his current positions. His research is focused on social enterprise and social innovation.

Assoc. Prof. Katharine McKinnon is the Director of the Centre for Sustainable Communities at the University of Canberra. She is a human geographer whose work engages with community economies, gender, development, and care. For the past 20 years, she has worked with a broad range of communities in Australia and the Asia-Pacific, engaging in qualitative and participatory social research. Katharine has published extensively on topics of community learning and development, and economies of care. She is the author of *Birthing Work: The Collective Labour of Childbirth (2020) and Development Professionals in Northern Thailand: Hope, Politics and Practice (2012)*.

Joanne McNeill, PhD, is a Senior Researcher, Impact Innovation with the Yunus Centre, at Griffith University in Australia. Her research and professional experience engage with new economy practices and concepts and with social innovation eco-systems. She is a Founding Director of the Community Economies Institute and has been a Churchill Fellow since 2008.

Batool Moussa has worked in law, public health advocacy, and behavioural sciences research. She holds a B Arts/B Laws (Hons) and a Master of Social Policy. She is currently a research assistant at the Centre for Social Impact (CSI), Swinburne University of Technology.

Sarah-Anne Munoz, PhD, is a health geographer, Professor of Rural Health and Acting Head of the Division of Rural Health and Wellbeing at the University of the Highlands and Islands (UHI). She has a PhD in Geography from the University of Dundee. She has worked in rural health geography with UHI since 2007. Sarah-Anne's research is focused on two areas: i) community engagement, co-production, and participation in rural healthcare services and ii) the relationships between landscape, nature, the outdoors, and wellbeing. She is primarily a qualitative researcher with expertise in participatory, creative, and mobile methods.

Gillian Murray, PhD, is a Research Fellow at the Yunus Centre for Social Business and Health at Glasgow Caledonian University. Her research focuses on the history of Scotland's social economy from the 1970s. From 2014 to 2018, Gillian worked on the CommonHealth research programme. Since then, working closely with the GCU Archive Centre, she has been PI on a Scottish Government funded project to develop the Social Enterprise Collection (Scotland).

Michael J. Roy, PhD, is Professor of Economic Sociology and Social Policy at the Yunus Centre for Social Business and Health at Glasgow Caledonian University, Glasgow, UK. He leads the Social Economy Research Group at GCU and is internationally respected for his research on social enterprise, health, and wellbeing, on 'ecosystems' of support for social enterprise and social entrepreneurship, and for his critique of innovative funding mechanisms such as Social Impact Bonds. He is Editor-in-Chief of *Social Enterprise Journal*, Associate Editor of the *Journal of Social Entrepreneurship*, and has published extensively in major scientific journals, including *Stanford Social Innovation Review, Public Management Review, Journal of Social Policy, Review of Social Economy*, and *Social Science and Medicine and Health and Place*. His research has been funded by a range of major funders including the Economic and Social Research Council, Scottish Government's Chief Scientist Office, National Institutes for Health Research, Australian Research Council, and the Canadian Federal Government.

Jillian Scott is a recent graduate of McMaster University's School of Earth, Environment & Society's Masters of Geography program in Hamilton, Ontario, Canada. Her MA research combined her interests in social sustainability and inclusive workplaces with her 20-plus years of experience working as an American Sign Language interpreter in a variety of community settings. Jillian is thrilled to contribute this, her first co-authored published work, to this fascinating collection of research and ideas.

Dr Roksolana Suchowerska is Research Fellow at the Centre for Social Impact, Swinburne University of Technology. Her research examines the intersections between public, private, community, and social enterprise sector efforts to address social and economic disadvantage. Roksolana completed her PhD in 2017 at the University of Melbourne (School of Social and Political Sciences). Prior to academia, Roksolana worked in Australian Industry Participation Policy at the Australian Department of Industry.

Robert Wilton is a professor in the School of Earth, Environment & Society at McMaster University. His research focuses on understanding the social geographies of people living with disability, mental ill health, and addiction. His research is broadly concerned with the social geographies of disabled people and the barriers they face with respect to social inclusion and belonging. He has led, and collaborated on, numerous research projects over the past two decades examining disabled people's experiences finding and keeping paid employment in both market and social economies; accessing and maintaining housing; and negotiating state benefits systems.

1 Social Enterprise, Health, and Wellbeing

A Timely Topic for Uncertain Times?

Michael J. Roy, Jane Farmer, and James M. Mandiberg

Introduction

When we first had the idea for this book, just like everyone else we did not expect the world to be gripped by a global pandemic. In any number of different ways, COVID-19 has brutally exposed just how the economy and the health and wellbeing of the population are intimately intertwined. Although they were clearly apparent before the present crisis, deeply entrenched forms of inequality, especially in relation to health and wellbeing outcomes, have been brought to the fore of public consciousness like never before. As a result, there has been an incessant clamour for new ways of working and organising the economy. In the vein of imagining a better future, rather than simply re-erecting the same models that were considered not to work very well for the great majority of people, 'social enterprise' has been presented as having a critical role to play in the post-COVID-19 recovery (Gallick, 2021; Hermant, 2021; OECD, 2020).

Drawing on a number of prominent research projects, in this book, we present what could be termed the 'state of the art' of research on social enterprise, health, and wellbeing with a view to stimulating interest in generating the next wave of research in this field. In this opening chapter, we will introduce social enterprise and its emergence; summarise evidence about social enterprise, health, and wellbeing; highlight why this is a significant topic with important avenues for further exploration; and introduce some of the key themes that we see recurring throughout the book.

The Rise of Social Enterprise

Organisations combining commercial and social missions have been with us for centuries, but in recent decades, governments internationally have started to explicitly promote 'social enterprise,' often as a welfare policy instrument for transitioning individuals and communities out of

DOI: 10.4324/9781003125976-1

disadvantage (Barraket, 2014; Farmer *et al.*, 2016; Muñoz *et al.*, 2015; Teasdale, 2010). Acknowledging that social enterprise is an inherently contested concept, varying with history, geography, culture, and context (Defourny *et al.*, 2020; Kerlin, 2013; Teasdale, 2012), here we define social enterprise as 'organisations with an explicit aim to help the community, initiated by a group of citizens and in which the material interest of capital investors is subject to limits,' and which place 'a high value on their autonomy and on economic risk-taking related to ongoing socio-economic activity' (Defourny and Nyssens, 2006, p. 5).

Social enterprises exist worldwide, operate in most industrial sectors of the economy, and manifest in multiple shapes and sizes. Contemporary social enterprises are the descendants of the first cooperative forms of business which were founded in the late 18th century, emerging as a reaction to the grim working conditions, social upheaval, and power inequities of the Industrial Revolution. More recently, terms such as community business, community enterprise, social venture, or even 'affirmative business' (particularly in North America) have been used to capture the idea of trading for a social purpose. Global figure and Nobel Peace Laureate, Muhammad Yunus conceptualises his particular brand of 'social business' as targeted to address a social problem, financially sustainable and with profits generated to be reinvested in the business and aimed at social impact, with no financial dividend for business owners (Yunus *et al.*, 2010). A variety of terminology is used to capture the social enterprise sector in different countries—for example, Francophone and Hispanophone countries use the terms '*economie sociale*' (social economy) and '*economie solidaire*' (solidarity economy) (Utting, 2015) to describe trading for social purpose.

Broadly speaking, there are two main traditions of social enterprise apparent in contemporary academic discourse (Defourny and Nyssens, 2010) which evolved more or less independently of each other. On the one hand, there is an Anglo-American Business School perspective that emerged from social enterprise education courses at, for instance, Harvard Business School in the early 1990s (Austin and Rangan, 2019), from social entrepreneurship education at the Fuqua School of Business at Duke University (Dees, 1998), and the Skoll Centre at Oxford University. This tradition, spread across the world through social innovation networks such as Ashoka (Drayton, 2011; Teasdale *et al.*, 2020), often conveys social enterprise as driven by the work of charismatic, 'heroic' social entrepreneurs who found and run social businesses (Ruebottom, 2013). The second tradition is rooted in the work of the EMES (*EMergence d'Entreprise Sociale en Europe*) international research network which began in Europe during the 1990s (Borzaga and Defourny, 2001; Defourny and Nyssens, 2006). Rather than focusing on outstanding individuals, this tradition links back to cooperative origins, emphasising the importance of the collective, democratic governance, and meaningful involvement by intended beneficiaries in the operation of social enterprises.

Most of the chapters in this book discuss social enterprise activity in Scotland, Canada, and Australia. These countries represent varying specific country contexts but share a relatively consistent notion of social enterprise as an organisational form. Scotland is regularly presented as having 'the most supportive environment in the world' for social enterprise (Roy *et al.*, 2015) with an ambitious ten-year strategy for social enterprise development co-produced with sector representatives (Scottish Government, 2016). Although there now exists clear policy identifying the envisaged contribution of social enterprise in Scotland's economic and social fabric, the term 'social enterprise' arrived surprisingly late to Scotland's policy discourse, almost a full decade after then UK Prime Minister Tony Blair recognised its potential to operationalise his 'Third Way' New Labour Government agenda bridging socialism and capitalism (Haugh and Kitson, 2007). Social enterprise in contemporary Scotland is the latest incarnation of a 'community business' tradition (Murray, 2019) designed to address community economic development.

Meanwhile, in Australia, interest in social enterprise has waxed and waned, and currently the interest varies between the different states. Barraket and colleagues stated that social enterprise only started to emerge during the 2000s in response to a mix of federal and state government policies to stimulate non-governmental organisations to provide social services and to diversify their income streams (Barraket *et al.*, 2010). The state of Victoria is currently regarded as the most active for promoting and incentivising social enterprise development with recent policies promoting social procurement among a range of pro-social enterprise measures (Barraket *et al.*, 2017).

Like Australia, enthusiasm to support social enterprise differs markedly between provinces of Canada, with their different cultures shaping how social enterprise is conceptualised and enacted. There is a strong emphasis on the social economy tradition in Francophone Quebec (Mendell and Neamtan, 2010; Quarter *et al.*, 2009), while Anglophone provinces such as Alberta and Ontario tend to look to the United States and Anglo-American traditions. Social enterprise has recently been formally recognised as a significant policy instrument in Atlantic Canada (Lionais, 2015), with new provincial policies in places including in Nova Scotia, which have a long history of innovative community economic development approaches.

The development of social enterprise practice in the last 30 years has seen a parallel rise in academic research interest. Reflecting the field's influence from policy movements, much of the emphasis of early research about social enterprise featured *defining* and *counting* social enterprises and rudimentary attempts to *measure their impact*. As policy interest has evolved to apply social enterprise to address specific societal needs, such as to create jobs or address environmental goals, so too research interest has moved to examine the role of social enterprise in these areas. While past studies have considered the impacts of social enterprise on individuals, communities, and regions, most recently there has been interest from policymakers and researchers about roles for social enterprise at the level of the political economy. The role of social enterprise in wider economic discussions is one of the themes picked up in different chapters across this book, and we will reflect more upon this in the concluding chapter.

The Growth of Work Integration Social Enterprise

One type of social enterprise that has come to the forefront as a policy tool for leveraging individual and community benefit is the work integration social enterprise (WISE). Several of the studies covered in this book feature WISEs. WISEs tend to be established to prepare people deemed as having insufficient capability to enter the open labour market, providing *pathways* to mainstream employment (Campi *et al.*, 2006; Spear and Bidet, 2005; Vidal, 2005), or providing *alternatives* to mainstream employment. WISEs are sometimes termed 'social firms'—a concept that captures broadly similar types of organisations (Warner and Mandiberg, 2006).

Those proposed to benefit from WISEs through gaining work experience, skills, and employment could include people who: have lower educational attainment or lack networks; experience disabilities or long-term illness; or are exiting institutions such as prison or mental health facilities. With experiencing gaps in their capabilities, such people often also experience work exclusion due to stigma. In their enabling role, WISEs could be regarded as 'special' workplaces established to address the failure of mainstream organisations to accommodate the inclusion of participants who need particular supports for periods of time or ongoing, including mentoring and flexibility in roles or working conditions (Evans and Wilton, 2019).

Such special workplaces are needed because the conditions of capitalism generally mean that only those who can comply or 'compete' effectively will fit within the mainstream system. Capitalist production demands speed and efficiency as necessary qualities of workers, with work defined into specified roles that are not easily modifiable to accommodate diverse capabilities. With the development of capitalism and industrialisation, those who were considered incapable were often consigned to institutions and undertook work within these. Inmates of prisons or asylums were generally required to work, including on farms and in workshops and factories within the institutions, growing and making the things needed by them. Such 'required labour' by people experiencing poverty and disability, in institutions and communities, has a mixed history. The requirement to labour is recognised as exploitative, but there is also recognition that involvement in work can support recovery and wellbeing. Required labour in institutions evolved into remedial sheltered workshops, a now-obsolete model where portions of a production process are subcontracted to the workshop to be performed by people with disabilities. In sheltered workshops, the workers are isolated from non-disabled workers and the general population, the type of work is limited, people are paid by how efficient they are rather than the hours they work, and the work is typically repetitive and boring. In some circumstances, sheltered workshops have been replaced by placing workers with a disability into competitive jobs, supported in those jobs by counsellors (Murphy and Rogan, 1995). Some sheltered workshops have evolved into WISEs, with the isolation of the workshop replaced by embedding people with disabilities with non-disabled people in forms of community businesses (Krupa *et al.*, 1999, 2003).

The development of the WISE as a coherent model draws from multiple prior traditions. Perhaps the earliest long-standing example of what today is called a WISE is the Salvation Army's repair and sale of donated materials, initially in London and beginning in 1865. This and other similar early examples of the charity shop (United Kingdom)/thrift shop (United States)/opportunity shop (op-shop) (Australia) model provide a prototype internationally for social purpose businesses that provide work opportunities for people with varying capabilities. Work is not subject to the pressures of efficiency, and the workforce is often a mix of people who experience workforce disadvantages alongside those who do not.

Early examples of charity shops such as those of the Salvation Army were initially created with religious motivations. Social service organisations, secular and faith-based, took longer to recognise that there could be a role for social purpose business in the wellbeing and recovery of disadvantaged people. Required labour in institutions and asylums for people with mental illnesses and disabilities became industrial therapy programs, with the view that work was therapeutic (Black, 1970). Once deinstitutionalisation began internationally in the post-Second World War period, community-based industrial therapy-like sheltered workshops became a dominant model. These were often associated with vocational readiness evaluation programs that purported to be able to determine what kinds of work could be performed by people experiencing various forms of disadvantage.

The relative failure of these models (Mandiberg, 2012) led to two approaches to work for those disadvantaged in the mainstream system. The first approach, generally called 'supported employment,' found people jobs with competitive employers, with the workers trained and supported on the job by social service staff until they could perform the tasks independently. This model has the limitation that workers need to conform to the inflexible requirements of the job. The second approach was to generate businesses, controlled by social service organisations, that could provide training and long-term employment, adjust work to fit worker capability, ensure interaction with the broader community to mitigate stigma, and balance the capabilities of disadvantaged workers by hiring other employees with complementary abilities. These practices have become standard in WISEs (Mandiberg and Edwards, 2016).

In the 1960s and 1970s, WISEs began to be created internationally. Examples that developed and thrive to this day include the Minnesota Diversified Industries in the United States, a manufacturing WISE employing people with a disability and non-disabled workers. It has prospered in part through an ongoing contract with the U.S. Postal Service to manufacture plastic bins (Du Rand, 1990), an early example of what today is called *social procurement*, or the capitalising of WISEs through favourable supportive contracts with governments and corporations (Barraket *et al.*, 2015). Also begun in the 1970s, former patients and staff of the San Giovanni Hospital in Trieste, Italy, created a cooperative to clean public buildings. Other cooperative businesses of former patients and staff in Trieste soon followed, over time including restaurants, cafés, a hotel, a childcare centre, a furniture business, and others (Mezzina, 2014). Many of these have prospered to this day, and the model they created, *social cooperatives*, has become a dominant model of WISEs in continental Europe (Defourny *et al.*, 2014; Laville *et al.*, 2006; Spear and Bidet, 2005).

Applying Social Enterprise for Impact

Based on the growth of social enterprise and increasing evidence of its potential impacts for disadvantaged individuals and communities, governments began to embrace the idea of instrumentally applying social enterprise. It represented a novel way to address social ills and is infused with ideas of mutual support and co-operation from its community and cooperative roots while also compatible with neoliberal ideals of self-help, engagement in work, and entrepreneurialism. Since the 1990s, some governments internationally have experimented with incentivising growth of the social enterprise sector, including WISE, through targeted funding streams, loans, establishing, and encouraging the formation of social enterprise networks and intermediary organisations, and through enabling welfare clients to use their own self-directed grants to 'purchase' experiences at social enterprises.

An excerpt from the State Government of Victoria (Australia) Social Enterprise Strategy is emblematic of how contemporary governments construe social enterprise within welfare policy as a way to engage people of different capabilities in work, to progress inclusion, and with the potential to impact at scales of individual, community, and region:

> Social enterprise activity improves workforce participation, often for the most disadvantaged in our community. The efforts of social

enterprises also improve social cohesion, a key asset culturally and economically. They create jobs and boost productivity by assisting more Victorians into work and by delivering innovative solutions to some of our most complex problems. Their reach extends right across the state, employing people from disadvantaged groups and regions.

(Victoria State Government, 2017, p. 8)

Such policy is built on the premise that having a job is an effective way of accessing multiple direct and indirect benefits. It provides income and something to do, provides structure and routine, social connection, goal-setting and achievement, identity, and physical activity. Jahoda (1981) argues it is this wide range of social and psychological benefits that means people prefer to work, even when working conditions are relatively poor, because 'unemployment is psychologically destructive' (p. 188).

Exploring work in WISEs, Cooney (2011) suggests that low rates of pay are a significant challenge. She found, too, little evidence that job experience from WISE employment provided pathways to 'mainstream' employment. Nonetheless, Cooney concludes that within prevailing thinking 'The workfirst welfare ideology posits that any job is a good job and is likely to lead to a better job over time' with 'the poor . . . encouraged to work in any job available' (Cooney, 2011, pp. 186–189). Canadian researchers Evans and Wilton (2019) conclude that valuing work has become so pervasive in contemporary society that people associate employment with acceptance as a 'legitimate citizen.' In their study of people with mental illnesses working in social enterprises, they attribute some of the positive outcomes found to employees perceiving themselves as useful to society because they have a job. Evans and Wilton suggest this is one manifestation of a shift in thinking from a collective to a self-directed society:

shift from 'welfare' to 'workfare' . . . has reconstituted long-standing socially conservative concerns regarding the 'moral hazard' of welfare dependency and spurred a reframing of the problem of unemployment: no longer seen as a by-product of economic restructuring, unemployment is understood as the direct result of the personal failings, deficits, and limitations of the unemployed themselves.

(Evans and Wilton, 2019, p. 91)

Valued for its role in individual self-improvement, social enterprise is also proposed as significant for addressing disadvantage at place, community, or regional levels. The encouragement of social enterprise in the Highlands and Islands region of Scotland provides a good example (Social Value Lab, 2019). In this rural area, the local development agency has long embraced the social enterprise sector as providing work opportunities for vulnerable people in fragile community settings, congruent with the sustainability ethos of the region (Kelly *et al.*, 2019). In marginal places, social enterprise can provide economic and social stimulus through providing paid work and skills enhancement at community and regional scales while simultaneously providing access to needed goods and services (Bosworth *et al.*, 2019).

In countries with different political drivers to neoliberal Australia, Canada, and the United Kingdom, which are prominent settings for the research in this book, social enterprises may have similar benefits but arising from different ideological roots. For example, as expressions of collectivism and solidarity through alternative forms of economic organising in areas recovering from war and/or having suffered from colonial oppression (e.g. in Latin America) (Calvo and Morales, 2017; Peredo and McLean, 2010; dos Santos and Banerjee, 2019).

Social Enterprise, Health, and Wellbeing

Thus far, we have mainly reflected that social enterprise has proposed economic and social benefits, but now we turn to considering why there has also come to be an interest in social enterprise as having health and wellbeing impacts. We first discuss how we understand the concepts of health and wellbeing and then consider research to date regarding social enterprise, health, and wellbeing. Others writing chapters in this book may use varying terminology and conceptualisations (particularly regarding wellbeing), but these will be explained in their specific chapters.

We understand health according to the World Health Organisation's (WHO, 1948) definition as 'a state of complete physical, mental and social wellbeing and not merely the absence of disease or infirmity.' This definition embraces multiple perspectives, including social attributes. Despite this, in day-to-day parlance, the idea of health tends to have clinical connotations and to be overly associated with (absence of) physical medical conditions. Due to its scientific underpinning and disciplinary stance, health (in a Western biomedical paradigm) as a set of practices tends to align with a quantitative stance of measuring episodes of care, levels or acute-ness of conditions, lengths of stay in the hospital, quantities of drugs prescribed, and so on. This capacity for measurement enables biomedical health to be neatly legitimised as 'scientific' and 'objective,' giving its resolution or treatment a tangibility appreciated by bureaucracies used to paying by episodes of care or quantities of drugs.

This tangibility of medical outcomes is in contrast to social outcomes such as sense of belonging, feelings of self-worth, or security which may arise from social enterprise engagement. Intangible, these are harder impacts to measure convincingly, and they align somewhat uncomfortably with standard outcomes-based evaluation systems.

Further, biomedical understandings of health tend to construe health as a resource residing at the level of the individual (Catlaw and Sandberg, 2018).

According to tenets of health promotion, individuals can reduce their risk of poor health by deciding to eat more healthily, take more exercise, or grow their knowledge. While we cannot dismiss this notion altogether, focusing on risk factors alone ignores or obfuscates the structural elements that influence health at a societal or group level, such as culture, peer and family pressure, or accepted local norms. For its very measurability and the potential to align inputs with outcomes, and with individuals, health status is an attractive indicator, also meaning that financial costs versus benefits can be tallied. This ready facility for measurement and costing could be one reason that policymakers and academics are interested in the role of social enterprise in affecting health outcomes. That social enterprise could be viewed as a health 'treatment' is also a useful idea for social enterprise practitioners who need to convince governments to fund them and for researchers who can apply to more lucrative health funding sources to support their research. However, the path from social enterprise to health has been unclear and hard to unpack, making this a complex area of study.

There are challenges of proving one clear-cut causal path from social enterprise to health outcomes. The idea of 'social determinants of health'—with relevant variables including income, education, housing, access to public spaces, employment and conditions of work—is well established (Marmot and Wilkinson, 2006; Solar and Irwin, 2010), with good access to these resources associated with better health measured as freedom from illness and longevity. However, the largely qualitative, exploratory research and inductive analysis regarding health impacts and outcomes of social enterprise has, to date, tended to surface a range of descriptive, fuzzy, benefits: see the 'intermediate effects' in Figure 1.1 (adapted from Roy *et al.*, 2014). This state of affairs has led to the almost overwhelming conclusion that social enterprise is beneficial to health. However, there is still a stubborn lack of precision about the extent to which social enterprise produces direct health benefits (and which these would be) versus indirect benefits via the income, access to housing, employment, or training generated by working at a social enterprise. Although such dissection may seem academic at times, it is significant to identify pathways from social enterprise to health outcomes and which outcomes attach to which antecedent variables. A framework or theory derived from such dissection would also make it easier to compare social enterprise with other types of public health intervention. Exploring this 'black box' of variables, pathways, and causation processes is one of the themes of this book.

One promising conceptual space within which to explore and analyse the 'black box' between social enterprise and health impacts is the idea of wellbeing. Wellbeing suffers from being frequently added onto the word health (i.e. 'health and wellbeing'), as if—it seems—to extend the notion of health beyond the physical and biomedical, to include social

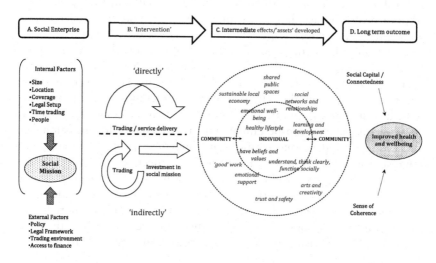

Figure 1.1 Pathways between engagement with a social enterprise and health and wellbeing impacts

Source: Adapted from Roy *et al.* (2014)

and psychological dimensions of health. Established thinking distinguishes between objective wellbeing (measurable via social or standard of living indicators) and subjective wellbeing or self-reported feelings and perceptions: for example, feelings of happiness, belonging, or self-worth (Fleuret and Atkinson, 2007). Relatedly, wellbeing can be examined at individual, community, and regional/national scales, while Prilleltensky (2005) suggests three sites of wellbeing as personal, relational, and collective, reflecting that wellbeing of groups may emerge as more than simply the sum of population wellbeing.

There has been a dramatic increase in interest by academics, policymakers, and civil society in the concept of wellbeing in recent years (Bache and Scott, 2018). Following the Commission on the Measurement of Economic Performance and Social Progress involving leading economists Joseph Stiglitz, Amartya Sen, and Jean-Paul Fitoussi (Stiglitz *et al.*, 2009), the OECD (2019), for example, developed the Better Life Index which has 11 topics of material living conditions (housing, income, and jobs) and quality-of-life indicators (community, education, environment, governance, health, life satisfaction, safety, and work–life balance) and provides rich-country comparisons of wellbeing. There has been considerable interest in the fact that, despite growing wealth, people in rich countries are not getting happier; it has been known for several decades, for example, that a focus on measures such as Gross Domestic Product

(GDP) does not guarantee advances in feelings of 'wellbeing' for people as they earn more, at least beyond a relatively minimal level (the so-called 'Easterlin Paradox'—see Easterlin 1974, 1995). And yet, the focus of rich-world national economies (and public policies) remains firmly focused—almost obsessively—upon growing GDP, rather than focusing on the wellbeing of people and the planet (Büchs and Koch, 2017; Dalziel *et al.*, 2018). Interest has turned in some countries (e.g. New Zealand, Scotland, Iceland, Wales, and most recently Finland) to the improvement of wellbeing as a central socio-economic policy priority, as an alternative to focusing solely upon hard economic measures such as GDP (Gregory, 2019; Hough-Stewart *et al.*, 2019; Trebeck, 2020). Although the Easterlin Paradox is regularly disputed, it also generates a discussion that wellbeing has self-generative elements beyond tangibles like income. Drawing from the 'positive psychology' movement, this stream of thinking has encouraged commentary and research about subjective wellbeing and how people could improve their own feelings of wellbeing (Fleuret and Atkinson, 2007).

For the purposes of this introductory chapter, we explain and understand wellbeing based on the ideas and conceptualisation of Atkinson (2013) who (drawing on an ancient tradition that stretches back to Aristotle) discusses an individual's experience of wellbeing as having what it takes 'to lead a good and flourishing life' (p. 137) or, as Andrews *et al.* (2014, p. 212) say, wellbeing is about 'being-well: content . . . and in a good place in life.' Atkinson highlights that wellbeing is not static, a set outcome or 'sets of entities to be acquired as internalised qualities of individuals' (Atkinson, 2013, p. 142), but rather fluid and fluctuating over time and influenced by relationships with people, materiality, and culture with wellbeing as an 'assemblage,' if you will:

> wellbeing is always and necessarily situated and relational, an effect of mutually constitutive interactions amongst the material, organic and emotional dynamics of places.
>
> (Atkinson, 2013, p. 138)

This way of understanding wellbeing requires a shift in thinking from the individual acquisition of attributes, to how to enhance the social and material environment, and how to enable interactions between people and their social and material worlds so that wellbeing is enhanced. The best way to address wellbeing, in short, is to address those aspects that evidence suggests assist wellbeing generation. This applies at the level of societal structures and policies, at organisational level about designing jobs and workplaces, and at group and community level, where attention can be paid to connecting, caring, helping each other to self-actualise, and to feel secure.

While unwilling to limit or restrict wellbeing to a set of components, Atkinson acknowledges that a framework can be useful for research purposes 'at least in the medium-term. . . [to] . . . enable the measurement of wellbeing through which to identify trends and associations and to evaluate interventions' (Atkinson, 2013, p. 139). With Sebastian Fleuret, Atkinson developed 'spaces of wellbeing' theory (Fleuret and Atkinson, 2007) which will be explored later in this book. Taking a geographical and relational perspective, the theory suggests that wellbeing forms in and through 'spaces' that help to realise social integration, capability, security, and therapy. 'Spaces,' in this sense, are relationally formed from assemblage (or bricolage) of components that make up our lived experiences. Built from key theories of wellbeing including the human capabilities approach (Sen, 1992) and relative standards theory (Diener and Lucas, 2000), the attraction of Atkinson's understanding of wellbeing, and spaces of wellbeing theory in particular, is that it is transdisciplinary and applicable across different contexts and paradigms. Recently, Atkinson (2020) has voiced frustration with the dominant ways in which wellbeing is conceptualised and practised, suggesting it may even have 'toxic' effects, mainly due to its mobilisation emphasising the need to 'perform a competent self' and detracting from structural and ideological issues that influence individual, relational, and collective wellbeing. Indeed, the fact that there are different understandings of wellbeing which can be mobilised to suit different agendas makes the 'politics of wellbeing' an inherently contentious topic (Bache and Scott, 2018). Notwithstanding these controversies, we continue to find wellbeing a useful concept for understanding social enterprise impacts, particularly as the interdisciplinary nature of the concept of wellbeing (Fleuret and Atkinson, 2007) is well suited to the hybridity of social enterprise forms and effects.

As social enterprise practice and research moves to a desire to understand the wider benefits of social enterprise—that is, beyond jobs, some income, and work experience—wellbeing (and in its relationship to health) could represent a useful pathway, acceptable to policy, through which to express both benefits and causation. Crudely, the challenge at this stage is twofold: first of all, to pin down the 'theory of change' whereupon social enterprises impact upon wellbeing and thereafter health (at individual and community levels); and second to identify and somehow measure this or at least to make wellbeing components more tangible so that changes can be appreciated. In providing the very latest research, and drawing on innovative methods, this book makes considerable headway in addressing these two challenges. Before turning to the broad content of the book, we next turn attention to the established 'state of the art' of what has become known about social enterprise, health, and wellbeing.

The State of the Evidence About Social Enterprise, Health, and Wellbeing

A small number of reviews in the last decade considered social enterprise, health, and wellbeing, each with different foci. Roy *et al.* (2014) examined social enterprise as a public health intervention using a systematic review methodology, finding two 'high-quality' studies about physical health changes and five studies examining mental or psychological health impacts. Simultaneously, all studies included in the review provided evidence of social benefits including employment, involvement, and improvement of living conditions, which Roy *et al.* (2014) categorised within three domains of 'social determinants of health': employability, reduction of stigma, and social integration. Calò *et al.* (2018) took a different tack, with a systematic review of social enterprise beneficiary outcomes, where beneficiaries included customers receiving services or employees participating for work experience. Comparing social enterprise provision with 'usual care' (in the public sector), across 18 studies they found social enterprises providing positive outcomes of connectedness, confidence, empowerment, interactions, inclusion, engagement, social support, and self-worth. Again, they found little evidence of clinical health benefits. Suchowerska *et al.* (2019) undertook a scoping review considering organisational aspects of social enterprises that influence experiences of social determinants of health (i.e. improvements to housing, employment, income, social networks, and stigma). They found that social enterprise team morale, interpersonal relationships, and a good work environment impacted improvements to social determinants. A recent systematic review examined research focusing upon a distinct subset of social enterprises, which they refer to as 'community businesses' (Bagnall *et al.*, 2020) and found 'moderate evidence' from qualitative and quantitative studies of positive impacts on social cohesion, civic participation, and individual wellbeing as well as moderate evidence from qualitative studies of positive impacts on quality of life, health, mental health, employment, and volunteering.

Drawing across other recent work, some studies have focused on specific groups of beneficiaries and contexts (Macaulay *et al.*, 2018): for example, rural contexts (Kelly *et al.*, 2019); asylum seekers and refugees (Barraket, 2014); community food initiatives (Gordon *et al.*, 2018); older people (Henderson *et al.*, 2019); street-living youth (Ferguson, 2007, 2012); and people experiencing mental illness (Krupa *et al.*, 2019). Examples of theoretical and methodological innovation include work employing the aforementioned Spaces of Wellbeing theory (Farmer *et al.*, 2016; Muñoz *et al.*, 2015). There has also been discussion on how actions at the local level can be thought about as influencing systemic change; to look much further 'upstream' (to use a phrase used commonly when considering the social determinants of health) to the level of the political economy itself (Roy and Hackett, 2017).

What is clear, even from this very brief summary, is the relatively nascent, emergent, even 'fuzzy,' state of this field to date. While the considerable work done recently seems to be leading to clearer ideas about 'what happens'—a theory of change and the implications of a relationship between social enterprise and health—this is a field that is only now starting to emerge from exploratory stages. It is a field where researchers are trying to systematise what is going on and to understand relationships between the consistently described beneficial social and subjective 'feelings' effects and 'hard' (measurable) health outcomes. Indeed, to date, perhaps the best gloss we can place on the evidence is that there seem to be health and wellbeing effects produced through/by the social enterprise (although these may be an unintended consequence or by-product of the central focus of social enterprise—see Roy *et al.*, 2017) but relatively inconclusive evidence of measurable physical and psychological health effects. The social effects described as related to social enterprise appear to be wide-ranging, but this could simply be due to inconsistent use of terms; some can be classified as social determinants of health (housing, income, and jobs), while others appear more related to wellbeing effects (self-confidence, self-worth, self-efficacy, social connectedness—see e.g. Chan, 2016).

The field is characterised, in the main, by qualitative studies. A key issue raised is how to compare findings when organisations are of different types and sizes, organisational forms, in different sectors, and how to compare findings across organisations where participants may have a widely varying capability, including participants with cognitive disabilities, physical disabilities, mental illnesses, or experiencing other forms of marginalisation. A second element of confusion is introduced around the unit of analysis or defining who is meant to be benefitting: whether it is the customers who purchase the goods and services, the marginalised participants of the social enterprise, or the whole team including staff and managers, and even the communities in which such social enterprises are situated.

The collective benefits of social enterprise at a community level that are identified in individual studies include the rehabilitation and increased inclusiveness of civic spaces resulting from social enterprise operations in rural communities (Barraket and Archer, 2010). In a pilot study of one Australian social enterprise, Farmer *et al.* (2016) examined the impacts of social enterprise on the wellbeing of its participants as well as wellbeing impacts on other local citizens. They found that a role for the social enterprise was 'acting to knit disconnected people into community life, thus protecting community functionality' (Farmer *et al.*, 2016, p. 246). Goods or services provided by social enterprises and learning provided to participants increased community capability.

Recent Programmatic Studies and This Book

Some programs of study about social enterprise, health, and wellbeing have been conducted and completed in the last five or six years, producing a wave of findings that, we propose, might be regarded as consolidating a 'first wave' of research in this field. This book draws together findings across several substantial research initiatives conducted in Scotland, Australia, and Canada and simultaneously draws on related contemporary studies. The main research programmes drawn on here are:

- *CommonHealth*, Scotland (2014–2018) funded jointly by the UK's Medical Research Council and Economic and Social Research Council. Led by Cam Donaldson at Glasgow Caledonian University's Yunus Centre for Social Business and Health and involving a host of university and sector partners across Scotland, the programme considered social enterprise as a complex form of health and wellbeing 'intervention.' It is covered in detail in Chapter 10.
- *Improving Health Equity of Young People: The role of social enterprise*, Australia (2018–2021). Funded by the Australian Research Council and VicHealth (a health promotion agency in Victoria, Australia), this study worked with four social enterprises in two Australian states and explored social enterprise as addressing health equity for young people, specifically focusing on organisational features that influence outcomes. This work was led by Jo Barraket, Australasia's leading social enterprise researcher and Director of the Centre for Social Impact at Swinburne University of Technology, Melbourne.
- *Mapping the impact of social enterprise on regional city disadvantage*, Australia (2017–2020). Funded by an Australian Research Council Discovery project, this study examined four social enterprises in two regional cities (population 80,000–100,000 people) in two Australian states and used qualitative GIS mapping methods to explore impacts on individual and community wellbeing using spaces of wellbeing theory and social capital theory. This project was led by Jane Farmer, Director of the Swinburne University of Technology Social Innovation Research Institute, based in Melbourne. The project involved researchers in Australia and Scotland, including Sarah-Anne Munoz (University of the Highlands and Islands, Scotland), Katharine McKinnon (University of Canberra, Australia), Chris Brennan-Horley (University of Wollongong, Australia), Jo Barraket (Swinburne University, Australia), Michael Roy (Glasgow Caledonian University, Scotland), and Sue Kilpatrick (University of Tasmania, Australia).

Taken together, the chapters of this book provide a certain international focus, albeit dominated by a research tradition from the global north, where the development of social enterprise, we fully recognise, has been heavily influenced by neoliberal ideology (Laville and Eynaud, 2019). The research featured draws on multiple disciplines and work that is highly interdisciplinary in nature, with studies involving researchers spanning sociology, public health, regional development, geography, urban planning, management, political economy, and anthropology. Further, most of the studies feature considerable input to study design and findings interpretation, from the practice and policy sectors, often with intensive work spent on-site at social enterprises. These features seem to align closely with the hybridity and intrinsically networked nature of social enterprise and its impacts.

Conclusion

The research reported in this book in many ways reflects the journey of discovery and sophistication in ideas around links between social enterprise and health and wellbeing. Although it may have been attractive to measure social enterprise in terms of its health impacts as a health intervention, thinking about 'what social enterprise does' in this book reflects developing complexity in application and understanding of the term 'wellbeing' that has been increasingly unpacked, explored, and critiqued over the last decade, in line with the arc of this book's research content.

The content reflects also a moment in time where public health as a discipline has begun to explore new thinking, with divergence from outmoded biomedical models to:

> re-orientate public health more closely towards enabling the growth of what nourishes human life and spirit, and supporting life's own capacity for healing and health creation . . . building upon the potential strengths of individuals and communities . . . rather than focusing on individual risk factors such as smoking, alcohol, diet and exercise alone.
>
> (Roy, 2017, p. 455)

In line with this opening up of thinking about public health, the ways that social enterprise is analysed in this book provides scope to move beyond thinking about social enterprises as part of 'formal' health systems or, alternatively, as some sort of quirky, marginal component of a local commercial system that has some ill-defined 'social value.' As evidenced herein, the inherent 'hybrid' nature (Doherty et al., 2014) of the social enterprise seems to enable it to cross boundaries of providing useful cost-effective products and services and providing safe and supported spaces for inclusion. The social enterprise appears to have potential as a space of inclusion at the organisational, but also at the community, level by 'helping to bridge "otherness" and "sameness"' (Evans and Wilton,

2019, p. 100). It provides an exciting experimental space for showing how social interventions impact health and wellbeing. Further, in enabling contractual relationships with the social sector, while offering a 'solution' for getting people into work, social enterprise fits well with the prevailing policy climate, at least in the advanced neoliberal contexts from which our examples are primarily drawn. Social enterprise has become accepted as an organisational model in society. Interestingly, our studies also show that by this very hybrid space that social enterprise represents, it is a space where researchers from different disciplines come together and contribute their expertise, helpfully producing new knowledge that is transdisciplinary and holistic, more insightful, and innovative than the sum of individual studies undertaken in individual disciplines.

References

Andrews, G.J., Chen, S. and Myers, S. (2014), "The 'Taking Place' of Health and Wellbeing: Towards Non-Representational Theory", *Social Science & Medicine*, Vol. 108, pp. 210–222.

Atkinson, S. (2013), "Beyond Components of Wellbeing: The Effects of Relational and Situated Assemblage", *Topoi*, Vol. 32 No. 2, pp. 137–144.

Atkinson, S. (2020), "The Toxic Effects of Subjective Wellbeing and Potential Tonics", *Social Science & Medicine*, available at: https://doi.org/10.1016/j.socscimed.2020.113098.

Austin, J. and Rangan, V.K. (2019), "Reflections on 25 Years of Building Social Enterprise Education", *Social Enterprise Journal*, Vol. 15 No. 1, pp. 2–21.

Bache, I. and Scott, K. (2018), *The Politics of Wellbeing: Theory, Policy and Practice*, Springer, Cham, Switzerland.

Bagnall, A.-M., South, J., Southby, K., Freeman, C., Jones, R., Rithalia, A., Pennington, A., *et al.* (2020), *A Systematic Review of the Community Wellbeing Impact of Community Business*, What Works Centre for Wellbeing, Leeds/Liverpool, available at: https://whatworkswellbeing.org/wp-content/uploads/2020/05/Community-business-full-report-May2020.pdf.

Barraket, J. (2014), "Fostering Wellbeing of Immigrants and Refugees? Evaluating the Outcomes of Work Integration Social Enterprise", in Denny, S. and Seddon, F. (Eds.), *Social Enterprise: Accountability and Evaluation Around the World*, Routledge, Abingdon, Oxon, pp. 102–120.

Barraket, J. and Archer, V. (2010), "Social Inclusion through Community Enterprise? Examining the Available Evidence", *Third Sector Review*, Vol. 16 No. 1, pp. 13–28.

Barraket, J., Collyer, N., O'Connor, M. and Anderson, H. (2010), *Finding Australia's Social Enterprise Sector: Final Report*, Social Traders, Queensland University of Technology, Brisbane.

Barraket, J., Douglas, H., Eversole, R., Mason, C., McNeill, J. and Morgan, B. (2017), "Classifying Social Enterprise Models in Australia", *Social Enterprise Journal*, Vol. 13 No. 4, pp. 345–361.

Barraket, J., Keast, R. and Furneaux, C. (2015), *Social Procurement and New Public Governance*, Routledge, Abingdon, Oxon.

Black, B.J. (1970), *Principles of Industrial Therapy for the Mentally Ill*, Grune & Stratton, Oxford, England, pp. ix, 190.

Borzaga, C. and Defourny, J. (Eds.). (2001), *The Emergence of Social Enterprise*, Routledge, London.

Bosworth, G., Steiner, A. and Farmer, J. (2019), "Rural Social Enterprise— Evidence to Date, and a Research Agenda", *Journal of Rural Studies*, Vol. 70, pp. 139–143.

Büchs, M. and Koch, M. (2017), *Postgrowth and Wellbeing: Challenges to Sustainable Welfare*, Springer Berlin Heidelberg, New York, NY.

Calò, F., Teasdale, S., Donaldson, C., Roy, M.J. and Baglioni, S. (2018), "Collaborator or Competitor: Assessing the Evidence Supporting the Role of Social Enterprise in Health and Social Care", *Public Management Review*, Vol. 20 No. 12, pp. 1790–1814.

Calvo, S. and Morales, A. (2017), *Social and Solidarity Economy: The World's Economy with a Social Face*, Routledge, Abingdon, Oxon.

Campi, S., Defourny, J. and Grégoire, O. (2006), "Work Integration Social Enterprises: Are They Multiple-Goal and Multi-Stakeholder Organizations?" in Nyssens, M. (Ed.), *Social Enterprise: At the Crossroads of Market, Public Policies and Civil Society*, Routledge, Abingdon, Oxon, pp. 29–49.

Catlaw, T.J. and Sandberg, B. (2018), "The Quantified Self and the Evolution of Neoliberal Self-Government: An Exploratory Qualitative Study", *Administrative Theory & Praxis*, Vol. 40 No. 1, pp. 3–22.

Chan, A. (2016), "Personal Wellbeing of Participants of Social Purpose Enterprises: The Influence of Social Support", *Voluntas: International Journal of Voluntary and Nonprofit Organizations*, Vol. 27 No. 4, pp. 1718–1741.

Cooney, K. (2011), "An Exploratory Study of Social Purpose Business Models in the United States", *Nonprofit and Voluntary Sector Quarterly*, Vol. 40 No. 1, pp. 185–196.

Dalziel, P., Saunders, C. and Saunders, J. (2018), *Wellbeing Economics: The Capabilities Approach to Prosperity*, Palgrave Macmillan, Cham, Switzerland.

Dees, J.G. (1998), *The Meaning of Social Entrepreneurship*, Duke University— Fuqua School of Business, Durham, NC.

Defourny, J., Hulgård, L. and Pestoff, V. (2014), "Introduction to the 'SE Field' ", in Defourny, J., Hulgård, L. and Pestoff, V. (Eds.), *Social Enterprise and the Third Sector: Changing European Landscapes in a Comparative Perspective*, Routledge, Abingdon, Oxon, pp. 1–14.

Defourny, J. and Nyssens, M. (2006), "Defining Social Enterprise", in Nyssens, M. (Ed.), *Social Enterprise: At the Crossroads of Market, Public Policies and Civil Society*, Routledge, Abingdon, Oxon, pp. 3–26.

Defourny, J. and Nyssens, M. (2010), "Conceptions of Social Enterprise and Social Entrepreneurship in Europe and the United States: Convergences and Divergences", *Journal of Social Entrepreneurship*, Vol. 1 No. 1, pp. 32–53.

Defourny, J., Nyssens, M. and Brolis, O. (2020), "Testing Social Enterprise Models Across the World: Evidence From the 'International Comparative Social Enterprise Models (ICSEM) Project' ", *Nonprofit and Voluntary Sector Quarterly*, available at: https://doi.org/10.1177/0899764020959470.

Diener, E. and Lucas, R.E. (2000), "Explaining Differences in Societal Levels of Happiness: Relative Standards, Need Fulfillment, Culture, and Evaluation Theory", *Journal of Happiness Studies*, Vol. 1 No. 1, pp. 41–78.

Doherty, B., Haugh, H. and Lyon, F. (2014), "Social Enterprises as Hybrid Organizations: A Review and Research Agenda", *International Journal of Management Reviews*, Vol. 16 No. 4, pp. 417–436.

dos Santos, L.L. and Banerjee, S. (2019), "Social Enterprise: Is It Possible to Decolonise This Concept?" in Eynaud, P., Laville, J.-L., dos Santos, L.L., Banerjee, S., Avelino, F. and Hulgård, L. (Eds.), *Theory of Social Enterprise and Pluralism: Social Movements, Solidarity Economy, and Global South*, Routledge, New York; Abingdon, pp. 3–17.

Drayton, W. (2011), "Everyone a Changemaker—Social Entrepeneurship's Ultimate Goal", in Petit, P.U. (Ed.), *Creating a New Civilization Through Social Entrepreneurship*, First Transaction Publishers/Goi Peace Foundation, Piscataway, NJ, pp. 53–62.

Du Rand, J. (1990), *The Affirmative Enterprise*, MDI, St. Paul, Minneapolis.

Easterlin, R.A. (1974), "Does Economic Growth Improve the Human Lot? Some Empirical Evidence", in David, P.A. and Reder, M.W. (Eds.), *Nations and Households in Economic Growth: Essays in Honor of Moses Abramovitz*, Academic Press, New York.

Easterlin, R.A. (1995), "Will Raising the Incomes of All Increase the Happiness of All?" *Journal of Economic Behavior & Organization*, Vol. 27 No. 1, pp. 35–47.

Evans, J. and Wilton, R. (2019), "Well Enough to Work? Social Enterprise Employment and the Geographies of Mental Health Recovery", *Annals of the American Association of Geographers*, Vol. 109 No. 1, pp. 87–103.

Farmer, J., De Cotta, T., McKinnon, K., Barraket, J., Munoz, S.-A., Douglas, H. and Roy, M.J. (2016), "Social Enterprise and Wellbeing in Community Life", *Social Enterprise Journal*, Vol. 12 No. 2, pp. 235–254.

Ferguson, K.M. (2007), "Implementing a Social Enterprise Intervention with Homeless, Street-Living Youths in Los Angeles", *Social Work*, Vol. 52 No. 2, pp. 103–112.

Ferguson, K.M. (2012), "Merging the Fields of Mental Health and Social Enterprise: Lessons from Abroad and Cumulative Findings from Research with Homeless Youths", *Community Mental Health Journal*, Vol. 48 No. 4, pp. 490–502.

Fleuret, S. and Atkinson, S. (2007), "Wellbeing, Health and Geography: A Critical Review and Research Agenda", *New Zealand Geographer*, Vol. 63 No. 2, pp. 106–118.

Gallick, S. (2021), "Opportunity Amid Crisis: Eight Pandemic-Prompted Lessons on Driving Social Change", *Pioneer's Post*, 13 January, available at: www.pioneerspost.com/news-views/20210113/opportunity-amid-crisis-eight-pandemic-prompted-lessons-on-driving-social-change.

Gordon, K., Wilson, J., Tonner, A. and Shaw, E. (2018), "How Can Social Enterprises Impact Health and Well-Being?" *International Journal of Entrepreneurial Behavior & Research*, Vol. 24 No. 3, pp. 697–713.

Gregory, A. (2019), "Governments Should Put Wellbeing of Citizens Ahead of GDP in Budget Priorities, Iceland PM Urges", available at: www.independent.co.uk/news/world/europe/iceland-gdp-wellbeing-budget-climate-change-new-zealand-arden-sturgeon-a9232626.html.

Haugh, H. and Kitson, M. (2007), "The Third Way and the Third Sector: New Labour's Economic Policy and the Social Economy", *Cambridge Journal of Economics*, Vol. 31 No. 6, pp. 973–994.

Henderson, F., Steiner, A., Mazzei, M. and Docherty, C. (2019), "Social Enterprises' Impact on Older People's Health and Wellbeing: Exploring Scottish Experiences", *Health Promotion International*, p. daz102.

Hermant, N. (2021), "Social Enterprises Lobbying for Part in Australia's Post-Covid-19 Economic 'Bounce Back'", *Abc.Net.Au*, 11 January, available at: www.abc.net.au/news/2021-01-12/social-enterprises-want-funding-in-post-covid-19-recovery/13047256.

Hough-Stewart, L., Trebeck, K., Sommer, C. and Wallis, S. (2019), "What Is a Wellbeing Economy?" *Wellbeing Economy Alliance*, December, available at: https://wellbeingeconomy.org/wp-content/uploads/2019/12/A-WE-Is-WEAll-Ideas-Little-Summaries-of-Big-Issues-4-Dec-2019.pdf.

Jahoda, M. (1981), "Work, Employment, and Unemployment: Values, Theories, and Approaches in Social Research", *American Psychologist*, Vol. 36 No. 2, pp. 184–191.

Kelly, D., Steiner, A., Mazzei, M. and Baker, R. (2019), "Filling a Void? The Role of Social Enterprise in Addressing Social Isolation and Loneliness in Rural Communities", *Journal of Rural Studies*, Vol. 70, pp. 225–236.

Kerlin, J.A. (2013), "Defining Social Enterprise Across Different Contexts: A Conceptual Framework Based on Institutional Factors", *Nonprofit and Voluntary Sector Quarterly*, Vol. 42 No. 1, pp. 84–108.

Krupa, T., Lagarde, M. and Carmichael, K. (2003), "Transforming Sheltered Workshops into Affirmative Businesses: An Outcome Evaluation", *Psychiatric Rehabilitation Journal*, Vol. 26 No. 4, pp. 359–367.

Krupa, T., McCourty, K., Bonner, D., Von Briesen, B. and Scott, R. (1999), "Voices, Opportunities & Choices Employment Club: Transforming Sheltered Workshops Using an Affirmative Business Approach", *Canadian Journal of Community Mental Health (Revue Canadienne De Santé Mentale Communautaire)*, Vol. 18 No. 2, pp. 87–98.

Krupa, T., Sabetti, J. and Lysaght, R. (2019), "How Work Integration Social Enterprises Impact the Stigma of Mental Illness", *Social Enterprise Journal*, Vol. 15 No. 4, pp. 475–494.

Laville, J.-L. and Eynaud, P. (2019), "Rethinking Social Enterprise Through Philanthropic and Democratic Solidarities", in Eynaud, P., Laville, J.-L., dos Santos, L.L., Banerjee, S., Avelino, F. and Hulgård, L. (Eds.), *Theory of Social Enterprise and Pluralism: Social Movements, Solidarity Economy, and Global South*, Routledge, New York; Abingdon, pp. 18–43.

Laville, J.-L., Lemaitre, A. and Nyssens, M. (2006), "Public Policies and WISEs in Europe", in Nyssens, M. (Ed.), *Social Enterprise: At the Crossroads of Market, Public Policies and Civil Society*, Routledge, Abingdon, Oxon, pp. 272–295.

Lionais, D. (2015), "Social Enterprise in Atlantic Canada", *Canadian Journal of Nonprofit and Social Economy Research*, Vol. 6 No. 1, pp. 25–41.

Macaulay, B., Mazzei, M., Roy, M.J., Teasdale, S. and Donaldson, C. (2018), "Differentiating the Effect of Social Enterprise Activities on Health", *Social Science & Medicine*, Vol. 200, pp. 211–217.

Mandiberg, J.M. (2012), "The Failure of Social Inclusion: An Alternative Approach Through Community Development", *Psychiatric Services*, Vol. 63 No. 5, pp. 458–460.

Mandiberg, J.M. and Edwards, M. (2016), "Business Incubation for People with Severe Mental Illness Histories: The Experience of One Model", *Journal of Policy Practice*, Routledge, Vol. 15 No. 1–2, pp. 82–101.

Marmot, M.G. and Wilkinson, R.G. (2006), *Social Determinants of Health*, Oxford University Press, Oxford.

Mendell, M. and Neamtan, N. (2010), "The Social Economy in Quebec: Towards a New Political Economy", in Mook, L., Quarter, J. and Ryan, S. (Eds.), *Researching the Social Economy*, University of Toronto Press, Toronto, pp. 63–83.

Mezzina, R. (2014), "Community Mental Health Care in Trieste and Beyond: An 'Open Door—No Restraint' System of Care for Recovery and Citizenship", *The Journal of Nervous and Mental Disease*, Vol. 202 No. 6, pp. 440–445.

Muñoz, S.-A., Farmer, J., Winterton, R. and Barraket, J. (2015), "The Social Enterprise as a Space of Wellbeing: An Exploratory Case Study", *Social Enterprise Journal*, Vol. 11 No. 3, pp. 281–302.

Murphy, S.T. and Rogan, P.M. (1995), *Closing the Shop: Conversion from Sheltered to Integrated Work*, Paul H Brookes Publishing Co, Baltimore, MD.

Murray, G. (2019), "Community Business in Scotland: An Alternative Vision of 'Enterprise Culture', 1979–97", *Twentieth Century British History*, Vol. 30 No. 4, pp. 585–606.

OECD. (2019), "Better Life Index", available at: www.oecdbetterlifeindex.org/about/better-life-initiative/.

OECD. (2020), *Social Economy and the COVID-19 Crisis: Current and Future Roles*, OECD Publishing, Paris, available at: www.oecd.org/corona virus/policy-responses/social-economy-and-the-covid-19-crisis-current-and-future-roles-f904b89f/.

Peredo, A.M. and McLean, M. (2010), "Indigenous Development and the Cultural Captivity of Entrepreneurship", *Business & Society*, Vol. 52 No. 4, pp. 592–620.

Prilleltensky, I. (2005), "Promoting Well-Being: Time for a Paradigm Shift in Health and Human Services", *Scandinavian Journal of Public Health*, Vol. 33 No. 66_suppl, pp. 53–60.

Quarter, J., Armstrong, A. and Mook, L. (2009), *Understanding the Social Economy: A Canadian Perspective*, University of Toronto Press, Toronto.

Roy, M.J. (2017), "The Assets-Based Approach: Furthering a Neoliberal Agenda or Rediscovering the Old Public Health? A Critical Examination of Practitioner Discourses", *Critical Public Health*, Vol. 27 No. 4, pp. 455–464.

Roy, M.J., Baker, R. and Kerr, S. (2017), "Conceptualising the Public Health Role of Actors Operating Outside of Formal Health Systems: The Case of Social Enterprise", *Social Science & Medicine*, Vol. 172, pp. 144–152.

Roy, M.J., Donaldson, C., Baker, R. and Kerr, S. (2014), "The Potential of Social Enterprise to Enhance Health and Well-Being: A Model and Systematic Review", *Social Science & Medicine*, Vol. 123, pp. 182–193.

Roy, M.J. and Hackett, M.T. (2017), "Polanyi's 'Substantive Approach' to the Economy in Action? Conceptualising Social Enterprise as a Public Health 'Intervention'", *Review of Social Economy*, Vol. 75 No. 2, pp. 89–111.

Roy, M.J., McHugh, N., Huckfield, L., Kay, A. and Donaldson, C. (2015), "'The Most Supportive Environment in the World'? Tracing the Development of an

Institutional 'Ecosystem' for Social Enterprise", *Voluntas: International Journal of Voluntary and Nonprofit Organizations*, Vol. 26 No. 3, pp. 777–800.

Ruebottom, T. (2013), "The Microstructures of Rhetorical Strategy in Social Entrepreneurship: Building Legitimacy Through Heroes and Villains", *Journal of Business Venturing*, Vol. 28 No. 1, pp. 98–116.

Scottish Government. (2016), *Scotland's Social Enterprise Strategy 2016–26*, Scottish Government, Edinburgh, UK, available at: www.gov.scot/Resource/0051/00511500.pdf.

Sen, A. (1992), *Inequality Reexamined*, Harvard University Press, Cambridge, MA.

Social Value Lab. (2019), *2019 Social Enterprise Census Data for the Highlands and Islands Region*, Social Value Lab, Glasgow, available at: www.hie.co.uk/media/6300/social-enterprise-in-scotland-census-2019-area-report-highlands-islands.pdf.

Solar, O. and Irwin, A. (2010), *A Conceptual Framework for Action on the Social Determinants of Health*, World Health Organisation, Geneva, available at: http://whqlibdoc.who.int/publications/2010/9789241500852_eng.pdf.

Spear, R. and Bidet, E. (2005), "Social Enterprise for Work Integration in 12 European Countries: A Descriptive Analysis", *Annales de L'économie Publique, Sociale et Coopérative*, Vol. 76 No. 2, pp. 195–231.

Stiglitz, J.E., Sen, A. and Fitoussi, J.-P. (2009), *Report by the Commission on the Measurement of Economic Performance and Social Progress*, available at: https://ec.europa.eu/eurostat/documents/118025/118123/Fitoussi+Commission+report.

Suchowerska, R., Barraket, J., Qian, J., Mason, C., Farmer, J., Carey, G., Campbell, P., *et al.* (2019), "An Organizational Approach to Understanding How Social Enterprises Address Health Inequities: A Scoping Review", *Journal of Social Entrepreneurship*, pp. 1–25.

Teasdale, S. (2010), "How Can Social Enterprise Address Disadvantage? Evidence from an Inner City Community", *Journal of Nonprofit & Public Sector Marketing*, Vol. 22 No. 2, pp. 89–107.

Teasdale, S. (2012), "What's in a Name? Making Sense of Social Enterprise Discourses", *Public Policy and Administration*, Vol. 27 No. 2, pp. 99–119.

Teasdale, S., Roy, M.J., Ziegler, R., Mauksch, S., Dey, P. and Raufflet, E.B. (2020), "Everyone a Changemaker? Exploring the Moral Underpinnings of Social Innovation Discourse Through Real Utopias", *Journal of Social Entrepreneurship*, available at: https://doi.org/doi.org/10.1080/19420676.2020.1738532.

Trebeck, K. (2020), "Agenda: Working Towards an Economy That Is Focused on Wellbeing", *The Herald*, available at: www.heraldscotland.com/opinion/18177452.agenda-working-towards-economy-focused-wellbeing/.

Utting, P. (Ed.). (2015), *Social and Solidarity Economy: Beyond the Fringe?* Zed Books, London.

Victoria State Government. (2017), *Social Enterprise Strategy*, Victoria State Government, Melbourne, available at: https://djpr.vic.gov.au/__data/assets/pdf_file/0008/1435868/10371_DEDJTR_EDEI_Social_Enterprise_Brochure_A4_WEB_FINAL.pdf.

Vidal, I. (2005), "Social Enterprise and Social Inclusion: Social Enterprises in the Sphere of Work Integration", *International Journal of Public Administration*, Vol. 28 No. 9–10, pp. 807–825.

Warner, R. and Mandiberg, J. (2006), "An Update on Affirmative Businesses or Social Firms for People with Mental Illness", *Psychiatric Services*, Vol. 57 No. 10, pp. 1488–1492.

WHO. (1948), "Constitution adopted by the International Health Conference held in New York from 19 June to 22 July 1946, signed on 22 July 1946 by the representatives of 61 States (Off. Rec. Wld Hlth Org., 2, 100) and entered into force on 7 April 1948", World Health Organisation, available at: http://apps. who.int/gb/bd/PDF/bd47/EN/constitution-en.pdf.

Yunus, M., Moingeon, B. and Lehmann-Ortega, L. (2010), "Building Social Business Models: Lessons from the Grameen Experience", *Long Range Planning*, Vol. 43 No. 2–3, pp. 308–325.

Section 1

Applying Theory for Insights

2 Social Enterprises as Spaces of Wellbeing

A Spatial and Relational Exploration of Where and How Wellbeing Realises

Tracy De Cotta, Jane Farmer, Peter Kamstra, Viktoria Adler, Chris Brennan-Horley, and Sarah-Anne Munoz

Introduction

This chapter explores how social enterprises help individuals to realise wellbeing by documenting the physical locations and associated work tasks that promote wellbeing. We use findings from a larger study called 'Mapping the impact of social enterprise on regional city disadvantage' (2017–2020) which applied a mixed methodology and drew on the geographical concepts of relational space and spaces of wellbeing. By adopting these theoretical frameworks, we were able to develop a typology of social enterprise 'spaces' that support and nurture individual wellbeing. We use our findings to highlight practical examples of spaces that helped individuals to realise wellbeing and consider how these types of spaces can be applied to other social enterprises to foster wellbeing. While social enterprises have been linked increasingly with health and wellbeing impacts, the causal mechanisms, extent of effects, and timeframe over which outcomes might realise have been hard to pin down (Roy and Hackett, 2017). Few quantitative studies of social enterprises as 'clinical interventions' have occurred, and most qualitative studies comment descriptively on developments in social and wellbeing dimensions, including feelings of belonging and identity, enhanced social interaction, inclusion, and social status (Elmes, 2019; Mason *et al.*, 2015; Roy *et al.*, 2014).

Addressing methodological challenges of exploring social enterprise wellbeing impacts and how these arise, in this study, we deployed a methodology that uses qualitative geographical information systems (GIS) techniques (Kamstra *et al.*, 2019). The mixed-methods approach that incorporated data from observation, different types of interviews, and focus groups is useful in helping to explain what happens, where it happens, and how certain spaces do (or do not) contribute to wellbeing.

DOI: 10.4324/9781003125976-2

Building on our analysis, we consider what this suggests for the design of current and future social enterprises, particularly in terms of optimising the outcomes from these organisations as spaces of wellbeing.

Background

When applying relational thinking to the concept of wellbeing, the health and social effects that might realise for people are viewed as emergent. This means that a person's wellbeing is produced and re-produced over time through multiple interactions with different types of spaces through that person's lived experiences. This way of seeing the world involves viewing social enterprises and spaces within these not as bounded geographical entities that are stuck in time and possess fixed characteristics (Cummins *et al.*, 2007) but rather as nodes in fluid networks of social, economic, historical, and cultural forces that change across space and time (Massey, 1985, 2005). Understanding space in this way helps to make sense of how places—in this case the spaces provided by/in social enterprises and the way that they function—impact health. We suggest that it helps to understand that health varies in relation to the social interactions and physical spaces experienced by people during different situations, and at particular times. In this way, '[p]lace, as well as the characteristics of individuals, contributes to health variation' (Cummins *et al.*, 2007, p. 1825). Understanding the mechanisms through which places and spaces influence health, as well as quantifying the impact of mechanisms, is significant for understanding causation and for identifying useful interventions to address health inequity (Cummins *et al.*, 2007).

Relational spaces, therefore, can be understood as spaces that emerge through social interaction, where varying lived experiences of wellbeing are constituted by how people interact with spaces. 'Spaces of health,' for example, can manifest from the assembled features of places and spaces—such as the therapeutic landscape of a particular health spa (Foley, 2014). Other health geographers have explored the idea of wellbeing as a relational outcome (e.g. Conradson, 2005), with Munoz and colleagues (2015) specifically studying wellbeing in relation to social enterprise.

In the study reported here, we deployed relational thinking alongside spaces of wellbeing theory (Fleuret and Atkinson, 2007) to provide a methodological and conceptual framework that enables the 'disentangling' of the interrelated effects that help wellbeing realisation. Following Atkinson (2013), we understand wellbeing as the resources required to live a good life and emerging from 'situated and relational effects' between 'complex assemblages of relations' involving people, material objects, and other aspects of places such as 'atmosphere, histories and values' (Atkinson, 2013, p. 142).

Our author team used the framework to conduct a pilot study of one social enterprise as a space of wellbeing (Munoz *et al.*, 2015; Farmer *et al.*, 2016), and elsewhere, we have also explored social integration and segregation (Farmer, De Cotta *et al.*, 2020), social enterprise and capability (Farmer *et al.*, 2019), and compared micro-geographies of wellbeing at three different regional social enterprises (Farmer, Kamstra *et al.*, 2020).

For this chapter, the physical locations that people in social enterprises associate with wellbeing are used as an entry point to understand where wellbeing realises (in relation to social enterprises) and how it is constituted. We use physical locations in social enterprises as prompts for data collection, and the location-related data produced were used to 'map' wellbeing using qualitative GIS methods. Jung and Elwood (2010) understand the visualisations in qualitative GIS as the gathering together of socio-spatial components to form specific geographies that are 'woven together in ways that enable greater understanding' (p. 67).

Methods

The study uses *Spaces of Wellbeing Theory*, with its dimensions of *capability, integration, security*, and *therapy*, to guide data collection (Fleuret and Atkinson, 2007). The theory builds off the hypothesis that satisfying needs is a prerequisite to wellbeing. In particular, in generating the theory, Fleuret and Atkinson (2007) drew from three traditions of wellbeing theory: 1. Theory of needs—where individuals are required to have emotional, social, and material needs fulfilled to realise wellbeing (Maslow, 1954; Diener and Lucas, 2000; Chambers, 1997); 2. Relative standards theory—where individuals' experiences are dependent on the wider context, meaning wellbeing is relative and subjective (Wilkinson, 1996; Layard, 2005) and; 3. Human capabilities approach focuses on self-actualisation of attainable and valuable skills to enable a flourishing life (Sen, 1992).

From a thorough review of the wellbeing literature, Fleuret and Atkinson (2007) identified the four consistent and interrelated emerging ideas/ themes of Spaces of Wellbeing Theory which we have employed and adapted. Explained by Fleuret and Atkinson (and with our shorthand adapted term in parentheses here), these are: Capability (self-actualisation) is independent thinking or gaining technical or life skills to achieve one's fullest capacity; Integration (social connection) is building relationships and trust to become embedded in networks with mutual valuing; Security (feeling comfortable in the world) can be both, feeling protected from physical and social risk or secure ontologically through comfort and predictable routines; and Therapy (recovery/healing) where spaces and places offer physical, mental, or emotional feelings of wellness or healing.

The study used physical locations as a spatial context to identify the emergence of these aspects of wellbeing. By linking wellbeing to locations, we analysed and mapped wellbeing to show the factors that contribute to individual's experiences of wellbeing at the scale of a social enterprise. Using qualitative GIS, we produced visual micro-geographies of wellbeing in terms of social enterprise organisational floor plans, heat maps, and topographies at one work integration social enterprise (WISE) called 'Farm.' We validated the findings for Farm by comparing with two other social enterprises where the same methods were used (see Table 2.1).

Sampling

The three social enterprises included are all work integration social enterprises (WISEs) and are located in two Australian regional cities (population <100,000) and given the pseudonyms here: Farm and Catering (City 1) and AssistAll (City 2). Assist All is established as an alternate workplace for those who are excluded from the mainstream labour market due to disability or vulnerability; it is a Type B WISE according to Vidal's (2005) typology. Farm and Catering aims to act as Type A WISEs: (Vidal, 2005) that is, they are a stepping stone for employees to enter 'mainstream' employment. However, in reality, few employees make the transition, and rather both WISEs also tend to provide an alternate workplace for excluded people.

Staffing at the social enterprises ranged from four to nine supervisory staff, with employee 'beneficiaries' ranging from 25 to 110 people. Farm and AssistAll operate across multiple sectors including woodworking, customised mail-outs and light manufacturing, shops, and car-washing, while Catering focuses only on the production of food for commercial sale. In this chapter, we present micro-geographical mapping and in-depth analysis of one case study Farm, with Table 2.1 illustrating that similar, supportive evidence about wellbeing was collected for Catering and AssistAll.

Data Collection

Data were collected in two stages, with the first stage collecting data from the three social enterprises, comprising 240 hours of observation, 12 supervisory staff interviews, and 13 'go-along interviews' with employees. 'Go-along interviews' can be walking interviews, although they can also be ride-alongs in cars or alongside mobility aids, where researchers follow participants on their everyday routines without the restriction of just a walk (Carpiano, 2009; Lager, Van Hoven, and Huigen, 2015; Ottoni *et al.*, 2016). Kusenbach (2003) describes the go-along as a 'hybrid between participant observation and interviewing' (p. 457).

The second stage involved presenting analysed data at focus groups with 32 employees and staff to verify and extend findings. Data collection centred on asking about and observing aspects relating to *promoting* or *not promoting* wellbeing in the social enterprises, with the four aspects of wellbeing (capability, social integration, security, and therapy) used as a framework to guide questioning and note-taking. This was done in relation to *physical locations* (i.e. spaces) within the social enterprises. All interview and focus group data were audio-recorded with consent.

Data Analysis

Multiple researchers were involved in coding data to themes related to wellbeing aspects extending a previous coding framework (Munoz *et al.*, 2015) and then for location (where location relates to the spaces being discussed). Once data were coded, the number of *mentions* of the wellbeing aspects was linked to a location on a mapped floor plan of each social enterprise using the spatial software program ArcGIS 10.6.1. *Mentions* are quotes from interviews or observation field notes that were related to a space in the social enterprise. Micro-geographical maps show quantities of wellbeing aspects mapped in relation to the locations, to show 'heat-maps' of *where* wellbeing realised. We examine the hotspots of mentions by exploring the underlying qualitative data, enabling explanation of *why* the hotspots of wellbeing may be occurring (or not). Thus, the maps reveal previously hidden spatial relationships between wellbeing and spaces in the social enterprise that help wellbeing to realise. Full explanation of the methodology and micro-geographical maps for all of the social enterprises are provided elsewhere (e.g. Farmer, De Cotta *et al.*, 2020; Farmer, Kamstra *et al.*, 2020).

Findings

In this section, we begin with a set of micro-geographical maps, generated through our study, of where wellbeing aspects of capability, social integration, security, and therapy were mentioned within Farm. We then explore how the micro-geographies of wellbeing emerged at Farm, contextualising with descriptive quotes from the primary data. Table 2.1 summarises results from AssistAll and Catering (the two other social enterprises studied) to validate evidence from Farm.

Considering the three-dimensional map of Farm (see Figure 2.1), the garden is the space with the highest number of wellbeing mentions. It is the largest physical space at Farm, and, as such, it accommodates multiple employees working on different tasks simultaneously. Noticeably, the garden also contributes multiple mentions of wellbeing

Table 2.1 Aspects helping wellbeing to realise at Catering and AssistAll social enterprises

	Spaces and Objects	Behaviours, Narratives, and Tasks
Capability		
Catering	• Workspaces in the kitchen signify progression, autonomy and responsibility • Whiteboards note goals	• Triaging people for what tasks they can manage at first, and progress to • Staff/supervisor ethos of guiding/pushing
AssistAll	• Op-shop: learning ironing, laundry skills • Kitchen: cooking skills that can be used at home • Notice board highlights progress and targets	• Work roster is rotating so that employees learn various skills and don't get bored • Employees encouraged to flag things they want to learn • Staff stay in the background while employees work
Social integration		
Catering	• Couch at reception: 'bumping spaces' • Kitchen: communal workspace • Uniforms: create a sense of belonging	• Joking conversations as well as discussions of inclusion, diversity, and sexuality • More experienced people help novices • Delivering meals offers the opportunity to meet people in the community
AssistAll	• Worktables: employees talk while working • Buddy seat: designated sitting area • Fire pit: place where employees gather	• Employees are on a fund-raising board and meet donors and supporters • Employees deliveries good to the community • Workplace code of conduct sets guidelines for workplace interactions
Security		
Catering	• Supervisor's office and administration area are places employees know they can go to at any time to seek help or to rest	• Established routines and practices • Supervisors watch from a distance, encouraging autonomy and self-confidence
AssistAll	• Supervisor's office: employees know that they can go here at any time to seek help • Safety gear in workshops	• Established routines and practices • Helping people to start tasks by demonstration: 'we'll do the first line for them'
Therapy		
Catering	• Boxroom: recovery spaces and to be alone	• Music and laughter encouraged in a supportive environment
AssistAll	• Toilets: recovery spaces and to be alone • Buddy seat: designated space to talk	• Regular exercise at work and discussions about healthy behaviours • Staff invite health promotion professionals

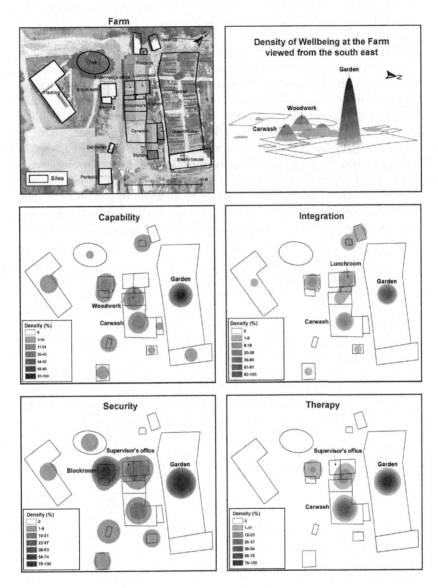

Figure 2.1 Mapped micro-geographies of wellbeing at Farm

across the entire range of wellbeing aspects. Together, the garden, carwash, supervisor's office, and blockroom contribute 76 per cent (245/321) of all the wellbeing mentions coded for Farm, suggesting the relevance of the qualities offered by these workspaces for employee wellbeing.

We now proceed to explore how qualities of the different spaces within Farm helped to realise aspects of wellbeing.

Capability: The garden had the highest mentions for capability and exhibits many of the features consistently associated with capability building across the social enterprises studied. For example, capability is associated with spaces where there are multiple work-task types, meaning that employees can find work that fits their experience, skills, and fluctuations in confidence. As some employee's mastery increases, they can 'progress' to more complex tasks within the same space, giving a sense of progression (e.g. moving from basic weeding to planning garden layout or masonry projects). The garden is also a space where employees engage in group and individual problem-solving. This is similar to the carwash, where employee teams divide their work responsibilities into washing, polishing, and detailing tasks. A sense of progressing and mastery, within teams, leads to individuals' feelings of achievement and self-worth, as highlighted:

> You start off new and you learn the ropes, and then you specialise on an area . . . nowadays, I specialise in the harvest . . . and then I've got more confidence. I did an admin course and did the public speaking thing. I could never had done it at school.
>
> [Farm_employee_1]

Mentoring or partnering more experienced employees with novice learners was also mentioned in the garden and woodwork spaces. Here, expressions about personal learning and self-worth were associated with gaining new skills and experiences as both learners and teachers:

> A few months ago, I learned how to build a wall and then I showed the local school kids how to build this path. They were pretty good, and I felt really good about it.
>
> [Farm_employee_2]

Associated with capability-building was the opportunity to use complex tools and apply creativity in the woodwork and welding spaces. The block-room is a space of more simple, repetitive tasks such as folding hospital laundry and painting mining stakes. However, some employees with mobility or cognitive difficulties reach high levels of capability and a sense of mastery at this space because it involves repetitive tasks in which they are adept.

Capability at the deliveries space was associated, by employees, with their being selected by supervisors as sufficiently responsible to pick up and return cars to client organisations that are located 'outside' of the social enterprise and in the community. Also, acknowledgement of individuals' achievement as responsible and capable, being seen within the social enterprise as undertaking worthwhile 'mainstream' tasks, gave a sense of self-worth to employees.

Thus, at Farm, data highlight that capability is realised through a range of relationally linked elements including being seen accomplishing a task both individually (e.g. individual tasks in the blockroom) and collectively (e.g. as a team at the carwash). This includes goals being formally recorded and marked off on noticeboards that display employee achievements. In terms of performativity, work practices of goal-setting, development planning, and marking-off goals as they were achieved were notable examples of achieving a sense of capability through structured and collective recognition.

Supportive supervisors also deployed 'hands-off' strategies—providing employees with autonomy, unless they required help. Supervisors reinforced the importance of encouraging employees to try new tasks and not worrying about making mistakes: 'it's a safe environment to try'; we have 'flexibility without pressure'; 'oh, I can't do that [they say]'—[I say] 'you want to come over here, this is how it's going to be—and they do it.'

Michael, for example, who had started as shy and awkward, gained gardening skills and now sought to study horticulture at college, and Jared, an Indigenous young man whose artistic talents had been nurtured such that he was considering applying for a small business start-up grant. The relational interactions between these employees and their supervisors created a supportive environment, where the employees were able to realise their capabilities. This could manifest as additional skills, working to their capacity or the confidence to think independently and solve problems (Farmer *et al.*, 2019).

Social integration: The map in Figure 4.1 shows that spaces with high mentions of social integration are also located across the Farm. We noted two types of social integration: ongoing social connections between people already known to each other and opportunities to make new and diverse connections. We found that the garden had a particularly high number of mentions—in part due to supervisors facilitating new connections through generating 'bumping spaces' (e.g. multiple people weeding close enough so that they chat with each other), and what we termed 'strategic pairing' where supervisors would partner people up together for work tasks—making assessments that they were likely to bond. For instance, a Farm supervisor noted:

> If you had two people on a row, they'll end up both at different ends, not necessarily talking to each other. If you put three or four on, they all sit there together and they're all weeding along together. It's funny how it works.
>
> (Farm_supervisor1)

Negotiating problem-solving tasks in teams was a good way to enable employees to build trust and the habit of working and talking with each other, through negotiating complex work tasks. One volunteer described sharing his existing knowledge with employees:

> Andrew [volunteer] is teaching Sam [employee] how to plant leek seeds—the seeds were gathered from last season's crop. Andrew explains to Sam how they were collected, how to tell the difference between the seed and the husk and how to separate the husks by blowing on them. He then shows Sam how to plant them, why it needs seed-raising mix. Sam listens intently and follows his instructions methodically and works slowly and intently. When asked if he's enjoying it, Sam says 'yep'.
>
> (Farm_Observation_050917)

Similarly, at the garden, we found various groups of people from different backgrounds working together in close proximity, including employees, school students, and volunteers. We found that people having incidental conversations helped to navigate difficult discussions involving diversity and health, for example. This included one conversation where an employee was insisting that 'Dr Who' (the television character) could not be a woman, while a staff member took the opportunity to discuss gender role stereotypes.

Another interesting example of relational wellbeing emerging at Farm was from background noise produced by a radio that facilitated lively discussions, helping to establish social connections between employees and staff at the carwash. Similarly, when the radio was on at the blockroom, employees sitting around a large table, but working on individual tasks, would exchange glances, smiles, and empathetic body language in response to radio discussion. In this sense, the blockroom provides a space where people are 'doing together' but not actively negotiating or working on interconnected tasks. In the lunchroom, however, we noticed situations where integration was stymied in settings that would seem inherently 'prosocial'; for example, where employees, volunteers, and school students would take their lunch breaks separately or undertake projects in their segregated groups—that is, *not* facilitating social integration. What was perhaps most significant for social integration was staff practices of implementing strategic pairing of employees to work in 'bumping spaces' that facilitate collective problem-solving.

Security: The garden, blockroom, and supervisor's office had the highest mentions of security. At the garden, security was associated with repeated, habitual routines and tasks. The Supervisor's office is associated with support from a designated 'support team'—some of whom expressed that they make themselves available to employees around the clock, via providing their mobile phone number:

> You're chatting to them every day pretty much, whether it's just say gidday, how you going or whatever, or helping them out. They might be looking for something, you give them a hand to find things and things like that.
>
> (Farm_staff_3)

Supervisors discussed assisting employees with matters outside of work such as finding safe accommodation and helping with form-filling and bureaucratic hurdles, leading to mentions of security both within and outside of the social enterprise. A key example was where an employee had experienced physical violence and bullying in her community life but insisted on coming to work the next day as she associated the social enterprise with a feeling of security and caring.

Similarly, two employees expressed that they feel safe in the social enterprise because they are able to work together:

> It's hard to say, because we work in a lot of different areas. Like every other day or every week. Sometimes we get shifted. Sometimes we're on the same job for a long time. Pretty much wherever we go is where we feel comfortable . . . Sometimes we go into the Blockroom. We do sometimes staple or stack some blocks and all that. So, we mostly, in a way, me and him just want to feel comfortable when we're working together.
>
> (Focus Group_Farm_employee)

Security at Farm was also realised in the supervisor's office, which was associated with being a place of both mental and physical safety. Ongoing and predictable work practices, the supportive attitudes of supervisors, and knowing where to find supervisors were significant elements. A range of supervisors interviewed made mention of supports like:

> they [employees] can always come and talk.
>
> (Farm_Staff_3)

> I help with tax—anything really.
>
> (Farm_Staff_2)

> we looked at accommodation and supports—I had permission to phone the people he was living with.
>
> (Farm_Staff_4)

Therapy: The highest number of mentions for therapy were associated with the Supervisor's office. This was discussed as a place where employees received therapeutic counselling and immediate attention. Mentions of therapy in the garden were associated with sensory pleasure from the green space and connection with natural processes. For example, one employee described the joy of watching seedlings germinate. Other comments about the garden were appreciation that it was a 'tranquil,' quiet, and peaceful space. Some of these therapeutic experiences could be through symbolic associations of, for example, gardens, nature, and green space, with health and wellbeing as closely associated to these spaces. This includes employees' involvement in cooking using produce from Farm, thereby endeavouring to influence employees to grow food and eat healthier outside of Farm, also contributing to the relational nature of wellbeing. At times, there was a counternarrative to therapy that emphasised the social enterprise as a business and need to do work, highlighting the tension between the dual social and economic missions of social enterprise.

The blockroom also had mentions of therapy relating to the predictable, routine nature of work tasks there—which were found to be calming. Mentions were from employees who more generally carry out more complex work, such as picking ripe produce in the garden. These workers said they sometimes felt a bit overwhelmed by the pressure of their work tasks and so would turn to the blockroom's repetitive work that enabled them to calm down and de-stress while also feeling useful.

Spaces of Wellbeing Across Three Social Enterprises

To validate that wellbeing realises through similar mechanisms for employees across each of the social enterprises, Table 2.1 summarises data and excerpts from the two other WISEs studied—Catering and AssistAll. Table 2.1 shows that spaces, practices, and narratives across the social enterprises could be similarly associated with the wellbeing aspects; for example—regarding capability and social integration:

Capability: At all three social enterprises, there was a high number of mentions of capability in spaces that enabled a variety of people with various skill sets to work together such as the garden and the blockroom at the Farm, the kitchen at Catering, and the communal worktable at AssistAll. Common to all those spaces is that employees can engage in a variety of tasks which allow them to work to their own capability and achieve self-actualisation in various ways.

Social integration: All three sites have delivery services. At these, employees drive or accompany other members of the social enterprise in a car or van into the community. In all three social enterprises, this opened up the opportunity for employees to engage with others in the car/van, such as co-workers or staff members in a more intimate space. Additionally, through the deliveries, employees are in contact with

Table 2.2 Typology of spaces contributing to wellbeing and their key characteristics

Types of space	Characteristics	Wellbeing aspect
Green spaces	Gardens, open spaces, or even vegetable boxes can provide positive sensory, learning, and team-building experiences.	Social Integration Capability Therapy
Spaces of diversity	Where a range of people with different skill sets or experiences work together in the same area or where different tasks are being completed at the same time.	Social Integration Capability
Spaces for community engagement	When employees travel out into the community or when the community comes into the social enterprise.	Social Integration Capability
Skill development spaces	Areas where employees work on complex tasks that allow room for progression, upskilling, or independent thinking.	Capability
Supported spaces	Spaces of support that not only include office spaces or places where employees know of to get support in relation to their work or in terms of their private lives from supervisors but also high-skilled spaces that can be under constant supervision.	Security Therapy Capability
Spaces of repetition	Repetitive tasks are those that employees were familiar with, which they can do on their own do not generally need others to assist them.	Security Capability
Incidental spaces	Spaces that either have an assigned use but are co-opted for alternative use by employees or non-spaces that employees can appropriate for their own use.	Security Therapy Social Integration

community members that they would not normally encounter in their daily lives.

A Typology of Spaces Contributing to Wellbeing

Following the aforementioned analysis describing how wellbeing is realised in spaces, we now draw together the consistent types of workspaces that *emerged* as promoting wellbeing realisation. This typology of spaces, how they are constituted, and what occurs within them are provided here to give some practical ideas for designing social enterprises to optimise wellbeing. Table 2.2 outlines the types of spaces and the wellbeing aspects to which the spaces contribute.

The typology does not necessarily mean that each of these spaces should be 'designed in' as physical locations, but they can be considered to arise through compositions of activities, organisational narratives, and ephemeral spaces. This section is intended as a helpful practical checklist—emergent from the research evidence—for social enterprises that seek to 'design in' elements that evidence suggests are associated with individual wellbeing realisation. In offering this typology of spaces, we try to translate abstract ideas about 'spaces of wellbeing' into more concrete designs for locations in social enterprises as well as work practices.

Green Spaces

Green and 'eco' spaces can have positive effects, as interactions with nature are shown to have therapeutic impacts on health (Sugiyama *et al.*, 2008; Bell *et al.*, 2018). Green spaces (gardens) were found at Farm and AssistAll, in our study, and were spaces of social interaction, as they provided multiple opportunities for forging new social relations, mentoring, and problem-solving among small groups. They were significant to capability realisation in providing multiple types of tasks, and repetitive routines in these spaces also influenced security. Experiences in the garden provided opportunities for education about life skills, from how to produce food, to understanding healthy eating.

The seasonality of green spaces also produces emergent changing impacts, for instance, when holding focus groups in spring, we found that the shade houses where seedlings were raised were noted as significant to wellbeing; however, this had not been identified during original data collection which was in winter.

Spaces of Diversity (Including Diverse Tasks and People With Diverse Backgrounds)

Having people with diverse backgrounds working in close proximity with each other exposes employees to discourses of inclusion and accounts of diverse experiences and world views. For example, we observed a conversation where an employee was working alongside visiting students from an assisted learning school and initiated a conversation with them around respect and why there were certain expectations placed on them by their parents. Because the employee was doing the same task with the students in the space, the students engaged with him intently and asked him questions they may not have asked of another adult. The garden at Farm represents a space of diversity. Volunteers, who were often retirees, might assist with weeding and pruning, and members of the community might visit to learn about the enterprise, purchase services, and produce. Employees, volunteers, school students, staff, and visiting community members then have opportunities to work together or engage with one another. Thus, these spaces of diversity afford opportunities for community social inclusion.

Spaces for Community Engagement

People living with a disability or who experience poor health can be excluded from many aspects of everyday community life. In our study, delivery vans, a carwash, market gardens, and 'op-shops' were, in a sense, portals through which employees moved into the community and external clients moved into the 'world' of the social enterprise. Other spaces of community engagement are created when community members visit the social enterprises in roles as customers to purchase goods and services. Employees, volunteers, and community members, then, are able to engage with each other in new spaces.

In the study, employees were engaged in activities that included delivering and picking up client's cars to be cleaned—tasks requiring a combination of practical and social skills. We gained evidence that being deemed responsible to work in the community and representing the social enterprise nurtured a sense of progression and achievement. Employees experience a secure exposure to the community through these encounters when it is part of their work and when it is navigated and supported by social enterprise supervisors.

Through engagements like these, employees are signified to the community as capable and valid 'working citizens.' Convivial encounters (where strangers encounter one another through a temporary shared experience or identity) often emerge between employees and community members of different backgrounds who might not otherwise meet and 'encounter with strangers . . . provides possibilities for people from minority or excluded groups to become recognised and known within communities' (Wiesel and Bigby, 2016, p. 201).

Skill Development Spaces

Spaces for skills development are those areas where employees learn and implement new and advanced skills by working on a range of complex tasks. Such spaces offer opportunities for developing confidence, a sense of achievement, independence, and creative thinking. For example, employees at Farm who made furniture in a workshop explained how they had learned to use tools such as nail guns, drills, and woodworking tools, and how this provided a sense of capability and pride at achievement. For an individual employee, spaces for skill development allow for a sense of progression through an organisation where being seen to develop and improve, by others including employees, staff, and visiting community members, could lead to feelings of accomplishment and satisfaction.

Spaces of Support

The existence of ongoing support and knowing where it can be readily accessed is significant to employees' sense of security and underpins the whole of the social enterprise experience. In our study, support was associated with particular staff members including designated support workers, supervisors, and managers and also associated with certain physical spaces like staff offices or secluded rooms (such as delivery vans or small kitchen areas). Employees appreciate knowing where support staff are located without having to specifically ask for them.

Spaces associated with learning skills that are under constant, but at 'arms-length,' supervision (like the kitchen at Catering) are also potential spaces of support. Employees working in these spaces feel secure that they can gain help immediately if needed. This helps them to feel confident and underpins their growth of capability by enabling employees to attempt new tasks. At all the social enterprises, kitchens emerged as spaces of security where employees and supervisors work side by side. Working on tasks together—in familiar surroundings—also supports conversations and discussions that cover personal issues while still undertaking productive activities.

Spaces of Repetition

Physical spaces of repetitive tasks generate security and capability through multiple people working together to provide tangible outputs. Our data showed this can lead to feelings of independence and achievement for people as individuals and in their sense of pride and achievement as part of a team (e.g. this was observed at communal worktables at Farm and AssistAll).

Repetitive tasks provide a sense of ontological security, or 'knowing what is expected,' which can give comfort. For example, painting stakes and folding laundry (tasks at Farm) allows employees with a range of abilities to undertake tasks together and autonomously with little input from supervisors. This gives employees a sense of capability and responsibility. Spaces of repetitive tasks could involve multiple people sitting together but working independently from each other—these can be termed 'together-alone' spaces (Littman-Ovadia, 2019), which are shown to be supportive as part of human wellbeing—where individuals who could not or did not want to interact, could still work as part of the team.

Incidental Spaces

Incidental spaces are physical locations where employees can take time out from formal tasks or being with other employees if this was found stressful. Incidental spaces could variously be places to calm down and take time out and/or to be social with other employees in non-work situations. We found incidental spaces across the three social enterprises. Some had a formal designated role as social spaces, whereas others were co-opted or 'created' for 'alternative use' by employees—such as the box room at Catering. This was a space used to fold boxes, but it was also the space (and task) that people chose to do when they wanted to get away from the stress of the commercial kitchen to have quiet or listen to music. Alternatively, some spaces were 'non-spaces' that employees had appropriated for use (e.g. under the big tree at Farm). Incidental spaces could also be hidden (e.g. such as toilets) or in places that are 'out of the way' (e.g. apparently unused or non-productive spaces such as next to the car wash at Farm) that were used for short breaks or socialising, away from 'the gaze' of supervisors.

In a sense, these spaces are adopted and given meaning by the employees themselves. They appear to provide employees with a sense of privacy or a perception that they are not being surveilled, and evidence suggests these were significant for employees' sense of their independence and control.

Discussion

We found that wellbeing was realised in and by the social enterprises studied. Significantly, by initially considering *where* wellbeing realises through harnessing a relational understanding of wellbeing and qualitative GIS methods, the study helps to show *how* social enterprises produce wellbeing effects. Understanding how social enterprises impact on employee wellbeing helps in considering how to design social enterprises for optimal impact and progresses thinking about meaningful ways to evaluate social enterprise outcomes.

Physical spaces and objects, behaviours, practices, and the narratives told and re-told, within the social enterprises studied, come together to help shape individuals' wellbeing. This occurs through supporting self-actualisation (capability), helping to connect employees to other and different people and organisations in the community (social integration), building comfort and a place of refuge (security), and caring about each other while building in aspects to enhance wellness such as the encounters with green space we found (therapy). While spaces within a social enterprise can be designed to help realise wellbeing, the wider symbolic understanding of social enterprises in contemporary society, as a type of socio-economic 'intervention,' serves to reinforce these effects. This understanding associates social enterprises with providing work opportunities, with being a worker, a crucial aspect that our society values (Evans and Wilton, 2019).

Findings suggest that social enterprises help to realise the upstream wellbeing effects that could be foundational to downstream improvements in physical and mental health. Wellbeing effects in themselves are likely to influence self-confidence, feelings of self-worth, belonging, and social status. Wellbeing aspects of social integration, capability, and security provide stepping stones for developing the agency to seek formal educational qualifications, develop social networks, adopt health behaviours, and to approach people and services for support.

The research techniques we used help to understand social enterprise causal mechanisms partly by enabling intangible wellbeing effects to be made tangible through visualisation and elements of quantification. This making the intangible 'real' helps to reveal wellbeing effects and make them more comprehensible (Brennan-Horley, 2010). By associating wellbeing effects with the places where they arise and then explaining the assembled elements that come together to make wellbeing experiences, we can draw a convincing line from theory to evidence with the aim of better understanding relationships between social enterprise aspirations and actual benefits.

Showing that some workspaces are more effective at producing wellbeing or aspects of wellbeing compared to others again helps to verify the idea that the effects revealed through the spatial and qualitative GIS methodology are valid. Previous studies have tended simply to suggest positive effects rather than showing varying levels of impact and variations fluctuating in relation to what occurs within or outside social enterprises. The study therefore helps to highlight how wellbeing might be enhanced by tangible inputs and new design ideas.

Atkinson and Robson (2012) highlight that wellbeing should not be regarded as simply a set of components that either exist or do not, but rather as a fluid process realised by and through interweaving and fluctuating effects. Atkinson also notes, however, that expressing wellbeing as components can be helpful as a shorthand to aid understanding of how wellbeing realises. In this study, we sought to identify and describe wellbeing by examining the aspects of social integration, capability, security, and therapy that are suggested by spaces of wellbeing theory. It is clear from findings that these aspects are interwoven and that—for example—feeling secure through experiencing and participating in work routines and interacting with supportive staff, helps to develop the confidence to make new relationships. New social relationships, in turn, serve to further embed feelings of security, and then both security and social relationships are helpful for developing capability as it is understood in this chapter.

Using our findings to develop a typology of spaces that encourage the realisation of wellbeing helps to translate the abstract idea of spaces of wellbeing into tangible design considerations. Taking into account specific types of physical spaces, objects, activities, and organisational narratives within the typology, social enterprises can not only 'build in' ways to nurture individual wellbeing realisation, but the typology can also be used as a checklist to assess the ways this may be occurring already within the organisation.

While increasing evidence about how wellbeing realises, the study and methodology have limitations. A 'measure' of wellbeing realisation that enables benchmarking and comparison across social enterprises, to understand which 'produces the most wellbeing,' is not given. Rather, the methodology and findings are most useful in enabling individual social enterprises to reflect on their practices and design, helping them to consider any changes that could be made to optimise and support wellbeing.

Applying spaces of wellbeing theory in data collection and analysis could be argued to produce a sort of self-fulfilling prophecy in terms of results, in that evidence of social integration, capability, security, and therapy are specifically sought out. However, the theory does appear to have validity as a frame to guide study, having been developed from a multidisciplinary literature review and used in multiple studies (Rotheram, McGarrol, and Watkins, 2010; Munoz *et al.*, 2015; Farmer *et al.*, 2016). Further, our data collection and analysis were open to other emergent themes and we found evidence of varying impacts on wellbeing. For more evidence about these varying and sometimes negative impacts (see Farmer *et al.*, 2019) which reflects on how the business-oriented emphasis and practices of the social enterprises studied could sometimes be detrimental to time spent developing social benefits.

The study did not address the temporality of wellbeing. Due to the cross-sectional nature of the study, we did not observe wellbeing over time, did it grow or fluctuate, and in relation to what effects? Also, little is known about what happens to wellbeing once employees leave the social enterprise—are there lingering or ongoing benefits? Does a social enterprise predicate 'a better life' for employees thereafter? Or do impacts dissipate when an employee leaves? Future study would usefully consider the fluid and fluctuating nature of wellbeing in relation to longitudinal employment in, and after, social enterprise experiences (see Elmes, in this book).

Conclusions

The study reported here draws on established geographical theory and mixed methodology to introduce a new way to understand and evaluate how social enterprises help to realise wellbeing for employees. The study addresses the major gap in assessing how social enterprises enable well-being realisation. Further, findings show, quite practically, the elements that social enterprises can embed, design-in, and evaluate with a view to nurturing and enhancing wellbeing. Consistently capturing wellbeing impacts across the three social enterprises helps to show the benefit of applying a consistent set of previously tested wellbeing indicators. We suggest it is significantly more likely that there is a relationship between upstream wellbeing effects from social enterprise, compared to showing downstream outcomes of physical and mental health clinical changes. Thus, focusing on measuring a consistent set of wellbeing indicators may be a useful way ahead both for convincing policymakers and others of wellbeing impacts from social enterprise and for progressing towards measurement and benchmarking methods.

Fruitful next steps to progress this research area would be considering how wellbeing changes over time and particularly the longitudinal effects for employees of social enterprise involvement. This would require exploring how the findings and methodology can feed into useable routine tools for evaluating and benchmarking social enterprise impacts.

References

Atkinson, S. 2013, 'Beyond components of wellbeing: the effects of relational and situated assemblage', *Topoi*, 32, 137–144.

Atkinson, S. and Robson, M. 2012, 'Arts and health as a practice of liminality: managing the spaces of transformation for social and emotional wellbeing with primary school children', *Health & Place*, 18(6), 1348–1355.

Bell, S.L., Foley, R., Houghton, F., Maddrell, A. and Williams, A.M. 2018, 'From therapeutic landscapes to healthy spaces, places and practices: A scoping review', *Social Science & Medicine*, 196, 123–130.

Brennan-Horley, C. 2010, 'Multiple work sites and city-wide networks: a topological approach to understanding creative work', *Australian Geographer*, 41, 39–56.

Carpiano, R.M. 2009, 'Come take a walk with me: the "go-along" interview as a novel method for studying the implications of place for health and well-being', *Health & Place*, 15, 263–272.

Chambers, R. 1997, *Whose reality counts? Putting the first last.* Intermediate Technology Publications, London.

Conradson, D. 2005, 'Landscape, care and the relational self: therapeutic encounters in rural England', *Health & Place*, 11(4), 337–348.

Cummins, S., Curtis, S., Diez-Roux, A.V. and Macintyre, S. 2007, 'Understanding and representing "place" in health research: a relational approach', *Social Science & Medicine*, 65, 1825–1838.

Diener E. and Lucas R.E. 2000, 'Explaining differences in societal levels of happiness: relative standards, need fulfilment, culture, and evaluation theory', *Journal of Happiness Studies*, 1, 41–78.

Elmes, A.I. 2019, 'Health impacts of a WISE: a longitudinal study', *Social Enterprise Journal*, 15(4), 457–474.

Evans, J. and Wilton, R. 2019, 'Well enough to work? Social enterprise employment and the geographies of mental health recovery', *Annals of the American Association of Geographers*, 109(1), 87–103.

Farmer, J., De Cotta, T., Kamstra, P., Brennan-Horley, C. and Munoz, S.A. 2020, 'Integration and segregation for social enterprise employees: a relational microgeography', *Area*, 52(1), 176–186.

Farmer, J., De Cotta, T., Kilpatrick, S., Barraket, J., Roy, M. and Munoz, S. A. 2019, 'How work integration social enterprises help to realize capability: a comparison of three Australian settings', *Journal of Social Entrepreneurship*, 1–23.

Farmer, J., De Cotta, T., McKinnon, K., Barraket, J., Munoz, S-A., Douglas, H. and Roy, M. 2016, 'Social enterprise and wellbeing in community life', *Social Enterprise Journal*, 12(2), 235–254.

Farmer, J., Kamstra, P., Brennan-Horley, C., De Cotta, T., Roy, M., Barraket, J., Munoz, S.A. and Kilpatrick, S. 2020, 'Using micro-geography to understand the realisation of wellbeing: a qualitative GIS study of three social enterprises', *Health & Place*. https://doi.org/10.1016/j.healthplace.2020.102293.

Fleuret, S. and Atkinson, S. 2007, 'Wellbeing, health and geography: a critical review and research agenda', *New Zealand Geographer*, 63, 106–118.

Foley, R. 2014, 'The Roman—Irish Bath: medical/health history as therapeutic assemblage', *Social Science & Medicine*, 106, 10–19.

Jung, J.K. and Elwood, S. 2010, 'Extending the qualitative capabilities of GIS: Computer-aided qualitative GIS', *Transactions in GIS*, 14(1), 63–87.

Kamstra, P., Cook, B., Kennedy, M.D. and Brennan-Horley, C. 2019, 'Qualitative GIS to relate perceptions with behaviors among fishers on risky, rocky coasts', *The Professional Geographer*, 71, 491–506.

Kusenbach, M. 2003, 'Street phenomenology: The go-along as ethnographic research tool', *Ethnography*, 4(3), 455–485.

Lager, D., Van Hoven, B. and Huigen, P. 2015, 'Understanding older adults' social capital in place: obstacles to and opportunities for social contacts in the neighbourhood', *Geoforum*, 59, 87–97.

Layard, R. 2005, *Happiness: Lessons from a new science*. Penguin, London.

Littman-Ovadia, H. 2019, 'Doing—being and relationship—solitude: a proposed model for a balanced life', *Journal of Happiness Studies*, 20, 1953–1971.

Maslow, A. 1954, *Motivation and personality*. Harper & Row, New York.

Mason, C., Barraket, J., Friel, S., O'Rourke, K. and Christian-Paul Stenta, C-P. 2015, 'Social innovation for the promotion of health equity', *Health Promotion International*, 30(2), ii116–ii125.

Massey, D. 1985, *New directions in space. Social relations and spatial structures*. Springer, Dordrecht.

Massey, D. 2005, *For space*. SAGE, London.

Munoz, S.A., Farmer, J., Winterton, R. and Barraket, J. 2015, 'Social enterprise as a space of wellbeing: an exploratory case study', *Social Enterprise Journal*, 11(3), 281–302.

Ottoni, C.A., Sims-Gould, J., Winters, M., Heijnen, M. and McKay, H.A. 2016, '"Benches become like porches": built and social environment influences on older adults' experiences of mobility and well-being', *Social Science & Medicine*, 169, 33–41.

Rotheram, S., McGarrol, S. and Watkins, F. 2010, 'Care farms as a space of well-being for people with a learning disability in the United Kingdom', *Health & Place*, 48, 123–131.

Roy, M., Donaldson, C., Baker, R. and Kerr, S. 2014, 'The potential of social enterprise to enhance health and well-being: A model and systematic review', *Social Science and Medicine*, 123, 182–193.

Roy, M. and Hackett, M. 2017, 'Polanyi's "substantive approach" to the economy in action? Conceptualising social enterprise as a public health "intervention"', *Review of Social Economy*, 75(2), 89–111.

Sen, A. 1992, 'Capability and wellbeing', in Sen, A. and Nussbaum, M. (Eds.), *The Quality of Life*. Clarendon Press, Oxford, pp. 30–53.

Sugiyama, T., Leslie, E., Giles-Corti, B. and Owe, N.N. 2008, 'Associations of neighbourhood greenness with physical and mental health: do walking, social coherence and local social interaction explain the relationships?' *Journal of Epidemiology & Community Health*, 62, e9.

Vidal, I. 2005, 'Social enterprise and social inclusion: Social enterprises in the sphere of work integration', *International Journal of Public Administration*, 28(9–10), 807–825.

Wiesel, I. and Bigby, C. 2016, 'Mainstream, inclusionary, and convivial places: locating encounters between people with and without intellectual disabilities', *Geographical Review*, 106(2), 201–214.

Wilkinson, R.G. 1996, *Unhealthy societies: The afflictions of inequality*. Routledge, London.

3 Transcending Social Enterprise Understandings— Wellbeing, Livelihoods, and Interspecies Solidarity in Transformation to Postgrowth Societies

Eeva Houtbeckers

Introduction

> *No one is born here with an idea that my mission is to destroy this planet, cause suffering, [. . .] no one has this automatically inserted in their head. It is what our society feeds there, this contemporary model. [. . .] Social enterprise is threatening to some because it indicates that this model is not acceptable. [It is not acceptable that] you deprive, you exploit, you do whatever for cash. [But] what can I do to get enough cash and do good more? With [. . .] meaningful marketing [. . .] it is possible to speak to others at a deeper level.*
>
> (Self-employed clothing and textile professional,
interview in 2009)

This book chapter presents observations and emerging ideas from the past ten years of ethnographic fieldwork focusing on grassroots initiatives related to social enterprise and postgrowth organising in the global North. As concepts, social enterprise and postgrowth retain vast streams of the literature impossible to review in one book chapter. Thus, it is difficult to say anything certain about matters that are speculative, but yet undeniably practised daily, as the previous quote indicates.

Yet, there is a growing number of social and natural scientists and researchers who observe complex socio-ecological crises and argue for a transformation of mindsets and paradigms in order to address these (see e.g. Wiedmann *et al.*, 2020; Stengers, 2017; Steffen *et al.*, 2015). Because postgrowth societies are constructed and reconstructed constantly, a perspective elaborated later in this chapter, this text cannot determine what social enterprises are like in postgrowth societies that maximise wellbeing, rather than economic growth. Instead, I find it important to map the frontiers of social enterprise thinking in order to explore *how to transcend social enterprise understandings that enable transformation*

DOI: 10.4324/9781003125976-3

to postgrowth societies that maximise wellbeing. Rather than a comprehensive report, this chapter presents thinking in progress and, thus, can be read as a starting point for a better comprehension of the following interlinked observations.

Observation 1: Postgrowth Transformation Is Needed

While the prioritising of economic growth has brought wellbeing to some parts of humanity, it is said to exploit many people in less privileged positions, let alone other-than-human beings and ecosystems (Mellor, 2006). Scholars in various disciplines argue that there is a need for transformation, or more narrowly transition, towards postgrowth societies (Jackson, 2009; Latouche, 2009; Demaria *et al.*, 2013; D'Alisa *et al.*, 2015; Paulson, 2017; Raworth, 2017). This is validated by evidence related to the correlation between economic growth and ecological and social degradation studied, for example, in the field of ecological economics (see e.g. Kallis *et al.*, 2012). While a radical decrease in material throughput is needed, at least in the global North, transformation is to the most degree a transformation in thinking, as dominant (occidental) cultures are experiencing an existential crisis (Latouche, 2009).

Observation 2: Social Enterprises as Postgrowth Organisations

Social enterprise is at times mentioned as being one of the needed operational units for postgrowth societies. It is understood as, for example, a provider of jobs (Gibson-Graham *et al.*, 2013), a distributor of wealth (Foundational Economy Collective, 2018), and a place for developing solutions for local needs (Johanisova *et al.*, 2013). However, in these discussions, the ambiguity of social enterprise might be overlooked, most likely because of the attempts to envision a novel complex system in a single research article or book and because the authors might not have studied the everyday life of social enterprises. In short, despite the notion of social enterprise as a potential vehicle for postgrowth futures, some understandings of social enterprise seem incompatible with the nuances related to such transformations.

Observation 3: The Understanding of Wellbeing Varies

These seemingly separate fields of postgrowth and social enterprise are connected when it comes to ensuring wellbeing (see e.g. Büchs and Koch, 2017; Roy, 2021). In principle, both fields aim to maximise wellbeing, however it is understood. While in postgrowth thinking this is done while explicitly dismantling economic growth as the policy-making priority, in social enterprise thinking, economic growth is more of an implicit issue. In short, this creates a tension that challenges some straightforward interpretations of social enterprise as postgrowth organising (Houtbeckers, 2018). The maximisation of wellbeing remains an unsolved puzzle, often complicated by anthropocentric understandings.

The Organisation of This Book Chapter

As an engaged scholar (Burke and Shear, 2014), I feel that I need to explore this fluctuating terrain. In addition to the existing literature, this book chapter draws from my past and ongoing ethnographic fieldwork among people who run various initiatives because of their concerns related to socio-ecological crises. Some of them relate to the notion of 'social enterprise,' some to 'degrowth' or 'postgrowth,' and some to neither of these but other concepts such as 'self-sufficiency.' What is interesting for this book chapter is that in these initiatives people's perspectives towards work, consumption, production, economy, and wellbeing question many taken-for-granted assumptions and invite a reconsideration of transformation towards postgrowth societies. Especially, I focus on ensuring livelihoods and interspecies solidarity in order to map some themes that could provide leverage for changes in social enterprise understandings.

In order to trace these expanding themes in one book chapter, I use leverage points thinking familiar from systems theories (Meadows, 1999; Wright and Meadows, 2012) as a starting point to indicate the effects and possibilities of contemporary thinking that are related to social enterprise, postgrowth, and wellbeing as the joint goal. Before that, I briefly give an overview of my ethnographic work that grounds the observations used in this chapter.

Ethnographies of Initiatives Aiming to Maximise Wellbeing

This book chapter stems from observations in two consecutive ethnographies. I use institutional ethnography (Smith, 2005) to study everyday practices in initiatives that aim to maximise wellbeing, when they need to function in a society organised around growth dependency, which is an example of an institution. My research stems from an understanding that growth dependency does not happen at a 'macro-level' nor is it merely 'structural' but is manifested in everyday activities. Moreover, as an engaged scholar (Burke and Shear, 2014), I am interested in local initiatives that work in and for the transformation to postgrowth societies and especially the difficulties, and at times the success, they face. While I am driven by exploring postgrowth practices with global connections, the immediate focus of my work and this book chapter is in the global North.

The first ethnography (2009–2016) began when I attended various Finnish social enterprise events and became familiarised with social enterprise actors in the field. At that time, social enterprise had picked up again in Finland, and I entered the field without prior knowledge of the history related to cooperatives, third-sector social service providers, and work-integration social enterprises—practices that later helped me to contextualise my study. Instead, I met a loosely bound group of young people who were excited about a novel approach to economy, work, and livelihood that went beyond corporate responsibility jargon and multinational corporations. Some of them referred to themselves as social entrepreneurs, while they were neither functioning in the social and welfare sector nor running a work-integration social enterprise nor limiting profit distribution that at the time were among the key indicators for social enterprises (Defourny and Nyssens, 2010). Instead, they were deeply concerned about the socio-environmental crisis and wanted to use their professional know-how while ensuring a livelihood (Houtbeckers, 2016a). Finally, I focused on these young urban micro-entrepreneurs who identified with social entrepreneurship and studied their everyday work practices in Finland (Houtbeckers, 2016b). My findings concluded that many of them did not benefit financially from their work that aimed to change institutions; yet, they found the work important and meaningful.

The second, and ongoing, ethnography (2016 onwards) focuses explicitly on actors, initiatives, and work in and for the transformation to postgrowth societies. I have contacted people and projects through the Finnish Degrowth Movement and events related to self-sufficiency, land rights, and rethinking of forest ownership. The more I fumble, as is usual with ethnographic fieldwork, the more I realise the interconnectedness of the themes between my two ethnographies. Working towards postgrowth societies is about how people organise their livelihoods and navigate the diverse economy (Houtbeckers, 2018) while striving for a fundamental paradigm change. This takes various forms, including social enterprise.

Leverage Points

It is fair to conclude that social enterprise, as a concept and practice, is part of a complex system related to, for example, economy, livelihoods, work, and wellbeing. In 1999, Donella Meadows published an influential analysis of leverage points, a concept used by system theorists (Meadows, 1999), and it was subsequently complemented by a book (Wright and Meadows, 2012). The earth can be understood as a complex system that hosts several interconnected systems, whereas a bathtub can be understood as a simpler system affected by the intake of hot and cold water and the outflow of excess water. Any system strives to be in balance but depending on the system changes can be unpredictable.

The analysis by Meadows specifies several leverage points that indicate points to intervene in a system in an efficient manner. Intuitively, people look for leverage points that would ease any changes (Table 3.1).

Table 3.1 Grouped leverage points from 'shallow' to 'deep' leverage

Leverage points	System characteristics
12. Constants, parameters, numbers (e.g. subsidies, taxes, standards)	*Parameters*
11. The size of buffers and stocks, relative to their flows	
10. The structure of material stocks and flows (e.g. transport networks, population age structure)	
9. The length of delays relative to the rate of system change	*Feedbacks*
8. The strength of negative feedback loops relative to the impacts they are trying to correct against	
7. The gain around driving positive feedback loops	
6. The structure of information flows (who does and does not have access to what kinds of information)	*Design*
5. The rules of the system (such as incentives, punishments, constraints)	
4. The power to add, change, evolve, or self-organise a system structure	
3. The goals of the system	*Intent*
2. The mindset or paradigm out of which the system—its goals, structure, rules, delays, parameters—arise	
1. The power to transcend paradigms	

Source: Adapted from Abson *et al.* (2017)

According to Meadows, a leverage point is the silver bullet or the quick fix of a system that makes up many 'good hero journey' stories. At the shallow end, an intervention is simpler and is most likely to be easier to complete. Thus, the greater the leverage, the more that opposition is met because the possible changes are fundamental to ways of thinking.

However, people tend to work against leverage points, which makes leverage points often counterintuitive (Meadows, 1999). One example is the role of economic growth discussed in this text: reducing economic growth is considered outrageous, although the decoupling of growth from social and environmental deterioration has not succeeded (see e.g. Wiedmann *et al.*, 2020).

Many other researchers and disciplines have picked up on leverage points and used this particular list. In order to help transdisciplinary researchers, who work with sustainability topics, Abson *et al.* (2017) grouped the leverage points into four clusters: parameters, feedbacks, design, and intent. *Parameters* are usually targeted by policymakers, and they can seem tangible and mechanistic, such as subsidies, taxes, and stocks. *Feedbacks* inform on the interactions within a system. For example, negative feedback loops indicate that something is not right with a system: the bathtub is overflowing, a person may require more rest, or the chosen social security measures are not helping less privileged citizens. *Design* indicates the 'social structures and institutions that manage parameters and feedbacks' (Abson *et al.*, 2017, p. 32). *Intent* reflects the 'the norms, values and goals embodied within the system,' such as economic growth that can be understood as a systemic intent, although not necessarily shared by everyone (Abson *et al.*, 2017, p. 32).

Finally, Abson *et al.* (2017) warn against 'social engineering' when thinking about leverage points. Systems are complex and holistic and therefore they cannot be completely captured in models. In this chapter, I use leverage points to aid in asking questions about social enterprise research and its relation to the transformation to postgrowth societies that maximise wellbeing.

Transformation Towards Postgrowth Societies

Currently, many social policy changes, or the lack of them, are justified with economic impacts. The debate circles around whether we can afford to address structural unemployment, alleviate extreme poverty, or slow down climate change. In policy talk, it is argued that we could afford these—but only after the economy, that is, gross domestic product (GDP), has grown. This is argued despite the fact that, in terms of GDP, (occidental) societies are more affluent than ever.

Yet, the unchallenged expectation of continuous economic growth can decrease the wellbeing of humans and other-than humans (Jackson, 2009; Latouche, 2009; Raworth, 2017; Büchs and Koch, 2017). This is also a finding from system theorists: economic growth can be understood as a 'leverage point' that affects complex systems in a counterintuitive manner (Meadows, 1999). This is because maximising economic growth brings increasing wealth to some and also unwanted processes, like environmental degradation and social inequalities.

Indeed, research has shown that economic growth and material use cannot be decoupled completely (Wiedmann *et al.*, 2020), and as a result, one finite planet is not enough to feed exponentially growing economies infinitely (see e.g. Raworth, 2017). Researchers have for years warned about the overrun of some vital resources (Steffen *et al.*, 2015). Because some resources, such as fossil fuels, are limited, increasing economy, and subsequently wellbeing for some, cannot be based solely on the overuse of limited production materials. This is not a condition in the unforeseen future, but already contemporary levels of consumption, combined with political steering geared towards the interest of capital, result in resource scarcity that is a reality for Majority World, usually for the poor

(Swyngedouw, 2013). Therefore, it is crucial to rethink how to live in a socially just manner on earth that has a limited carrying capacity.

Degrowth and postgrowth debates bring together activists and scholars who criticise the economic growth paradigm and develop knowledge on transformation to postgrowth societies (D'Alisa *et al.*, 2015; Demaria *et al.*, 2013). In this text, I use the notion of postgrowth to refer to the debates about transformation to postgrowth. Although they form a versatile and multidisciplinary field with several ongoing debates, some common themes emerge.

First, whatever opinions one has about degrowth or postgrowth as a concept, experts argue that Europe—one of the affluent economies—has entered an era of slow or no growth (Jackson, 2018). Affluent economies will stagnate despite efforts to keep the machine going. Postgrowth activists and scholars argue that instead of uncontrollable decline, the economy could and should be used to conduct a more controlled transformation. Overall, it is argued that in affluent countries the level of wellbeing is high enough to decouple the maintenance of wellbeing from economic growth (Latouche, 2009). In Majority World countries with a less privileged history and presence, economic growth might still be needed (D'Alisa *et al.*, 2015).

Second, many urge the placing of wellbeing and care at the centre of policymaking, instead of economic growth (Büchs and Koch, 2017; Dengler and Strunk, 2018). When talking about economic growth, it is important to emphasise that GDP is a computational means to keep tally of economic transactions. Using money to value exchanges between households, enterprises, and nations is one way to understand the world and make decisions about common matters. In the end, people live their lives despite agreements on economic bookkeeping. This contradicts the taken-for-granted assumption that economic growth is a prerequisite for enabling wellbeing. As a result, the capacity for economic growth and the justification for it have decreased in occidental societies (Büchs and Koch, 2017). However, since many human societies and welfare systems are based on economic growth, transformation is difficult to make.

Maximising Wellbeing in the Transformation to Postgrowth Societies

In their important book *Postgrowth and wellbeing*, Büchs and Koch (2017) explore the nexus of wellbeing and postgrowth in order to advance postgrowth thinking. The core postgrowth argument is that 'economic activity should mainly aim at achieving long-term human wellbeing, not economic growth' (Büchs and Koch, 2017, p. 57). Postgrowth proponents relate to wellbeing with three main arguments (Büchs and Koch, 2017, p. 126). First of all, it is a moral imperative to move away from growth-based societies in order to meet the basic needs of future generations. Second, GDP is not clearly connected with subjective and objective wellbeing. Third, the contemporary understanding of wellbeing is based on a materialistic worldview and consumption.

In the postgrowth literature, wellbeing is used in various connections with various meanings. Büchs and Koch urge that basic human needs should be discussed in relation to postgrowth. This is because there is little understanding of how a degrowing economy affects subjective or objective wellbeing. For example, how is mindset to be changed, perhaps at a rapid pace, when a previous level of consumption is no longer possible for those who are used to it?

Despite enthusiastic and optimistic promises of a better life in post-growth societies, Büchs and Koch argue that there is a need to empirically and critically study the relationship between postgrowth and wellbeing. While it is argued that a voluntary transformation to postgrowth societies is more rational than waiting for a crisis, it is difficult to plan a systemic change that aligns with postgrowth thinking when there are no guarantees of outcomes. Therefore, it is difficult to argue for wellbeing enabled by postgrowth societies.

First, postgrowth thinking 'is based on a different time perspective compared to that usually applied in public debates and economic reasoning' (Büchs and Koch, 2017, p. 68). Although, in the long run, postgrowth may prove to be a sustainable solution, maximising wellbeing during the transformation can be challenging. There are many vested interests in maintaining the contemporary system.

Second, the authors acknowledge that wellbeing stagnates or decreases with GDP growth but remind that GDP growth is measured in log scales while wellbeing in linear scales (Büchs and Koch, 2017, pp. 68–69). This may explain the studies that show how people get used to certain levels of wellbeing or how increases in income do not increase perceived wellbeing. While post-materialistic values can shift the way people think about wellbeing, there are other mixed findings about the spread of these ideas in contemporary occidental societies. Moreover, the authors argue, contemporary growth-based societies seem to value certain ways of behaving, such as an accelerating pace of life, which people find less likeable in the long run. In addition, individualistic culture can alienate people from one another.

Third, while a radical redefinition of wellbeing can ease transformation, including for example grounding wellbeing in terms of less materialistic values, the wellbeing effects from slowing down are greater if everyone is in the same boat (Büchs and Koch, 2017, p. 77). For example, limiting one's waged labour now results in less social security in many welfare states. Therefore, 'a transformation to postgrowth society will require far-reaching changes of institutional frameworks, including more redistributive policies, and collective conceptions of wellbeing (which includes people's aspirations, values and identities) to counter-act possible negative wellbeing implications of contracting economies' (Büchs and Koch, 2017, pp. 79–80). This directs towards finding leverage points grouped as design and intent.

Overall, Büch and Koch (2017, p. 99) argue that the needed transformation in thinking and social interaction has been neglected in transformation literature: 'This transformation will require a fundamental reorientation of culture and embedded wellbeing conceptions towards the fulfilment of basic human needs, framed by the concern and care for the wellbeing of future generations.' They add that it is challenging to make the needed changes within the given timeframe without compromising current levels of wellbeing.

Büchs and Koch (2017, p. 111) review some solutions for transformation, including 'the need to replace today's global capitalistic system with economies based on principles of the cooperatives and social enterprise movement and orient towards local production and consumption cycles.' Moreover, they state that the means of meeting planetary limits and universal human needs include per capita limitations of emissions and consumption. This 'would require a new mix of property forms including communal, state and individual property and new divisions of labour between market, state and "commons", where markets would play a much lesser role than currently' (Büchs and Koch, 2017, p. 113). Finally, they conclude that reductions in time spent in paid work are needed in order to reduce unemployment, distribute work across the population, break the cycle of 'consuming because earning,' improve work-life balance, and free up time for unpaid activities, such as care and voluntary work.

Büchs and Koch rightly ask what groups would benefit from a transformation to postgrowth societies; they conclude that in wealthy countries people who experience precarious labour market conditions, for example, zero contract and gig economy workers, and people 'who have little prospect of fitting into mainstream patterns of lifecycle achievement—including career progression, home and car ownership, etc.—could be perceptive to alternative visions of life aspirations and socio-economic models beyond growth' (Büchs and Koch, 2017, pp. 131–132). However, these groups have little decision-making power compared to the ones who benefit from the contemporary system. Therefore, the dilemma in the needed transformation is that the welfare state does not only act as a counterforce to capitalism, but it also enables it and therefore locks the means of generating wellbeing for citizens (Büchs and Koch, 2017, p. 129). The authors conclude that while the promise of postgrowth societies is to improve work-life balance and even increase gender equality by shaking the male-breadwinner model, there are groups that may find these advances unacceptable.

Ambiguous Social Enterprise

Social enterprise has gained popularity as a way to address many contemporary problems, and it raises hope as a means, or even 'The Means,' to overcome serious social and environmental problems when other institutions seem to fail. Combining societal change with the means of business seems innovative and fresh because the focus is on doing. What is even more promising is the idea of scaling up local solutions to spread globally. Consequently, it is not unusual to establish a business with the aim of reducing the use of natural resources, social inequalities, or even advance radical societal change.

Because of its great promise, social enterprise is often mentioned as an example of a postgrowth or non-capitalist form of organising (see e.g. Gibson-Graham *et al.*, 2013; Johanisova *et al.*, 2013; Büchs and Koch, 2017; Foundational Economy Collective, 2018). Part of the social enterprise definition used in this edited book, which states that 'the material interest of capital investors is subject to limits,' aligns with this interpretation.

However, manifestations of social enterprise vary regionally and create confusion among practitioners (Safri, 2015). Moreover, according to critical studies, there is a danger that social enterprise is used as a neoliberal tool to increase capital interest instead of limiting it (Cook *et al.*, 2003). In this line of thinking, social enterprise is largely considered to be an individual process: people come up with a great idea that enables doing things differently. They experiment, gather resources, succeed (and also fail), but eventually, something ground-breaking emerges. With this, the line of thinking goes that the people involved experience how different ways of doing things are more effective and enable better lives. However, the effects of social enterprise are not portrayed as individualistic. Instead, social enterprise is represented as creating useful effects for collectives, which preferably should be evaluated with social impact analysis. Thus, in this view, individuals' efforts bring social good for many (for an analogy to micro-credit for women in the Majority World, see Cornwall, 2007).

Some examples of this process include the reduction of public expenditure by privatising social and welfare services to be provided by social enterprises (Eikenberry, 2009; Teasdale *et al.*, 2013). Moreover, the exploitation of people may take place not only by encouraging the establishment of social enterprises but also by the use of the notion 'social enterprise,' which places a burden on individuals to solve complex problems beyond their immediate reach (Jones and Murtola, 2012; Jones and Spicer, 2009).

But while these critical studies of social enterprise portray the ambiguities of social enterprise, they do not explicitly challenge the imperative of economic growth. Some growth-agnostic voices have emerged in studies that focus on health and social enterprise. Michael Roy combines contemporary research on wellbeing, health, and social enterprise with existing criticism towards the economic growth paradigm (Roy, 2021). He calls for the second wave of studies in this sphere that solves some of the 'conceptual, practical, and methodical' challenges related to addressing 21st-century questions in a point of no return. Next, I turn to some ripples that could result in larger waves.

Transcending the Understanding of Social Enterprise in Order to Maximise Wellbeing

Embedded within the ambiguities of social enterprise is the debate as to whether it treats the symptoms or addresses the root causes. From the perspective of leverage points, both of these approaches are needed. Yet, the power of social enterprise seems to be in its potential to challenge the taken-for-granted assumptions instead of small fixes (see also Roy, 2021).

Therefore, the social enterprise seems to have more potential than solely being a practical tool for delivering solutions in postgrowth societies. Returning to leverage points, I argue that currently, social enterprise understanding tends to emphasise shallower leverage points. For supporting transformation to postgrowth societies, this section focuses on possible paths ahead for social enterprise thinking in order to maximise wellbeing.

Social Enterprise in Ensuring Livelihoods

Paid labour is one of the taken-for-granted assumptions in occidental societies (Standing, 2010). As discussed earlier, it is the basis for social security and the welfare state model. Because work has become such an integral part of people's lives, people increasingly look for meaningful jobs. Yet, especially in growth-oriented societies, paid labour is disappearing from affluent nations, and production has been shifted to countries with lower pay levels.

As a result, livelihoods need to be gained independent of paid labour. In community economies thinking the aim is to map practices beyond other taken-for-granted economic activities, including paid labour (Gibson-Graham *et al.*, 2013; Miller, 2019). These examples include alternative paid labour—such as self-employment, cooperatives, reciprocal labour, in-kind, work for welfare, and indentured—and unpaid labour—such as housework, family care, neighbourhood work, volunteering, self-provisioning, and slave labour. While international agreements are not in favour of indentured or slave labour, these practices unfortunately exist in contemporary affluent societies.

Many consider self-employment as a reasonable labour market solution to employ oneself meaningfully, resulting in more micro- and small enterprises. In my first ethnography, I studied the everyday experiences of Finnish micro-entrepreneurs who employed themselves because they were concerned about socio-ecological crises and who related to the notion of social enterprise, although some in a critical manner (Houtbeckers, 2016a). Instead of leading their professional lives as if they did not know about these challenges, they decided to use their professional know-how to develop local solutions instead of working full-time for others. They set up a cooperative, a business name, or a limited liability company in the fields of textile recycling, open data, urban planning, and veganism. Their customers included consumers and organisations, such as educational institutions or cities. Some had their own shop, while others worked as an expert with their laptop. For them, waged labour was not possible nor desirable because there were no jobs available to address the socio-ecological crises they found troubling. Moreover, during the time of the study, no one was willing to pay for their accumulated expertise related to transforming the fields they functioned in.

In order to sustain themselves financially, at times the micro-entrepreneurs had part-time jobs elsewhere, alongside their own business. Because the turnover of their own enterprise was uncertain, they did not pay themselves or they invested profits back into their enterprise. Nevertheless, deep concerns about socio-ecological crisis united the micro-entrepreneurs who participated in my study. Although they worked in different sectors, one of the main challenges was how to ensure a livelihood.

Of course, some may refuse to take on the responsibility of employing themselves and try to get by via other means. Drawing from community economies thinking, Hirvilammi and Joutsenvirta (2020) mapped the diverse work practices in two initiatives that both relied heavily on alternative and unpaid labour. They conclude that social security and activation policies by the Finnish government both enable and disable the work for the studied initiatives. For instance, it was not beneficial for the research participants to openly display their means of livelihood to the employment officials because they did not consider community work as real work.

At times, when I report my own findings related to the work of micro-entrepreneurs, some consider their activities to be 'hobbies' or 'not real enterprises.' These comments conflict with the lived experiences of the micro-entrepreneurs who considered themselves as professionals working in (mostly) meaningful projects. Therefore, these comments, aligning with the employment officials' attitudes reported by Hirvilammi and Joutsenvirta (2020), reflect the taken-for-granted assumptions related to work and the economy. While in reality all economic activities are about navigating the diverse economy, a 'real' capitalist economy is often privileged (Gibson-Graham *et al.*, 2013).

I have observed that people may use their work time to advance post-growth transformation or they may act *as if* postgrowth societies already existed. As noted by Büchs and Koch (2017), the problem with the latter is that most others may not share the goal of postgrowth society. Instead of risking a comfortable pay level or social security tied to waged labour, they prefer to continue with business as usual. This requires democratic debates about the role of paid labour in the transformation (Barca, 2019). While universal basic income or more recently care income is offered as a solution, political commitment and practices are still emerging, despite government-led experiments, for example, in Finland. The COVID-19 outbreak has intensified the calls for care of basic human needs.

Therefore, an important discussion is needed on how social enterprise would be used to ensure livelihoods for people during transformation to postgrowth societies. Previous research has mapped some postgrowth work practices. First, workers may receive their payment in community currencies, which entail a (often) digital background system that keeps track of exchanges against payment organised by local time banks (Dittmer, 2015). Second, services are produced not only for exchange and increasing owners' assets but also for use (Kallis *et al.*, 2015, pp. 11–12). Third, such 'production for use' (Kallis *et al.*, 2015, pp. 11–12) entails the blending of producer-consumer roles, since the owners of enterprises and/or workers are those who, for example, need care for their children or transportation in remote areas. Such famous mixing of producer-consumer roles already exist in digital platforms such as Uber and Airbnb, but these initiatives do not exclusively strive for postgrowth societies, and they have been criticised for their commodification of involved workers and service providers.

Postgrowth examples could include 'community land trusts, credit unions, co-operative umbrella groups and village seed banks,' since they preserve activities outside profit interests (Johanisova *et al.*, 2013, p. 15). These are all communal initiatives, something I will turn to in the next subsection. As for now, gaining a living in a socially and ecologically just way, while 'minding one's own businesses' seems difficult. Moreover, it can be asked if the rewards of self-employment for postgrowth societies should be distributed within communities in order to achieve a more ecologically and socially just world. This contradicts strongly with the prevailing image of an individual hero (social) entrepreneur with an economic rationale.

Interspecies Solidarity in Understanding Wellbeing

The discussion of postgrowth societies so far has been anthropocentric. Focusing on the wellbeing of humans leaves one important question unanswered: What about the wellbeing of other-than-human beings? One way to rethink wellbeing and social enterprise is to include the work of animals (Coulter, 2016) and plants (Hall, 2011). This resonates with ecofeminist thinking, in which the treatment of humans in less-privileged positions is reflected in the treatment of other-than-human nature and vice versa (Warren, 2000). Moreover, it entails a more holistic understanding of wellbeing: the ill-treatment of other-than-humans is related to the ill-treatment of humans and vice versa.

For Coulter (2016, p. 150), interspecies solidarity is a goal that has ethical and political ramifications. Solidarity stands for support, despite differences, and the practice of empathy, that is, legitimising the experiences of others. While it is tempting to brush these matters aside, human and animal relations are not marginal. Instead, they are at the centre of policymaking related to socially and ecologically just societies. For instance, factory farming generates a high share of greenhouse gases (Coulter, 2016, p. 162).

Moreover, Coulter observes that people use animals in a less compassionate way because they may not have other ways to gain a livelihood. According to some analyses, transformation to postgrowth societies requires less use of fossil fuels and overall energy consumption, which means increased use of human muscle-power for work (Järvensivu, 2017). Therefore, it is likely that in postgrowth societies, the use of muscle-power for heavy lifting increases, which also entails making further ethical decisions on the willingness of human and other-than-humans to work together. Therefore, there is a need to imagine ways to get by through solidarity.

Beyond animals that work under the control of humans, there are other-than-humans that inhabit ecosystems that allow human societies to prosper. From a community economy perspective, the work of ecosystems is unpaid, and these processes can be considered as common property. Yet, interestingly the disruption of these ecosystems for profit-making purposes is currently justified, despite environmental laws in some regions of the world. In his book *Plants as Persons*, Hall (2011) explains how, based on scientific research, plants sense, move, and signal. The idea of plant intelligence challenges ideas of plants as passive and immobile inhabitants of the world and therefore subordinate to humans. Thinking plants to be lesser than humans has resulted in a lack of care towards plants and ecosystems, which has led to contemporary socio-ecological troubles. Therefore, there is a need for ethical considerations and practical steps to take place in order to reduce the harm done to vegetation.

Hall (2011) suggests restoration as one means to ensure plant diversity and overall wellbeing. Indeed, large-scale restoration projects could bring wellbeing for humans and other-than-human animals as well as in the forms of a livelihood for humans and a liveable habitat for all. In my ongoing ethnography, I have come across a Finnish initiative *Snowchange Cooperative* that conducts landscape-wide rewilding projects in collaboration with indigenous people living on the land. Such initiatives consider it important to understand wellbeing beyond humans and try to adopt a holistic perspective to living in solidarity.

Miller (2019) suggests that livelihood should be considered as something that is done communally, including more-than-humans. In addition to making a living as an individual, livelihood is about shaping others' lives and being shaped by others. His 'actual and possible' circle of livelihood incorporates many themes discussed earlier. Moreover, he promotes shifting economics into transdisciplinary livelihood studies. I see many opportunities for also shifting social enterprise research thinking towards this direction.

Conclusions

This book chapter started with three interlinked observations: (1) there is a need for postgrowth societies, (2) social enterprises are often framed as postgrowth organisations, and (3) the understanding of wellbeing varies. Many thinkers have challenged the primary nature of economic growth in policymaking and call for prioritising wellbeing in decision-making (see e.g. Büchs and Koch, 2017).

Overall, I argue that by focusing on 'constants, parameters and numbers' as leverage points (Meadows, 1999), the social enterprise movement may lose some of its potential. While it is important to also focus on 'shallower' leverages, they are not enough when striving towards postgrowth transformation. It is important to focus on the *design* and *intent* of the system (Abson *et al.*, 2017).

In order to continue to push paradigmatic debates in the domain of *intent*, this book chapter presented ideas related to social enterprise as a nexus for (1) ensuring livelihoods and (2) including interspecies solidarity in understanding wellbeing. In terms of livelihoods, I discussed how social enterprise could be detached from the notion of maximising profits in practice. In terms of interspecies solidarity, I have fewer concrete suggestions but rather hope to engage in paradigmatic debates about the interaction between humans and other-than-humans.

I have observed that many political, practical, and ideological alternatives are ignored with the argument that they do not focus on economic growth. This chapter promotes space for open discussions about taken-for-granted assumptions on increasing wellbeing based solely on economic growth. Many contemporary movements, such as social enterprise or postgrowth initiatives, may be downplayed as utopian, while the practitioners and activists already partially lead their lives based on their own understandings. In times of mounting ecological and social imbalances, we cannot afford to push already practised suggestions aside without allowing them to be explored.

The focus on social enterprise as a mechanism to maximise wellbeing, rather than economic growth, can open up debates related to the problematic nature of the growth paradigm and social justice related to global resource use and the treatment of other-than-human beings. Everyone navigates in the diverse economy. It is everyone's responsibility to try to minimise the exploitation caused by economic activities and maximise wellbeing, and the postgrowth economy should serve all humans and other-than-humans.

References

Abson, D.J., Fischer, J., Leventon, J., Newig, J., Schomerus, T., Vilsmaier, U., von Wehrden, H., Abernethy, P., Ives, C.D., Jager, N.W., Lang, D.J., 2017. Leverage points for sustainability transformation. *AMBIO* 46, 30–39.

Barca, S., 2019. The labor(s) of degrowth. *Capitalism Nature Socialism* 30, 207–216.

Büchs, M., Koch, M., 2017. *Postgrowth and Wellbeing: Challenges to Sustainable Welfare*. Palgrave Macmillan, Cham.

Burke, B.J., Shear, B., 2014. Introduction: Engaged scholarship for non-capitalist political ecologies. *Journal of Political Ecology* 21, 127–144.

Cook, B., Dodds, C., Mitchell, W., 2003. Social entrepreneurship—False premises and dangerous forebodings. *Australian Journal of Social Issues* 38, 57–72.

Cornwall, A., 2007. Of choice, chance and contingency: 'Career strategies' and tactics for survival among Yoruba women traders. *Social Anthropology* 15, 27–46.

Coulter, K., 2016. *Animals, Work, and the Promise of Interspecies Solidarity*. Palgrave Macmillan, Houndmills.

D'Alisa, G., Demaria, F., Kallis, G., 2015. *Degrowth: A Vocabulary for a New Era*. Routledge.

Defourny, J., Nyssens, M., 2010. Conceptions of social enterprise and social entrepreneurship in Europe and the united states: Convergences and divergences. *Journal of Social Entrepreneurship* 1, 32–53.

Demaria, F., Schneider, F., Sekulova, F., Martinez-Alier, J., 2013. What is degrowth? From an activist slogan to a social movement. *Environmental Values* 22, 191–215.

Dengler, C., Strunk, B., 2018. The monetized economy versus care and the environment: Degrowth perspectives on reconciling an antagonism. *Feminist Economics* 24, 160–183.

Dittmer, K., 2015. Community currencies. In: D'Alisa, G., Demaria, F., Kallis, G. (Eds.), *Degrowth: A Vocabulary for a New Era*. Routledge, New York, pp. 149–151.

Eikenberry, A. M., 2009. Refusing the market: A democratic discourse for voluntary and nonprofit organizations. *Nonprofit and Voluntary Sector Quarterly* 38(4), 582–596.

Foundational Economy Collective, 2018. *Foundational Economy: The Infrastructure of Everyday Life*. Manchester University Press, Machester, UK.

Gibson-Graham, J.K., Cameron, J., Healy, S., 2013. *Take Back the Economy: An Ethical Guide for Transforming our Communities*. University of Minnesota Press, Minneapolis; London.

Hall, M., 2011. *Plants as Persons: A Philosophical Botany*, SUNY series on religion and the environment. State University of New York Press, Albany.

Hirvilammi, T., Joutsenvirta, M., 2020. Diverse work practices and the role of welfare institutions. In: Eskelinen, T., Hirvilammi, T., Venäläinen, J. (Eds.), *Enacting Community Economies within a Welfare State*. Mayfly Books, pp. 47–70, available at: http://mayflybooks.org/?page_id=292.

Houtbeckers, E., 2016a. The tactics of ecopreneurs aiming to introduce new practices. *Small Enterprise Research* 23, 22–38.

Houtbeckers, E., 2016b. *Mundane Social Entrepreneurship: A Practice Perspective on the Work of Microentrepreneurs*, Aalto University Publication Series DOCTORAL DISSERTATIONS 171/2016. Aalto University, Aalto.

Houtbeckers, E., 2018. Framing social enterprise as post-growth organising in the diverse economy. *Management Revue* 29, 257–280.

Jackson, T., 2009. *Prosperity without Growth: Economics for a Finite Planet*. Earthscan, London.

Jackson, T., 2018. *The Post-Growth Challenge: Secular Stagnation, Inequality and the Limits to Growth*, CUSP Working Paper No 12. University of Surrey, Guildford.

Järvensivu, P., 2017. A post-fossil fuel transition experiment: Exploring cultural dimensions from a practice-theoretical perspective. *Journal of Cleaner Production* 169, 143–151.

Johanisova, N., Crabtree, T., Franková, E., 2013. Social enterprises and non-market capitals: A path to degrowth? *Journal of Cleaner Production* 38, 7–16.

Jones, C., Murtola, A.-M., 2012. Entrepreneurship and expropriation. *Organization* 19, 635–655.

Jones, C., Spicer, A., 2009. *Unmasking the Entrepreneur*. Edward Elgar Publishing, Cheltenham.

Kallis, G., Demaria, F., D'Alisa, G., 2015. Introduction: Degrowth. In: D'Alisa, G., Demaria, F., Kallis, G. (Eds.), *Degrowth: A Vocabulary for a New Era*. Routledge, New York, pp. 1–17.

Kallis, G., Kerschner, C., Martinez-Alier, J., 2012. The economics of degrowth. *Ecological Economics* 84, 172–180.

Latouche, S., 2009. *Farewell to Growth*. Polity Press, Cambridge.

Meadows, D., 1999. *Leverage Points: Places to Intervene in a System*. Sustainability Institute, Hartland, WI.

Mellor, M., 2006. Ecofeminist political economy. *International Journal of Green Economics* 1, 139–150.

Miller, E., 2019. *Reimagining Livelihoods: Life Beyond Economy, Society, and Environment*. University of Minnesota Press, Minneapolis, MN.

Paulson, S., 2017. Degrowth: Culture, power and change. *Journal of Political Ecology* 24, 425–448.

Raworth, K., 2017. *Doughnut Economics: Seven Ways to Think Like a 21st-Century Economist*. Random House Business Books, London.

Roy, M.J., 2021. Towards a 'wellbeing economy': What can we learn from social enterprise. In: Gidron, B., Domaradzka, A. (Eds.), *The New Social and Impact Economy: An International Perspective*. Springer International Publishing, Cham, pp. 269–284.

Safri, M., 2015. The politics of mapping solidarity economies and diverse economies in Brazil and the Northeastern United States. In: Roelvink, G., Martin,

K.St., Gibson-Graham, J.K. (Eds.), *Making Other Worlds Possible. Performing Diverse Economies*. University of Minnesota Press, Minneapolis, pp. 296–321.

Smith, D.E., 2005. *Institutional Ethnography: A Sociology for People*. Rowan Altamira, Lanham.

Standing, G., 2010. *Work after Globalization: Building Occupational Citizenship*. Edward Elgar, Cheltenham.

Steffen, W., Richardson, K., Rockstrom, J., Cornell, S.E., Fetzer, I., Bennett, E.M., Biggs, R., Carpenter, S.R., de Vries, W., de Wit, C.A., Folke, C., Gerten, D., Heinke, J., Mace, G.M., Persson, L.M., Ramanathan, V., Reyers, B., Sorlin, S., 2015. Planetary boundaries: Guiding human development on a changing planet. *Science* 347, 1259855–1259855.

Stengers, I., 2017. *Another Science is Possible: A Manifesto for Slow Science*. Polity, Cheltenham, UK.

Swyngedouw, E., 2013. Apocalypse now! Fear and doomsday pleasures. *Capitalism Nature Socialism* 24, 9–18.

Teasdale, S., Lyon, F., Baldock, R., 2013. Playing with numbers: A methodological critique of the social enterprise growth myth. *Journal of Social Entrepreneurship* 4, 113–131.

Warren, K.J., 2000. *Ecofeminist Philosophy: A Western Perspective on What it is and Why it Matters*. Rowman & Littlefield Publishers, Lanham, MD.

Wiedmann, T., Lenzen, M., Keyßer, L.T., Steinberger, J.K., 2020. Scientists' warning on affluence. *Nature Communications* 11. doi:10.1038/s41467-020-16941-y.

Wright, D., Meadows, D.H., 2012. *Thinking in Systems: A Primer*. Taylor and Francis, Hoboken.

4 Community Wellbeing and Social Enterprise

Place, Visibility, and Social Capital

Sue Kilpatrick and Sherridan Emery

Introduction

Social enterprise is recognised as developing wellbeing benefits and broadening life opportunities for their employee participants. This has been found to be the case in Australian and international studies (Bertotti, Harden, Renton, & Sheridan, 2012; Kilpatrick, Emery, Adler, & Farmer, 2019; Macaulay, Roy, Donaldson, Teasdale, & Kay, 2018; Roy, Donaldson, Baker, & Kerr, 2014). Work Integration Social Enterprises (WISEs) are framed as a form of 'empowering' community economic development intervention, which are constructed to draw upon the particular strengths of people and overcome barriers to work (Mason, Barraket, Friel, O'Rourke, & Stenta, 2015). Wellbeing benefits that realise for employees of social enterprises have been found to include increased capability, social inclusion, therapy, and a sense of security (Farmer *et al.*, 2019). Further, research has shown that employees of social enterprise benefit through the development of social capital resources which create opportunities for greater participation in society (Kilpatrick *et al.*, 2019).

Recent research has explored the benefits generated by social enterprises for the broader community and economy of their local region (Barraket & Archer, 2010; Birch & Whittam, 2008; Muñoz & Kimmitt, 2019; Richter, Fink, Lang, & Maresch, 2019). Wellbeing benefits that social enterprises develop with and for their broader communities are the focus of this chapter, which draws upon data from the study *Mapping the Impact of Social Enterprise on Regional City Disadvantage* (Farmer, Adler *et al.*, 2020) to consider in particular the question: how do social enterprises make use of social capital to realise wellbeing for the broader community?

There is growing awareness that the wellbeing benefits of social enterprises extend beyond the boundaries of the enterprise itself and ripple out into communities which interact with the enterprise (Borzaga & Sforzi, 2014). We are interested in the means and processes by which this occurs. In previous research, we investigated the role of social capital in

DOI: 10.4324/9781003125976-4

generating wellbeing for employees of social enterprises (Kilpatrick *et al.*, 2019). In this chapter, we take the community and local economy as a point of focus to consider the interplay between social capital and wellbeing arising from social enterprise interactions.

While there are many definitions of social capital (Bourdieu, 1990; Coleman, 1994; Putnam, 1993), we adopt an interpretation of social capital that refers to networks and other relational resources including trust, shared norms, and a shared vision (Evans & Syrett, 2007). The influences of social capital and networks literature on the social enterprise and social economy literature is modest as would be expected of a nascent field (Hulgård & Spear, 2006; Kay, 2006; Littlewood & Khan, 2018). We recognise that social capital can be simultaneously both built and used through interactions (Falk & Kilpatrick, 2000). Social capital at the community level can help explain the ease with which regional city communities can combine their diverse human capital and other assets for collective social and economic benefit (Evers, 2001; Szreter & Woolcock, 2004). This is achieved through 'a combination of close, bonding networks, bridging networks between community entities and linking networks that extend beyond community boundaries' (Kilpatrick, Farmer, Emery, & De Cotta, 2021). This chapter explores place-based means by which social enterprises can realise individual and collective, community wellbeing benefits. Such benefits arise through mobilising networks to share values, build a shared community identity, and to develop trust and norms of social inclusion and individual development (Kilpatrick, Field, & Falk, 2003; Uphoff, Pickett, Cabieses, Small, & Wright, 2013).

Community wellbeing is defined by Wiseman and Brasher (2008) as 'the combination of social, economic, environmental, cultural and political conditions identified by individuals and their communities as essential for them to flourish and fulfil one's potential' (p. 358). Community wellbeing, which typically encompasses aspects of health, economy, security, social relations, and social inclusion, is increasingly a policy objective for regional cities and communities (Morton & Edwards, 2013; McCrea, Walton, & Leonard, 2016). According to Atkinson and colleagues (2017), community wellbeing may emerge from the relations between individuals and place, drawing on emotional connections to place such as sense of belonging, cultural heritage, and opportunities for leisure, work, volunteering, and learning. Social enterprises can influence community wellbeing through emotional place attachment (Kibler, Fink, Lang, & Muñoz, 2015). Wellbeing benefits are not automatically generated by having a social enterprise located in a community: it is through the interactions between the social enterprise and the community that the wellbeing benefits arise. Here, we consider how social capital contributes to the wellbeing outcomes of interactions that are part of the day-to-day operation of social enterprises. Social capital is a well-known concept in relation to (health and) wellbeing discussions, both at the very local level and even up to the level of nations (Lomas, 1998; OECD, 2001; Stephens, 2008). We are interested in the geospatial distribution of social capital's contribution to wellbeing outcomes, particularly where benefits accrue to the community, beyond the social enterprise.

Methods

A multiple case study design (Baxter & Jack, 2008) provides the diversity of perspectives that are key to a rich understanding of how and why the phenomena under investigation occur. This approach is important when the context is likely to influence outcomes as it does for social enterprises. The four social enterprises in this study are located in two medium-sized Australian cities. 'Farm' and 'Catering' are located in City 1 in the state of Victoria; 'AssistAll' and 'Community Centre' in City 2 in the state of Tasmania. The first three of these organisations are work-integration social enterprises, while Community Centre is a community organisation through which several small social enterprise initiatives operate (such as sales of vegetable boxes and recycled clothing).

This study investigated the interactions that the four social enterprises activate for their employees both inside the organisation and within the broader community. Drawing upon observations, interviews, and focus groups conducted with social enterprise employees and staff, and people in the community who interact with the social enterprises, we employ Kilpatrick et al.'s (2003) social capital framework to analyse the role of bonding, bridging, and linking networks and associated social capital in facilitating the interactions to understand how social enterprises generate community wellbeing in regional cities.

Data Collection

The data collection for the study involved obtaining qualitative first-person accounts from all four social enterprises: employees (n = 17) and staff (n = 16), observations of employees work activities within the social enterprise premises and in the community, as well as accounts from community informants (n = 15) who were people within the local region who interacted with the social enterprise as a customer or in business or civic role. Community informants were purposively sampled by targeting social enterprise customers, business people, members of local business associations, and representatives from local councils and other levels of government who had interacted with the social enterprise.

Interviews were transcribed and coded using two key frameworks of analysis: spaces of wellbeing theory (Fleuret & Atkinson, 2007) and social capital (Bourdieu, 1990; Kilpatrick et al., 2003). Findings related to the social capital outcomes in this study of social enterprise have been published elsewhere (Kilpatrick et al., 2021). Following the data analysis, focus groups (n = 15) were conducted with employees and staff of the social enterprises as a way of sharing the emerging findings with the research participants, checking the reliability of the analysis, and obtaining further data. This process was facilitated with photographs of all areas of the social enterprise that were shared amongst research participants to serve as a prompt for discussion. The photo-elicitation yielded further information about the many different types of interactions generated by social enterprises both inside and outside their premises. Information received from social enterprise employees and staff also informed the interviews conducted with community informants, providing insights about interactions and civic involvement that could be further explored during the interviews.

Approaches to investigating community wellbeing have previously neglected spatial aspects (Atkinson, Bagnall, Corcoran, South, & Curtis, 2019; Atkinson, Bagnall, Corcoran, & South, 2017), and this study adopted a spatial methodology to accommodate interdisciplinary understandings and help explain what happens and why (Farmer, Kamstra et al., 2020). The data coded for social capital (bonding, bridging, and linking) were geocoded by noting the places that the participants referred to in discussing their interactions generated through the social enterprise. As an example, employees from AssistAll attended a social event at the local football ground organised through the social enterprise. The address of the football ground was coded to bonding social capital and entered onto a spreadsheet which provided the basis for mapping coordinates of locations where wellbeing was 'realised' in the regional city. The data were overlaid on maps of the two regional cities, and two maps are included in the findings for illustrative purposes.

This chapter includes maps depicting the social enterprises' use and creation of social capital and discusses the interactions where social capital is built and used. This type of mapping is innovative in the field of social capital research.

Findings

We first present two maps to illustrate where social capital was used and built in the community beyond the social enterprise and then go onto illustrate the wellbeing outcomes of the social capital interactions.

The maps geolocate places and journeys which contributed to wellbeing realisation in our data. Journeys are indicated according to the type of social capital (bonding, bridging, or linking) which was activated in realising wellbeing. For example, bonding social capital may be associated with employees playing team sports or engaging with sports clubs; bridging social capital tends to involve businesses and may include business association events attended by staff; and linking social capital includes

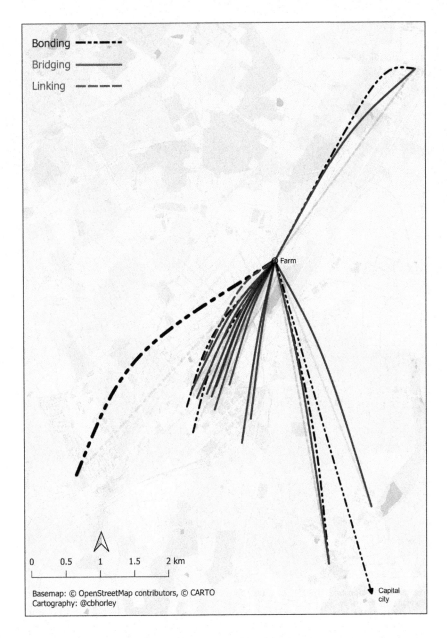

Figure 4.1 Social capital map for Farm in City 1

Figure 4.2 Social capital map for AssistAll in City 2

interaction with what might be termed 'the corridors of power' such as city council or state and Federal government representatives.

The maps help to show the spatial movement of employees from the social enterprises within the two regional cities. Map one, for example, charts where employees travel within City 1 as they distribute goods produced at Farm amongst other journeys and perform services for which the social enterprise is paid, such as mailbox distribution for the local fire, services, and delivery of produce growing at Farm to local restaurants. Business customer interactions provided opportunities for social enterprise employees to come into regular contact with employers, developing bridging social capital. In City 1, employees travelled to sporting fields where they played netball and cricket which is depicted on the map. These sporting interactions were occasions for generating bonding social capital.

While the maps show that linking social capital opportunities were few in number (one linking social capital interaction in City 1, two interactions in City 2), nevertheless, such linking capital opportunities are typically significant in terms of access to resources and opportunities for employees. Through such interactions, the social enterprises drew upon and generated bonding, bridging, and linking social capital (portrayed using lines of different colours) in geographically dispersed locations within the regional community. The map for City 2 includes where social enterprise employees travel to empty the clothing bins (for their charity clothing shop) and where they deliver client catering to. In the wood workshop at AssistAll, employees manufacture timber products, and the map shows where these are delivered. In addition, the map shows where employees go for recreational purposes through the social enterprise. For example, in City 2, the employees built and used bonding social capital as they attended sporting events at the football stadium and went ten-pin bowling together.

Interviews conducted with community informants revealed that these interactions that occur in different parts of the regional cities develop relationships and build bridging and linking networks that provide further opportunities for employment and social interaction for employees (Kilpatrick et al., 2021). The interview, observation, and focus group data reveal the visibility of social enterprise activities in regional cities and support our focus on the geospatial aspects of building and using social capital for wellbeing realisation. For example, participation in sporting activities outside of the social enterprise produced benefits including positive physical wellbeing benefits, forming bonding social capital through the friendships that developed, and beyond that, becoming visible in their communities. Bridging social capital also developed through the work that employees undertook, as in an example of gardening work undertaken by Farm employees at a neighbourhood church. This sets up new opportunities for employees to see themselves as contributing to the community as revealed in the interview with the community informant.

Analysis of the interactions revealed the multiple ways that social enterprises help to create conditions for community wellbeing. They generate interactions amongst diverse populations, creating social capital resources such as trust and norms of social inclusion. They foster inter-organisational trust and norms of working together while building and maintaining bridging and linking networks. These social capital resources create participation, employment, and economic opportunities for regional economies and enable organisations and institutions to broaden their reach and access new audiences. They help shape their city's identity and reputation.

Generating Interactions Amongst Diverse Populations

Community informants made reference to the multiple ways that social enterprises created opportunities for people from diverse social and cultural backgrounds to interact together in multiple locations, promoting social inclusion. One community informant from the government sector spoke of how the farmers' market social enterprise in City 1 created spaces for vibrant events that take advantage of the affordances of its place to create a space for social inclusion:

> So, the market concept of being an attractor for the purposes like, it's 'come to this market, because we've got great produce', and where— like you don't have to come here because you feel sorry for us, it's not about that at all. It's about, this is a great thing for [City 1]. So, if they can kind of crack into that space—that this is normal, this is what community looks like. It just so happens that these people aren't lonely and at home and behind closed doors.
>
> (Community informant 1, City 1)

In this quote, the informant explains how the farmers' market normalises the integration of people of different capabilities and backgrounds, and this normalising is part of the enrichment of community wellbeing in regional cities.

Another government representative from City 2 likewise commented about the inclusiveness of events staged in various spaces and places at the Community Centre:

> You just have to see the cross-section of people that are there [at the social enterprise] for community events and particularly [suburb], you'll see migrant communities being involved, a cross-section of migrant communities. You'll see people from close at hand in adjacent suburbs. You're not just talking about a random group of

people; you're actually seeing significant groups of people . . . It was not just the fact that there were lots of people there, but you looked around and you could see diversity in action. Very, very diverse group of attendees.

(Community informant 2, City 2)

As this informant reveals, the events at the social enterprise produced opportunities for employees to build bonding social capital, networks with other community members that promoted a shared norm of social inclusion. Bonding social capital was built out in the community, as the following example of social enterprise employees who were part of an all-abilities cricket team shows. One Farm employee explained how that team comprised 'just a few guys and girls . . . we're not sexist about who plays so it doesn't matter if you're a boy or girl.' Asked by the facilitator if the employees participated in social activities after the cricket games the employee replied,

Yeah, if we're doing travel—like we travel to Melbourne—we may just go to Macca's on the way home and social that way, [and] sometimes we'll have social events at the club to raise money for different things.

(Farm employee 3, City 1)

A community informant in City 2 spoke of the variety of interactions that are brought about through social enterprises. He gave an example of another social enterprise he was familiar with to articulate the multiple positive benefits of interactions that built emotional place attachment, in this case, through a positive experience around food at a local venue:

When we're talking about social enterprises, you can't overlook an organisation like the [migrant resettlement organisation] with their community kitchen enterprise which operates out of the [local pub]. Again, that produces a similar effect. You enjoy eating the food, but there is virtue in simply attending to be exposed to different experiences and also providing a measure of support for that community that's serving the food. I think the same considerations apply to both AssistAll and Community Centre.

(Community informant 2, City 2)

As alluded to in this quote, the community benefits from the social enterprise staging events that offer vibrant experiences for everyone to participate in while also providing increased visibility and a financial return for the enterprise. The community kitchen opportunity arose from a community-level bridging social capital network between the hotelier and the migrant resettlement organisation.

Social enterprise customers indicated that there were benefits that arose from their interactions with social enterprise employees in the community. One restaurateur in City 1, for example, indicated that through the relationship with the Farm enterprise his business was able to access herbs which were of better quality than those bought from their standard supplier. This informant explained that having a social enterprise employee interact regularly with his business as they delivered supplies fostered social inclusion through the bridging network transaction:

> They [social enterprise employees] come in and disperse all the deliveries. It's good for them because a lot of them . . . are struggling with social skills and it gives them an opportunity to get out and meet business owners who, in turn, get to meet them as well and we have an interaction. They tell us what they have for us, for the day, as far as the fresh herbs and things like that. Then, they hand over the dockets and I sign it off and off they go again.
>
> (Community informant 6, City 1)

The restaurateur commented on the quality of the product from Farm:

> The product itself is fantastic. So as far as quality and the longevity of the product—we get an extra couple of days of freshness out of their product than what we would from buying from the market in Melbourne, which was surprising to us at the time. So that's one of the benefits, also being able to give back to the community.
>
> (Community informant 6, City 1)

Through such regular interactions with the restaurant staff, social enterprise employees begin to form bridging networks with businesses, which is a further benefit to the social connections that they form through doing their deliveries. For the business customer, in addition to being able to access a product that was of better quality than product from their typical suppliers, interacting with the social enterprise provided a way for that business to support its local community and build social inclusion opportunities into its operation.

Creating Participation, Employment, and Economic Opportunities

Farm employees undertook a project on the request of a nearby church in their neighbourhood. A training facilitator who worked with Farm explained what took place in the native garden out front of the church:

> What we did as a project, over a few weeks we trimmed up all the garden. The church community provided us with some mulch and

we provided the plants that the [Farm employees] had grown. We replanted the garden for the community . . . We took lots of photographs and then the [Farm employees] put it together in a Power-Point presentation and we presented it to the church.

The church then played it to the congregation and it was gold. Because it was such a great outcome for them and for the [Farm employees], they had so much pride in doing this work outside the church. People would come past while we were working there saying, 'oh, wow, you're doing a great job. That looks fantastic.' It was all those sorts of comments which for a person who sometimes is getting a kick in the belly or a, 'you're not worthy' or whatever.

(Community informant 5, City 1)

In addition to this work opportunity improving the look and feel of this community asset, it generated feelings of accomplishment for Farm employees. A sense of identity as a valued worker was also experienced by another Farm employee who was a highly valued part of the team of one of Farm's corporate clients as a staff member explained:

One of our participants, Alan has been working out there [car washing corporate client's location] for about six years . . . They treat him like he belongs in the organisation. When they have the Christmas party, he's invited . . .

(Farm staff member 5, City 1)

Being part of the social network at work is part of the social inclusion goal of social enterprise and the growth of bonding and bridging social capital for this employee. Asked about the benefits social enterprises delivered specifically to regional communities, a government representative in City 2 indicated that many opportunities for participation were generated by social enterprises which 'have maintained a good reputation for the role that they play.' He explained further:

There are many different characteristics surrounding social enterprises. It's not just the provision of the services; it's also the involvement of people in the activities of the organisation, whether they're as employees, volunteers, or pro bono assistance to the organisation.

(Community informant 2, City 2)

This comment suggests there is external recognition of the social enterprise as making the most of resources in providing opportunities for realising wellbeing of employees and the broader community as a whole.

AssistAll general manager relayed a conversation she had with the manager of a university gallery about an initiative the social enterprise staged there:

> One of the things we were keen to do, was to engage the [City 2] community in the AssistAll anniversary celebrations. We staged a photographic exhibition down at the [university gallery] with the support of the university. The photos of our guys were up on the walls for a couple of weeks, and we had a cocktail party event down there. I was talking to the curator of the art gallery and he said over the course of the exhibition, they had people through the university who had never been there before. Because they wanted to see the photos. He said it was a great opportunity for the university to discover this whole other part of [City 2], which they hadn't had any dealings with, and the community got to interact through the photo exhibition with our employees. That worked really well. It's all sorts of bits and pieces we try and do and actively link them up.
>
> (AssistAll staff member 1, City 2)

These comments from AssistAll's general manager about the celebration staged at the university gallery revealed that this initiative brought people who might not traditionally access higher education to the university for an event related to a social enterprise celebration. The university gallery event offered an opportunity *for people who have traditionally been largely marginalised* from high-status institutions such as universities to gain familiarity with this setting. It also presented an opportunity for the university to access and gain exposure to non-traditional audiences which is relevant to the university's widening participation agenda aligning with the Federal Government's stated policy objectives for higher education (Bradley, Noonan, Nugent, & Scales, 2008). Social capital activated through bridging networks that included both university and social enterprise staff made the event possible, with benefits for social enterprise employees and the university.

City Identity, Reputation, and Social Inclusion

Community informants spoke about their experiences as customers of social enterprises. Here an organiser of a major community event describes the event's relationship with AssistAll:

> We've had a relationship with those guys now for probably about five years. Initially it started off with us utilising their catering facilities and it grew from that. We've actually utilised them twice in recent times . . . to design some . . . custom-made tables and then

build them for us . . . They did an initial lot of 50 and they were very, very successful and they've worked out ideal.

(Community informant 1, City 2)

This community informant describes the gap filled by AssistAll in the rural economy of City 2 and how its services and products add value to commercial food businesses and events which invigorate the city, adding to its liveability. In City 2, an informant credited Farm with changing the way that people were valuing the local food economy:

[Farm] is reaching out to a broader demographic who like farmers' markets to support that local food produce environment . . . it's recruiting people to eat local produce to understand it so they're able to charge a higher, more premium price for it.

(Community informant 3, City 1)

Further, this local food growing hub was acknowledged as a place that contributed a feeling of community and emotional place-attachment to the city as well as providing services that enhance its environmental sustainability qualities:

The [employees] they're at work and they feel incredibly empowered by that. Social enterprises also help deliver to the overall community and feel and I guess the visibility. [Farm] is a wonderful space . . . The social enterprises involved in collecting recyclables—again, taking what would otherwise end up in landfill and recycling it, delivering that social worth.

Social enterprises also reached out strategically to business and civic city infrastructure making use of linking and bridging social capital in the process. The manager of AssistAll was on the board of City 2's business organisation. The parent organisation of the two City 1 social enterprises had joined the chamber of commerce to build closer relationships with the business community to increase pathways to employment and customers for their services:

[Parent organisation] . . . have been involved in the chamber of commerce for many years . . . They decided to become a partner . . . their role was around shifting the mindset of employers, particularly the large employers, around the contribution of people with a disability in employment. . . [They] identified new host employers . . . there was a huge amount of growth for [social enterprise] in being exposed to new catering clients. I know a lot of the very large organisations here use them very frequently. We do.

(Community informant 2, City 1)

Social enterprises that have established long track records in regional cities attract external recognition for their capabilities to make the most of resources to benefit wellbeing of employees and broader communities according to a government representative interviewed in City 2:

> I know [Community Centre] has got a very good reputation as being a safe pair of hands in particular for receiving government funding. So, I think that speaks volumes for the way they're able to actually not just represent but involve the community.
>
> (Community informant 2, City 2)

Social enterprise staff were active in creating and growing the linking networks that support the growth and development of the social enterprise sector, particularly from an enterprise in the study which provided work for employees with disabilities. The staff member explained:

> We do a fair amount of policy and lobbying law reform work. I interact with local providers, I'm on the peak body for specialist service providers in the state, so I'm the deputy chair of that. That's regular trips to [capital city] and meeting with politicians, and other service providers in the state. Then I'm on a national disability and carer's advisory council, so I work on the federal level on that as well. There's a series of forums and events and meetings that we go to, which are around the disability sector.
>
> (AssistAll staff member 1, City 2)

These comments from both a community informant and from a social enterprise staff member demonstrate the important work that social enterprises do as they use linking networks that extend outside the City bringing visibility to the sector and promoting opportunities for fostering social inclusion. These advocacy activities simultaneously use existing social capital and build and strengthen social capital (Falk & Kilpatrick, 2000), as the state and federal bodies learn more about how policies should be shaped to work best for social enterprises like AssistAll, and AssistAll becomes aware of new opportunities for AssistAll and City 2.

Discussion and Conclusion

Community wellbeing is increasingly a stated aim of government and civic leaders in regional cities (Morton & Edwards, 2013; McCrea et al., 2016). Increasing inclusion and valuing of diversity is central to enhancing connectedness and respect amongst people. The data support our geospatial mapping of the location of activities to show the distribution of where social capital is used and built on an ongoing basis, as social enterprise actors interact with the broader community in a variety of locations within their cities. Our findings demonstrate that social enterprises bring together people of diverse abilities, backgrounds, and interests through their everyday interactions in regional cities to support wellbeing of employees and others through the establishment and maintenance of bonding networks. Social enterprises work with their community to build social inclusion through opportunities for people from different social and cultural backgrounds to interact together in a variety of places and spaces, such as the all abilities cricket club in City 1. Social inclusion in civic spaces has been recognised as a collective benefit (Barraket & Archer, 2010) and was promoted as a shared norm in City 1 and City 2 through the geographic diversity of places and spaces in which interactions occurred. The farmers' market and restaurant herb supply examples demonstrate how the commercial purpose of Farm and its market brought together people all going about their everyday business of buying and selling fresh produce in everyday trading and the market setting. The farmers' market draws on emotional place attachment (Kibler et al., 2015), creating a vibrant and attractive space for its employees and the wider community to interact.

Similarly, the enterprises at Community Centre present employment opportunities through the cleaning service and vegetable bag service that generate community interactions within the regional city. Community commercial or economic benefit and social inclusion are simultaneous outcomes of opportunities provided by social enterprises. Employment opportunities were often established through social enterprise bridging networks through participation in business associations or serving on organisational boards within the regional cities. Added to this, social enterprises built linking networks with multiple levels of government and were valued for their reputations as a 'safe pair of hands' for receiving government funding.

The findings from this study show the myriad ways that social enterprises support other businesses and also revealed how social enterprises provide services that enhance the lives of people in their communities. Social enterprises establish themselves as part of the local economy and society and intentionally work to achieve this through establishment and activation of social networks and social capital (Hulgård & Spear, 2006). This study starts to make visible the bonding, bridging, and linking networks that social enterprises activate (Szreter & Woolcock, 2004) and, through geospatial mapping, show the distribution of where different forms of social capital are generated and used. Through their activities, social enterprises can create conditions for the formation of emotional place attachment (Kibler et al., 2015) in regional cities. Emotional place attachment appears to engender a willingness to establish and activate social capital networks of all sorts (Falk & Kilpatrick, 2000). Community members are attracted to the farmers' market where bonding networks are developed; business associations and individual organisations (such as chambers of commerce and councils) are drawn to forming bridging and linking networks with social enterprises in 'their' city as the comments from government representatives show. The visibility of this activity across diverse locations (from farmers' markets, to community kitchens, church gardens, and corporate car washing in the city) incorporates social enterprises into people's emotional place attachment within the cities. Visibility is both geographic and in different fora (the spaces where people and groups interact, e.g. business associations).

Social enterprises strategically use the social capital networks of their place/city, along with trust and other social capital resources, to fulfil their joint social and economic mission. This contrasts with mainstream for-profit businesses which generally focus on an economic/commercial mission. Social enterprises draw on distributed place-based resources within their community, making themselves and their activities visible in the process. They proactively plan ways of increasing the interactions that are vital to the formation of social capital. Social enterprises are creative and flexible in their development of bridging and linking networks and other social capital resources; they demonstrate (and facilitate) emotional place attachment to achieve legitimacy of their social and economic mission.

References

Atkinson, S., Bagnall, A. M., Corcoran, R., & South, J. (2017). *What is community wellbeing? Conceptual review*. What Works Centre for Wellbeing, London.

Atkinson, S., Bagnall, A. M., Corcoran, R., South, J., & Curtis, S. (2019). Being well together: Individual subjective and community wellbeing. *Journal of Happiness Studies*, 1–19.

Barraket, J., & Archer, V. (2010). Social inclusion through community enterprise? Examining the available evidence. *Third Sector Review*, 16(1), 13–28.

Baxter, P., & Jack, S. (2008). Qualitative case study methodology: Study design and implementation for novice researchers. *The Qualitative Report*, 13(4), 544–559.

Bertotti, M., Harden, A., Renton, A., & Sheridan, K. (2012). The contribution of a social enterprise to the building of social capital in a disadvantaged urban area of London. *Community Development Journal*, 47(2), 168–183.

Birch, K., & Whittam, G. (2008). The third sector and the regional development of social capital. *Regional Studies*, 42(3), 437–450.

Borzaga, C., & Sforzi, J. (2014). Social capital, cooperatives and social enterprises. In A. Christoforou & J. B. Davis (Eds.), *Social capital and economics: Social values, power, and social identity* (pp. 193–214). Abingdon, Oxon: Routledge.

Bourdieu, P. (1990). *The logic of practice*. Stanford University Press, Stanford.

Bradley, D., Noonan, P., Nugent, H., & Scales, B. (2008). *Review of Australian higher education: Final report*. Canberra, ACT: Commonwealth of Australia.

Coleman, J. S. (1994). *Foundations of social theory*. Cambridge, MA: Harvard University Press.

Evans, M., & Syrett, S. (2007). Generating social capital? The social economy and local economic development. *European Urban and Regional Studies*, *14*(1), 55–74.

Evers, A. (2001). The significance of social capital in the multiple goal and resource structure of social enterprises. In C. Borzaga & J. Defourny (Eds.), *The emergence of social enterprise* (pp. 296–311). London: Routledge.

Falk, I., & Kilpatrick, S. (2000). What is social capital? A study of interaction in a rural community. *Sociologia Ruralis*, *40*(1), 87–110.

Farmer, J., Adler, V., De Cotta, T., Kilpatrick, S., MacKinnon, K., Barraket, J., . . . Munoz, S-A. (2020a). *Mapping the impact of social enterprise on disadvantaged individuals and communities in Australia's regional cities: Final report*. Hawthorn: Swinburne University of Technology Social Innovation Research Institute.

Farmer, J., De Cotta, T., Kilpatrick, S., Barraket, J., Roy, M., & Munoz, S. A. (2019). How work integration social enterprises help to realize capability: A comparison of three Australian settings. *Journal of Social Entrepreneurship*, 1–23.

Farmer, J., Kamstra, P., Brennan-Horley, C., De Cotta, T., Roy, M., Barraket, J., . . . Kilpatrick, S. (2020b). Using micro-geography to understand the realisation of wellbeing: A qualitative GIS study of three social enterprises. *Health & Place*, available at: https://doi.org/10.1016/j.healthplace.2020.102293

Fleuret, S., & Atkinson, S. (2007). Wellbeing, health and geography: A critical review and research agenda. *New Zealand Geographer*, *63*(2), 106–118.

Hulgård, L., & Spear, R. (2006). Social entrepreneurship and the mobilization of social capital in European social enterprises. In M. Nyssens (Ed.), *Social enterprise: At the crossroads of market, public policies and civil society* (pp. 85–108). Abingdon, Oxon: Routledge.

Kay, A. (2006). Social capital, the social economy and community development. *Community Development Journal*, *41*(2), 160–173.

Kibler, E., Fink, M., Lang, R., & Muñoz, P. (2015). Place attachment and social legitimacy: Revisiting the sustainable entrepreneurship journey. *Journal of Business Venturing Insights*, *3*, 24–29.

Kilpatrick, S., Emery, S., Adler, V., & Farmer, J. (2019). *Social enterprises and wellbeing for disadvantaged people in Australian regional towns*. National Rural Health Conference, Better Together, Hobart.

Kilpatrick, S., Farmer, J., Emery, S. & De Cotta, T. (2021), Social enterprises and regional cities: Working together for mutual benefit. *Entrepreneurship & Regional Development*, available at: https://doi.org/doi.org/10.1080/0898562 6.2021.1899293.

Kilpatrick, S., Field, J., & Falk, I. (2003). Social capital: An analytical tool for exploring lifelong learning and community development. *British Educational Research Journal*, *29*(3), 417–433.

Littlewood, D., & Khan, Z. (2018). Insights from a systematic review of literature on social enterprise and networks. *Social Enterprise Journal*, *14* (4), 390–409.

Lomas, J. (1998). Social capital and health: Implications for public health and epidemiology. *Social Science and Medicine*, *47*(9), 1181–1188.

Macaulay, B., Roy, M. J., Donaldson, C., Teasdale, S., & Kay, A. (2018). Conceptualizing the health and well-being impacts of social enterprise: A UK-based study. *Health Promotion International, 33*(5), 748–759.

Mason, C., Barraket, J., Friel, S., O'Rourke, K., & Stenta, C. P. (2015). Social innovation for the promotion of health equity. *Health Promotion International, 30*(Suppl_2), ii116–ii125.

McCrea, R., Walton, A., & Leonard, R. (2016). Developing a model of community wellbeing and resilience in response to change. *Social Indicators Research, 129*(1), 195–214.

Morton, A., & Edwards, L. (2013). *Community wellbeing indicators: Measures for local government.* Sydney: Australian Centre of Excellence for Local Government, University of Technology.

Muñoz, P., & Kimmitt, J. (2019). Rural entrepreneurship in place: An integrated framework. *Entrepreneurship & Regional Development, 31*(9–10), 842–873.

Organisation for Economic Co-operation and Development. (2001). *The well-being of nations: The role of human and social capital.* Paris: OECD Centre for Educational Research and Innovation.

Putnam, R. (1993). The prosperous community: Social capital and public life. *The American Prospect, 13*(4), 35–42.

Richter, R., Fink, M., Lang, R., & Maresch, D. (2019). *Social entrepreneurship and innovation in rural Europe.* Abingdon, UK: Routledge.

Roy, M. J., Donaldson, C., Baker, R., & Kerr, S. (2014). The potential of social enterprise to enhance health and well-being: A model and systematic review. *Medicine, 123,* 182–193.

Stephens, C. (2008). Social capital in its place: Using social theory to understand social capital and inequalities in health. *Social Science and Medicine, 66*(5), 1174–1184.

Szreter, S., & Woolcock, M. (2004). Health by association? Social capital, social theory, and the political economy of public health. *International Journal of Epidemiology, 33*(4), 650–667.

Uphoff, E. P., Pickett, K. E., Cabieses, B., Small, N., & Wright, J. (2013). A systematic review of the relationships between social capital and socioeconomic inequalities in health: A contribution to understanding the psychosocial pathway of health inequalities. *International Journal for Equity in Health, 12*(1), 54.

Wiseman, J., & Brasher, K. (2008). Community wellbeing in an unwell world: Trends, challenges, and possibilities. *Journal of Public Health Policy, 29*(3), 353–366.

5   Community Economies of Wellbeing

How Social Enterprises Contribute to 'Surviving Well Together'

Katharine McKinnon and Melissa Kennedy

Introduction

How do individuals, households, and communities 'survive well together'? This question drives both the scholarship and the practice of community economies. The concern for 'surviving well' builds on J.K. Gibson-Graham's work to articulate a post-capitalist vision of the economy (2006). Subsequent collaborations with Jenny Cameron and Stephen Healy to operationalise this postcapitalist vision in relation to community, led efforts to rethink and reshape livelihoods (Gibson-Graham et al. 2013). Their work asks for a reconsideration of what constitutes the foundations of a livelihood that does not just allow people to survive but to survive *well*, a livelihood that takes into consideration all that is necessary to assure wellbeing and a quality of life not just for the individual but the other people and communities that individual is connected with. The addition of the term 'together' signals the central interest in how livelihoods are shaped with others (Gibson-Graham et al. 2015). Community economies scholars place interdependence and reciprocity at the heart of economic relations, elaborating the complex ways in which making a living for ourselves cannot occur without also making livings *for* others and receiving a living *from* others (Miller 2019). Although competition and the 'open market' are supposed to be the foundation for economic success, in fact, all livelihoods depend to some extent on the collective outcomes of how human communities negotiate efforts to 'survive well together' (and alongside our more-than-human planetary companions). As an ethical praxis and a (non-essentialist) political approach, community economies scholarship advocates for consideration of all livelihood endeavours as an opportunity to question if and how they enable us to survive well together.

Social enterprises have a particular role to play in economic relations that support efforts to survive well together as they are a form of enterprise that places social or environmental concerns at the heart of their functions. Many social enterprises operate in a similar way to other capitalist firms. They are privately owned, have a Board of Directors

DOI: 10.4324/9781003125976-5

and a CEO that controls operations, and makes decisions about how to appropriate and distribute the surplus that is gained from the enterprise's productive activities, that is, the profits accrued after the costs of production are covered and workers are paid. In a capitalist firm, the surplus is usually distributed to shareholders and to senior management in the form of bonuses. Decisions are often driven by a desire to maximise the benefits that accrue to shareholders. In a social enterprise, decisions are likewise made by the executive group, but rather than seeking to satisfy shareholders and maximise the surplus available for distribution, it is the social or environmental mission of the enterprise that determines how surplus is distributed. Social enterprises do not put surplus into individual pockets but seek to reinvest in support of the core aims of the organisation. Within a diverse economy framing, social enterprises are thus categorised as *more-than-capitalist* enterprises:

> In the 'more than capitalist' firms that may have many attributes of mainstream business, what surplus there is left over from distributed payments to all the claimants on surplus is deployed to a range of ends, not only private accumulation. This could include to 'other' ends, such as the national commonwealth, the environment, a social grouping that may be marginalized, registered members of a tribe, or a constituency of stakeholder producers or consumers.
>
> (Gibson-Graham & Dombroski 2020, p. 12)

Community economies scholarship opens up the consideration of decisions about how to distribute surplus as part of a series of ethical negotiations. Each decision point in the operation of any enterprise is understood to hold the possibility of an ethical praxis, the possibility of taking decisions that contribute to (rather than detracting from) efforts to build sustainable and equitable livelihoods for all.

This chapter draws on a study of four social enterprise case studies, exploring the ways in which they contribute to this ethical praxis of building community economies. Of particular interest to us is the place that the production of wellbeing holds within each of these case studies. The research was conducted in collaboration with a team of other researchers, each investigating different aspects of wellbeing in social enterprises. The research was underpinned by a shared interest in how wellbeing can be understood *spatially*—that is, how the experience of wellbeing emerges in the physical spaces of the enterprise and how that wellbeing might spread, flowing into the wider community through social and economic relations. The project conducted interviews with employees in the enterprises, and some of their clients, gaining insights into how people experienced wellbeing in different ways. Drawing on a shared database, the three subgroups within the research project analysed the data, in turn, using Spaces of Wellbeing Theory (SOWT, see Chapter 2, this book), theories of social capital (see Chapter 4, this book), and, in our case, a community economy framing. Our analysis explored how the experiences of workers reflected the multidimensional forms of wellbeing necessary for surviving well together.

First of all, we offer a more thorough explanation of a community economy theorisation of wellbeing and its place at the centre of the open-ended ethical negotiations that are understood to be crucial to the praxis of surviving well together. We then offer a brief elaboration of our methods and analysis and then explore the empirical evidence from the research to elaborate how the creation of wellbeing is integrated into the everyday functioning of these more-than-capitalist enterprises. We argue that while many forms of wellbeing are certainly being produced for workers within the social enterprises, everyday experiences of the workplace were not always good for wellbeing. Among these complex experiences, however, are examples that suggest pathways for workplaces of all kinds to do more to place wellbeing at the centre of economic activities.

Theorising Wellbeing in Community Economies

Community economies scholarship emerges from the assumption that the economies that provide human livelihoods are part of a 'diverse economy.' Based on the ground-breaking work of J.K. Gibson-Graham, diverse economies scholarship recognises that the ways we sustain and nurture ourselves and our families involve a vast array of practices that are seldom acknowledged in standard discussions of 'the economy.' The diverse economy is made up of a myriad of economic practices. It includes wage labour and capitalist enterprises but also unpaid work, bartering, subsistence production, gifting, gleaning, and scavenging. These activities are understood to take place in multiple types of enterprises including cooperatives, community gardens, non-profits, and households. Further, the economic benefits that they produce are understood to be much more than just financial. Social enterprises are one example of a form of enterprise that generates surpluses to be directed towards social or environmental benefits alongside running a viable business. Social enterprises fit into a type of enterprises 'whose "core business" is not to maximise private benefit but to produce community wellbeing directly, particularly for marginalised groups' (Gibson-Graham & Cameron 2007, p. 21).

J.K. Gibson-Graham (2006) argue in 'A Post Capitalist Politics' that the diverse economic practices that provide for our existence are not only shaped around concerns for maximising efficiency or profit. They also entail making ethical decisions around how our economies impact human and planetary others. As these decisions are made, there are opportunities to shape practice around the health and wellbeing of human and non-human communities rather than a concern for profit margins. This is what they term a 'community economy.' In collaboration with Stephen

Healy and Jenny Cameron, Gibson-Graham extend the engagement with community economy as a set of practices that enable us to 'survive well together' beyond meeting material ends (Gibson-Graham et al. 2013). Community economies scholarship seeks to identify the range of livelihood practices and enterprise forms within the diverse economy that enable more sustainable and equitable economic relations and lifeways: 'identifying, gathering, and amplifying ethical economic practices that already exist—and that prefigure "the world we want to live in"' (Gibson-Graham et al. 2017).

As a starting point for orienting practice towards building community economies, J.K. Gibson Graham et al. (2017) identify a cluster of ethical concerns or 'coordinates' around which community economies are being (and might be) built:

1. Survival: What do we really need to survive well? How do we balance our own survival needs and wellbeing with the wellbeing of others and the planet?
2. Surplus: What is left after our survival needs have been met? How do we distribute this surplus to enrich social and environmental health?
3. Transactions: What is the range of ways we secure things we cannot produce ourselves? How do we conduct ethical encounters with human and non-human others in these transactions?
4. Consumption: What do we really need to consume? How do we consume sustainably and justly?
5. Commons: What do we share with human and non-human others? How do we maintain, replenish, and grow these natural and cultural commons?
6. Investment: What do we do with stored wealth? How do we invest this wealth so that future generations may live well?

A concern for wellbeing underpins each of these coordinates through attention to both human and planetary wellbeing, care for each other, and the implicit (and at times explicit) recognition of interdependence and collective responsibility. One example, as Kelly Dombroski has highlighted, is the distributed interdependent caregiving that defines the work of Cultivate Christchurch. Cultivate is a social enterprise that operates a community garden to address youth mental health following the devastating earthquakes that destroyed much of the Christchurch CBD in 2010 and 2011 (Dombroski 2020; Dombroski et al. 2019). In Cultivate, Dombroski argues:

> the diverse forms of labour and compensation and the diverse forms of care work form a hybrid caring collective that acts to improve not just youth mental health, but environmental health and the wellbeing

of staff, volunteers, restaurants and the general public who purchase the organic vegetables.

(Dombroski 2020, p. 159)

As members of Cultivate and their clients interact, and as the garden is worked, decisions are made about how the goods are produced and sold and about how the benefits are shared and reinvested in the garden and its people. As these decisions are made, it is the orientation towards a concern for a shared wellbeing that positions this enterprise as part of the community economy.

This chapter contributes to the community economies literature by providing a systematic consideration of how the case study social enterprises *produce* and *distribute* wellbeing as part of the day-to-day function of the organisation. We propose that these coordinates require negotiation not just of the production and distribution of material benefits but also of the social, emotional, and cultural benefits that are both the foundation for, and the result of, the different ways that human beings shape their livelihoods. Key to this analysis is the community economy scholarship that positions markets and marketplaces not just as sites of the exchange of goods and services but as the circumstances through which relationships are built and communities fostered. This is in contrast to much of the policy focus on social enterprises that follows mainstream business models and 'the market' to address social issues (Cameron 2010; Cameron & Hendriks 2014). Community economy scholarship has questioned the conventional presentation of markets as a neutral arbiter of supply and demand, arguing that this desocialised framing obfuscates human encounters and interactions. Buyers and sellers getting together to negotiate prices is one example: an everyday occurrence in the marketplace that also constitutes a form of social relationship (Gibson-Graham 2006; Gibson-Graham et al. 2013). Rather than viewing the market as an entity to procure goods and services that people cannot provide for themselves, community economy scholarship places market transactions amongst the broader suite of ethical economic actions that help us to 'survive well together' with our human and nonhuman cohabitants (Diprose 2020; Gibson-Graham et al. 2013). From a social enterprise perspective, attention to transactions widens the scope of understanding beyond the ethical aspirations of the organisation itself, to how wellbeing might flow more widely between workers or producers and the consumers of social enterprise goods and services more broadly within the community.

Methodology

For this chapter, we draw on analysis of the shared data produced within the collaborative research project, 'Mapping the impact of social enterprise on regional city disadvantage,' a project funded by the Australian

Research Council (DP170100388). The project involved interviews and participant observation with four social enterprises in two regional cities in Australia.

The study included enterprises located in city suburbs with high relative disadvantages. Two cases (Farm and Catering) were in City 1 and two (AssistAll and Community Centre) in City 2. Farm, Catering, and AssistAll are Work Integration Social Enterprises (WISEs) that provide work integration for people with a disability and/or disadvantage (*supported workers*). Community Centre operates as an entity that supports a number of small social enterprises as part of its mission to support its disadvantaged community. In Farm and AssistAll, supported workers undertake light manufacturing, mail outs, assembly, cleaning, and maintenance, and AssistAll also provides a catering service and second-hand store. Farm has the most diverse work environment incorporating a market garden, art studios, a store, and a restaurant, all open to the public. Farm also draws on the services of community members who volunteer in the garden and work with the social enterprise participants. Catering is a dedicated catering business, while enterprises that operate within Community Centre offer home cleaning, a recycled clothing shop, and a vegetable box delivery service.

The research methods in this project involved semi-structured interviews with staff, supported workers, and community leaders (such as business representatives, customers, politicians, and non-profit sector representatives). 'Go-along' interviews (Bergeron et al. 2014; Carpiano 2009) were also conducted with supported workers through the site and in the community to better understand their perspectives on their role and achievements in relation to the social enterprise and the impacts that their involvement had on their lives in the wider community. Interview transcripts were coded in NVivo for emerging representations of wellbeing under the frame of 'surviving well together.' Gibson-Graham et al. (2013) propose that in order to survive well together, communities and organisations need to work on an ongoing basis to balance five different types of wellbeing that enable holistic livelihoods.

1. Material wellbeing, which comes from having the resources to meet our basic needs and being satisfied with the resources we have.
2. Occupational wellbeing, which comes from a sense of enjoyment of what we do each day, whether in a conventional job or as a student, a parent, a volunteer, or a retiree.
3. Social wellbeing, which comes from having close personal relationships and a supportive social network.
4. Community wellbeing, which comes from being involved in community activities.
5. Physical wellbeing, which comes from good health and a safe living environment.

Our preliminary analysis identified that missing from these five elements was a notion of psychological or spiritual wellbeing (see McKinnon et al. 2020). In the context of WISE's, and particularly those that work with people with disabilities, psychological health is extremely important; thus, we added a sixth component of wellbeing in our exploration:

6. Psychological and spiritual wellbeing, which moves 'beyond a physiological or biomedical notion of health to encompass the emotional, social and, in some cases, spiritual dimensions of what it means to be human' (Conradson 2012, p. 16).

In our analysis, we used this typology of six types of wellbeing to ask: 'How are social enterprises generating the wellbeing needed for 'surviving well' together?' The broad findings (Farmer, De Cotta, Kilpatrick et al. 2020) highlight that while social enterprises are uniquely positioned to contribute to individual and community wellbeing and support holistic livelihoods, the benefits that accrue to workers are not without accompanying problems and drawbacks. This paper draws on the analysis to focus particularly on how the different kinds of wellbeing produced in the case studies created opportunities for each social enterprise to contribute to building stronger community economies.

Creating and Distributing Wellbeing Benefits

In this section, we consider examples from each community economy wellbeing type, in turn, exploring how wellbeing benefits are created and distributed throughout the social enterprises and the communities in which they are situated. Particular attention is paid to the ways that wellbeing benefits are negotiated within the context of enterprise and the markets within which they operate.

Material Wellbeing

Material wellbeing involves 'having the resources to meet our basic needs and being satisfied with the resources we have' (Gibson-Graham et al. 2013, p. 21). Material wellbeing—having enough to live on—is the cornerstone of survival for people and their families. One of the key questions that shapes community economy engagements with survival is the question of how to balance one's own survival needs and wellbeing with the wellbeing of others and the planet.

For the social enterprises in this study, providing the opportunity of wage work for disadvantaged or disabled members of the community was a core focus. For Grace at Farm (City 1), the social enterprise provided a pathway to paid employment from voluntary work, allowing her capacities to be recognised and rewarded in a way that the open job market failed to do:

> I did a lot of volunteering work, study, I looked for work that wasn't there. I was in a field of not disabled enough but not able enough either . . . I was still volunteering here, and when that fell through they said, you're no longer a volunteer, we're going to pay you for what you do now. Then they added the cleaning jobs on top of that.

Grace's experience was one example of how people employed in social enterprises have difficulty finding work in the open market. Often, those workplaces were unable to accommodate well the material and other needs of people with disabilities. While the social enterprises enabled Grace to get employment, her wages and those of other supported workers were low.

Wages are at award rates to begin with, and in the case of Catering and Farm, the award rate is also scaled according to the independence of each supported worker. Employment Assistance Plans (EAPs) assess the capacity each supported worker has to complete, the individual tasks required for their work, and the more support they need from staff, the less wages they receive. Staff in these organisations worked hard to ensure supported workers received as much pay as possible, as Zoe from Catering reflects:

> the EAP is basically about their wage assessment so it's how we can work to get a higher wage, for them to get a higher wage and what can we do and we can improve on and what we can really work at.

Part of the justification for the scaling of wages is that workers were expected to eventually transition into the open labour market. The Work Integration Social Enterprise model followed by Catering and Farm is based on the assumption that through their jobs here, supported workers could gain the experience and skills needed to transition in the open job market. In reality, this happens infrequently:

> They don't want to leave here once they're sort of here . . . There's not that many that have moved into other employment. I don't think there is that much around (City 1) for it.
>
> (Zoe, Catering)

One of the challenges in relation to material wellbeing is the low wages that workers receive. For many supported workers, the jobs they had within these social enterprises were crucial to their survival, but wages were low both for supported workers and for staff. For workers who rely on the social enterprise for their main income, this creates difficulties.

Graeme, a staff member from one of the non-governmental organisation (NGO) involved with AssistAll, spoke about the low wages:

> Now, we have a lot of volunteers, we also have a lot of relatively lowly paid staff members. We'd love to pay more, but we can't, there's simply not enough food in the tin so to speak . . . But overall, people do this because they love to do it.

Ultimately, some of the people who work at these social enterprises were only just meeting their own survival needs and had very little surplus left over after those needs were met. They did this both because they chose to (in the case of staff who had chosen to take work at the enterprise over other better-paid positions in the commercial sector) or, like Grace, had few other places they could seek paid work.

Occupational Wellbeing

People doing the work 'because they love to do it' is indicative of the strong sense of occupational wellbeing that emerged for both the paid staff and the supported workers within the case study social enterprises. Occupational wellbeing entails 'a sense of enjoyment in what we do each day' (Gibson-Graham et al. 2013, p. 21). For most respondents, staff, and employees alike, the work they did in the social enterprise was a source of pleasure and fulfilment, although often for different reasons. For employees, part of this appears to be simply the satisfaction of having an occupation. For Liam, for example, the motivation to look for a job was about, 'Just get[ting] out of the house for a while' (City 1). This appears to be the case for many, as Farm staff member Luna commented: 'Everyone wants something to do. That is probably 99 per cent of the response.' For others, however, the joys of work were about engaging in new challenges and learning new skills, such as cooking, or working with something that they love, such as animal care.

For many, the routine of work was also connected with experiences of occupational wellbeing. As one of the employees, Jessica from AssistAll stated, having a job to go to was a way to 'get out there. It got me into a routine.' However, along with the sense of enjoyment, being at work also brought inevitable stresses and difficulties. The converse to occupational wellbeing was the necessity to deal with things that detracted from a sense of enjoyment. For many supported workers, tasks that had to be completed under time pressure were the least enjoyable. One example is from Maggie, for example, an employee at Farm, who found packing and delivering garden produce for local restaurants stressful:

> I like the garden, but I don't like doing the restaurant orders. I find that a bit stressful. I like the weeding and the planting, and the

watering and all that . . . you don't have the stress of cleaning up, and there's no time limit.

Because she found the restaurant orders too stressful, Maggie's work at the Farm was adjusted to enable her to spend more time in the garden. What was happening at the Farm, and in other social enterprises, was that workplace conditions were often adjusted to the particular needs of employees. Staff would utilise the resources at hand, changing rosters, creating supportive spaces, or allowing people to move between different branches of the enterprise (from Catering to Farm, for example, or from gardening work to car washing), in response to individual needs and vulnerabilities.

A sense of enjoyment in the workplace was evident through the interviews with staff and supported workers alike. The sense of wellbeing that arises from having something to do and getting out of the house however sits sometimes in tension with the pressures that come with having an occupation, particularly the pressure of performing tasks to deadlines. Yet because the social enterprises make more space for care through flexibility and responsiveness to the needs of employees, conditions of work could, to some extent, be adjusted. This highlights how, within the organisation, transactions of labour could be conducted with an ethical concern for maximising the wellbeing of workers. Normal labour relations within workplaces are made up of (more or less) calculated decisions by enterprises to purchase labour power in order to produce goods and services. In these enterprises, the purchase of labour power was not a straightforward transaction between employer and employee. For supported workers in particular, their wages are subsidised by government welfare payments through the National Disabilities Insurance Scheme. In amongst the complexities of these remunerative relations, (and the added complications of EAPs at Catering and the Farm), considerations of occupational (and other) forms of wellbeing were added into the negotiations around work tasks and rosters.

Social Wellbeing

Social wellbeing is associated with 'having close personal relationships and a supportive social network' (Gibson-Graham et al. 2013, p. 22). For employees, the workplace itself is a place where they are able to build social networks and connect with others. Several interviewees—both staff and supported workers—recognised that one of the biggest benefits of involvement in the enterprise was an expansion of employees' social connections. This related to their increasing ability to interact socially with others and to extend themselves through new forms of social connection beyond the workplace as well. Leah from Catering reflects on how she noticed the change in an employee through increased social interaction:

> She's very softly spoken and very shy. The first time she came in the car she didn't say anything to me at all. Then as it's gone on she will even initiate conversations with me so telling me about things she does in her personal life. She might do activities. I've seen that, just their social interaction grow. They can speak to the customers now.

This change was also experienced by Rachel, a supported worker at Catering who observed the fostering of social relationships in the workplace:

> I kind of kept to myself but now I'm here I don't keep nothing to myself. I'm like a person that always keeps talking. You've virtually got to tell me to shut up. . . [I feel] so comfortable here I could talk to anybody about anything that needs to be going or family or friends or anything like that. If anything happens I can always talk to [staff member].

Study participants observed how the sociality of the workplace extended into other activities outside of the social enterprise for employees, such as playing netball and cricket and going out for dinner or to the movies.

The sociality of the workplace was recognised among staff across the case studies, highlighting the central contribution that each enterprise was making to the lives of supported workers. Unfortunately, commercial imperatives also place a limit on how much the social relationships could be fostered as William from AssistAll highlighted:

> Look, at the end of the day, we're all about providing employment, but at the same time we're about trying to generate money to keep the company and that going. I'd love to put the guys on the bus and take them fishing for a day or take them to a local game of football or just something like that, because it's rewarding and a lot of them don't get an opportunity to do that.

These restrictions are, in part, determined by the funding schemes within which the social enterprises are embedded. The funding model is dependent not only on financial turnover from trade but also on the funding brought in by employees through the National Disability Insurance Scheme. As a result, there are limitations to what they can do. Adrian, a politician from City 2 explains why:

> Funding is now typically on a fee-for-service or on an item-based— for example, in healthcare, unless you've got an MBS (Medicare Benefits Schedule) provider number and an item number, you are

restricted to providing particular services that are chargeable. There's less funding for a service based upon block funding, or to do a range of social goods which are not chargeable by an item. I think that's a real risk going forward.

Because there is space to attend to the value of social connection alongside the commercial purposes of the social enterprises, these organisations provide an example of how the workplace may become a site of ethical negotiation between business imperatives and creating conditions that allow social benefit to emerge, such as compromising on productivity or income in order to enable greater social connections to be fostered. In these enterprises, the sociality that is always a part of work is often allowed to take priority. The care and welfare role of these organisations enable them to place significance on practices that enable social interactions, with a view to enhancing the broader health and wellbeing benefits for supported workers. The struggle, however, is that the enterprises lack ways to value this sociality within a system defined by financial flows and benefits and shaped around chargeable service delivery.

Community Wellbeing

Community wellbeing is attributed to involvement in community activities (Gibson-Graham et al. 2013, p. 22). Not all social enterprises fostered opportunities for increased community involvement as part of their operations, but both Farm and AssistAll sought to provide spaces and moments in which staff and supported workers had opportunities to encounter and connect with members of the wider community. Farm in City 1, for example, actively works to bring the community 'in' through weekend market days and through the presence of volunteers (often retirees) who help tend to the garden. As staff member Penny explained:

> Social interaction I think is a big one, especially for the volunteers. They're all retirees . . . so you could sit at home day in day out and not see a soul really if you wanted to. But they come down, even if it's only for half an hour, an hour, you get to have a cuppa and a chat and then they go home and they're happy. Even the supported workers [employees] I think for them it's a big thing too.

The social enterprises also create community wellbeing in other ways through market transactions via the goods and services that are offered. For instance, through the value of the nutritious take-home meals prepared at Catering, the fresh fruit and vegetable boxes provided through

(AssistAll) or offering garden maintenance services for isolated clients as Isaac, at Community Centre Social Enterprise, reflects:

> Some of, especially the older people we used to go to, they mightn't see anybody. They were so happy to see someone come around just to sit and yak to for half an hour. Some days two guys would be out cutting the grass and I'd be, please now I've got to get going. They just wanted to talk. I'll sit and have a cuppa with you.

As reflected in the previous discussions of wellbeing, the practice of care provided within the social enterprise working environment nurtured employees' sense of wellbeing. Through transactions with clients across the cities, the social enterprises are also offering an opportunity for those purchasing goods and services to participate in relationships that build wellbeing. Clients of Catering and Farm, for example, identified that the decisions to purchase from the social enterprises were a conscious act of engaging in transactions that offered greater benefits to members of the community, and directed their consumption around a desire for shared benefit. As the following consumers reflected:

> Well I think they are not cheap with their catering. I mean they're not overly expensive, they're on a par with everybody else and a few people have said, 'Why do we use them?' and we go, 'Well it's an opportunity for the people of [City 1] to be involved in something that is employing people that otherwise may not be able to get employment'. So, I think that's really important.
>
> (City 1, Catering Client 1)

> The sense of reinvesting in community was really important to us.
>
> (City 1, Catering Client 2)

These clients highlight the ethical decisions that are being made in transactions with social enterprises. Such transactions offer the potential for communities to 'survive well together' beyond conventional framings of markets that act in the pursuit of self-interest and the lowest price. The ethical negotiations that underpin this are highlighted by Melanie, a staff member at Farm, who explained how the cost of the social enterprise goods and services was met with varying levels of support in the community.

> We gave them a brochure explaining what [we] do, that it's helping the community and—because we're employing people with a disability or people with a disadvantage. Some people were amazing, they really wanted to try to help us. Then the other side of that

was sometimes they thought that [it] didn't cost them very much. It doesn't work like that.

For some, there is an expectation that the social enterprise would be cheaper, yet others actively endorse the social value returned to the community through market transactions. As a procurer of the services from Farm reflected:

> You can put me on your wellbeing because it feels good to know that I'm doing something worthwhile as well.
>
> (Nicole, City 1)

When viewed through the lens of market transactions, such insights help to enlarge understanding of the diverse ways that community wellbeing can be ethically negotiated through social enterprises.

Physical Wellbeing

Physical wellbeing—good health and a safe living environment—was supported by social enterprises in a variety of ways. In all the organisations, there was a focus not just on developing skills for the workplace but in helping employees to learn the skills they needed beyond the workplace in order to live healthy lives. For instance, at AssistAll, a number of talks were instigated to support physical wellbeing around topics, such as family planning, mental health, and personal hygiene. Fulfilling these needs was taken on as part of the organisation's responsibilities. AssistAll acknowledged that supported workers often needed support, not only in their working lives but also for their health and wellbeing in their personal or home life, and took on responsibility for that:

> The employees have varying, like any human being, complex personal lives and complex health issues . . . so there have been times an employee's health and wellbeing is not well. That means doing things like making sure that they're okay in the bathroom. . . . A whole bunch of personal care stuff around that. Supporting them to make life, hopefully wise life choices, without being intrusive.
>
> (Jessica, City 2)

Simultaneously, these organisations were also engaging employees in learning new habits of good health within the workplace, particularly around the habits of doing exercise, eating fresh produce, and cutting down on fast foods, for instance at Catering, Christine reflects:

> We try to teach them to cook healthier at home, or not have takeaway, or they're saying about they eat Maccas [McDonalds] and things like that. You don't eat that stuff, you know.
>
> (Christine, Staff, Catering)

Because the social enterprises are dealing with people with disabilities or health issues, the social enterprises have room to consciously engage in providing targeted support for the broader physical health of employees. For Farm and Catering, they also have a mandate to provide care supported through the NDIS funding that they receive. But as Jessica from AssistAll highlighted, the needs of the supported workers are not so different from the needs of anyone. Indeed, all people, regardless of ability, have moments in time and periods of life when they are vulnerable and in need of care and support. As Julie Stephens (2011) and Puig de la Bellacasa (2017) have both argued, the need to receive the care of others is a fundamental part of the human experience from birth. Ensuring that an organisation's workers are healthy and well while at work is widely recognised as an obligation of all workplaces and is regulated by state and federal governments (although to varying degrees in different jurisdictions globally). These organisations, however, took the responsibility for physical health and wellbeing a step further by seeking to support workers learn how to lead more healthy lives within and beyond the workplace. This constitutes not only an investment in the capacity and productivity of employees, ensuring their workers were able to undertake their assigned tasks, but also an investment in their ability to live healthy lives. The interest in health beyond the workplace could also be seen as an investment in the common good that comes with a population that is physically well and healthy, a benefit shared with the wider community beyond the workplace.

Psychological and Spiritual Wellbeing

Psychological and spiritual wellbeing is the foundation for a balanced emotional life and a sense of purpose or meaning in being human. For some participants, working at the social enterprises allowed more than just a sense of enjoyment and satisfaction with their activities. Their work afforded an opportunity to create a different sense of themselves and the world they are living in:

> It is good for your heart. It's good for all of you. Makes you think. You get home and you think geez that was a good day. That's how it's been because of it.
>
> (Carol and Sue, Community Centre, City 2)

The ways that the work and workplaces enable a deeper sense of contentment and meaning in the world are multiple and varied, depending on the individual workers. For some, simple repetitive tasks provided a meditative space that helped them to achieve a sense of calm in a world that otherwise was often experienced as too chaotic and demanding. Peeling potatoes for example is a favourite task for some workers at Catering, while at Farm folding paper bedding for the hospital or shredding paper served a similar purpose. Staff at Farm, for example, noticed that the job of shredding paper was soothing:

> Some of them just sit there all day and that's what they enjoy doing. That's fine if that makes them comfortable within themselves as well . . . I think it's soothing. . . [for supported worker] . . . the part of his disability is he just needs that shut the world out type of stuff.
> (Melanie, Farm, City 1)

Not only is the experience acting in a positive way for the workers, but it also had an impact on the world of which they are a part of. One small example of this is in the garden at Farm. In the garden, employees found spaces of calm and happiness in relation to the plants they cultivate and harvest. Michael, a supported worker at Farm, for example, spoke about the happiness that came from seeing a plant he had sowed and cared for grow into produce for sale at the weekly market: 'Because I know like I've done that. Yeah.' The wellbeing that arose in relation to the garden was also a mutual relationship. On its own, the garden itself did not induce the sense of calm or happiness that respondents spoke about. It happened through and with people's work with the soil, the seeds, and the plants and work to grow the garden and harvest the produce. Staff member Luna at Farm reflected on her realisation of how important the relationships with the garden were for volunteers and supported workers at Farm:

> In my head, it was, like, the garden would be there, and that garden would provide the therapy. But, no, the therapy is creating the garden.

These examples demonstrated how psychological wellbeing could be fostered in the midst of the activities that underpinned the social enterprises' production of goods and services. As workers interacted with each other, with the spaces of the enterprise (a quiet corner for peeling potatoes, a garden), and with the materials with which they work (the shredder, the peeler, and the plants), these encounters were moments in which psychological wellbeing could be found and fostered. The importance of having spaces for a quiet time out, and spaces for social interaction, was one of the key findings from the analysis conducted by Farmer et al. (2019) and Farmer, De Cotta, Kamstra et al. 2020). From a community economies perspective, what becomes important is how enterprises deliberately consider how spaces and encounters can be designed so as to provide opportunities for emotional safety and support.

Conclusion

In this chapter, we have explored the place of wellbeing at the foundations of community economies. Alongside the basic need to make a living, a concern for mutual wellbeing takes a central position in efforts to create community economies; wellbeing that is an outcome of care for others and of conscious engagements with the interdependence of those connected through economic activity and processes of production and distribution of goods and services. Gibson-Graham and the Community Economies Collective propose that in order for humans to survive well together, economic activities—whether of individuals, households or enterprises—ought to be shaped around the negotiation of a series of 'ethical coordinates,' open-ended questions about how to most sustainably and equitably ensure survival, distribute surplus, conduct transactions with others, consume, replenish the commons, and invest for health and wellbeing of future generations.

In the four case studies on social enterprises discussed in this chapter, there is evidence of efforts to shape the day-to-day functioning of the enterprise around all of these considerations. And one clear outcome of these efforts is the experience of multidimensional wellbeing among those that work at each enterprise. We began this chapter with the question: 'How are social enterprises generating the wellbeing needed for "surviving well" together?' In our case studies, material wellbeing is presented through the income provided, where alternative jobs are hard to find, and through the provision of new skills. At the same time, workers found it difficult to transition to mainstream jobs, and jobs on offer were often given low wages. For many employees, supported workers, and staff alike, the work provided occupational wellbeing, it was generally a source of pleasure and fulfilment, it was work that had meaning, gave a sense of routine, and involved the practice of care as the norm. Social wellbeing came with an expansion of opportunities for social connection, while at the same time the pressures to focus on productive work and constrained funding models could also limit time for connection. Community wellbeing was closely connected with the relationships that the social enterprises built through clients in the wider community. Through the various transactions, each social enterprise provided essential services for the wider community; facilitated encounters between diverse people; and spread wellbeing through products/services delivered which may have inherent benefits (healthy food, veggie boxes). The physical health and wellbeing of workers was a central concern for the social enterprises, which sought to build skills for healthy lives, acknowledging these are significant to work as well as home, life; benefits to workplace and society, as well as individuals. Finally, the psychological and spiritual wellbeing of workers was provided for through the type of work tasks assigned to suit individual worker's needs, for example, in the meditative value of simple repetitive tasks; calmness in garden work.

Across all of the social enterprises, some of these wellbeing outcomes were a part of deliberate and conscious action, while others were simply accidental. The experiences of different types of wellbeing in the enterprises are by no means uncomplicated. Alongside each story of a positive benefit, there were also stories of challenges and difficulties. One person's opportunity for calm and contemplation by peeling potatoes could be another person's moment of boredom and frustration. What is highlighted for us is the degree to which these workplaces suggest pathways for workplaces of all kinds to do more to place wellbeing at the centre of economic activities. As the stories from these social enterprises show, wellbeing is multi-dimensional as well as both individual and relational. To facilitate the conditions for 'surviving well together' in these social enterprises involves negotiating these different and perhaps competing aspects within the commercial demands of the enterprise.

We suggest that wellbeing could be given an even more prominent place in the ethical coordinates that inform community economies praxis. Wellbeing, in these examples, was not only a by-product of the workplace but something produced by and in it, alongside the goods and services that are the core economic activity of each organisation. We wonder if wellbeing could even be understood as one of the products that was exchanged through transactions with clients across the community? If so, it suggests that as social enterprises shape their organisational purpose and practice, some additional coordinates might be worth considering in relation to how the production and distribution of wellbeing could be foregrounded at the organisational level:

- How can (multi-dimensional forms of) wellbeing be produced alongside the core activities of the enterprise that enable workers to **survive well**?
- Can wellbeing benefits be counted as part of the **surplus** that an enterprise produces and reinvests, thus enabling the enterprise to formally acknowledge and value the social relations that emerge through economic activities?
- How can relationships across the community distribute wellbeing more widely through the types of **transactions** the enterprise has with volunteers and clients?
- How might wellbeing be factored into the **consumption** decisions of those procuring social enterprise goods and services?
- How does the enterprise contribute to shared wellbeing beyond the enterprise itself, helping to create **common** health and wellbeing from which everyone benefits?
- In what ways can the enterprise **invest** in building the emotional, psychological, and spiritual wellbeing of workers?

References

Bergeron, J., Paquette, S. & Poullaouec-Gonidec, P. (2014), 'Uncovering landscape values and micro-geographies of meanings with the go-along method', *Landscape and Urban Planning*, vol. 122, pp. 108–121.

Cameron, J. (2010), 'Business as usual or economic innovation? Work, markets and growth in community and social enterprises', *Third Sector Review*, vol. 16, no. 2, pp. 93–108.

Cameron, J. & Hendriks, S. (2014), 'Narratives of social enterprise: Insights from Australian social enterprise practitioners', in H. Douglas & S. Grant (eds), *Social Innovation, Social Entrepreneurship and Social Enterprise: Context and Theories*, Tilde University Press, Melbourne, pp. 342–358.

Carpiano, R.M. (2009), 'Come take a walk with me: The "Go-Along" interview as a novel method for studying the implications of place for health and wellbeing', *Health & Place*, vol. 15, pp. 263–272.

Conradson, D. (2012), 'Wellbeing: Reflections on geographical engagements', in S. Atkinson, S. Fuller & J. Painter (eds), *Wellbeing and Place*, Ashgate, Surrey, pp. 15–34.

Diprose, G. (2020), 'Framing essay: The diversity of transactions', in J. K. Gibson-Graham & K. Dombroski (eds), *The Handbook of Diverse Economies*, Edward Elgar, Cheltenham, UK and Northampton, MA, pp. 195–205.

Dombroski, K. (2020), 'Caring labour: Redistributing care work', in J. K. Gibson-Graham & K. Dombroski (eds), *The Handbook of Diverse Economies*, Edward Elgar, Cheltenham, UK and Northampton, MA, pp. 154–162.

Dombroski, K., Diprose, G., Conradson, D., Healy, S. & Watkins, A. (2019), *Delivering Urban Wellbeing through Transformative Community Enterprise*, National Science Challenge 11, Building Better Homes, Towns and Cities, viewed 9 August 2020, <www.buildingbetter.nz/publications/urban_wellbeing/Dombroski_et_al_2019_delivering_urban_wellbeing_through_transformative_community_enterprise.pdf>.

Farmer, J., De Cotta, T., Kamstra, P., Brennan-Horley, C. & Munoz, S. A. (2020), 'Integration and segregation for social enterprise employees: A relational micro-geography', *Area*, vol. 52, no. 1, pp. 176–186.

Farmer, J., De Cotta, T., Kilpatrick, S., Barraket, J., Brennan-Horley, C., McKinnon, K., Adler, V., Kamstra, P., Emery, S., Kennedy, M., Munoz, S.-A. & Roy, M. (2020), *Mapping the Impact of Social Enterprise on Disadvantaged Individuals and Communities in Australia's Regional Cities*, Swinburne University of Technology, Melbourne.

Farmer, J., De Cotta, T., Kilpatrick, S., Barraket, J., Roy, M. & Munoz, S.-A. (2019), 'How work integration social enterprises help to realize capability: A comparison of three Australian settings', *Journal of Social Entrepreneurship*, pp. 1–23.

Gibson-Graham, J. K. (2006), *A Postcapitalist Politics*, University of Minnesota Press, Minneapolis.

Gibson-Graham, J. K. & Cameron, J. (2007), 'Community enterprises: Imagining and enacting alternatives to capitalism', *Social Alternatives, Special Issue on Counter Alternatives*, vol. 26, no. 1, 20–25.

Gibson-Graham, J. K., Cameron, J. & Healy, S. (2013), *Take Back the Economy: An Ethical Guide to Transforming our Communities*, University of Minnesota Press, Minneapolis.

Gibson-Graham, J.K., Cameron, J. & Healy, S. (2015), 'Pursuing happiness: The politics of surviving well together', in *On Happiness: New Ideas for the Twenty-First Century*, UWA Publishing, Crawley, pp. 116–131.

Gibson-Graham, J. K., Cameron, J., Dombroski, K., Healy, S., Miller, E. & Community Economies Collective. (2017), 'Cultivating community economies',

TheNextSystem.Org, viewed 9 August 2020, <https://thenextsystem.org/cultivating-community-economies>.

Gibson-Graham, J. K. & Dombroski, K. (2020), 'Introduction to the handbook of diverse economies: Inventory as ethical intervention', in J. K. Gibson-Graham & K. Dombroski (eds), *The Handbook of Diverse Economies*, Edward Elgar, Cheltenham, UK and Northampton, MA, pp. 1–24.

McKinnon, K., Kennedy, M., Barraket, J. & De Cotta, T. (2020), 'Is being in work good for wellbeing? Work integration social enterprises in regional Australia', *Australian Geographer*, pp. 1–15.

Miller, E. (2019), *Reimagining Livelihoods: Life Beyond Economy, Society and Environment*, University of Minnesota Press, Minneapolis.

Puig de la Bellacasa, M. (2017), *Matters of Care: Speculative Ethics in More than Human Worlds*, University of Minnesota Press, Minneapolis.

Stephens, J. (2011), *Confronting Postmaternalism*, Columbia University Press, New York.

Section 2

Extending Methodological Frontiers

6 Spatialising Wellbeing Through Social Enterprise

Approaches, Representations, and Processes

Chris Brennan-Horley, Tracy De Cotta, Peter Kamstra, and Viktoria Adler

Introduction

Social enterprise research is turning towards the importance of space and place for understanding social enterprise operations and how geographically informed research might aid understanding of the sector. One stream of research looks to understanding spatial aspects such as scale and spread (Buckingham et al. 2012) and the geography of impact (Castellas 2017), while a second is interested in why impact arises, especially when disadvantaged clients engage with Work Integration Social Enterprise (WISE) (Munoz et al. 2015; Wilton and Evans 2016).

Economic and social accounting methodologies are a mainstay in the social enterprise literature. However, to gain a greater understanding of what social enterprise can offer communities and the economy, a wider range of impact pathways must be attended to (Munoz 2010). Wellbeing is an emerging lens through which to understand how health—as one type of social enterprise impact—is generated through WISE work. Fleuret and Atkinson's (2007) Spaces of Wellbeing framework has been adapted and used in WISE research for apprehending health and wellbeing as simultaneously relational and geographic achievements (Munoz et al. 2015). We draw upon this framework in this chapter to understand how therapy, safety, capability, and social integration might come together spatially in three WISEs to produce wellbeing and encourage social capital.

More specifically, this chapter explores how maps can aid understanding about social enterprise operations from a wellbeing and social capital perspective. Indeed, in the research that this chapter draws from, mapping became a central means for thinking spatially about WISE operations, with a variety of mapping techniques employed across all stages of the research process. We use cartographic visualisation to think through how to best convey findings to diverse audiences. We also introduce a range of topographic and network metaphors to convey understandings of the relational, unbounded, and multi-scalar nature of the WISE.

DOI: 10.4324/9781003125976-6

In presenting this work, this chapter answers Sarah-Anne Munoz's (2010) call for greater geographic engagement with social enterprise—especially using Geographic Information Systems (GIS)—to contend and understand these enterprises as embedded within, and therefore generative elements of, local and regional economies and geographies. We use mapping and GIS to engage with two particular elements raised in Sarah's *Area* piece: First, the examination of micro-geographies (how space is made and modified by a social enterprise) and second, the spread and scale of WISE operation and impact.

This chapter also contributes to methodological conversations between spatial researchers and social enterprise scholars by indicating pathways for WISE managers to think spatially with their supported workers and staff about how wellbeing can be cultivated in their enterprise. To enable this, we provide a detailed discussion of the mixed-methods approach employed with WISE employees and managers. The main results section then follows, as we step through various cartographic strategies that help us think about how wellbeing and social capital emerged. But first, we begin with a brief introduction to mapping and why it is worth considering as a heuristic.

Why Mapping?

Mapping and cartography have occupied a dominant position within multiple knowledge systems across millennia, principally as tools for organising and displaying locational information. Bio-evolutionary and cultural factors undergird the map's success as a knowledge instrument. We are innate spatial problem solvers (Sinton et al. 2013), as our bodies continually engage in three-dimensional spatial decision-making at multiple scales (e.g. the bodily capacities and spatial reasoning required to pick up a cup or drive a car). Consequently, humans have evolved a visuospatial cortex dedicated to processing and making sense of visual patterns (Ware 2010). It is unsurprising then that mapping—abstracting the observed world via scale-reduced signs—has evolved as a 'cultural universal' (Stea et al. 1996) with archaeological evidence of map-making stretching back into prehistory.

As map viewers, humans are able to simultaneously observe and make decisions from the multiple pieces of information available within a single map image (Mennecke et al. 2000). Placing data in its geospatial context permits the viewer to quickly take in both the data and its spatial component, permitting inferences to be made about spatial relationships (distance, scale and rotation, concentration, and direction) across a data set (Bertin 1967). This efficiency has led mapping to become the preferred choice for displaying information with an underlying locational component, above and beyond other common approaches including tables, graphs, or text. In short, maps can permit decision-makers to quickly make sense of otherwise complex geospatial issues.

Pivoting off our innate capacities to understand and interpret maps, what role might they play in understanding the health and wellbeing impacts of social enterprise? In this chapter, we looked to mapping and geographic information systems (GIS) to help us achieve this aim. GISs are specialist computer programs that handle the storage, retrieval, analysis, and display of geographic information. In a GIS, mapping is both the process and an endpoint. This technology has emerged primarily from earth sciences and demography and is perhaps most well-known for its seemingly quantitative powers, Cartesian spatial routines, and visualisation capacities. However, when this research project began, quantitative statistics or spatial data about spaces of wellbeing in WISE settings were non-existent. Additionally, we recognised the power of qualitative interviews and narrative to enable thick description and understanding about space and place (Geertz 1973). In an effort to work productively with both approaches, we turned to qualitative GIS.

Qualitative GIS can be envisaged as a mixed-methods framework that bridges between analytical approaches familiar to spatio-statistical research with alternate and qualitative ways of knowing that embrace complexity and the situated and partial nature of knowledge (Cope and Elwood 2009). Qualitative GIS thus permits the grounding of contextual knowledge about place, can unearth previously hidden spatial processes, and aid in understanding the inherent complexity of our socially constructed worlds. In short, Qualitative GIS can be used to generate spatial narratives of place and draw upon the analytical and cartographic possibilities of GIS to reveal alternate geographies. Studies that have produced grounded data from working closely with participants include producing creative geographies from statistically 'invisible' workers (Brennan-Horley and Gibson 2009); understanding the impact of place for at-risk youth (Mennis et al. 2013); and mapping the relational nature of risk (Kamstra et al. 2019). Based on these diverse applications, Qualitative GIS offered a tantalising possibility for revealing the hidden geography of wellbeing generation in WISE.

The WISEs we report on in this chapter are from three regional cities (service centres with 80–100,000 population) in Victoria and Tasmania, Australia. The WISEs included are code-named Farm, Catering, and AssistAll. All three are not-for-profit organisations (in Australia, not-for-profits operate across a multitude of domains, can take on a range of legal structures, and can qualify for a range of tax concessions but may not be tax-exempt). One (AssistAll) is also a registered charity (charities are a not-for-profit, that is tax-exempt). Farm contains an on-site kitchen, grows and sells produce to restaurants and the general public, has an art studio, and produces light manufacturing, assembly, and packaging. Off-site work includes a courier and mail service, car washing, and garden maintenance. As the name suggests, Catering offers catering services using produce grown at Farm. AssistAll produces timber products, conducts clothing recycling, handles mail outs and print finishing, assembly work, data entry, catering, and room-hire. Across the three sites we studied, employees are considered 'supported workers' that are either excluded from, or preparing themselves for, work in the mainstream economy.

Gathering and Ground Truthing Spatial Wellbeing Data

Data gathering was informed by a Qualitative GIS framework and involved collecting primary data through sketching, observation, interviews, focus groups, and mobile methods to secondary quantitative data from social enterprise management.

Over a six-month period in 2017–2018, participant observations were conducted at Farm, Catering, and AssistAll (approximately 80 hours at each social enterprise), using primarily field notes, photographs (with consent), and sketch mapping to record pertinent workspaces and practices both on-site and out in the community. This began with research participants sketching a 'mental map' of their commute with the researcher and then talking 'through their map.' Mental mapping involved employees sketching their spatial knowledge and experience on a blank page, drawing from the extensive mental and cognitive mapping tradition in planning and behavioural geography (Lynch 1960; Gould and White 1974). Mental maps of their commute helped employees to express their sociospatial experiences of wellbeing along that journey (Gieseking 2013). In some instances, mental mapping also emerged as a useful icebreaker and itinerary generator for subsequent go-along interviews.

'Go-along' interviews, lasting around 90 minutes, then followed and were conducted with employees on-site and in the community during social enterprise-related activities (Farm n = 4; Catering n = 5; AssistAll n = 5). These interviews used informal discussion techniques to target specific micro-spaces like a workshop, the lunchroom, or the car washing area. Go-along journeys ranged from navigating the WISE to accompanying staff in delivery vehicles or on public transport. During the go-alongs, employees were encouraged to describe objects, how they felt moving through different places, as well as providing an explanation of their experiences via storytelling and taking photographs. Collectively, these techniques allowed employees to 'show' and 'tell,' allowing the researcher to develop a rich, place-based retelling of employees' experienced wellbeing micro-geographies (Bergeron et al. 2014; Carpiano 2009). Employees were sampled to represent a mix of competency and experiences but with the capacity for informed consent (as assessed by staff). Due to varying employee literacy, verbal consent was obtained, and audio recorded. All interview data and go-along interviews were audio-recorded.

Semi-structured interviews with staff (around 60 minutes each) promoted discussions of employee wellbeing, the role workspaces play in generating wellbeing, and staff perceptions of activities that influence employees' wellbeing.

Analytically, data were coded in Nvivo 11 to Fleuret and Atkinson's (2007) wellbeing aspects of integration, capability, security, and therapy and to aspects of social capital (Kilpatrick et al. 2003). The coded data were then mapped to the corresponding micro-spaces in GIS. The aim of this approach was to spatially represent qualitative responses and perform both spatial and visual analyses (Knigge and Cope 2006). These visualisations revealed spatial patterns that are then contextualised by quotes, providing a 'triangulated' spatial understanding of where wellbeing occurred in tandem with specified explanations as to why.

A secondary data set was also obtained from Farm and Catering management detailing off-site work and sales across a single month. This spreadsheet contained data including addresses, customers, tasks, and sales. Street addresses were geocoded (turned into latitudes and

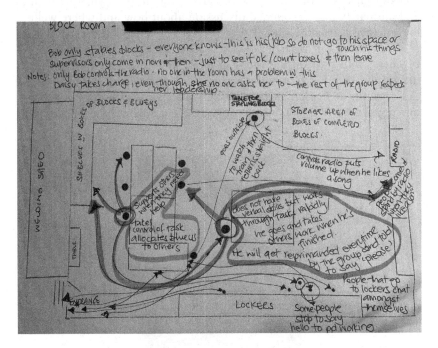

Figure 6.1 An early sketch of workplace activities, movements, and wellbeing emergence at Farm from participant observation

longitudes) using the Google API for subsequent map visualisation and road network trip routing.

After coding and analysing the interview data, 32 focus groups were held to verify (in GIS parlance—to 'ground truth') and extend our findings across all three sites. These took place during work hours at the premise of the social enterprises. The number of participants ranged from 2 to 4 people as larger groups could not be released from work at the same time. Focus groups lasted 40–120 minutes and were audio-recorded for later transcription. In most cases, focus groups were conducted with either only employees or only staff members.

We used interactive visual aids to prompt memories and instigate discussions amongst focus group participants. We designed these aids to also support participants with intellectual and physical capabilities to create an inclusive method which allowed us to hear a diverse range of voices and experiences. Colour-coded printouts of floor plans, site maps, and a simplified version of the space of wellbeing framework and photos of spaces within the social enterprises were used to visualise different aspects of wellbeing realising in the social enterprises.

Spatial thinking and reasoning came to the fore with our focus group participants. The maps and other visual aids were active agents in the focus groups, assisting in drawing participants into a dynamic, haptic, and ultimately more grounded discussion about how and where wellbeing emerged across the sites.

Results from our participant observation were generally agreed upon by clients and staff during focus groups. New insights gained through the ground-truthing activities were around temporal changes (e.g. activities done in the market garden during winter versus summer), the varying popularity of certain tasks amongst employees, and spatial and

Figure 6.2 Identifying spaces of wellbeing with a simplified map of the WISE

operational changes or changes in personnel since the data were first gathered. Furthermore, we gained deeper insights into the importance of relationships and their positive impact on employees' experiences of the social enterprises as a whole. Where possible these findings were fed back into the coding and data analysis strategy.

The multiple rounds of fieldwork and ground-truthing produced an abundance of detailed qualitative, quantitative, and spatial data. We turn now to the spatial analysis and visualisation strategies we employed to make sense of such rich and varied information. To make this manageable, we will proceed by making an artificial distinction between wellbeing data gathered on-site as a surface versus wellbeing generated off-site as a network. These are dealt with in turn.

Cartographic Stylings for Mapping Within Enterprises

A 500-year cartographic arc spanning Descartes to Google Maps has primed us to associate a planimetric (top-down) view when we think of maps. Indeed, this 'god's eye' viewpoint is what lends the map its seemingly objective, disembodied, and authoritative stance (Haraway 1988). There is nothing inherently wrong with planimetric maps—indeed you will see examples peppered throughout this chapter. But from a visualisation perspective, there is a fascination for three-dimensional (3D) representation of 'real-world' objects like city skylines or landscapes popularised by digital globes such as google earth and increasingly as part of gaming and virtual reality settings. These aspect views remain relatively novel compared to planar maps (Haeberling et al. 2008) and can convey particular affordances to visual storytelling beyond the two dimensional. 3D provides an extra-dimensional perspective, transforming data into a volumetric property that makes size comparisons between objects easier to decipher. 3D also plays upon our inherent stereoscopic capabilities that permit everyday depth perception, pulling the mind down from the orthogonal 'god's eye' view from above into a more embodied position looking over an imagined terrain. A landscape of peaks, valleys, and hills can thus emerge from otherwise 'flat' data (Brennan-Horley et al. 2010).

Pivoting off this fascination, this first results section engages with the possibility of using 3D visualisation to convey micro-geographies of wellbeing (Munoz et al. 2015) that emerged from within the bounds of the WISE. Two speculative cartographies that lean on topographical metaphors—mountains and icebergs—are introduced. Both exaggerate data about the z-axis to produce pseudo-terrains of wellbeing and integration.

Scaling the Peaks of Wellbeing

The first cartographic styling—mountains—is based upon data gathered from participant observation and interviews with key contacts (staff and employees) at each WISE. All data were recorded as point locations, coded against the four various wellbeing types (capability, security, integration, and therapy), and summed to produce an overall metric of wellbeing against each point location (refer to Farmer et al. 2020 for full details of this breakdown and analysis). From here, the sites were defined geographically in a spatial database by tracing their outline from aerial imagery and the metrics joined to the centroid (geographic centre) of each micro-site such as a building or work zones found within (refer to Figure 6.3).

As we have highlighted earlier, one of the key strengths of a spatial approach is that by associating tabulated data with geolocation, spatial context becomes a preferable ordering strategy for understanding the data. Rather than only presenting the data in tabulated form (a format that essentially wrests the data away from its spatial context), map visualisations permit spatial patterns to become evident.

Two alternate point distribution rendering strategies were iterated through (proportional circles and 2D graphs) before settling on the design shown in Figure 6.3: a 3D kernel density surface. Density surfaces

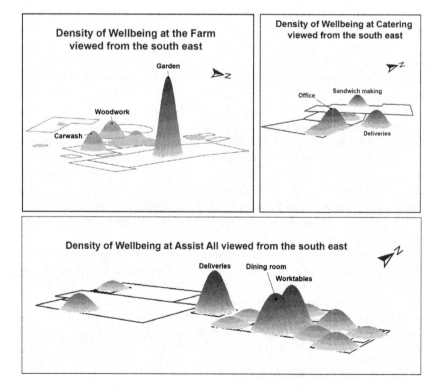

Figure 6.3 3D wellbeing topographies across the three WISE sites

permit the map reader to quickly make sense of the underlying pattern of a point distribution, revealing concentrations and spatial proximity more effectively. The kernel is the weighted radius drawn around each point which drives the shape of the resulting density surface. The bigger the kernel, the more a point overlaps with its neighbours, with greater overlap influencing the intensity of the resulting output. Default kernel radii were defined by ArcGIS in proportion to the overall extent of each WISE. A kernel is not an evenly weighted radius. Instead, greater importance/weight is assigned in a bell curve shape as you move towards the centre. These kernel density analyses were weighted by the wellbeing score at that location. Essentially, this means that differences in wellbeing mentions arose in the relative weightings of wellbeing at each point. The resulting output densities of wellbeing were then symbolised as percentages of density, with a colour ramp expressing darker shades as concentrations of wellbeing mentions increased. Jenks natural breaks scheme set divisions along the colour ramp to clump like values most efficiently before importing the data set into ArcScene, the 3D viewing extension of ArcGIS.

The 3D renderings in Figure 6.3 represent the total of all four wellbeing sub-types, but the resulting measure of wellbeing intensity across the WISE sites was used not only to drive a darkening colour scheme of increasing shades as the weightings and kernel interactions increased but also by height above ground level, creating a pseudo-topography of wellbeing. The resulting visualisations reveal varying micro-scale wellbeing topography operating within the bounds of the given WISE. Transforming the data by exaggerating the third dimension allows viewers to make a rapid assessment of prominence, absence, and the varying gradations of wellbeing across the WISE sites.

At Farm, for example, the garden registered the largest 3D peak of wellbeing across all three WISE, towering over smaller peaks at Farm. After visualising such a dominant peak, staff at Farm can explore using contextualising qualitative quotes to understand why the garden was so successful in generating wellbeing and use lessons learned to promote wellbeing at other sites. Conversely, the highest 3D peaks at Catering and AssistAll lie at a similar elevation, meaning wellbeing is more evenly distributed across these WISE. At Catering, the office has an observable larger peak than the other sites, but the next highest peak of wellbeing generated at the sandwich-making area and delivery areas is similar. AssistAll also demonstrates similar peaks of wellbeing at the deliveries area, dining room, and work tables. Although the rendering shown in Figure 6.3 is static, the software used to render the perspective 3D view (ArcScene) permits one to fly and move through the WISE wellbeing landscape and observe the data from different vantage points. This is particularly useful when taller terrain elements might block the views of other wellbeing concentrations.

Icebergs—What Lies Beneath

This section builds upon instances of wellbeing generation at certain sites around the Farm WISE but pivots to looking predominantly at one facet from spaces of wellbeing theory—integration and its inverse, segregation.

The data come from coding of the same observational data gathered at Farm, only this time, it was done by looking specifically for instances of spatial integration and segregation of employees and staff. An example of employees' mentions of social integration included interactions with other employees as well as with visiting volunteers, school students, and/ or 'members of the public.' An example of employees mentioning feelings of segregation included individuals co-occupying the same space but not interacting with one another. Coded excerpts of integration and segregation, like these, were then quantified and mapped to corresponding locations within the social enterprise. This enabled a visual 'spatial narrative' (Kwan and Ding 2008) of social integration and segregation across Farm. This 'spatial narrative' is an aggregation of where employees: (a) experienced social integration and segregation behaviours (from observation); (b) discussed integration/segregation (employee interviews); and (c) were perceived by staff to experience integration/segregation (staff interviews).

Our method for understanding the micro-geography of integration and segregation is given in Figure 6.4, which maps these data within Farm. In the planimetric/orthogonal view, sites are coloured along a diverging ramp, with white denoting an equal number of mentions of both integration and segregation. Sites diverge away from this middle value towards poles of either more integration (solid greys) or segregation (cross-hatched greys).

Visualising from a top-down vantage point was helpful but could potentially be enhanced by also creating terrains of integration versus segregation. Thinking of the notion of an iceberg led us to again extrude the data about the z-axis, with integration mentions running as a topography in the positive direction, but with negative values sinking below ground level, representing the bathymetry of segregation. The only problem here was in how to display both terrains at once, as a pseudo-3D terrain rendering on a 2D page could not simultaneously display both effectively without leaving half the data invisible beneath ground level. To effectively show both together in a static image, a transect was run across the site from north to south, slicing the 3D data like a cake to reveal both the positive and negative intensities in a single 2D image. The resulting outcome topography is shown as an inset in Figure 6.4.

Figure 6.4 revealed integration and segregation as not mutually exclusive phenomena, rather they emerged in varying and uneven intensities across the Farm. The Market Garden, for example, contained 15 mentions of integration, while simultaneously, having the greatest number of mentions of segregation. Whereas the workshop, car wash, and

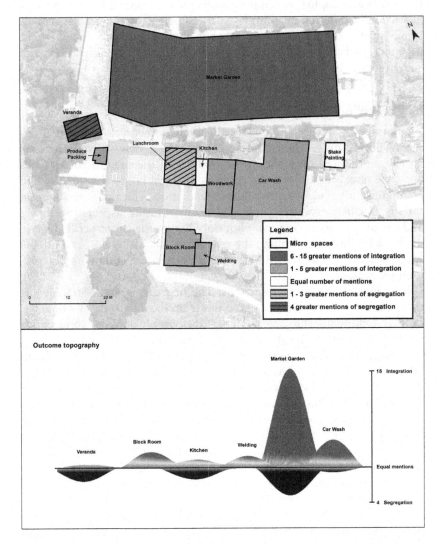

Figure 6.4 Integration versus Segregation at Farm WISE, incorporating 2D and
    3D visualisation strategies

block-room all attracted more mentions of integration, compared with
segregation mentions. Conversely, the lunchroom and veranda (areas for
taking breaks) were revealed as the most bottom-heavy in mentions of
segregation when compared to integration.

The variable nature of integration and segregation mentions, at times
in the same micro-space, highlights wellbeing as a relational achievement.
The transect is visual evidence of subtle power differentials operating

between staff, employees, support workers, and volunteers that are held in tension in differing magnitudes and geometries across the Farm. This brings to the fore questions about what physical phenomena, activities, practices, or behaviours influence this variability in social relations and subsequent sense of place (Massey 2012).

Unbounding the WISE

The mountain and iceberg terrains in the previous section mapped on-site wellbeing only. These produced a bounded view of wellbeing—as an effect produced only within the confines of the site. To counter this view, we now look beyond the confines of the WISE to the surrounding community for evidence of wellbeing generation. The aim of this section then is to cartographically unbound positive health aspects (wellbeing and social capital) as occurring not only within the circumscribed space of the WISE but also through the operations, the deliveries, and off-site work tasks that our studied WISEs carry out in the community, across multiple scales.

It is divided into two subsections. The first cartographic style details the expansion of wellbeing geographies from the day-to-day work geographies (lightning). The second (spider) cartography looks at connections in the context of social capital stretching out from the WISE.

Both of these data codings and subsequent cartographies lent themselves to representation as lines rather than as terrain or topography, principally because we wanted to show connection between the WISE and a range of sites spread across sometimes large geographic areas. The cartographic goal then was to use a geographic primitive that best encapsulated this relationship between a centre (the WISE) and a series of nodes (work sites, customers, and so on). Lines have the semiotic capacity to convey a sense of linkage, with our visuospatial cortex attuned to follow connections, thereby seeing nodes as part of a connected whole (Lechner 2020).

Regularly deployed in multiple sub-fields of human geography and data visualisation more broadly, flow or network maps graphically detail linkages and movement across space between nodes in a connected network. They can be used to visualise relationships between any manner of linked agents, such as capital, workers, materials, energy, waste, data, products, or services. The flow maps in this section were all generated with reference to a Cartesian projection as opposed to aspatial network graphs focused on connection alone. This permits distance measurement between nodes, allowing the scalar nature of WISE impact to become evident (Munoz 2010). Additionally, flow maps can reveal spatial arrangement and connective strength between nodes by deploying differences in line colour and thickness.

Lightning—Sparking Connections in the Community

Many WISEs offer products or services off-site, necessitating employees and supported workers to move about in the wider community. Multiple WISEs studied in this research offered activities including gardening and landscaping, cleaning services, recycling collection, and secondment for office administration roles. Additionally, catering and fresh produce deliveries grown and prepared on-site at the WISE were delivered regularly to a spectrum of customer groups (private, government, and not-for profits) locally and beyond. To contend with these multi-scalar geographies and their potential for generating client wellbeing, we began by flow-mapping one month of WISE deliveries and off-site jobs in Figures 6.5 and 6.6.

The underlying data for both figures were sourced from Farm's managers, detailing customer addresses and frequency over a one-month period. This table was transformed into spatial data through geocoding the address column (transforming written addresses into their respective latitude and longitude pairs). Next, lines tracing along the road network from the WISE to each latitude/longitude pair were routed using the Google Maps API. These routes were overlaid and symbolised so that lighter sections of the road network indicate the most often-used routes, although this process does not result in an exact map of where drivers may go. A more accurate data set would require GPS tracking of vehicles

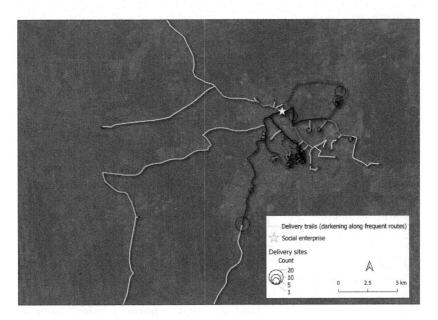

Figure 6.5 Delivery journeys

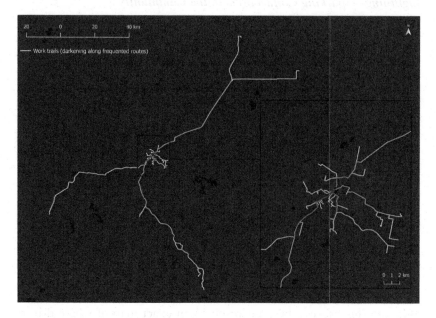

Figure 6.6 Off-site work locations

which was not viable within this project. Finally, these visualisations were triangulated with interview data gathered from employees and staff about WISE transport aspects and mobile work.

Figure 6.5 is a network map of one month of Catering sales made to public sector, not-for-profit, and private customers, revealing the multi-scalar nature of social procurement supporting this particular WISE. Figure 6.6 then shows 152 individual mobile jobs occurred across Farm's network. Gardening is a key mobile business arm of Farm, including mowing, weeding, and planting on both private properties and public land. The majority were single jobs per month in and around the town. Gardening work is a chance for employees to experience and build well-being, specifically 'capability' through learning and performing manual tasks up to operating and maintaining gardening machinery and liaising with customers. Cleaning jobs were also prominent, predominantly within the same regional town and within a short drive of the main WISE site.

The mobile work tasks and sales displayed in the lightning maps are primarily clustered in the downtown commercial district, a fine-scaled pattern broadly reflective of land use—that is, business clients requiring office work or cleaning services are located predominantly on commercially zoned land, while gardening tasks performed on public land or private property are more dispersed, occurring in areas zoned for residential or greenspace use. However, the end points of the lightning trails are not confined to the town itself but stretch out into the town hinterland and beyond to neighbouring towns in a 50-kilometre radius. Social procurement practices of primarily local businesses underpin the success of this WISE's off-site work tasks, yet regional relationships remain important.

However, the lightning maps need not be read solely as economic artefacts. Rather than thinking of interactions between WISE employees and customers/work hosts as trades of goods and services, the trails and overall map can also be seen as representing the frequency and spatiality of opportunities for meaningful social interactions.

For example, community food delivery puts employees in direct contact with multiple diverse people, providing interactions with new people and places that employees may not otherwise have access to. This opportunity to get out into the community and perform 'normal work' and interacting with customers is appreciated by employees:

> I think they're [employees] excited. They are always so excited to come for a drive. Always. You never have to ask twice. Sometimes they'll put their hand up to come for a drive and they're like, can we go? They're always just excited. No-one ever seems nervous. It's good. They get to come outside in the fresh air and speak to the customers and look at where we go and they all love it. They really do.
>
> (Catering Staff 3)

Similarly, another Catering staff member spoke of how it gave supported workers a chance to build capacity by mixing with their customers:

> I think it's good that they go out on delivery sometimes, so they get to see the people that they're feeding and they get the confidence of meeting other people they don't know, but they've also got [Amy or Sarah] as a support there for them, instead of one of us. I think it teaches them to be a bit more confident in speaking to people and that—I think that's great.
>
> (Catering Staff 4)

In economically depressed regional areas where many WISEs operate, opportunities to mix socially with the wider community may be less available, particularly for those experiencing multiple disadvantages (Burkhardt et al. 1999). Performing work tasks amongst the wider community permits WISE employees to interact socially from an alternate subject position to the label of 'disadvantaged' while learning new capabilities and potentially generating social capital. Capacity exists then for mobile WISE work to redress public perceptions about social exclusion and disadvantage.

From a spatial perspective, capturing these social interaction opportunities in a network map is significant because they visualise potential changes to support workers' functional activity space. Social exclusion and activity space are linked phenomena (Kamruzzaman and Hine 2012), and before engaging with the Farm WISE, some employees were known to be spatially constrained in their everyday travel capacities. A restricted activity space is perhaps indicative that some places also do not convey a sense of belonging, leading to alienation and a decreased sense of wellbeing. Therefore, time spent as WISE workers on the move presents a chance to claim a wider activity space, cultivating spatial knowledge through familiar routines of delivery and social interaction. These shifts to everyday activity space may potentially combat alienation, cultivate belonging, and contribute to enhancing topophilia—a deeper sense of place attachment (Tuan 1999). In this sense, then, network maps become a record of the spread, scale, and frequency of wellbeing potential.

An earlier cartographic choice involved using direct lines from the central WISE hub out to each node. However, a decision was made instead to convey movement by car along the road network because qualitative evidence hinted the vehicle itself was acting as a mobile site of wellbeing generation. The following quote details a transition towards wellbeing relayed by a support worker:

> She's very softly spoken and very shy. The first time she came in the car she didn't say anything to me at all. Then as it's gone on, she will even initiate conversations with me so telling me about things she does in her personal life. She might do activities. I've seen that, just their social interaction grow. They can speak to the customers now.

Thinking from a wellbeing perspective, for this supported worker, the car became a therapeutic space (Foley 2011), permitting a sense of safety and security and growing confidence towards conversing with staff to emerge. The delivery vehicle was not simply a mobility device but a site of care and for developing interpersonal relationships while on the move (Waitt and Harada 2016).

With these thoughts of activity spaces and care in mind, the lightning maps in Figures 6.5 and 6.6 are not only showing a map of well-worn routes and routines but fine-grained maps of both activity space and wellbeing potential. These maps hug the road because the journey matters.

Spiders: A Relational Social Capital Web

This section also utilises network mapping, but for revealing a network where fine-scale journey, routing matters less. It is based upon a separate coding of the WISE staff interviews that looked for themes of social capital production. As organisations, social enterprises build and use bridging and linking social networks to provide opportunities for employees. Off-site work and on-site interactions connect staff and employees to external business or community groups, with the results of developing trust and social inclusion.

WISE staff described off-site work interactions as integral for engaging directly with the community. Staff at Farm, for example, referenced interactions with representatives from public, private, and not-for-profit sectors. Employee benefits were often related to strong bonding networks and trust between employees, staff, and people encountered in the community.

These interactions, particularly those that happen off-site, have geography worthy of examination. This spider visualisation style (so named for the 'legs' stretching out from a central 'body') does the work of locating businesses or sites in the community that display social capital generating connections with the WISE. Rather than hug the road like the lightning maps, these social capital connections are sometimes one-way (workers going to a site), sometimes reciprocal relationships (external organisation representatives perhaps coming to the WISE site), and sometimes connections fostered during working hours that go on to flourish after hours.

The spider maps shown in Figure 6.7 attempt to capture and visually reinforce the notion that the WISE is a generative hub, spurring a

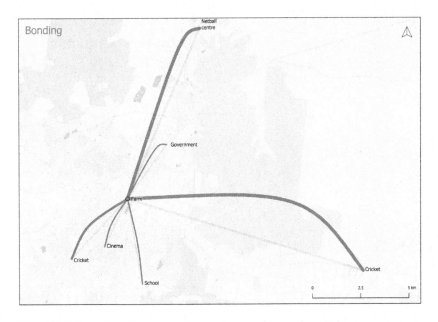

Figure 6.7 Farm bonding networks

range of social capital connections. Figure 6.7 illustrates how bonding networks expand outside work hours, including playing sport or simply using cultural infrastructures like the cinema. Figure 6.8 details the bridging networks that essentially cross social divides for supported workers as they engaged with a number of private, not-for-profit, and public sector end points.

In these spider maps, line thickness denotes an increasing magnitude of connections mentioned in interviews while also conveying direction, scale, and clustering of social capital linkages. Subtle iterative work was done in adjusting the curvature of the legs and placing 2D shadows at ground level to add perspective depth. This generates the pseudo-3D effect, lifting the lines up and out of the background and enhancing figure-ground separation. Finally, the curve also implies a subtle sense of movement as the eye tracks back and forth along lines, further reinforcing a mental association between end points and the centre.

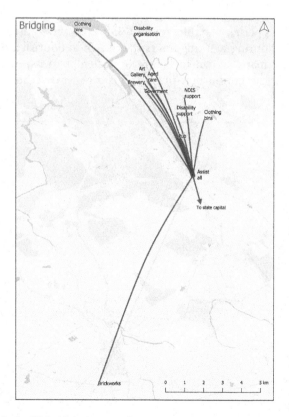

Figure 6.8 AssistAll bridging networks

Discussion and Conclusion

This chapter presented a range of performative data visualisations about wellbeing generated through social enterprises. A Qualitative GIS framework gave us the means to incorporate a true variety of primary and secondary data sources (quantitative, qualitative, observed, and ground-truthed) and wherever possible foregrounded the experiences of individuals. A productive 'collision of epistemologies' occurred (Brown and Knopp 2008), as we recursively moved between and combined quantitative and qualitative ways of knowing through spatial visualisation.

This chapter illustrated Qualitative GIS as able to cultivate new understandings and geographies of previously hidden phenomena such as wellbeing, which has the capacity to generate empirical health impacts. The in-depth research was conducted against a backdrop of ever-increasing big data streams, machine learning, and immersive data visualisations. We are hopeful this chapter illustrates that rich data produced by considered and grounded work with small numbers of individuals can also produce performative visualisations that shape how we think about space and place, but perhaps more importantly, can tell us why certain patterns emerge.

The map's performative capacities aided in conveying narratives of transition, concentrations of wellbeing, and social capital connection by grounding these in spatial representations that we, as spatial thinkers, are primed to understand and grasp in nonlinear ways that text cannot convey as quickly. With this in mind, these sorts of cartographic outputs can play a role as alternative backgrounds or as pseudo-metrics of wellbeing success stories, in place of or alongside more orthodox benchmarks of WISE success such as profit and loss statements, products sold, or customers served.

Wellbeing emerged in the various mappings as simultaneously networked and site-specific. The surface-like terrain maps showed where and how wellbeing was generated and concentrated in positive ways. Yet equally, we were able to drill down and uncover the understanding of how segregation operated spatially to decrease wellbeing. The spider and lightning network maps then graphically unpicked the bounds of the social enterprise—visualising it not only as a bounded space but rather a highly networked and relational organisation, undergirded and generative of socio-economic relationships with multiple local organisations, groups, and individuals. WISE impact was also revealed as multi-scalar, producing wellbeing interactions downtown, in the regional hinterland, in intrastate towns, and far-flung urban capitals. From a theory-generating standpoint, the mappings produced new spatial understandings of WISE as a truly relational achievement.

For WISE practitioners, mapping should be thought of as a spatial decision support tool for altering the layout or programming of the social enterprise to maximise wellbeing. For example, by providing space for downtime and solitude/security, providing spaces away from surveillance, and mixing up activities so that different groups get a chance to work together and cultivate social connection. A simple paper map for collaborative drawing with WISE employees and staff could achieve this. It would permit understanding about how tasks, objects, and relationships come together spatially to achieve a sense of wellbeing in their particular WISE. An online self-assessment mapping toolkit is also available for WISE practitioners to complete this style of planning at https://social-enterprisewellbeing.com.au/.

The lightning maps were particularly adept at conveying the geographies of everyday activity space activation and the link to potential wellbeing generation. While the visualisation strategy was somewhat advanced, social enterprise managers seeking to maximise their supported workers' activity space should not be discouraged from mapping where their customers are located. This can happen relatively easily, from literal pushing of pins onto a large-format paper wall map to dropping virtual pins on a google map. Spatial thinking would allow rudimentary understanding of any underlying spread and scale to emerge, without needing specific cartographic or GIS training. From this point, managers could aim to cultivate future social procurement opportunities by looking for customers in underserved parts of the map. Recording these changes over time (e.g. monthly photographs or screenshots of the map) would also create a metric of place activation for supported workers.

We hope that our qualitative mapping approach helps others think afresh about work-integrated social enterprises as networked social infrastructure that can seed social connectedness, belonging, and sense of place relationally from comparatively small physical footprints. They are vital place-making organisations for disadvantaged community members.

Acknowledgements

This research was funded by the Australian Research council 2017–2020, DP170100388.

References

Bergeron, J., Paquette, S. and Poullaouec-Gonidec, P., 2014. Uncovering landscape values and micro-geographies of meanings with the go-along method. *Landscape and Urban Planning*, 122, pp. 108–121.
Bertin, J., 1967. *Se'miologie graphique: Les diagrammes, les re'seaux, les cartes.* Paris: Mouton.
Brennan-Horley, C. and Gibson, C., 2009. Where is creativity in the city? Integrating qualitative and GIS methods. *Environment and planning A*, 41(11), pp. 2595–2614.

Brennan-Horley, C., Luckman, S., Gibson, C. and Willoughby-Smith, J., 2010. GIS, ethnography, and cultural research: Putting maps back into ethnographic mapping. *The Information Society*, 26(2), pp. 92–103.

Brown, M. and Knopp, L., 2008. Queering the map: The productive tensions of colliding epistemologies. *Annals of the Association of American Geographers*, 98(1), pp. 40–58.

Buckingham, H., Pinch, S. and Sunley, P., 2012. The enigmatic regional geography of social enterprise in the UK: A conceptual framework and synthesis of the evidence. *Area*, 44(1), pp. 83–91.

Burchardt, T., Le Grand, J. and Piachaud, D., 1999. Social exclusion in Britain 1991–1995. *Social Policy & Administration*, 33(3), pp. 227–244.

Carpiano, R.M., 2009. Come take a walk with me: The "go-along" interview as a novel method for studying the implications of place for health and wellbeing. *Health & Place*, 15(1), pp. 263–272.

Castellas, E., Barraket, J., Hiruy, K. and Suchowerska, R., 2017. *Map for Impact: The Victorian Social Enterprise Mapping Project*. Hawthorn, Australia: Centre for Social Impact Swinburne.

Cope, M. and Elwood, S., 2009. *Qualitative GIS: A Mixed Methods Approach*. London: SAGE Publications Ltd.

Elwood, S. and Cope, M., 2009. Introduction: Qualitative GIS: Forging mixed methods through representations, analytical innovations, and conceptual engagements. *Qualitative GIS: A Mixed Methods Approach*, pp. 1–12.

Farmer, J., Kamstra, P., Brennan-Horley, C., De Cotta, T., Roy, M., Barraket, J., Munoz, S.A. and Kilpatrick, S., 2020. Using micro-geography to understand the realisation of wellbeing: A qualitative GIS study of three social enterprises. *Health & Place*, pp. 102–293.

Fleuret, S. and Atkinson, S., 2007. Wellbeing, health and geography: A critical review and research agenda. *New Zealand Geographer*, 63(2), pp. 106–118.

Foley, R., 2011. Performing health in place: The holy well as a therapeutic assemblage. *Health & Place*, 17, 470–479.

Geertz, C., 1973. *The Interpretation of Cultures* (Vol. 5019). New York, NY: Basic Books.

Gieseking, J.J., 2013. Where we go from here: The mental sketch mapping method and its analytic components. *Qualitative Inquiry*, 19(9), pp. 712–724.

Gould, P. and White, R., 1974. *Mental Maps*. Abingdon: Routledge.

Haeberling, C., Bär, H. and Hurni, L., 2008. Proposed cartographic design principles for 3D maps: A contribution to an extended cartographic theory. *Cartographica: The International Journal for Geographic Information and Geovisualization*, 43(3), pp. 175–188.

Haraway, D., 1988. Situated knowledges: The science question in feminism and the privilege of partial perspective. *Feminist Studies*, 14(3), pp. 575–599.

Kamruzzaman, M. and Hine, J., 2012. Analysis of rural activity spaces and transport disadvantage using a multi-method approach. *Transport Policy*, 19(1), pp. 105–120.

Kamstra, P., Cook, B., Kennedy, D.M. and Brennan-Horley, C., 2019. Qualitative GIS to relate perceptions with behaviors among fishers on risky, rocky coasts. *The Professional Geographer*, 71(3), pp. 491–506.

Kilpatrick, S., Field, J., and Falk, I.H., 2003. Social capital: An analytical tool for exploring lifelong learning and community development. *British Educational Research Journal*, 29(3), 417–433.

Knigge, L. and Cope, M., 2006. Grounded visualization: Integrating the analysis of qualitative and quantitative data through grounded theory and visualization. *Environment and Planning A*, 38(11), pp. 2021–2037.

Kwan, M.P. and Ding, G., 2008. Geo-narrative: Extending geographic information systems for narrative analysis in qualitative and mixed-method research. *The Professional Geographer*, 60(4), pp. 443–465.

Lechner, V.E., 2020. What a line can say: Investigating the semiotic potential of the connecting line in data visualizations. In Engebretsen, M. and Kennedy, H. (eds) *Data Visualization in Society* (pp. 329–346). Amsterdam: Amsterdam University Press. doi:10.2307/j.ctvzgb8c7.26

Lynch, K., 1960. *The Image of the City* (Vol. 11). Cambridge, MA: MIT Press.

Massey, D., 2012. Power-geometry and a progressive sense of place. In Bird, J., Curtis, B., Putnam, Robertson, G. and Tickner, L. (eds) *Mapping the Futures* (pp. 75–85). Abingdon: Routledge.

Mennecke, B., Crossland, M. and Killingsworth, B., 2000. Is a map more than a picture? The role of SDSS technology, subject characteristics, and problem complexity on map reading and problem solving. *MIS Quarterly*, 24(4), pp. 601–629. doi:10.2307/3250949.

Mennis, J., Mason, M.J. and Cao, Y., 2013. Qualitative GIS and the visualization of narrative activity space data. *International Journal of Geographic Information Science*, 27(2), pp. 267–291. doi:10.1080/13658816.2012.678362

Munoz, S.A., 2010. Towards a geographical research agenda for social enterprise. *Area*, 42(3), pp. 302–312.

Munoz, S.A., Farmer, J., Winterton, R. and Barraket, J.O., 2015. The social enterprise as a space of well-being: An exploratory case study. *Social Enterprise Journal*, 11(3), pp. 281–230 doi:10.1108/SEJ-11-2014-0041.

Sinton, D., Bednarz, S.W., Gersmehl, P., Kolvoord, R.A. and Uttal, D.H., 2013. *The People's Guide to Spatial Thinking*. Washington, DC: National Council for Geographic Education.

Stea, D., Blaut, J.M. and Stephens, J., 1996. Mapping as a cultural universal. In Portugali J. (eds) *The Construction of Cognitive Maps. GeoJournal Library*, vol. 32. Dordrecht: Springer.

Tuan Y-F., 1999. *Topophilia: A Study of Environmental Perception, Attitudes, and Values*. New York: Columbia University Press.

Waitt, G. and Harada, T., 2016. Parenting, care and the family car. *Social & Cultural Geography*, 17(8), pp. 1079–1100.

Ware, C., 2010. *Visual Thinking for Design*. Burlington, MA: Morgan Kaufman Publishers.

Wilton, R. and Evans, J., 2016. Social enterprises as spaces of encounter for mental health consumers. *Area*, 48, pp. 236–243. https://doi.org/10.1111/area.12259

7 WISE Working Conditions Matter for Health and Wellbeing

Aurora Elmes

Introduction

Work integration social enterprises (WISEs) have a primary social purpose of creating meaningful employment opportunities for people who are marginalised in the open employment market (Lysaght et al. 2018). While WISEs are diverse and aim to generate employment pathways for different groups of people, this chapter has a particular focus on people with mental illness. Existing research suggests that WISEs may improve access to employment for people with lived experience of mental illness by creating inclusive workplaces, constructing new types of jobs for disadvantaged workers (Buhariwala, Wilton & Evans 2015), and providing meaningful work that contributes to health and wellbeing (Roy et al. 2014). The body of research evidencing the social, economic, health, and wellbeing impacts of social enterprise is growing as is policy interest in social enterprise as a means of increasing health equity (Roy et al. 2014). There is currently limited evidence of the longer term economic, social, health, and wellbeing outcomes of WISE employment and the mechanisms by, and contexts in which, these outcomes are achieved (Roy, Baker & Kerr 2017). This chapter begins by briefly discussing the existing evidence and gaps. It then presents the methodology and empirical findings from a longitudinal case study of the WISE—Vanguard Laundry Services, located in Toowoomba, a regional Australian town.

Background

Employment is widely recognised as one of the major social conditions that influences peoples' health, connecting to other influential structural and social conditions including education, income, social status, and material circumstances that are known collectively as the social determinants of health (Solar & Irwin 2010). Social determinants of health frameworks such as that of Solar and Irwin (2010, p. 6) recognise that structural factors including social values, cultural norms, and policies inform the (in)equitable distribution of occupational opportunities,

DOI: 10.4324/9781003125976-7

safe environments, financial, and social resources. These kinds of social determinants of health ultimately contribute to disparities in health and wellbeing. Internationally, people with mental illness are among those most excluded from work (Buhariwala, Wilton & Evans 2015). Employment is associated with higher income, increased social support, sense of purpose, and improved health (Butterworth et al. 2011). Thus, employment is recognised as a potential area for action on social determinants of health. WISEs represent one type of organisation that can respond to the employment barriers disproportionately experienced by people with mental illness.

While much research within and beyond the social enterprise field has surfaced findings about the benefits of employment for people with mental illness (Svanberg, Gumley & Wilson 2010), evidence about the effects of employment specifically on peoples' mental health is mixed (Doroud, Fossey & Fortune 2015). Effects have been found to depend on factors including the nature of employment, quality of the work, and whether the employment meets individuals' needs (Butterworth et al. 2011). Multiple researchers have explored the workplace features that are valued by people with mental illness in the context of WISE employment. These include facilitating successful employment, flexibility, security, support (Buhariwala, Wilton & Evans 2015), a balance between task demands and rewards, regular hours, positive workplace interactions (Williams et al. 2016), and an environment that promotes 'feelings of belonging, success, competence and individuality' (Svanberg, Gumley & Wilson 2010, p. 482).

Some research has identified that social enterprises are more inclined than mainstream employment services to engage people with higher levels of social exclusion—and this may be where the 'added value' of WISEs lie (Hazenberg, Seddon & Denny 2014, p. 897). This suggests that WISEs may fulfil a distinctive need by actively recruiting people with mental illness who would otherwise be excluded from the open labour market and providing work environments that are designed for people with mental illness as the norm rather than the exception (Buhariwala, Wilton & Evans 2015). While some have questioned the degree of economic opportunity that WISEs provide, due to the often low-skilled, minimum wage work, or limited amount of hours available (Buhariwala, Wilton & Evans 2015), others argue that WISEs provide benefits of increased income, social networks, and wellbeing through their provision of inclusive employment (Roy et al. 2014).

Research findings consistently suggest that WISEs primarily affect health through facilitating suitable employment, increasing access to social or financial resources, and offering experiences of capability and belonging (Farmer et al. 2016; Macaulay et al. 2018). While research into the health and wellbeing effects of social enterprise continues to grow, the evidence base has limitations. These include a scarcity of studies using repeat measures or longitudinal designs (Williams et al. 2016), a relative lack of studies using health outcome measures (Macaulay et al. 2018), and a need for more empirical research that incorporates beneficiaries' perspectives (Roy, Baker & Kerr 2017). The current study responds to these limitations. It is a mixed-methods longitudinal evaluation that uses a critical realist evaluation approach (Maxwell & Mittapalli 2010) and health outcome measures to better understand the effects of a WISE on economic participation, social inclusion, health, and wellbeing for participants over time.

This chapter's three research questions, in relation to health, wellbeing, economic participation, and social inclusion, are: What are the effects of WISEs on these factors? How do WISEs influence outcomes? What other mediating or contextual factors influence outcomes?

Methods

Vanguard Laundry Services (henceforth, Vanguard) is an Australian WISE commercial laundry service based in the regional town of Toowoomba, with a population of 167,657 (Toowoomba Regional Council 2019), in the state of Queensland, Australia. Vanguard has a core social purpose of providing jobs and employment pathways for people with mental illness who have a history of unemployment (identified here as their 'target staff') (Elmes 2019). Vanguard employs people with (around 60 per cent) and without (around 40 per cent) experience of mental illness and has a transitional employment model, aiming for target staff to eventually move into mainstream employment.

All current staff of Vanguard were invited to participate over the three years of the longitudinal study reported on here, and current staff who left the WISE between 2017 and 2019 were followed up. The study had Human Research Ethics Committee approval. Table 7.1 shows the Vanguard staff participants who participated each year. Overall, 48 target staff participated for at least one data collection period, and seven

Table 7.1 Evaluation of participants and attrition rates from 2017 to 2019

	Year 1 (2017)	Year 2 (2018)	Year 3 (2019)	Number discontinuing by 2019	Total attrition % by 2019
Target staff participants in 2017 cohort	23	19	18	5	21.7
Target staff participants in 2018 cohort	–	14	12	2	14.3
Target staff participants in 2019 cohort			11	–	–
Total staff participants	23	33	41	7	14.6

left the study by 2019—an attrition rate of 14.6 per cent between 2017 and 2019.

Three existing questionnaires were selected based on the following criteria: validation as a measure of the relevant outcome; previous use in an Australian population or a similar SE context; and enabling comparability of results with other data, such as established population scores (Elmes 2019). The first questionnaire was an adapted version of the Personal Wellbeing Index–Adult (PWI–A) (International Wellbeing Group 2013), incorporating an additional question about job satisfaction (Elmes 2019). The second was the RAND SF-36 Health Survey 1.0 (The RAND Corporation 1992), a publicly available health and functioning scale, which measures overall self-assessed health and health changes, and functioning across physical, mental, and social activities (Elmes 2019). The final validated questionnaire was the Kessler-10 (K-10) measure of psychological distress (Kessler et al. 2002), which has been widely used in national health surveys and clinical mental health practice in Australia, and in international epidemiology research (Australian Bureau of Statistics 2001; Elmes 2019). In addition to these three questionnaires, a detailed custom questionnaire was developed based on Vanguard's theory of change to collect information on participant demographics, health conditions, housing, income, sources of social support, confidence, motivation, and health service use (Elmes 2019). Interview schedules were informed by previous conceptual models of social enterprise effects (Roy, Baker & Kerr 2017; Roy et al. 2014), the impact goals of Vanguard's theory of change, and Solar and Irwin's (2010) social determinants of health framework (Elmes 2019).

Descriptive and inferential statistical analysis was conducted. Since most data were not normally distributed, nonparametric tests were used for statistical analysis, as they do not assume normally distributed data and are robust with smaller sample sizes (Pek, Wong & Wong 2018). For analysis of validated questionnaires, published guidelines for handling data were followed—for further details see Elmes (2019).

Thematic analysis was conducted for qualitative data using an abductive approach (Dubois & Gadde 2002) to generate and refine thematic codes (Elmes 2019). Data were coded concurrently for sentiment to help differentiate between positive and negative mechanisms and effects.

Quantitative Findings

Findings included here relate to the effects of the WISE on target staff with lived experience of mental illness; mechanisms contributing to these effects; and contextual factors influencing participants' experiences and outcomes. Findings are reported for 41 target staff unless otherwise specified.

Of the target staff involved in the study in 2019, 25 (61 per cent) were male; the median age was 41; and 22 (62.9 per cent of $n = 35$) had been unemployed for more than one year. About half (20 staff, 48.8 per cent) reported mental health conditions only, while another 13 (31.7 per cent) reported both physical and mental health conditions. In 2019, the most commonly reported types of mental health condition experienced by staff were mood disorders such as depression or bipolar disorder (53.7 per cent); schizophrenia or schizoaffective disorder (34.1 per cent); and anxiety (29.3 per cent). This pattern remained quite consistent from 2017 to 2019.

Income and Jobs

Target staff typically worked between 10 and 20 hours per week at Vanguard. Related-samples McNemar Change tests (Salkind 2010) ($n = 39$) showed that changes in staff earning over the relative poverty line (50 per cent of median income) were significant since employment with Vanguard ($p < .01$). However, the majority of staff still remained within the lowest earnings bracket for Australia, in which people are more likely to experience financial stress (McColl, Pietsch & Gatenby 2001).

Spending more than 30 per cent of income on housing can be an indicator of housing stress (Australian Bureau of Statistics 2015). Over the three years of the study, there was a consistent pattern of reduced housing stress by this measure. A Related-Samples McNemar Change Test (Salkind 2010) ($n = 30$) showed that this difference in housing stress was statistically significant ($p < .01$).

As of 2019, 100 per cent of target staff participants had reached six months' employment with Vanguard, and 77.1 per cent had reached one year. However, just 14 (29.2 per cent) of the total 48 staff surveyed proceeded to get a job outside Vanguard between 2017 and 2019. Organisational records (encompassing all target staff, including people who did not participate in the evaluation) detailed a total of 33 people who had transitioned to jobs outside of Vanguard during the study period. The most common job roles of transitioned target staff included cleaning (25.6 per cent), repair and maintenance (12.8 per cent), supporting people with disability (10.3 per cent), and laundry production (10.3 per cent).

Health and Wellbeing

Compared to RAND SF-36 Health Survey normative scores for Australians with depression, mean scores for staff were higher than national norms. For the 2017 participant cohort who were followed up across three years, there were no significant differences between Physical

Table 7.2 Health and wellbeing quantitative findings

	Before employment with Vanguard	Since employment with Vanguard
Self-assessed change in health (n = 48*)		
Participants reporting better health compared to a year ago	–	34 (70.8%)
Queensland Health hospital data (n = 25) for one year before and since employment with Vanguard		
Participants with any emergency department visits	6 (24%)	9 (36%)
Participants with any hospital admissions	7 (28%)	5 (20%)
Total number of days in hospital across the group *(n = 25)*	339 days	98 days
Smoking (n = 31)		
Quit smoking	6 (19.5%)	9 (26.8%)
Median cigarettes smoked per day (for daily smokers)	15	10

* A total of 48 target staff participants completed at least one period of data collection after commencing at Vanguard, and they were asked to rate their health now in comparison to one year ago (a time before they were working at Vanguard).

Component Summary (PCS) and Mental Component Summary (MCS) mean scores at year 1, 2, or 3 of the study.

In 2019, K10 scores indicated that just under half (44 per cent) of target staff participants experienced high or very high levels of distress. Participants' psychological distress scores did not differ significantly over time, even among the small group of participants who left Vanguard and became unemployed again. However, as psychological distress could not be measured prior to involvement with Vanguard, it is possible that differences in psychological distress before and after Vanguard involvement may have existed but could not be detected.

Self-reported primary care and community health appointments were not significantly different before, during, or after employment with Vanguard. Of the 25 participants with complete Queensland Health (i.e. state health department) data available, only a minority had any Emergency Department (ED) presentations or hospital admissions in the year before or since Vanguard. The reduction in hospital days was highly concentrated among a few participants, rather than being a general pattern of decreased hospital days across the whole group. Related-Samples Wilcoxon Signed Rank tests (Smalheiser 2017) showed no statistically significant differences in ED visits or hospitalisations before and since involvement with Vanguard, as the majority of participants' hospital episodes did not change. Due to the small sample size and high variability of the hospital data, it is possible that actual significant effects were not able to be detected. Equally, any changes could be due to chance or other factors beyond Vanguard.

Across all years of the study, Vanguard's target staff had mean scores on the Personal Wellbeing Index (PWI) (68.6 in 2019) that were lower than the Australian average (75.5 on a scale of 0–100), but higher than the Australian normative scores for those with a current mental health condition (65.2), and higher than the normative scores for people who are unemployed (58.6). Despite having lower wellbeing scores than the general Australian population, it is likely that employment and additional income positively affected the wellbeing of Vanguard staff as was generally reflected in participant interviews. For participants with multiple years of data, PWI scores did not significantly differ over time, but wellbeing could not be measured prior to participants commencing at Vanguard, which may have contributed to the lack of change detected.

Motivation for regular paid work decreased from 95.7 per cent in 2017 to 78 per cent in 2019. Some of this change may be attributed to participants joining or leaving the study over time. Spearman's rank-order correlations (Salkind 2010) with data from the 41 target staff involved in the 2019 evaluation showed moderate negative correlations between the level of psychological distress and motivation to be in regular paid work ($rs = -.462, p < .01$); and level of self-reported health and motivation to be in regular paid work ($rs = -.346, p < .05$). These correlations were both statistically significant, with higher levels of distress and worse self-rated health correlated with lower motivation to be in regular paid work.

Qualitative Findings

Income

From 2017 to 2019, participants spoke about the differences that extra income had made in their lives. The key themes included decreased financial stress, increased financial security, and freedom to spend money on things that were important to themselves or loved ones in addition to meeting basic needs (Elmes 2019):

> it's made a lot of difference in [my mental health] because I'm not worried about—I'm not living on $150 a week. I'm now planning to save up for a car and those sorts of things.

Social Capital

The themes related to social capital, connections, and support across the three years were largely about decreased feelings of isolation, expanded social networks, and some strengthening of existing relationships

(Elmes 2019). Participants reflected on the benefits of meeting new people and supportive colleagues. However, social experiences were not all positive, with some participants feeling excluded and reporting negative effects on their desire to connect with others.

> if I can make someone else feel good I will. There's been a couple of people that have been a bit down and I've been able to just say to them, 'Hey look, it might not get better today but it will eventually get better.' And other people have done that for me too.
>
> When I was first going there I was the person who actually wanted to go to work . . . And, then by the end, of maybe a year or less, I was like, 'Nah, this is not right'. I think it was just the feeling of I didn't feel wanted and that I knew that I could do the job but they won't let me, and are not actually giving me the opportunity.

Health and Wellbeing

Across three years, many participants spoke about positive changes in their mental and physical health, such as the alleviation of mental health symptoms, improved mood, or increased physical fitness. There were also some instances of negative effects on physical or mental health:

> I feel so much better that my brain is active, I'm active . . . You know, when you sit around and do nothing all the day what else have you got to think about but your illness?
>
> I was feeling very painful around here . . . So because I could not move my arm there's a dislocation here and . . . that's when I decided to leave.

Participants cited multiple positive effects on their wellbeing since working at Vanguard, including a renewed sense of purpose and capability and valuing the social contact, structure, and status that work provided. However, some participants reported stressful experiences linked with negative interpersonal interactions, having their work hours cut, or not having access to equal work opportunities:

> I felt like there was pressure to apply for jobs and I felt used in a way because of wage subsidies. I don't feel right about it because they should just employ people regardless if they're right for the job. I felt like my hours dropped off after the subsidy finished. I got hurt by this and feel like the last person to be considered. I don't feel important here . . . Most days I hate coming here—a year ago I loved coming here.

A pattern of deterioration in health influencing the decision to resign from work was also observed in participant interviews and copies of exit interviews obtained from Vanguard:

> Well I've recently moved out of my unit because of my schizophrenia affecting [me]. I'm now at the community care units which are supported. It's temporary . . . and I'll find my own unit again. I no longer work at Vanguard anymore because I've had issues going on with my life.

Barriers and Enablers in the Work Environment of the WISE

From 2017 to 2019, many of the findings emphasised target staff participants' views that employment with Vanguard provided a vital opportunity for social and economic participation through a work environment that offered award-waged work, flexibility, supportive relationships, acceptance and understanding, and practical and social support. Overall, staff reported positive work experiences, with some areas for improvement identified through the evaluation, including ensuring a consistently safe work environment and culture. Some target staff described a division in the opportunities available to staff with and without mental illness. From 2017 to 2019, several target staff expressed that they wanted to apply for a permanent role at Vanguard but did not feel that this opportunity was open to them, given Vanguard's transitional employment model:

> there are lots of people out there in the category of [target staff] who are highly productive, good team players, able to make good permanent employees, but they're not given the opportunity. It's like a glass ceiling.

In 2018, a shift in recruitment criteria brought a stronger focus on employing target staff with high motivation and readiness for transition opportunities. A slightly larger number of staff reported negative experiences in 2019, including having hours cut, witnessing discriminatory comments or bullying from co-workers, or feeling that there were unequal opportunities available for staff with mental illness to progress their career at Vanguard if they chose.

The Australian Disability Discrimination Act (1992) legislates against discrimination such that if a person with a disability wants to apply for a job and has the capacity to fulfil the inherent requirements of the job after reasonable adjustments, they should have equal opportunity to apply and be considered for the job alongside others. Following feedback from the 2019 evaluation, Vanguard's management confirmed that all vacant roles were being explicitly advertised to existing staff, and by December 2019, three existing casual target staff were employed in permanent part-time positions.

Other Factors Influencing Employment Outcomes

When participants had experienced life challenges or deteriorations in health, many commented that having supportive and flexible paid employment at the WISE provided a valued sense of stability and hope. A small number of staff made the decision to end their employment due to a deterioration in mental or physical health. In most cases, participants described this as unrelated to Vanguard, but in a few cases, participants reported that bullying from peers or dissatisfaction with their treatment at work had affected their health negatively:

> This guy was basically mocking me and imitating me at work . . . and he just carried on like that for months and months, and I put up with it. And then he started calling me names, and that's when I made a complaint and they're like, 'Oh yeah, I spoke to him about it and he said it was just a joke.' And I'm like, 'Yeah, that's not a joke . . . it's not funny.' It took the joy out of my entire workday. It took everything out of it, I didn't even want to be here.

Discussion

This longitudinal mixed-methods study adds the dimension of time to existing conceptualisations of the health and wellbeing effects of WISEs. Qualitative and quantitative data showed improvements in many social determinants of health, including increased income, sustained employment, improved living standards, enhanced social connections, reduced health service use, and improved health and wellbeing. However, these effects did not all persist over time, and they varied in relation to the organisational environment, the quality of the working conditions, and other contextual factors including individuals' health, and broader social norms which continued to limit participants' opportunities outside of (and sometimes also within) the WISE.

Contextual Factors Influencing the Effects of the WISE

The primary influential factors identified at the level of social context were the labour market and other employers. These findings underline the influence of structural factors, such as cultural and social norms of stigma and discrimination disproportionately limiting the occupational opportunities of people with mental illness (Reavley, Jorm & Morgan 2017). Accordingly, the main pathway through which the WISE was perceived to influence social contextual factors, was through engaging with other employers, supporters (such as customers of the WISE), and the broader community to find and build more work opportunities for target staff.

Several individual-level contextual factors were identified as either supporting or constraining positive outcomes, with the main theme being the fit of opportunities to the individual as found in research on job tenure for people with mental illness (Williams et al. 2016). Other individual-level contextual factors that participants identified as influencing outcomes included their health, and material circumstances (e.g. stable housing), which are known to affect employment (Reavley, Jorm & Morgan 2017). These findings illustrate that the organisational context, the broader social context, and individual contexts all influenced the effects of the WISE.

Mechanisms of the WISE

Findings showed consistencies and changes over time in the mechanisms and effects of the WISE. In 2017, the first year of operations, the majority of participants reported positive experiences and gratitude for opportunities for flexible, supportive employment. Many of the workplace features known to facilitate successful employment for people with mental illness—such as flexibility, support, security (Buhariwala, Wilton & Evans 2015), well-matched levels of task demand and rewards, regular hours, and positive workplace interactions (Williams et al. 2016)—were observed frequently in qualitative data. Most of these mechanisms align with what is known about aspects of 'good' work that support health (Butterworth et al. 2011). However, the changes observed in participants' experiences and outcomes over time add a new dimension to existing conceptualisations of the effects of WISE, which are largely based on cross-sectional research or retrospective studies. Rather than viewing the effects of a WISE as static (Farmer et al. 2016), these findings suggest that the mechanisms and effects of a WISE can vary over time.

Aspects of 'good' work such as supportive relationships with co-workers, access to practical and social support, flexibility, acceptance, and understanding were the mechanisms most commonly associated with positive sentiment. Most often associated with negative sentiment were issues with the work culture or environment that presented risks to mental or physical health and limited opportunities for career progression or permanent employment for target staff. These findings emphasise that the quality of the work environment and employment offered represent the primary mechanisms by which WISEs can act on social determinants of health. Through 'good' work other positive effects occur.

The WISE had both positive and negative effects on health and health behaviours depending on working conditions. When participants experienced acceptance and inclusion, this contributed to positive work experiences and a sense of capability and belonging. When participants experienced the work environment as unsafe (e.g. from bullying), this contributed to negative experiences of work, a sense of being excluded or viewed as incapable, and (in some cases) led to participants disengaging from work or resigning. This highlights some limitations in the social inclusion facilitated by the WISE. While the WISE provided opportunities for employment of people with mental illness, these opportunities were largely limited to casual, entry-level work, with limited increases to income and economic mobility.

Findings indicate that the WISE did not always provide a 'mentally healthy,' stigma, and discrimination-free environment. Therefore, even within a WISE with a social mission of creating employment pathways for people with mental illness, disclosure of mental illness sometimes led to experiences of stigma and discrimination—as has been found to occur in open employment (Reavley, Jorm & Morgan 2017). These findings contrast with previous research that has characterised WISE as reducing stigma (Roy, Baker & Kerr 2017)—suggesting that the mechanisms at work in different WISE might be highly variable and deserving of the closer examination that a longitudinal case study such as this allows.

Effects of the WISE Over Time

Findings from this study support many of the effects that have been identified in previous research on social enterprise—including increased employment, income, and social capital (Roy et al. 2014). However, there were some mixed and inconclusive findings regarding the effects of the WISE on health, wellbeing, and social determinants of health.

Despite employment with the WISE significantly increasing their income, target staff remained at an income level at which people may still struggle to meet basic needs (McColl, Pietsch & Gatenby 2001). Findings indicated that target staff participants' health and wellbeing did not increase to the level experienced in the general population, but health and wellbeing scores were higher than the normal range expected for Australians experiencing depression or unemployment. Some support was found for positive effects on health behaviours such as increased physical activity and reduced smoking. There was some evidence of reduced total hospital admissions and days in the hospital, but statistical tests comparing change for the same individuals over time found no significant differences, making this finding inconclusive.

To some degree, the findings regarding mental health were consistent with other evidence—that good-quality employment within a WISE can contribute to positive subjective experiences of health and wellbeing that align with elements of mental health recovery, including through opportunities to contribute and connect with others (Doroud, Fossey & Fortune 2015; Svanberg, Gumley & Wilson 2010). However, as noted, there was also evidence of negative effects on mental health, which have not been as apparent in evidence about WISEs and mental health to date.

Other researchers have questioned whether social enterprises are changing the 'upstream' structural conditions influencing the social determinants of health or largely responding to the 'downstream' effects of health inequities (Roy, Baker & Kerr 2017). Here, health and wellbeing effects of the WISE largely sit within the intermediary social determinants of health (Solar & Irwin 2010)—material circumstances (primarily working conditions), psychosocial factors, behaviours, and interactions with the health system—with some effects on social cohesion, social capital, and income. There was little evidence of structural change in the open labour market. The WISE primarily affected health and wellbeing through working conditions, and these conditions and effects could be positive and negative. These findings emphasise that many of the processes by which WISEs impact health, wellbeing, and social determinants of health are shared with the features of good quality work (Butterworth et al. 2011). If the ability of the WISE to provide good-quality work is compromised so is its ability to generate positive health and wellbeing outcomes.

Interviews suggest some missed opportunities for increasing staff employability (e.g. through providing access to more diverse training and higher-skilled work opportunities within the WISE). Some of the most frequent criticisms of transitional WISEs is that these models largely do not seem to improve participants' employment prospects beyond low-status, low-waged work (Buhariwala, Wilton & Evans 2015). The findings of this study support arguments that opportunities to develop and move into higher status (often higher-waged) roles are vital in supporting larger changes in social capital and socioeconomic position (Buhariwala, Wilton & Evans 2015). Where a social gradient operates within the WISE and people with mental illness are disproportionately employed in insecure, lower status jobs, this can constrain their opportunities for occupational advancement, improvements in economic participation, social inclusion, health, and wellbeing.

Conclusion

This longitudinal study illustrates how the effects of a WISE on health and wellbeing can vary over time, building on previously conceptualised pathways for WISE impacts on social determinants of health (Roy, Baker & Kerr 2017) by using quantitative data to measure changes in participants' health, wellbeing, and health service use over multiple years. Findings indicate that health and wellbeing were primarily impacted through the WISE itself facilitating employment for people—providing increased income, opportunities for social connection, and participation in work that supported physical and psychosocial health (Elmes 2019).

However, impacts on health and wellbeing were negative, where existing structural inequities (such as limited occupational opportunities) were recreated within the social context of the WISE (Elmes 2019). There was little evidence of structural inequities changing outside of the WISE.

Many of the mechanisms that were found to support positive outcomes are the same as those that are known to be present in 'good' work (Butterworth et al. 2011) and with employers who treat staff with mental illness well (Reavley, Jorm & Morgan 2017). Yet, even within this single WISE over time, the employment provided was not always experienced as 'good' or inclusive. Findings emphasise the centrality of employment and workplace conditions in mediating the effects of a WISE on health and wellbeing. This study finds that effects on health and wellbeing are not static; they can change over time. Findings support the call for WISEs to facilitate sustainable economic participation and promote full social inclusion, health, and wellbeing through access to secure, inclusive, flexible, and supportive work environments with fair working conditions for all (Lysaght et al. 2018; Williams et al. 2016). Further longitudinal research, which enables comparison of health outcomes before and after involvement with a WISE, will advance knowledge of the health and wellbeing effects of WISEs. In part, this will continue through this ongoing longitudinal evaluation. In addition, longitudinal research with other WISEs and other types of social enterprise will broaden our understanding of the contexts and mechanisms that support social enterprises to generate positive effects on health and wellbeing over time.

References

Australian Bureau of Statistics 2001, *4817.0.55.001 — Information Paper: Use of the Kessler Psychological Distress Scale in ABS Health Surveys, Australia, 2001*, Commonwealth of Australia, viewed 28 August 2020, <www.abs.gov.au/ausstats/abs@.nsf/papersbyReleaseDate/4D5BD324FE8B415FCA2579D500161D57>.

Australian Bureau of Statistics 2015, *6553.0—Survey of Income and Housing, User Guide, Australia, 2013–14*, Commonwealth of Australia, viewed 28 May 2020, <www.abs.gov.au/ausstats/abs@.nsf/Lookup/by%20Subject/6553.0~2013-14~Main%20Features~Housing~4>.

Butterworth, P, Leach, LS, Strazdins, L, Olesen, SC, Rodgers, B & Broom, DH 2011, 'The psychosocial quality of work determines whether employment has benefits for mental health: results from a longitudinal national household panel survey', *Occupational and Environmental Medicine*, vol. 68, no. 11, p. 806.

Buhariwala, P, Wilton, R & Evans, J 2015, 'Social enterprises as enabling workplaces for people with psychiatric disabilities', *Disability and Society*, vol. 30, no. 6, pp. 865–879.

Doroud, N, Fossey, E & Fortune, T 2015, 'Recovery as an occupational journey: A scoping review exploring the links between occupational engagement and recovery for people with enduring mental health issues', *Australian Occupational Therapy Journal*, vol. 62, no. 6, pp. 378–392.

Dubois, A & Gadde L.-E 2002, 'Systematic combining: An abductive approach to case research', *Journal of Business Research*, vol 55, no. 7, pp. 553–560.

Elmes Aurora, I 2019, 'Health impacts of a WISE: A longitudinal study', *Social Enterprise Journal*, vol. 15, no. 4, pp. 457–474. © 2019, Emerald Publishing Limited.

Farmer, J, De Cotta, T, McKinnon, K, Barraket, J, Munoz, S-A, Douglas, H & Roy, MJ 2016, 'Social enterprise and wellbeing in community life', *Social Enterprise Journal*, vol. 12, no. 2, 2016, pp. 235–254.

Hazenberg, R, Seddon, F & Denny, S 2014, 'Investigating the outcome performance of work-integration social enterprises (WISEs): Do WISEs offer "added value" to NEETs?' *Public Management Review*, vol. 16, no. 6, pp. 876–899.

International Wellbeing Group 2013, *Personal Wellbeing Index*, Australian Centre on Quality of Life, Deakin University, Melbourne, VIC.

Kessler, RC, Andrews, G, Colpe, LJ, Hiripi, E, Mroczek, DK, Normand, SL, Walters, EE & Zaslavsky, AM 2002, 'Short screening scales to monitor population prevalences and trends in non-specific psychological distress', *Psychological Medicine*, vol. 32, no. 6, pp. 959–976.

Lysaght, R, Roy, MJ, Rendall, JS, Krupa, T, Ball, L & Davis, J 2018, 'Unpacking the foundational dimensions of work integration social enterprise: The development of an assessment tool', *Social Enterprise Journal*, vol. 14, no. 1, pp. 60–70.

Macaulay, B, Mazzei, M, Roy, MJ, Teasdale, S & Donaldson, C 2018, 'Differentiating the effect of social enterprise activities on health', *Social Science & Medicine*, vol. 200, Mar, pp. 211–217.

Maxwell, JA & Mittapalli, K 2010, 'Realism as a Stance for Mixed Methods Research', in A Tashakkori & C Teddlie (Eds.), *SAGE Handbook of Mixed Methods in Social & Behavioral Research*, SAGE, Thousand Oaks, CA, pp. 145–168.

McColl, B, Pietsch, L & Gatenby, J 2001, *Australian Economic Indicators, Jun 2001*, Australian Bureau of Statistics, 1350.0, viewed 15 June 2020, <www.abs.gov.au/AUSSTATS/abs@.nsf/94713ad445ff1425ca25682000192af2/793d1402ee51ba8bca256a5d0004f5d5!OpenDocument>.

Pek, J, Wong, O & Wong, ACM 2018, 'How to address non-normality: A taxonomy of approaches, reviewed, and illustrated', *Frontiers in Psychology*, vol. 9, no. 2104, 6 November.

The RAND Corporation 1992, 'The RAND 36-item short form health survey (SF-36)', viewed December 2017, <www.rand.org/health/surveys_tools/mos/36-item-short-form.html>.

Reavley, NJ, Jorm, AF & Morgan, AJ 2017, 'Discrimination and positive treatment toward people with mental health problems in workplace and education settings: Findings from an Australian national survey', *Stigma and Health*, vol. 2, no. 4, pp. 254–265.

Roy, MJ, Baker, R & Kerr, S 2017, 'Conceptualising the public health role of actors operating outside of formal health systems: The case of social enterprise', *Social Science and Medicine*, vol. 172, pp. 144–152.

Roy, MJ, Donaldson, C, Baker, R & Kerr, S 2014, 'The potential of social enterprise to enhance health and well-being: A model and systematic review', *Social Science & Medicine*, vol. 123, pp. 182–193.

Salkind, NJ 2010, *Encyclopedia of Research Design*, SAGE Publications, Thousand Oaks, CA.

Smalheiser, N 2017, 'Chapter 12 — Nonparametric Tests', in *Data Literacy: How to Make Your Experiments Robust and Reproducible*, Elsevier Science & Technology, San Diego.

Solar, O & Irwin, A 2010, *A Conceptual Framework for Action on the Social Determinants of Health*, Discussion Paper Series on Social Determinants of Health, World Health Organization, Geneva, Switzerland.

Svanberg, J, Gumley, A & Wilson, A 2010, 'How do social firms contribute to recovery from mental illness? A qualitative study', *Clinical Psychology and Psychotherapy*, vol. 17, no. 6, pp. 482–496.

Toowoomba Regional Council 2019, 'Toowoomba region annual report 2018–2019', viewed 28 August 2020, <www.tr.qld.gov.au/ar/images/AR2018-19.pdf>.

Williams, AE, Fossey, E, Corbiere, M, Paluch, T & Harvey, C 2016, 'Work participation for people with severe mental illnesses: An integrative review of factors impacting job tenure', *Australian Occupational Therapy Journal*, vol. 63, no. 2, Apr, pp. 65–85.

8 Designing Work Integration Social Enterprises That Impact the Health and Wellbeing of People Living With Serious Mental Illnesses

An Intervention Mapping Approach

Terry Krupa, Rosemary Lysaght, and Michael J. Roy

Introduction

Work integration social enterprises (WISEs) are commercial ventures with dual financial and social goals (Vidal, 2005; Spear & Bidet, 2005). They produce goods and services to achieve sustainability to improve employment and social integration opportunities for people who have experienced significant marginalisation from the community workforce.

As one form of initiative within the broader social enterprise field, they have been studied as a highly complex form of public health 'intervention,' having the potential to positively promote health and wellbeing (Roy et al., 2014). Like all complex interventions, WISEs have multiple interacting components operating at individual, community, and organisational levels.

One of the challenges facing the WISE field is reaching consensus about what constitutes the critical ingredients of a WISE (i.e. when is an initiative called a WISE actually a WISE?) while recognising the inherent need for sensitivity to local contexts and planned adaptation. Explicitly identifying similarities and differences in WISE structures and processes is necessary for the design of evaluation processes that can demonstrate, with validity, their impact on health and wellbeing outcomes.

Intervention mapping, a systematic process for the development, implementation, and evaluation of interventions, has the potential to contribute to advancing WISE as a public health initiative. It originated with the goal of capturing the complexity of public health interventions (Eldredge et al., 2016; Fernandez, Ruiter et al., 2019; Kok & Mesters, 2011).

DOI: 10.4324/9781003125976-8

With intervention mapping, there is an explicit effort to develop the link between theory and practice, with a particular focus on 'ecological' theories (e.g. Krieger, 2001) that can attend to multiple levels of factors, from those focused on the individual to broader social interactions and societal structures (Eldredge et al., 2016). Attention to local factors influencing design and adaptation is integral to the process. In this way, intervention mapping could support both the development of consensus on critical features of WISE and recognise differences in specific applications across settings.

In this chapter, we aim to demonstrate an application of intervention mapping to WISE. We focus on WISEs designed specifically to address the needs of people living with serious mental illnesses (SMI) and the health and wellbeing outcomes associated with their employment in a WISE. The chapter begins with a brief overview of work integration and SMI and a profile of WISEs and their connection to health and wellbeing. This is followed by a description of the intervention mapping process and the application of this systematic framework to WISEs for people with SMI. Two examples of WISEs in Canada developed for people with mental illnesses are offered as examples of how the intervention mapping approach can be applied to reveal consistency with general WISE objectives and performance features while remaining sensitive to local contexts.

Serious Mental Illnesses and Work Integration

SMI is not a homogeneous health condition but a concept used to define a collection of features related to pervasive and persistent mental disorder and significant activity limitations and participation restrictions (Brennaman & Lobo, 2011). Challenges may be directly associated with the mental disorder (e.g. difficulties with mood, thought processes, perceptions, and so on) but also may comprise psychological challenges such as those related to coping and resilience as well as social-environmental issues such as stigma, poverty, and institutionalisation (Krupa & Chen, 2013).

Compromised participation in the community workforce is a prevalent issue among those who experience SMI. Employment rates for people with SMI have been consistently lower than those of people experiencing other disabilities or health conditions, and evidence suggests that employment rates for this group are getting worse over time (National Alliance on Mental Illness, 2014). In the United States, Bureau of Labor Statistics figures evidenced a net drop in employment figures for this population between 2003 and 2012, from 23 per cent to 17.8 per cent, and a similar rise in rates of unemployment. Actual employment rates for this population maybe even worse than suggested given that labour force participation rates are determined based on the numbers of individuals who are actively looking for work or working. Many individuals with SMI who are not employed have given up looking for work (Kozma et al., 2011), so not only do they not receive the benefits of being part of formal job search programs but they are no longer counted as a job seeker. Furthermore, due to compromised continuity in their identities as workers, and the associated public and self-stigma, many do not see themselves as capable of work (Elstad & Johannsen, 2017).

Workforce engagement of people with SMI is complicated by the fact that, as a population, they have low levels of previous labour market attachment: that is, they are not on disability leave from jobs, have no employment setting awaiting their return, and most are dependent on government financial assistance for daily living (Jakobson, Lysaght & Krupa, 2017). Evidence shows, however, that most want to work, and at least 60 per cent could succeed at work if provided with appropriate support (SAMHSA, 2009). To reconcile this difference between actual employment participation and desire to work, the Mental Health Commission of Canada has named the population the 'aspiring workforce' (Mental Health Commission of Canada, 2013).

Employment has been identified as a key factor in promoting and maintaining health and wellbeing among the general population. The benefits of employment, both 'latent and manifest' (Jahoda, 1981), are well known. There is no reason to believe that participation in employment would not provide health and wellbeing benefits to people with SMI. Indeed, employment might have additional benefits such as promoting personal illness management and recovery, distracting from troubling symptoms, and reducing negative personal experiences associated with stigma and discrimination (Dunn, Wewiorski & Rogers, 2008). Concerns that the demands of employment may lead to a worsening in mental health have not been supported, and the case has been made that the stress experiences of unemployment are associated with poor health and wellbeing outcomes for this population (Marrone & Swarbrick, 2020).

WISEs and the Connection to Health and Wellbeing

Roy, Baker, and Kerr (2016) identified seven mediating variables that explain how engagement in a social enterprise acts to produce health and wellbeing outcomes including: (1) engaging people in meaningful work; (2) engendering a supportive and safe work environment; (3) improving knowledge and skills; (4) expanding social networks; (5) accessing information and welfare; (6) raising public awareness; and (7) building self-worth. Their work is based on the empirical study of a range of social enterprise types; that is, their model development is based on businesses with social purpose outcomes, but which engage a broad range of populations in businesses with varying social goals. The models and causal pathways identified offer an important but broad stroke conceptualisation of how WISEs, through their activities, can influence health and wellbeing. However, they lack direct reference to the circumstances that create specific employment challenges for particular sub-groups.

There are important historical forces that have contributed to the employment marginalisation of people with SMI and serve as critical barriers to successful workforce engagement (Elmes, 2019; Gidron & Monnickendam-Givon, 2017). This is an important point because, without attention to these underlying conditions, the potential of WISEs to impact health and wellbeing may be neutralised or WISEs could unintentionally sustain marginalising forces.

Employment-related interventions for people with SMI have largely been delivered within the context of mental healthcare systems. Conceptual models for WISEs thus need to position them relative to other employment interventions and approaches designed for this population if they are to have any significant impact on practice, policy, and funding. For example, the primary evidence-based approach to work integration in the mental health field is supported employment, and specifically the Individual Placement and Support Model (IPS) which focuses on rapidly placing people into mainstream employment and providing the continuous support necessary to successfully sustain employment (Bond, Drake & Becker, 2012). IPS, unlike WISEs, is delivered using a 'service' approach which is more familiar to mental health professionals than the market-oriented approaches of social enterprises.

Intervention Mapping Applied to WISEs

Intervention mapping includes the following six process steps (Fernandez, ten Hoor et al., 2019; Eldredge et al., 2016): (1) needs assessment/problem analysis; (2) developing proximal intervention objectives; (3) selecting theory and related methods and practical strategies; (4) development of the intervention plan; (5) adoption and implementation; and (6) evaluation planning. Here, we apply each of these six process steps to WISEs for people with SMI in relation to health and wellbeing outcomes.

1. Needs Assessment/Problem Analysis

The needs assessment in intervention mapping focuses on developing a comprehensive understanding of the problem. More than a cursory appraisal of the gap between what exists now and a desired state, the needs assessment process engages intervention developers with a range of stakeholders to consider the problem from multiple perspectives. For example, the assessment might include the following questions: What is the nature of the problem in context? What is the lived experience of relevant stakeholders? How is this a community issue? What are the consequences, and who is affected? The needs assessment also considers what interventions are already in place and how a new intervention might add value to what already exists.

Although there has been a long history of efforts to advance the work participation of people with SMI, these resulting programs have been subject to challenges and critique. The development of WISEs as a legitimate and effective option needs to attend to these issues. These challenges, described in the following, include ongoing segregation; sustained patient identities; limited potential for advancement; and exploitation of workers.

Segregation

The employment segregation of people with SMI has historically been in the form of work in institutional settings. Even with the growth of community care, employment for this group evolved to include work activities that exist in community service contexts 'parallel' to the broader community. Contemporary efforts to promote employment integration are charged with designing initiatives that facilitate regular, positive contact between people with SMI and the general public which will then raise their profile as contributing citizens.

Patient Identities

When work opportunities are developed within mental health or social service structures, they can be perceived by the public, the service sector, and people with SMI as 'service programs.' This situation can contribute to the population being viewed as 'patients,' rather than legitimate workers, dependent on service systems. In this way, their work activities and products become viewed as a form of charity, rationalising their exclusion from employment, because it lends support to the widely held stigma that individuals with SMI do not have the capacity to work to expected standards and that health, social, and economic structures (such as government pensions) are in place to meet their needs (Krupa et al., 2009). There has historically been little opportunity for worker voice and control, contributing to the ongoing disempowered status of the population.

Limited Potential to Grow and Demonstrate Competence

Work-related interventions accessed by people with SMI have largely involved them in the creation of products and services that are associated with low-status jobs and industries. This has resulted in situations of limited worker pride, a fractured sense of work identity, and self-stigma. There can also be limited attention to structures that support career or personal development, thus sustaining and perpetuating this position of low social status.

Exploitation

Historically, there has been a tendency to place lowered expectations related to work processes such as efficiency, and product quality, on people with SMI. This practice results in undervaluing of the capacities of these workers as well as the products of their labour. Devaluing of products and services in turn devalues the workers themselves, both in terms of social status and compensation for work performed, which may fall below legal market standards.

Our own research on WISEs for people with SMI has revealed that even with the best of intentions, particular processes in these businesses can be experienced as sustaining the forces of employment marginalisation (Krupa, Sabetti & Lysaght, 2019; Krupa & Lysaght, 2016). This point is echoed by Garrow and Hasenfeld (2014) who recognise that if the business practices and culture of the WISE are too heavily dominated by a 'market logic,' this can result in vulnerable workers being treated as a commodity to be exploited. WISEs thus need to be social in both their means (i.e. their internal processes) *and* in their ends to prevent unintended consequences from arising, hence our point earlier about the importance of consensus on critical ingredients (see Lysaght et al., 2018). Developing WISEs as an intervention strategy that promotes health and wellbeing requires them to be developed in a way that not only provides opportunities for participation in work activities but also attends to the forces that sustain inequities, devaluation, disadvantage, and exclusion. In this way, WISEs can be positioned to go beyond economic and social goals to serve socio-political goals related to changing the very nature of economic development, promoting inclusivity, diversity interdependence, and democratisation (Campi, Defourny & Grégoire, 2006; Laville & Nyssens, 2001).

2. Specifying the Proximal Objectives That Will Result in the Desired Health Outcomes

The second step in intervention mapping is the identification of performance objectives which will lead to the desired and likely health and wellbeing objectives. Performance objectives lead to both individual behavioural changes and environmental changes (Eldredge et al., 2016). Performance objectives for WISEs will need to recognise both the economic and the social mission of the approach. The performance objectives should be aligned with the needs assessment and problem analysis. So, in the case of WISEs, the objectives would be developed to recognise the forces that have operated to marginalise people and align with the optimal health and wellbeing outcomes.

Our research has suggested seven distinct but interrelated organisational elements of WISEs requiring specific performance objectives to ensure the likelihood of maximising health and wellbeing outcomes (Lysaght et al., 2018). These are identified in Table 8.1.

The performance objectives are aligned with both a market-oriented approach and a range of foundational social values, including inclusion, equity, fairness, community integration, flexibility, empowerment, personal growth, and sustainability. So, for example, WISEs that create the conditions for interdependence among workers, the production of quality products and services, fair pay, worker engagement, and direct contact with the public have the potential to increase the likelihood that individuals with SMI will experience expanded social networks, a commitment to illness management, improved family dynamics, and decreased public and self-stigma. Similarly, WISEs that are structured to be legally registered, focus on quality of products or services for marketing, consider both economic and social factors in decision-making, use a market orientation, and have work processes that attend to worker safety, are likely to promote worker pride and identity, decrease workplace injury or harm, and contribute to the public's perception that the WISE is a 'real business.' All these behavioural and environmental outcomes are associated with health and wellbeing outcomes, such as improvements in indicators of recovery, physical and mental health, and quality of life.

3. Intervention Design: Selection of Theories and Evidence-Based Methods and Strategies

The third step in the intervention mapping process involves selecting theories that are well aligned with the problem analysis and emerging objectives and suggest related theory-based methods and strategies for change. This step involves intervention developers in considering what theories, if applied, have the potential to increase intervention effectiveness. The identification and application of theory can be considered particularly important for WISE in this sector due to the contextual history of entrenched negative assumptions and stigmatising attitudes and history of marginal, low-status employment. Without ongoing attention to theory that underlies the expected change, complacency is likely and WISEs risk replicating practices of marginalisation.

In the case of WISEs developed for people with SMI, three philosophically aligned theoretical frameworks are identified: community economic development; empowerment-community integration; and recovery.

Community Economic Development

Community economic development (CED) emerged as a response to failures of predominantly market-based approaches that are ill-suited to the needs of local communities; failures which led to populations and communities struggling with unemployment, poverty, and ruin of

Table 8.1 Performance objectives

7 Elements of WISE	Performance objectives	Expected behavioural and environmental outcomes	Health and wellbeing outcomes
Products/ services	Production of good-quality products and services Products and services based on interests and skills of workers (personally meaningful) and market needs (socially meaningful) Costing of product/service aligned with local market rates Production meets societal workplace standards for safety, equity and fairness	*Individual behavioural changes* Develop a broad range of new knowledge and skills is developed Improve work efficiency Contribute to the production of quality goods and services Demonstrate reliability and responsibility Follow standards for safe and inclusive workplaces Contribute own voice to aspects of business operation Demonstrate pride in work of the WISE Increase knowledge about rights and resources related to government disability income benefits Attend WISE meetings Provide support to WISE colleagues Demonstrate practices of respect and inclusion for WISE employees and customers	Improved physical health (e.g. stamina, physical health practices) Improved self-perception of mental health Improvements in indicators of recovery including hope, coping and resilience, positive identity, empowerment, self-efficacy Decrease in use of intensive mental health services (such as hospitalisation, crisis services) Increased income Improvements in quality of life Improved access to community resources available to all citizens

(Continued)

Structural model and business practices		
	Legally registered as a business based on legal local, regional, and national business requirements that govern commercial organisations and workplaces	Engage in social relations with WISE colleagues
	Marketing focused on the quality of the product/service, with its social mission marketed as a secondary benefit	Engage in personal self-care including illness management practices
	Flexible work processes and practices.	Increase social contacts, activities, and participation in the broader community
	Operating decisions based on sound business plans that balance financial and social goals	Contribute to positive family dynamics
	WISE strives to accommodate individual worker differences and preferences.	Balance work, home and community life
	The WISE capitalises on interdependence, shared learning, and mutual support to achieve social and economic goals	Participate in WISE community activities
	Education and training practices include attention to a broad range of competencies: job tasks, social, and management of personal health and wellbeing	Sustain work tenure
	WISEs operate in a manner that is economically, socially, and environmentally sustainable	Engage in longer term planning and activities related to career and community employment
	Workplace expectations and standards are clear and supported through transparent and respectful business principles and practices rather than clinical interpretations.	

Table 8.1 (Continued)

7 Elements of WISE	Performance objectives	Expected behavioural and environmental outcomes	Health and wellbeing outcomes
Advancing inclusion	Businesses practices welcome and support diversity, including the inclusion of all individuals regardless of gender orientation, race, and culture WISE business practices maximise opportunities for all workers to have positive contacts with the public WISEs seek involvement in activities that demonstrate their contribution to their communities. Collaborations with individuals and organisations in the broader community to advance both financial and social goals		
Compensation structures and practices	Pay meets standards for fair and equitable compensation Opportunities to advance in the pay scale Compensation strategy recognises implications of earned income relative to government income supports and associated benefits (e.g. drugs, housing)	*Environmental-level changes* Public perceives WISE employees as competent and contributing citizens rather than as patients of a service system Customers purchase WISE products/services because they perceive them as worthy and valuable	

Worker engagement	Workers have the opportunity to influence the policies that govern conditions of employment, day-to-day business practices, and decisions related to the growth and development of the business. Benefits counselling/training engages workers in maximising finances through employment	The public perceives the WISE as a legitimate business Mental health systems and services respect the value of WISEs for the people they serve The local community perceives the WISE as community-minded, contributing to a socially and economically vibrant community
Career Progression	WISE offers opportunities for all workers to develop their interests, gain knowledge, learn new skills, and achieve goals. Affirmative policies are in place to ensure that all employment positions within the WISE are open to people with mental illnesses. Policies and practices are in place to promote progression through the ranks WISE has processes in place to support individual workers in transitioning to other employment positions if they desire	Stigma and social distancing by the public is reduced Decrease public view of WISE workers as recipients of charity Family members view WISE involvement positively and encourage participation Family social dynamics improve and family burden decreases
Relationship to mental health services	The WISE is independent and distinct from mental health service agencies Collaborative relationships with mental health services support access to care for workers Natural supports in the workplace are enabled Specialists in the particular business/trade of the WISE support workers	People outside of the individual's kin network socialise with WISE workers WISE workers with SMI have increased access to practical, emotional, esteem, and informational support through social networks

local economies (Lamb, 2011). CED offers a conceptualisation of how to address these failures to reduce disparities and to improve the social and economic lives of people with SMI. Applied to people with SMI, the mainstream economy is viewed as failing them by way of structures that systematically deny their access to employment and its associated social and material privileges. Specific marginalising forces in the market economy include: 1) judgements that people with SMI do not have the personal abilities necessary to meet the efficiency standards necessary for employment; 2) competition and pressure to grow in scale along with lower costs, and; 3) a profit orientation that sees wealth distributed to investors outside of business production (Enns, 2018; Krupa et al., 2009). Furthermore, given their low social status and levels of poverty, people with SMI are viewed as an economic burden and not as a population worthy of focused market attention (Mandiberg & Warner, 2012). CED principles that are particularly applicable to WISE include local reinvestment of profits, local control, grassroots development, cooperative approaches to ownership and business development, recognition of community assets, local skills development, business practices that support the local economy, and operations based on dignity and respect (Enns, 2018).

Empowerment and Community Integration

The empowerment and community integration theoretical paradigm was developed to address the limitations of traditional medical and rehabilitation understandings of mental illnesses (Jorge-Monteiro & Ornelas, 2016; Nelson, Lord & Ochocka, 2001). This perspective is concerned with the extent to which guiding frameworks in the mental health sector construct 'social relations in ways that maintain power and control in the hands of professional institutions' (Nelson, Lord & Ochocka, 2001, p. 17). It is this aspect of the empowerment and community integration theoretical paradigm—the power relations between people with SMI and the mental health and social sectors developed to serve them—that both aligns with and distinguishes it from the grassroots approach espoused in community economic development. Values underlying this paradigm that are relevant to WISE include a goal of increasing power, choice, and control by people with SMI in their relations with professionals as well as the development of autonomous organisations. The second value is community support and integration, which is operationalised through self-help, mutual aid, and a focus on strengths. Finally, the value of social justice is demonstrated through access to valued community resources and opportunities, including employment (Nelson et al., 2001). The actual implementation of empowerment theory ideals in practice requires nuanced attention to the ways in which the professional domination of the social relations of people with SMI occurs in the context of WISE.

Recovery

The recovery concept has gained international recognition as a guiding vision in the mental health field. Unlike definitions that focus on cure, current conceptualisations of recovery evolved from the writings of Patricia Deegan, herself a woman with SMI, who described recovery as 'a way of living a satisfying, hopeful and contributing life even with limitations caused by illness' (Deegan, 1988, p. 11). While there is no one agreed upon 'theoretical model' of recovery, there has been some consensus about the key elements of recovery-oriented practice. These elements include a focus on strengths, identity, hope and dignity, empowerment, social supports, and participation in meaningful roles and activities. What recovery as a guiding vision adds to the theory underlying WISE is the focus on catalysing the awareness by people with SMI of the self as active in the process of creating a life beyond illness, including active self-management of one's mental illness. This has led to the development of a range of methods and strategies. For example, psychoeducation interventions have been developed to enable people with SMI and their families to learn about their illnesses and to devise and share strategies for coping with illness as they proceed in their recovery journey. WISEs focused on the employment integration of people with SMI will need to attend to how, through their processes and practices, worker agency in illness management will be supported while maintaining their profile and practices as a business entity.

4. Developing the Intervention

While the previous steps lay a foundation for the intervention, the fourth step in the process recognises that developers need to carefully consider the broad range of factors that will influence the translation of intervention plans to implementation of related materials and activities. In relation to WISE, some of the likely contextual factors that need to be considered include local labour laws and whether there are wage standards that are required to be upheld. Where wage standards are not present, prevailing societal norms and beliefs related to income will need to be considered and appropriately articulated in business documents such as by-laws and employee handbooks.

Some of the variability in WISEs internationally emerges from the forces pressing for the development of community alternatives to institutional opportunities. For example, in Italy, work integration enterprises developed in response to the country-wide closure of psychiatric hospitals (Burti, 2016). WISE development will be influenced by environmental context. For example, where WISEs are developed in prisons, they will be limited in their ability to operationalise performance objectives that see individual workers interacting directly with the broader public but may be able to consider indirect ways of connecting to community. One such business saw offenders with SMI in a prison-based sewing enterprise donate headscarves to a local cancer organisation to contribute to the community (Davidson, 2010). Similarly, WISE development will be influenced by the experiences and needs of particular subgroups. Ferguson's (2018) work has highlighted that social enterprises developed for homeless youth, many of them with mental illnesses, could benefit from strong peer mentorship elements to counter the high distrust of this population for helping professionals. In this instance, it was also important to focus on business ideas and practices geared to youth culture.

The local funding regime or funding opportunities may well influence the way that WISEs are required (or choose) to describe or market themselves, an important requirement for building legitimacy with local stakeholders or funders (Dey & Teasdale, 2016). Some funding sources are based on 'poverty-alleviation' goals, while others may be more focused on 'inclusion and community integration.' In some jurisdictions, like in Quebec or Ireland, social and economic policy that has prioritised the social economy has served as a catalyst to the development of social enterprises for people with SMI outside the medical realm (Mendell & Neamtan, 2010; O'Shaughnessy & O'Hara, 2016).

Local standards related to the social economy may also need to be considered. For example, in some areas (such as with Italian 'type B' social cooperatives), there are requirements related to the percentage of WISE employees that must have a type of disadvantage, such as living with SMI (Warner & Mandiberg, 2006). The population of people with SMI working in the WISE may present other situations or conditions meriting consideration, such as a history of involvement with the justice system, substance abuse, or intellectual disability. Beyond disability associated with mental illnesses, other sources of disadvantage also need to be considered, such as gender, race, or ethnicity, with care given to ensure that business product/service ideas do not exclude certain groups of people.

5. Implementation and Adoption Planning

Eldredge and colleagues (2016) highlight that even with interventions that are theory and evidence-based, implementation can require several levels of adoption and negotiation. At its most basic, implementation and adoption planning involve ensuring sufficient clarity with regard to the specific elements of the initiative, the multiple stakeholders involved and their activities, and the necessary structures and resources. The adoption of new interventions can also require considerable system and organisational change. The implementation and adoption of WISEs for people with SMI will necessarily include a broad range of structural and organisational considerations. We identify only a few of these considerations subsequently.

WISEs focused on people with SMI will require clarity with respect to the relationship with the mental health system and mental health service providers. This can take many forms; for example, WISEs may wish to provide information and training related to the roles of mental health professionals in relation to supporting WISEs and WISE workers. Several logistical issues may merit explicit attention, including space agreements, business licences, corporate naming, bank loans, and so on, with a view to ensuring control over central features.

WISE implementation also calls for clarity related to the relationship between the available employment interventions. For example, what is the relationship between WISE and other vocational support services, such as Individual Placement and Support, job coaching, on-the-job supports? Career counselling is an important consideration in relation to implementation of values of supporting growth and advancement of workers yet a difficult one practically. WISEs will be forced to balance their efforts to support worker career development with the need for attention to economic sustainability and the challenges posed by the loss of valued and reliable employees. In some mental health systems, clarity with respect to relationships with local unions will be required as well as transparency with respect to procurement of services. Consideration will also need to be directed to identifying opinion leaders who could champion the development and implementation of WISEs.

Implementation and adoption efforts will also depend on the clarity of communication, and feedback processes that have the capacity for rapid and supportive responses for issues as they arise, and for ongoing planning. WISEs may construct, for example, active committee structures and governance requirements for regular reports related to business processes and activities as well as providing evidence of worker health and wellbeing.

6. Evaluation Plan

The purpose of this step is the development of an evaluation plan based on the previous steps of the intervention mapping process. Evaluation is considered an invaluable step in the process, both to move advance an evidence base for an intervention and to provide feedback for ongoing intervention development. Where an intervention, such as WISE, has been implemented without prior intervention mapping, mapping is important to explicate both the rationale of intervention as applied and to provide a clear articulation of the processes by which change is expected. As the WISE field advances and comes to an agreement on critical elements of the intervention approach, intervention mapping is advisable for individual WISE initiatives, given the influence of local conditions and contexts.

Evaluation of the association between WISE participation and health and wellbeing outcomes is itself a distinct and complex process. An important question to be addressed in the evaluation is the extent to which the WISE is reaching the intended population and who is being excluded. For example, there has been a concern in the mental health field that employment initiatives that are financially dependent on outcomes will tend to select those individuals deemed likely to be high performing, a phenomenon referred to as 'creaming' (McGrew et al., 2007), and a potential concern for WISEs that are under pressure to achieve financial sustainability. Evaluation plans also need to consider the extent to which the intended performance objectives are actually adopted, implemented, refined and maintained (Fernandez, Ruiter et al., 2019), and have the capacity to link particular WISE practices to outcomes. To this point, some scholarly work has suggested that the involvement of mental health professionals in the day-to-day operation of the WISE can lead to favouring the social over commercial activities while potentially compromising sustainability (Battilana et al., 2015), and so evaluation planning would need to be sensitive to this possibility. Evaluation planning for complex public health interventions requires careful consideration of the multiple stakeholders to engage. For example, the performance objectives and expected environmental changes outlined in Table 8.1 suggest the need to engage members of the public, business customers, other businesses, potential future employers, cross-sectoral partners, and family members in the evaluation process.

The involvement of the primary beneficiaries of WISEs, the employees with SMI, in evaluation planning and implementation related to health and wellbeing outcomes needs to be carefully considered. There are many examples of evaluation research accessing the perspective of people with SMI working in WISEs regarding their experiences with WISE and the impact on their wellbeing (Milton et al., 2015; Lanctôt, Duran & Corbire, 2012; Williams, Fossey & Harvey, 2010; Svanberg, Gumley & Wilson, 2010). However, evaluation of the health and wellbeing outcomes associated with participation in WISEs will depend on the development of participatory approaches to evaluation that engage those with SMI in the design and implementation of evaluation processes. The collection of much personal medical, health, and wellbeing data about individual employees is somewhat inconsistent with the running of a business but determining what information requires to be collected, and how, is an important consideration. The collection of information related to diagnoses, health service utilisation, and other health measures, for example, will ultimately depend on the involvement and acceptance of the WISE workers themselves and may be more appropriately conducted through a partnership with external evaluators.

Case Studies

This section presents brief studies of two WISEs developed to meet the needs of people with SMI. A full intervention mapping of both organisations is beyond the limits of this chapter, and so the studies are presented here as illustrations of how the construction of the elements of the intervention in practice were influenced by local contexts and situations. Although both WISEs were developed prior to the explication of the intervention mapping approach, their developmental processes aligned with multiple elements and associated performance objectives identified in Table 8.1. The specific context of their evolution, however, presented challenges pressing for ongoing adaptations in implementation. It is these challenges and examples of adaptations that focus the descriptions.

The Umbrella Organisation: Negotiating a Relationship With a Mental Health Agency

The 'Umbrella Organisation' is a not-for-profit corporation in a small city in Canada. The organisation oversees the development and implementation of businesses that aim to provide employment with fair renumeration for people with SMI, particularly those who have received services from specialised mental health services. It has been incorporated for more than 25 years and today oversees seven distinct businesses employing more than 75 individuals with SMI. Over the years, the businesses have ranged from cafes and catering to landscaping, car washes, packaging services, pet care and food, personal care and wellbeing products, and cleaning services.

The organisation emerged in response to government-imposed requirements to close sheltered workshops in favour of a community-based approach that capitalised on the strengths of workers and created real employment opportunities. A social business model was selected as one employment intervention option. Developers of this new social business approach were guided by a community economic development perspective, which provided a well-articulated counterpoint to traditional rehabilitation paradigms that focused almost solely on individual characteristics considered essential to employment by focusing on creating conditions and opportunities for employment.

Their initial challenge was to create a business organisational structure that was distinct from but linked to the parent mental health agency. Separation from the mental health service was formalised by the creation of an autonomous corporation with its own Board of Directors, with members recruited based on expertise related to both the economic and the social mission. With incorporation, business by-laws and policies were established, compensation and workplace practices were governed by local fair and safe workplace practice standards, and business decisions focused on community marketing and business sustainability. Work policies were developed with the involvement of workers themselves to create supportive conditions for employment while maintaining business productivity. For example, volunteer relief schedules were developed to address unexpected absences for health and wellbeing reasons, and jobs were held for workers on health-related leave.

From the beginning, the need for a formal link to the mental health agency was clear. Early business development depended on the transfer of resources from pre-existing sheltered workshops, including equipment and space, a commitment to the employment of individuals who worked in the workshops, and the involvement of vocational rehabilitation staff in key business positions. An 'affirmative business' approach, with its focus on the mutual benefits of partnerships, guided the development of the ongoing relationship with the mental health agency. Strategies included formalising the shared interests of both organisations in the employment of people with SMI through the creation of a liaison position. This person, employed by the mental health agency, was integral to facilitating communication and addressing challenges to business development; for example, reconciling union issues and advocating for the businesses in the context of hospital restructuring. More recently, the organisation has explicitly embraced a recovery philosophy, aligning its intentions with the broader mental health field.

Implementation over the years has seen multiple changes to the businesses being operated by the WISE in response to local economic considerations. Annual evaluations include attention to both business net income and payroll expenses, the latter indicating the direct financial benefit to workers. The ongoing development of partnerships with community organisations has spun off businesses within the broader community. Key management and supervision positions continue to be held by mental health agency staff, but the organisation has initiated an education award for employees to enable the career development of workers, and some supervisory/mentoring positions and jobs linked to special business initiatives have purposely been created to promote job advancement of people with SMI. The organisation has maintained a commitment to evaluation and has been instrumental in advancing understanding of how health and wellbeing are both supported and challenged by ongoing linkages with mental health agencies. For example, some businesses that are located within the grounds of the mental health agency have raised concerns about stigma against the businesses and the workers, yet these same businesses are viewed as having the potential to encourage the employment aspirations of those who are receiving treatment in hospital and have few opportunities to view people with SMI at work.

The Cleaning Business: Empowering Consumer/Survivor Identity and Pride

This business, located in a large Canadian city, has been in operation for over 25 years. The organisation aims to provide stable employment for consumer-survivors of the mental health system, along with job training and support, life skills training, and peer support. It is incorporated as both a community development corporation and a charity. The organisation employs approximately 90 workers in a range of cleaning and property management activities.

The organisation was founded by a group of mental health service users, supported by a community economic developer. A few local community agencies were supportive and were among the business's first clients. Falling outside the scope of most funding for mental health initiatives, the founders received start-up monies through anti-recession funding made available by a government keen on developing the strengths and capacities of consumer-survivor groups.

The Cleaning Business emerged in the context of the growth of a consumer-survivor movement that advocated for the importance of 'identity communities,' celebrating the interdependence among people with mental illnesses and countering the normalisation practices and service dependence inherent in vocational rehabilitation approaches (Mandiberg, 2012; Church et al., 2000; Trainor & Tremblay, 1992). Subsequently, the development of the business demonstrates a focus on empowering the collective strengths of consumer/survivors. This included policy requiring most Directors to identify as consumer-survivors and all employment positions to be filled by individuals who identify as mental health service users. As business demands increased, a management structure was created to enable a focus on developing practices, training, and conditions that can facilitate both getting the work done and worker growth and wellbeing. Emphasis is placed on explaining issues as work-related skills, rather than examples of mental illness. In addition to business practices focused on the delivery of quality services, the business includes opportunities for peer support and the development of a strong peer community. The need to move the business operation to a larger location has pressed the organisation to consider how the sense of community and peer support can be maintained.

The economic sustainability of the business has been supported by the creation of new specialised business options related to cleaning and property management in response to market needs. Much of the work is in sectors where daily contacts are often with other marginalised people. This cleaning work is focused on reducing a range of health and safety issues that can compromise stability and health in public housing. On the one hand, this is a source of pride for services offered and evidence of their skill and expertise to fulfil an important need. On the other hand, it is a source of concern related to how ongoing associations with marginalisation might negatively impact the employees' personal sense of social status and potential. The business employs a 'learning attitude' recognising the communication, skill, information, and problem-solving inherent in the services provided.

The consumer-operated business regularly implements evaluation of the economic sustainability of the business. Grants to the organisation are used to cover administrative and business development costs, while business revenues cover all costs related to the actual work of the business. While data related to mental illness and health are not routinely collected, the business has participated in evaluations that have demonstrated their positive impact on mental health, including reduced use of intensive mental health services.

Discussion

This chapter focuses on the potential of employment in Work Integration Social Enterprises to positively impact the health and wellbeing of individuals who have traditionally been marginalised from gainful work in the broader community. The chapter has a specific focus on WISEs developed for people with SMI.

WISEs have been identified as a type of complex public health intervention. They are complex because they operate from a hybrid model that balances both social and economic missions (Pache & Santos, 2013; Doherty et al., 2014; Battilana & Lee, 2014) and because they operate at multiple levels, including the individual, the organisation, the community, and broader society. In addition, they regularly serve several populations (and subpopulations) of disadvantaged people. The result of this complexity is that the field has lacked clear descriptions of the intervention approach, agreement on essential ingredients of the approach (including expected health and wellbeing outcomes), and ultimately this has compromised the implementation and interpretation of research meant to advance the field.

The chapter has proposed Intervention Mapping as a systematic process to guide the development, implementation, and evaluation of WISEs. One strength of the approach is its attention to theory underlying the intervention. WISE as an intervention approach for people with mental illnesses, for example, benefits from theories such as community economic development, empowerment and community integration, and recovery, which provide alternatives to traditional biomedical and rehabilitation views of employment and mental illness and are well aligned with business principles. The intervention mapping approach promotes the development of general WISE performance objectives and outcomes that attend to processes of change at both individual and environmental levels. Yet, it also provides the opportunity for WISEs to be sensitive to their local contexts and situations to explicate informed adaptations to the approach. In the brief case studies provided, these adaptations highlight the extent to which tensions are ongoing, beyond initial business development, and require constant consideration for informed implementation. While in this chapter there is no effort made to organise these local adaptations, there have been efforts to do so in the broader social enterprise literature. For example, Smith, Gonin, and Bersharov (2013) identify four categories of social-business tensions faced by social enterprises (performing, organising, belonging, and learning tensions) that may be useful in advancing the mapping of WISE interventions.

The routine application of intervention mapping in the WISE arena will not be without difficulties. In their conceptual review of intervention mapping, Kok and colleagues (2017) note that some authors describe the process using terms such as 'elaborate,' 'time-consuming,' and 'expensive.' In the WISE field, where business development is characterised by limited funding and often depends on the extended commitment of multiple stakeholders, the process may be challenging. However, in the long run, it may contribute to advancing the field in a way that positively influences practice, policy, and funding.

Conclusion

In this chapter, we used an intervention mapping approach to inform existing gaps in the conceptualisation of WISE as applied to populations with SMI. By positioning WISE as a complex and powerful 'intervention' that can address the long-standing employment marginalisation of this population, we have begun to unpack the particular challenges and imperatives associated with effective WISE development. We consider that this work lays the foundation for a systematic process guiding the development, implementation, and evaluation of WISEs, thus providing guidance for WISE practitioners and scholars.

References

Battilana, J., & Lee, M. (2014). 'Advancing research on hybrid organizing: Insights from the study of social enterprises'. *Academy of Management Annals* 8: 397–441.

Battilana, J., Sengul, M., Pache, A., & Model, J. (2015). 'Harnessing productive tensions in hybrid organizations: The case of work integration social enterprises'. *Academy of Management Journal* 58(6): 1658–1685. DOI: 10.5465/amj.2013.0903.

Bond, G.R., Drake, R.E., & Becker, D.R. (2012). 'Generalizability of the individual placement and support (IPS) model of supported employment outside the US'. *World Psychiatry* 11: 32–39.

Brennaman, L., & Lobo, M.L. (2011). 'Recovery from serious mental illness: A concept analysis'. *Issues in Mental Health Nursing* 32(10): 654–663. DOI: 10.3109/01612840.2011.588372.

Burti, L. (2016). 'Thirty-five years of psychosocial rehabilitation in Italy'. *International Journal of Mental Health* 45: 7–14.

Campi, S., Defourny, J., & Grégoire, O. (2006). 'Work integration social enterprises: Are they multiple-goal and multi-stakeholder organisations?' In:

Nyssens, M. (ed) *Social Enterprise: At the crossroads of market, public policies and civil society*, pp 29–49. Routledge: Abingdon Oxon.

Church, K., Fontan, J.M., Ng, R., & Shragge, E. (2000). 'Social learning among people who are excluded from the labour market part one: Context and case studies'. WALL Working paper no. 11, Centre for the Study of Education and Work, Ontario Institute for Studies in Education at the University of Toronto.

Davidson, T.A. (2010). 'Free spirit affirmative business: Employment for offenders with serious mental illness'. Masters Thesis, Queen's University, Kingston, Ontario.

Deegan, P. (1988). 'Recovery: The lived experience of rehabilitation'. *Psychosocial Rehabilitation Journal* 11(4): 11–19. DOI: 10.1037/h0099565.

Dey, P., & Teasdale, S. (2016). 'The tactical mimicry of social enterprise strategies: Acting "As If" in the everyday life of third sector organizations'. *Organization* 23(4): 485–504. DOI: 10.1177/1350508415570689.

Doherty, B., Haugh, H., & Lyon, F. (2014). 'Social enterprises as hybrid organizations: A review and research agenda'. *International Journal of Management Reviews* 16: 417–436.

Dunn, E.C., Wewiorski, N.J., & Rogers, E.S. (2008). 'The meaning and importance of employment to people in recovery from serious mental illness: Results of a qualitative study'. *Psychiatric Rehabilitation Journal* 32(1): 59–62. DOI: 10.2975/32.1.2008.59.62.

Eldredge, L.K. Bartholomew, Markham, C.M., Ruiter, A.C., Fernández, M.E., Kok, G., & Parcel, G.S. (2016). *Planning health promotion programs: An intervention mapping approach*, 4th edition. Jossey Bass: San Francisco.

Elmes, A.I. (2019). 'Health impacts of a WISE: A longitudinal study'. *Social Enterprise Journal* 15(4): 457–474. DOI: 10.1108/SEJ-12-2018-0082.

Elstad, T.A., & Johannsen, G.S. (2017). 'Mental health, participation and social identity'. In: Eide, A.H., Josephsson, S., & Vic, K. (eds) *Participation in health and welfare services: Professional concepts and lived experience*, pp. 156–169. Routledge: London.

Enns, S.W. (2018). *Community economic development in Manitoba: Theory, history, policy, and practice*. Canadian Centre for Policy Alternatives: Manitoba. Available from: www.policyalternatives.ca/publications/reports/community-economic-development-manitoba (Accessed April 8, 2020).

Ferguson, K.M. (2018). 'Using the social enterprise intervention (SEI) and individual placement and support (IPS) models to improve employment and clinical outcomes of homeless youth with mental illness'. *Social Work in Mental Health* 11(5): 473–495. DOI: 10.1080/15332985.2013.764960.

Fernandez, M.E, Ruiter, R.A.C., Markham, C.M., & Kok, G. (2019). 'Intervention mapping: theory- and evidence-based health promotion program planning: Perspective and examples'. *Frontiers in Public Health* 7. DOI: 10.3389/fpubh.2019.00209.

Fernandez, M.E., ten Hoor, G.A., van Lieshout, S., Rodriguez, S.A., Beidas R.S., Parcel, G., Ruiter, R.A.C., Markham, C.M., & Kok, G. (2019). 'Implementation mapping: Using intervention mapping to develop implementation strategies'. *Frontiers in Public Health* 7 DOI: 10.5465/amj.2013.0903.

Garrow, E.E., & Hasenfeld, Y. (2014). 'Social enterprises as an embodiment of a neoliberal welfare logic'. *American Behavioral Scientist* 58(11): 1475–1493. DOI: 10.1177/0002764214534674.

Gidron, B., & Monnickendam-Givon, Y. (2017). 'A social welfare perspective of market-oriented social enterprises'. *International Journal of Social Welfare* 26: 127–140. DOI: 10.1111/ijsw.12232.

Jahoda, M. (1981). 'Work, employment, and unemployment: Values, theories, and approaches in social research'. *American Psychologist* 36(2): 184–191. DOI: 10.1037/0003-066X.36.2.184.

Jakobson, K., Lysaght, R., & Krupa, T. (2017). 'Impacts on work participation of people with mental health disability'. In: Eide, A.H., Josephsson, S. & Vic, K. (eds) *Participation in health and welfare services: Professional concepts and lived experience*, pp 141–155. Routledge: London.

Jorge-Monteiro, M.F., & Ornelas, J.H. (2016). 'What's wrong with the seed? A comparative examination of an empowering community-centered approach to recovery in community mental health'. *Community Mental Health Journal* 52: 821–833. DOI: 10.1007/s10597-016-0004-8.

Kok, G., & Mesters, I. (2011). 'Getting inside the black box of health promotion programmes using intervention mapping'. *Chronic Illness* 7(3): 176–180. DOI: 10.1177/1742395311403013.

Kok, G., Peters, L.W., & Ruiter, R.A. (2017). 'Planning theory- and evidence-based behavior change interventions: A conceptual review of the intervention mapping protocol'. *Psicologia: Reflexão e Crítica* 30: 19. DOI 10.1186/s41155-017-0072-x.

Kozma C., Dirani, R., Canuso, C., & Mao, L. (2011). 'Change in employment status over 52 weeks in patients with schizophrenia: an observational study'. *Current Medical Research and Opinion* 27: 327–333. DOI: 10.1185/03007995.2010.541431.

Krieger, N. (2001). 'The ostrich, the albatross, and public health: An ecosocial perspective—or why an explicit focus on health consequences of discrimination and deprivation is vital for good science and public health practice'. *Public Health Reports* 116(5): 419.

Krupa, T., & Chen, S.P. (2013). 'Psychiatric/psychosocial rehabilitation (PSR) in relation to vocational and educational environments: Work and learning'. *Current Psychiatry Reviews* 9(3): 195–206.

Krupa, T., Kirsh, B., Cockburn, L., & Gewurtz, R. (2009). 'A model of stigma of mental illness in employment'. *Work* 33(4): 413–425. DOI: 10.3233/WOR-2009-0890.

Krupa, T., & Lysaght, R. (2016). 'Perspectives on how social business can engender work identity among people with mental illness'. *Journal of Policy Practice* 15(1–2): 36–57. DOI: 10.1080/15588742.2016.1109962.

Krupa, T., Sabetti, J., & Lysaght, R. (2019). 'How work integration social enterprises impact the stigma of mental illness'. *Social Enterprise Journal* 15(4): 475–494. DOI: 10.1108/SEJ-12-2018-0075.

Lamb, L. (2011). 'Voluntary participation in community economic development in Canada: An empirical analysis'. *Canadian Journal of Nonprofit and Social Economy Research* 2(1): 75–96. DOI: 10.22230/cjnser.2011v2n1a61.

Lanctôt, N., Duran, M., & Corbière, M. (2012). 'The quality of work life of people with severe mental disorders working in social enterprises: A qualitative study'. *Quality of Life Research* 21: 1415–1423. DOI: 10.1007/s11136-011-0057-7.

Laville, J., & Nyssens, M. (2001) 'The social enterprise. Towards a theoretical socio-economic approach'. In: Borzaga, C. & Defourny, J. (eds) *The emergence of social enterprise*, pp. 312–332. Routledge: London.

Lysaght, R., Roy, M.J., Rendall, J.S., et al. (2018). 'Unpacking the foundational dimensions of work integration social enterprise: The development of an assessment tool'. *Social Enterprise Journal* 14(1): 60–70. DOI: 10.1108/SEJ-11-2017-0061

Mandiberg, J.M. (2012). 'The failure of social inclusion: An alternative approach through community development'. *Psychiatric Services* 63: 458–460. DOI: 10.1176/appi.ps.201100367.

Mandiberg, J.M., & Warner, R. (2012). 'Business development and marketing within communities of social service clients'. *Journal of Business Research* 65(12): 1736–1742. DOI: 10.1016/j.jbusres.2012.02.015.

Marrone, J., & Swarbrick, M.A. (2020). 'Long-term unemployment: A social determinant underaddressed within community behavioral health programs psychiatric services'. *Psychiatric Services*. DOI: 10.1176/appi.ps.201900522.

McGrew, J.H., Johannesen, J.K., Griss, M.E., Born, D.L., & Katuin, C.H. (2007). 'Performance-based funding of supported employment for persons with severe mental illness: Vocational rehabilitation and employment staff perspectives'. *Journal of Behavioral Health Services Research* 34: 1–16. DOI: 10.1007/s11414-006-9045-z.

Mendell, M., & Neamtan, N. (2010). 'The social economy in Quebec: Towards a new political economy'. In: Mook, L., Quarter, J., & Ryan, S. (eds) *Researching the social economy*, pp. 63–83. University of Toronto Press: Toronto.

Mental Health Commission of Canada. (2013). *The aspiring workforce: Employment and Income for people with serious mental illness*. Available from www.mentalhealthcommission.ca/sites/default/files/2016-06/Workplace_MHCC_Aspiring_Workforce_Report_ENG_0.pdf (Accessed April 8, 2020).

Milton, A., Parsons, N., Morant, N., Gilbert, E., Johnson, S., Fisher, A., Singh, S., Cunliffe, D., & Marwaha, S. (2015). 'The clinical profile of employees with mental health problems working in social firms in the UK'. *Journal of Mental Health* 24(4): 242–248. DOI: 10.3109/09638237.2015.1057324.

National Alliance on Mental Illness (NAMI). (2014). *Road to recovery: Employment and mental illness*. NAMI: Arlington, VA.

Nelson, G., Lord, J., & Ochocka, J. (2001). *Shifting the paradigm in community mental health: Towards empowerment and community*. University of Toronto Press: Toronto.

O'Shaughnessy, M., & O'Hara, P. (2016). 'Social enterprise in Ireland—why work integration social enterprises (WISEs) dominate the discourse'. *Nonprofit Policy Forum* 7(4): 461–485. DOI: 10.1515/npf-2016-0015.

Pache, A.C., & Santos Insead, F. (2013). 'Inside the hybrid organization: Selective coupling as a response to competing institutional logics'. *Academy of Management Journal* 56: 972–1001.

Roy, M.J., Baker, R., & Kerr, S. (2016). 'Conceptualising the public health role of actors operating outside of formal health systems: The case of social enterprise'. *Social Science & Medicine* 172: 144–152. DOI: 10.1016/j.socscimed.2016.11.009.

Roy, M.J., Donaldson, C., Baker, R., & Kerr, S. (2014). 'The potential of social enterprise to enhance health and well-being: A model and

systematic review'. *Social Science & Medicine* 123: 182–193. DOI: 10.1016/j.
socscimed.2014.07.031.

SAMHSA. (2009). *Supported employment: Building your program.* Substance
Abuse and Mental Health Services Administration DHHS pub no SMA-08–
4364. SAMHSA: Rockville, MD.

Smith, W.K., Gonin, M., & Besharov, M.L. (2013). 'Managing social-business
tensions: A review and research agenda for social enterprise'. *Business Ethics
Quarterly* 25: 407–442. DOI: 10.5840/beq2C1323327.

Spear, R., & Bidet, E. (2005). 'Social enterprise for work integration in 12 European countries: A descriptive analysis'. *Annales de L'économie Publique, Sociale
et Coopérative* 76(2): 195–231. DOI: 10.1111/j.1370-4788.2005.00276.x.

Svanberg, J., Gumley, A., & Wilson, A. (2010). 'How do social firms contribute
to recovery from mental illness'. *Clinical Psychology and Psychotherapy* 17:
482–496. DOI: 10.1002/cpp.681.

Trainor, J., & Tremblay, J. (1992). 'Consumer/survivor businesses in Ontario:
Challenging the rehabilitation model'. *Canadian Journal of Community Mental Health* 11(2): 65–71. DOI: 10.7870/cjcmh-1992-0013.

Vidal, I. (2005). 'Social enterprise and social inclusion: Social enterprises in the
sphere of work integration'. *International Journal of Public Administration*
28(9–10): 807–825. DOI: 10.1081/PAD-200067347.

Warner, R., & Mandiberg, J. (2006). 'An update on affirmative businesses or social
firms for people with mental illness'. *Psychiatric Services* 57(10): 1488–1492.

Williams, A., Fossey, E., & Harvey, C. (2010). 'Sustaining employment in a
social firm: Use of the work environment impact scale v2.0 to explore views of
employees with psychiatric disabilities'. *British Journal of Occupational Therapy* 73(11): 531–539. DOI: 10.4276/030802210X12892992239.

9 'They See People in Need and Want to Help'

Social Enterprise and Wellbeing in Rural Communities

Sarah-Anne Munoz

Introduction

Almost half the world's population live in rural areas (World Bank, 2017) that share characteristics such as lower population densities, longer drive times to service centres, and economies that are more reliant on agriculture and land-based activities. However, it has long been recognised in the rural studies literature (drawing on sociological perspectives) that there is not one rural, but many (Halfacree, 2006), with different experiences of rural living that are influenced by wider socio-economic contexts, cultural norms, and governance structures (Woods, 2009). This chapter considers the experience of rural areas within the Global North by positioning evidence about social enterprise in rural Scotland, within wider rural social entrepreneurship and wellbeing literature.

Although the proportion of social entrepreneurship research that explicitly considers the rural context is relatively small (Farmer, Hill and Munoz, 2012; van Twuijver et. al., 2020), it has been shown that a variety of types of social enterprise exist within rural areas (Berkes and Davidson-Hunt, 2007; Senyard et. al., 2007). Some studies have considered the barriers and challenges faced by social entrepreneurs operating in rural areas; such as dispersed settlement patterns (Farmer, Steinerowski and Jack, 2008); particularly high and rising proportions of elderly, and very elderly (Munoz et. al., 2011); and small settlement size (Munoz and Steinerowski, 2012).

Researchers have, however, also highlighted the opportunities for social entrepreneurship in rural areas, such as dense social networks (Anderson and Jack, 2002) and high levels of social orientation, sense of place, and sense of community (Granovetter, 2005; Williams, 2007). There is a recognition within the literature that rural social enterprise both draws on and has the potential to enhance rural community social capital (Lang and Fink, 2016) and, by extension, individual and

DOI: 10.4324/9781003125976-9

community wellbeing. Van Twuijver et. al. (2020) in their systematic review of rural social enterprise literature shows that such organisations meet individual and community needs that would otherwise remain unmet by the public or the private sector—and that they do this partly by fostering 'strong local involvement.' Ritchter (2019) also demonstrates that rural social enterprises act as 'intermediaries'—strongly, locally embedded organisations that draw in different types of capital for the benefit of the rural regions within which they are based. The outcome of successful rural social entrepreneurship is summarised by Steiner and Teasdale (2019) as 'locally responsive services that fit the rural context.'

This chapter explores further these issues with reference to a case study social enterprise in rural Scotland as well as reflection on the author's wider experiences as rural health researcher, health geographer, and rural social enterprise scholar. It proposes that social enterprise, and processes of social entrepreneurship, do generate wellbeing in rural communities and for rural residents. The chapter demonstrates, through a case study example, some of the ways in which rural social enterprises can be conceptualised as spaces of wellbeing. In summary, the chapter argues for greater awareness of how social entrepreneurship in rural areas is bound up with what can be considered to be the everyday, the ordinary, and the unexceptional as well as with the performance of rural identity. It is argued that by understanding more about these processes and mechanisms, we can deepen our insight into the relationships between social enterprise and wellbeing in rural areas.

Rural Social Entrepreneurship as Everyday Life

As a rural health geographer based in the north of Scotland, I have had the opportunity to observe, work with, and try to make sense of the myriad of forms of social entrepreneurship that take place within rural communities. I've seen social innovation happen within rural community organisations, social businesses, and statutory services providers. I've seen it be driven forward by nurses, doctors, retired volunteers, single mothers, small business owners, and many others besides. I've seen rural social entrepreneurship attempt to tackle market failures and a perceived lack of public service provision in diverse sectors from elderly care and home care to the provision of affordable housing, employment for young offenders, community transport, and the reduction of social isolation. I've been involved in work that has tried to capture the processes of social entrepreneurship and social enterprise creation in rural communities (Farmer, Hill and Munoz, 2012). Some of the work that I have carried out within rural Scotland has suggested that there may be common processes to social enterprise development within rural areas, such as legitimacy and needs recognition (similar to those seen elsewhere in the social entrepreneurship literature) that are played out in specific rural ways (Munoz and Steinerowski, 2012):

> the rural community social entrepreneur must be able to promote the concept of service co-production and delivery . . . to audiences ranging from community members to the public sector. They must have the capacity to communicate with different stakeholders and take on a role in negotiating and building coalitions between the community and the public sector.
>
> (Munoz and Steinerowski, 2012, p. 71)

Looking back over the last 13 years of conducting research with rural communities, I see common threads running across several of the studies in which I have participated. One of the clearest themes (and most memorable in terms of my own experiences of being involved in data collection and analysis) is that successful rural social enterprises emerge and develop, at least partly, due to the determined hard work of individuals or small groups of rural residents who see a 'problem' or 'issue' within their own community and set out to address it. Depending on the individual context, sometimes it takes only one doggedly determined person to make a rural social enterprise viable, sometimes a group, and sometimes virtually a whole community. But without this 'catalyst,' the social enterprise does not take off:

> key citizens who were important in relaying information through informal community networks were identified. If these were not identified or failed to engage . . . then the process of social enterprise creation failed to gain legitimacy . . . key citizens were often also important in later stages, e.g. in facilitating community action and initiating/running a community social enterprise. When community members did not 'connect' with the Project Manager at this stage, it hampered or broke down the social enterprise development process.
>
> (Munoz, Steiner and Farmer, 2015, p. 485)

The ways in which rural social entrepreneurs have spoken to me, about the process of innovation or enterprise creation, most often centred around their experiences and knowledge of the rural community in which they live and work, rather than of business strategy. Their stories of social entrepreneurship are ones about their intuitive recognition that some variety of *doing things differently* (albeit a way that includes the trading of goods or services) may fix a problem or at least make some people's lives better within their community. This reflects what van Twuijver et. al. (2020) found in their systematic review when they wrote that 'rural social enterprises are characterised by strong local involvement.'

Most people that I have spoken with in Scotland's rural communities would not describe this type of activity as social entrepreneurship; they would not describe or see themselves as social entrepreneurs or their organisations as social enterprises. In formal interviews and during periods of participant observation, they have talked rather about their *rural way* of doing things. This is often described by them as a 'can do' attitude that they view as centuries old; a determination to keep their communities 'alive' and an instinctual, visceral response to doing so, that they 'felt in their bones':

> Most often, people talked about their own personal satisfaction that emerged from taking part in the service co-production development. They talked about it allowing them to help their community but also to contribute to something that they thought would help preserve their community and rural way of life.
>
> (Munoz, 2013, p. 281)

Our rural communities contain a lot of people who, either through a recent migration choice or a long history of their family living in the area, *want* to be there; they want to ensure that their elderly people, their young people, their single parents, their underemployed youth, and so on are cared for and remain living within the geographical boundaries of their community for as long as possible. To do so is to ensure that their community survives, and they instinctively know this. The words that people use to describe rural social entrepreneurship and social enterprise organisations regularly position both of these as rural community survival strategy:

> 'jobs, work [. . .] it's a major influence on people, families, remaining in the community [. . .] this initiative must address this [. . .] there's not a choice, or we'll [the village] die' (Community Interview 2).
>
> (Munoz, 2013, p. 282)

This suggests that rural social entrepreneurship research needs to consider this activity that could be characterised as quieter, smaller, and less vocal, but no less impactful than other forms of social entrepreneurship. This type of activity could be conceptualised as an intrinsic part of rural living, and, therefore, research around it would benefit from greater interaction with the methodologies and theories of rural sociology. I suggest this partly because I have found that, when working with rural community members, the way that they describe themselves and their organisations is through a rural, place-based, community-focused narrative. They explain their socially entrepreneurial activities as a *way of life*.

Is rural social entrepreneurship, therefore, one facet of a skill set for rural living that includes things such as how to talk to your neighbour;

how to assess community assets; how to liaise with the local public sector; and how to cope with doing at least two different jobs at the same time? There is scope for social entrepreneurship research to look more closely at this kind of rural social entrepreneur and entrepreneurship. I would welcome more research into this type of 'quiet' social entrepreneurship that I have observed taking place within rural communities, driven by those living there, who tend to have big hearts, a variety of skills, and a determination to help their communities thrive. It seems impossible to disentangle this form of social entrepreneurship from the wellbeing of rural communities and the individuals who live within them.

The Rural Social Enterprise

Previous research has shown that in rural areas, just as in urban localities, different types of social enterprises operate. I suggest that social enterprise in rural areas has multiple forms, income streams, and objectives out of *necessity*. In this way, rural social enterprise reflects the nature of rural citizens who wear multiple hats and do multiple jobs (paid and unpaid) in order to sustain themselves, their families, their local business and services, and their very communities.

Social enterprise has been offered as a new model of service provision that can address market failure or public sector cutbacks (Farmer, Hill and Munoz, 2012). However, little research has addressed the question of if (and, if so, then how) individual social enterprises can become sustainable in rural environments that cannot sustain commercial business and are too expensive for public sector budgets. It is sometimes suggested that social enterprises can operate in areas of market failure, such as rural areas because they do not need to make a profit—but neither does the public sector—and it too is struggling to provide services in rural areas, certainly in ways that meet citizen expectations. The underlying ethos of most rural social enterprises—to ensure rural community sustainability—means that they are also driven to treat staff well and to provide living wages and a high standard of working conditions; thus, keeping their costs fairly high. Rural social enterprises may not distribute profit to shareholders, but they are engaged in monetary exchange for goods or services. An example is the provision of home care.

I worked closely with one dispersed rural community on the issue of home care provision over the course of around 18 months—when I first met with community members to discuss this issue, they described the provision of home care services locally as 'inefficient and dysfunctional.' The public sector model of employing home carers was proving too expensive; therefore, the provision of home care was transferred to a private company. This brought a change to zero hours contracts, reduced holiday and sick pay, and reduced pension provision for home care staff. It brought a slightly more sustainable business model, but the company withdrew after a time due to insufficient profit generated. A group of community residents, therefore, sought to take over the provision of home care in their local area through the development and running of a social enterprise. They envisaged that this would allow them to provide home care in a more locally 'acceptable' way. They wished to run a home care service that paid a living wage and provided stable working hours for staff, alongside the provision of a reliable, high standard of care in terms of both personal care and additional help such as cleaning, gardening, or basic DIY tasks. But this business did not take off. The social enterprise encountered exactly the same problems as the public sector and the private sector providers had done within this geographical area (Munoz, 2013). For rural communities to 'take over' public sector provision as a social enterprise without any other fundamental shift in *how* services are delivered, or needs are met, is problematic.

Often, when working with social enterprises in rural areas, the staff members have talked to me about the need to constantly combine income streams—to have multiple income streams in order to survive. This means trading and also effectively utilising local volunteer labour, public sector contracts, and charitable funding. Mixing these income streams is seen as just how things are done within rural areas because income from trade is never going to be enough to keep a business sustainable:

> we wouldn't be here if it wasn't for the volunteers . . . and, good on them, you know . . . they give up their time to help; I think they want to give something back to the community. Maybe they've worked all their lives and now want to give something back. They see people in need and want to help. We're able to pay [employ] a few people, but we wouldn't be here without the volunteers.
>
> (Community interviewee. Excerpt from unpublished fieldwork diary of Munoz, 2019)

I argue that this reflects what van Twuijver et. al. (2020) summarise in their systematic review of the rural social enterprise literature when they say that 'rural social enterprises are characterised by . . . an ability to combine different goals and resources.' It suggests that social entrepreneurship in rural areas may be learnt informally as a rural community coping strategy. It begs the question that, if people already behave in these ways, why is social entrepreneurship, as a part of rural coping, not more widely recognised as such and taught as such within different levels of education and continuous professional development? This straddling of different income streams in order to sustain a social enterprise was also a key theme within work that I was involved in on modelling the process of rural social enterprise creation. Within this work, it was found that the successful rural social entrepreneur needed to be:

> Competent in both the civic discourse of the community (with aware-ness of local needs, cultures and social value) and the public discourse of the state (with an awareness of co-production, empowerment, pro-curement and budgeting). They must be competent and confident in shifting between the two and in reconciling their sometimes disparate focuses. Legitimacy with the public sector is particularly important in small, often dispersed rural communities where reliance on public sector grant funding and trading agreements is high.
>
> (Munoz, Steiner and Farmer, 2015, p. 490)

To this, I would now add (following further time spent living and researching within rural communities) a need to be competent and con-fident in the recruitment and effective integration of volunteers into the running of a rural social enterprise. In previous collaborative work, I sug-gested that 'a community development approach should be considered alongside more traditional forms of entrepreneurial support' within rural areas (Munoz, Steiner and Farmer, 2015). The call for this still holds true, and further research is needed into how to effectively make this happen.

Over the last decade, my research has focused on some of the key chal-lenges affecting rural areas within the Global North, such as the aging population, public sector austerity, and economic change. The power of social enterprise to bring impact in otherwise underserved rural areas is great. Some of the biggest challenges in our rural areas, however, cannot be solved solely by turning public sector service provision into a social enterprise—we need wider ranging social innovation than this. I have seen communities and individual social entrepreneurs attempt to take on service provision by simply trying to supplant traditional public sector services models into community ownership—when rural social enter-prises attempt to deliver services in the same way as the public sector, this often proves to be either extremely challenging or impossible. In my opinion, key change (and key success) comes when rural social entrepre-neurs do things differently and challenge the very nature and set up of ser-vice delivery within rural areas. Social enterprise research needs to engage with how social entrepreneurship will tackle the big challenges of rural areas over the coming decades. Including, perhaps, how the Global North can learn from the Global South, where things are already being done differently in rural areas out of necessity, determination, and innovation.

Rural Social Enterprise as a Space of Wellbeing

Rural social enterprises can be conceptualised as an integral part of eve-ryday rural life and the ways in which rural communities function. When rural social entrepreneurs have talked to me about their activities, through a discourse that situates their endeavour as central to the sustainability of their communities, they are drawing on a deep-seated understanding that organisations which span both social need and commercial opportunity are necessary in rural contexts to (a) sustain the rural economy and (b) sustain the very social and cultural fabric of rural communities. Thus, rural social enterprise contributes to multiple levels of individual and community wellbeing. I feel that it is possible to see the contribution of this organisational form to the four elements of the Spaces of Wellbeing Theory (Fleuret and Atkinson, 2007) that is outlined earlier in this book: capability, security, integration, and therapy.

This chapter now turns to consider an example of the ways in which rural social enterprises function as spaces of wellbeing through a case study from rural Scotland. The social enterprise in question runs a community transport service within the Scottish Highlands, primarily focused on servicing one small rural town and its surrounding hinterland. This social enterprise allowed me to carry out a period of ethnographic observation and interviewing over a four-month time span in 2019. This research was given ethical approval by the research ethics committee of the university that I work for. The study employed the same methodology as the 'social enterprises as spaces of wellbeing' studies by Farmer et al. described in Chapter 2 of this book. Thus, I started with a period of ethnographic observation and moved on to in-depth interviews with staff, volunteers, and service users that were both audio-recorded and tracked by GPS. After geo-coding the qualitative data collected, and subjecting it to a thematic analysis, the main themes were fed back to participants within focus groups that allowed for participant validation of the themes generated. As described elsewhere in this book, geo-coding the qualitative data allowed me to reflect on both the 'shape' and the 'nature' of wellbeing generation associated with this rural social enterprise. In summary, this Scottish case study found that various aspects of wellbeing were generated for staff, volunteers, and service users.

It seemed pertinent to explore the contribution of a social enterprise focused on transport in a rural area. In rural communities, public transport can be particularly poor, leaving many vulnerable people isolated and unable to reach locations in which their wellbeing may be enhanced such as lunch clubs, shops, libraries, and leisure centres. However, the case study social enterprise does not just replicate traditional public transport provision. Rather it provides a personalised, tailored service that goes way beyond that:

> So, I've got my sheet here with all the names of the customers that I'm going to pick up . . . and it [the software] churns out these timings of . . . these are the timings it thinks we should have, the minutes it thinks we should take [to collect a service user] and then move

on to the next one . . . and I'm just not going to, there's no way I'm
going to do that. I'm going to go right up to the door of the house,
I'm going to get out and probably have to ring the doorbell and go
inside and help them with their bags . . . and half the time, help them
switch the telly off and the lights off. And I'll make sure they are on
the bus, sitted down, with their belt on . . . and only then are we
going to the next place . . . otherwise what's the point? I'm not a taxi,
I'm not your [names private bus service], if I don't care about these
people, then what is the point?

[staff member A]

This person-centred approach was evident throughout the organisation—
when speaking with employees and volunteers alike, they were very
clear that they are doing what they do in order to help people within
their community. I was told, and overheard, many stories about how the
transport provided by the social enterprise was a 'lifeline' particularly for
older residents:

I couldn't get out if it wasn't for the minibus . . . because it comes
right down to my house, you see, into the cul-de-sac. The public bus
only stops up there on the main road . . . it's like, what, 18 feet from
my house? But it's up a slope, and in the winter, in the ice and if I had
to carry shopping, I wouldn't make it

[service user F]

When staff members talked about the organisation, they not only discussed the benefits that they felt were clearly evident to the service users
but also expressed their own feelings of pride, comfort, and self-worth
that were generated by working for an organisation that cared about its
community and its staff:

Here [working for this social enterprise], I can be more than a bus
driver, much more than just a bus driver. It gives me the chance to
care for folk.

[staff member A]

It matters to work for a social enterprise, definitely, you know . . . I
had my own troubles, it was one reason I left my last position . . . I
had stress and anxiety and just that feeling that you're just not valued, as a person . . . and it's just not like that here.

[staff member B]

Thus, both staff and volunteers talked about valuing working for an
organisation that treated its employees and volunteers well. However,
they also spoke about the value of the organisation having a community

conscience—being a transport service that is quietly, diplomatically, and in a person-centred manner, negotiating the needs of rural citizens as well as the challenges of working within a rural community:

> We have to be careful, we have to do it carefully you know. We are very aware that there are other people trying to make a living here. We're not competing with the taxi company. People are employed as bus drivers . . . we're not trying to take away the public bus service. We're trying to provide a service for those people who don't have anything else. The taxi man can focus on the tourists, he can focus on young folk going home from the pub. The public bus service is fine for people who can get to the bus stop, for who that suits . . . we're going to be there for the people who need a bit extra.
>
> [staff member C]

Its success and, therefore, its generation of wellbeing comes from the particular way in which the organisation, through its staff, board, and volunteers, combines their social mission with business (and charitable sector) practices to meet rural citizen need without competing against other rural small businesses. By geo-coding the qualitative data, it was possible to identify *where* participants talked to me about the four elements of wellbeing within the Spaces of Wellbeing Theory (see Figure 9.1).

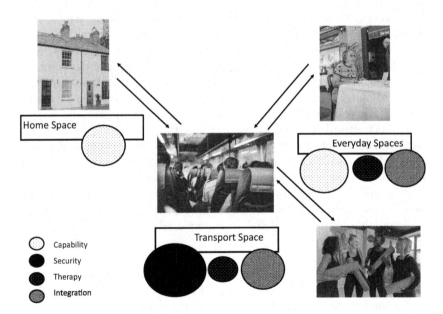

Figure 9.1 Types of wellbeing facilitated by a rural community transport social enterprise

Unsurprisingly, many of these conversations happened whilst on the bus—or consisted of talking about being on the bus. These elements of the qualitative data set were geo-coded to 'community transport.' What was more surprising was that the strongest theme (in terms of frequency among the coding) was 'security' (this will be explored in more detail shortly). The second strongest theme was around 'integration' which is a much more intuitive finding—that staff, volunteers, and, in particular, service users talked about the bus enabling them to stay part of local, social networks, to interact with other people, and to the generation of feelings of self-worth through conversations with others:

> Aye, it's fine of a morning, coming on here because you a'ways ken (know) you'll see the same folk (people) . . . we like to sit in the same seats you see [chuckles]. That's my seat . . . and we'll have a good gossip and it doesn't matter if you shout across the bus 'cause we're the only folks (people) in it, and we like to have a natter (conversation).
> [service user D]

Thus, the 'integration' aspect of wellbeing was generated for service users by not only the physical act of the bus transporting them to local activities or services but also through the social interaction that travelling on the minibus allowed with their peers. Service users also described the importance to them of interacting with the minibus driver in terms of social contact.

However, as mentioned earlier, the aspect of wellbeing which was coded to the most within the 'community transport' space (the bus) was 'security.' This was due to the number of conversations, stories, and anecdotes that involved service users speaking about how the community transport social enterprise shielded them from risk. It was spoken about as 'safe' but also 'safer' than regular public transport or a taxi service. The way in which the transport service is set up, and the way in which its staff and volunteers behave, allows the older people to negotiate what can be classified as their perceived 'social and environmental risks.' One risk that was frequently discussed was that of adverse weather—particularly cold, snow, ice, and rain that service users associated with anxiety and risk of falling and injury. There were many other ways that people talked about the service offering 'security' by generating feelings of being able to go out 'safely,' an example relates to the behaviour of the bus driver:

> It's usually always him [the driver] but if it's not him it's another one [driver] that I know. They all know me. They know where to come for me. They make sure I pull my door shut . . . he's a wee star though, he makes sure I get on the bus, in my seat with my

belt on . . . there's no having to fish my pass out quick . . . there's no bus moving off before I've even sat down. I hate that, a normal service they just pull right on off, I'm scared I'll break something [taps her hip].

[service user C]

Oh, I've used it for a long time, yes . . . they take me right to the door of [the shop] and I know that [the driver] will always put my bags in for me [to the bus] and then into the house. Normal bus driver wouldn't do that, you know.

[service user B]

Feelings of safety were also generated by the fact that the service users had got to know the other people on the bus—they contrasted this with the experience of getting on public transport on which they perceived that there may be numerous strangers and people who may behave erratically. Thus, the community transport social enterprise emerges as a space in which 'safety' wellbeing is realised due to the way in which it goes about providing its service.

Although the instances were fewer in number, I did code some of my ethnographic notes and conversational data collected whilst on the bus (or discussing the experience of being on the bus) to the 'therapy' aspect of wellbeing. I found this interesting because before I started the research, I thought that I may not find any instances of therapeutic experience associated with a community transport social enterprise. Spaces of Wellbeing Theory conceptualises the therapeutic aspect of wellbeing as resources that help with physical, mental, and emotional healing. The text coded to the 'therapy' aspect related mostly to the mental and emotional dimensions of this—particularly in relation to the bus service acting as a space in which people found the resources necessary to combat isolation, loneliness, and even feelings of depression and anxiety:

I dinnae (don't) want to be stuck in the house. Just sat there, with the telly (television) for company . . . it's no good. I slip into a bad place when I don't get out of the house.

[Service User D]

This gets me out of the house . . . I just wouldn't get to these activities otherwise. It's terrible when you're getting older, and you're used to being out and about and then suddenly you can't anymore. It's a real feeling of being cut off . . . because the bus comes to the end of my lane, I can get on it. It stops me staring at the four walls. It's my little bit of chat, on here.

[Service User G]

During the fieldwork, I spent time sitting on the bus and speaking with the employed and volunteer drivers as well as with several service users who came on and off the bus at various points. However, I also journeyed with six service users from the point of their home to the point of their destination. Thus, in journeying *with* people, I also generated data in their own homes and conversations with them about their home lives. It was possible to geo-code these data to the 'home' location. By far the strongest theme that emerged in, and about, the home space was that of 'capability' wellbeing. In general terms, the 'capability' aspect of wellbeing can be conceptualised as abilities and skills that enable individuals to lead a flourishing and satisfying life. The text that was coded to 'capability' within the home space, overwhelmingly related to service users' discussions of how their interactions with the transport social enterprise had the positive effect of keeping them physically and mentally active and, therefore, living well and independently within their own homes:

> I go every week to the exercise class [on the mini bus] . . . it helps with balance and keeping us supple and moving about. And it makes your brain work.
>
> [Service User F]

> As long as the bus still comes to get me, I'll be able to go and get my messages.[1] It keeps me going, a little routine, and I'm happy in my own house. No one wants to leave their own house. I can still get my messages and cook for myself.
>
> [Service User G]

This theme relates closely to a 'capability' wellbeing theme that was geo-coded to the everyday and leisure spaces that the community transport social enterprise takes people to. As part of my fieldwork, I was kindly invited to come in and observe some of these activities and talk to the people taking part. Inevitably, I sometimes took part in the activities informally as well (my favourite being afternoon tea with an old-time song sing along). Talking with service users, and observing what happened in these activities, demonstrated that they too contributed to keeping people mentally and physically active (and well). In these everyday and leisure spaces, there was also, perhaps unsurprisingly, many discussions and discourses of 'integration' wellbeing as people who used the transport service spent social time with each other and with other members of the community who had used other transport methods to get to the leisure spaces. 'Therapy' wellbeing emerged as a lesser theme in these spaces too, particularly through people's discussions of the informal peer support that they experienced:

> You know what happened to me, don't you? I was in an accident, it was a really bad time. . . [details removed by researcher] . . . I was really unwell but these guys, they helped me get through it.
>
> [Service User H]

In geo-coding the qualitative data, it was possible to see that service users talked about the wellbeing enabling effect of the social enterprise in, not surprisingly, the bus (where they talked with friends and the driver and about how the bus enabled them to get to social activities and everyday spaces such as the pharmacy and the supermarket). It also demonstrated that service users value the enabling effect of the bus service to leave their own homes and keep mentally and physically active. The 'capability' generated by interacting with the social enterprise was talked about in the home space in terms of independent living, that is, supporting them to age well. Thus, the transport space itself (the bus) brought 'security,' 'therapy,' and 'integration.' The everyday and leisure activities with which the transport service connected service users generated 'capability,' 'therapy,' and 'integration' within these spaces and their own homes. We have also seen that wellbeing was generated for staff and volunteers who talked about finding fulfilment from working for an organisation that cares and is making a difference in their rural community. Volunteers' wellbeing, in particular, was seen to be generated from being mentally and physically active in ways that they find rewarding.

In summary, I would characterise the success of this social enterprise (that has been operating for around 20 years) to the specific ways in which its staff, and volunteers, understand how to operate within a rural community with a place-based social and cultural awareness that means they do not, in the words of one interviewee, 'ruffle any feathers.' The case study social enterprise manages to do this in a way that meets the needs of older citizens; brings multiple wellbeing benefits; provides employment conditions and volunteering opportunities that suit rural lives and generate individual self-esteem alongside civic pride; and contributes to rural identity as resilient and self-sufficient. The fieldwork carried out at this social enterprise produced qualitative data that were overwhelmingly positive, in that it demonstrated the benefits to all those who came into contact with the social enterprise. The fact that I did not encounter some of the more negative tensions seen by Kelly et al. in their 2019 study may reflect the relative maturity of the organisation and that it had already 'weathered' some of the issues around sustainability and volunteer fatigue that have been observed elsewhere (Yarker, Heley and Jones, 2020; Colibaba, Skinner and Furgal, 2019).

Overall, I feel that it is through sensitively balancing the elements seen within the case study, that rural social enterprises generate economic activity that enables rural people to live in the villages and dispersed settlements that they want to, whilst at the same time providing the services that they, their neighbours, their families, and their friends need. In this way, the existence of rural social enterprise and social entrepreneurship is intimately connected to deep-seated notions and feelings of wellbeing that are bound up with rural identity—feelings of safety and security generated through activities that are seen as contributing to the continuation of rural place and rural way of life. I would characterise this as the wellbeing of 'through this, we will survive' alongside 'I have done good for those I care about.' Thus, rural social enterprises are providing health, care, and wellbeing services to rural communities, but they are also facilitating wellbeing indirectly, through their activities, for rural individuals and communities.

Conclusions

The rural context remains underrepresented in social entrepreneurship literature, despite some key studies that have sought to engage with understanding the drivers for, and barriers to, social enterprise in rural areas. As a health geographer, and rural scholar, I have argued in this chapter for a greater consideration of the ways in which place-based ruralities interact with social entrepreneurship. My own research in this area has suggested certain key themes that may be progressed in future work. There is the potential to look at rural social entrepreneurship as a part of the sociology of rural life; and, considering the key challenges for rural areas over the coming decades, the potential role for social entrepreneurship in devising and mobilising social innovations to tackle these. Rural social entrepreneurship does many of the things that we see social enterprise do in other, urban, contexts (such as build social capital), but it is also intimately connected to the creation and maintenance of rural space, place, community, and identity.

Through consideration of one rural Scottish case study, this chapter has demonstrated some of the ways in which rural social enterprises generate wellbeing for their service users, volunteers, paid staff, and wider communities. Through the geo-coding of qualitative field notes and interview transcripts, it was possible to see that rural social enterprises generate different kinds of wellbeing not only within their spaces of service provision (in our example, a transport service with buses) but within the homes and other everyday public spaces to which they are connected. Our example showed the ways in which one rural social enterprise generated experiences of 'security,' 'therapy,' and 'integration' within its service space and how it generated, in particular, the 'capability' aspect of wellbeing within home and everyday public spaces. This case study has not only demonstrated how the enterprise acts as a space of wellbeing but how it reflects wider themes in rural social entrepreneurship literature such as local embeddedness (Richter, 2019), responsiveness to rural context (Steiner and Teasdale, 2019), and the balancing of diverse goals and resources (van Twuijver et. al., 2020).

There is the potential, therefore, for a rural social entrepreneurship research agenda that pushes forward spatial thinking in order to understand the role of these organisations in the creation of rural place and identity. This could be achieved through a greater engagement by social enterprise scholars with spatial and sociological theory on the construction of space and place. Ultimately, I am arguing for rural social entrepreneurship research that engages with how rural communities can be sustained. This will involve greater consideration of the rural resident as social entrepreneur or social innovator as they, through sometimes everyday practice, reshape the social and economic processes at work within their communities (a type of rural bricolage that draws on place-based cultural, social, and economic resources). This calls for research into the very nature of rural communities—starting with the realities of rural communities as experienced by those who live within them, not with their deficiencies or problems as perceived from an urbane outside.

Acknowledgements

Many thanks to the rural residents who so kindly gave up their time to engage with me during my fieldwork in 2019. The work could not have happened without the support of the University of the Highlands and Islands, my colleagues within the Division of Rural Health and Wellbeing, and the Highlands and Islands Enterprise School of Health grant funding.

Note

1 "Messages" is a colloquialism for grocery shopping.

References

Anderson, A., Jack, S., (2002) 'The articulation of social capital in entrepreneurial networks: A glue or a lubricant?' *Entrepreneurship and Regional Development*, 14, pp. 193–210.
Berkes, F., Davidson-Hunt, I. J., (2007) 'Communities and social enterprises in the age of globalisation', *Journal of Enterprising Communities: People and Places in the Global Economy*, 1 (3), pp. 209–221.

Colibaba, A., Skinner, M. W., Furgal, C., (2019) 'The challenges and opportunities of sustaining volunteer-based rural libraries', *Public Library Quarterly*, 38 (4), pp. 410–427.

Farmer, J., Hill, C., Munoz, S., (2012) *Community Co-Production: Social Enterprise in Remote and Rural Areas* (Boston: Edward Elgar).

Farmer, J., Steinerowski, A., Jack, S., (2008) 'Starting social enterprises in remote and rural Scotland: best or worst of circumstances?' *The International Journal of Entrepreneurship and Small Business*, 6 (3), pp. 450–464.

Fleuret, S., Atkinson, S. (2007) 'Wellbeing, health and geography: A critical review and research agenda', *New Zealand Geographer*, 63 (2), pp. 106–118.

Granovetter, M., (2005) 'The impact of social structure on economic outcomes', *Journal of Economic Perspectives*, 19 (1), pp. 33–50.

Halfacree, K., (2006) 'Rural space: Constructing a three-fold architecture', in Cloke, P., Marsden, T., Mooney, P., *The Handbook of Rural Studies* (London: Sage).

Kelly, D., Steiner, A., Mazzei, M., Baker, R., (2019) 'Filling a void? The role of social enterprise in addressing social isolation and loneliness in rural communities', *Journal of Rural Studies*, 70, pp. 225–236.

Lang, R., Fink, M., (2016) 'Social entrepreneurs as change agents in regional development: the role of linking social capital', paper presented at the *RSA Annual Conference, Graz (Austria)*, available online: www.regionalstudies.org/uploads/RSA_2016_Lang_Fink.pdf, accessed 03/08/2018.

Munoz, S., (2013) 'Co-producing care services in rural areas', *Journal of Integrated Care*, 21 (5), pp. 276–287.

Munoz, S., (2019) *Unpublished Fieldwork Diary*. Observation and interviews carried out with one social enterprise organisation in Highland Scotland between August and November 2019.

Munoz, S., Steiner, A., Farmer, J., (2015) 'Processes of community-led social enterprise development: learning from the rural context', *Community Development Journal*, 50 (3), pp. 478–493.

Munoz, S., Steinerowski, A., (2012) 'Socially entrepreneurial skills and capabilities in a rural community context', in Farmer, J., Hill, C., Munoz, S., *Community Co-Production: social enterprise in remote and rural areas* (Boston: Edward Elgar).

Munoz, S., Steinerowski, A., Farmer, J., Stephen, K., (2011) 'Social enterprise as a response to the needs of ageing rural populations', *Journal of Social Management*, 9 (2), pp. 23–44.

Richter, R., (2019) 'Rural social enterprises as embedded intermediaries: The innovative power of connecting rural communities with supra-regional networks', *Journal of Rural Studies*, 70, pp. 179–187.

Senyard, J., Pickernell, D., Clifton, N., Christie, M. (2007) 'Grant maintained or grant restrained? Rural social enterprise in Ceredigion, Wales', *Journal of Rural Enterprise and Management*, 3 (1), pp. 5–23.

Steiner, A., Teasdale, S., (2019) 'Unlocking the potential of rural social enterprise', *Journal of Rural Studies*, 70, pp. 144–154.

Van Twuijver, M., W., Olmedo, L., O'Shaughnessy, M., Hennessy, T., (2020) 'Rural social enterprises in Europe: A systematic literature review', *Local Economy*, 35 (2), pp. 121–142.

Williams, C., (2007) 'Socio-spatial variations in the nature of entrepreneurship', *Journal of Enterprising Communities*, 1 (1), pp. 27–37.

Woods, M., (2009) 'Rural geography: blurring boundaries and making connections', *Progress in Human Geography*, 33 (6), pp. 849–859.

World Bank (2017) available online: https://data.worldbank.org/indicator/SP.RUR.TOTL.ZS, accessed 03/08/18.

Yarker, S., Heley, J., Jones, L., (2020) 'Stewardship of the rural: Conceptualising the experiences of rural volunteering in later life', *Journal of Rural Studies*, 76, pp. 184–192.

Section 3

New Insights for Practice

10 How Do Social Enterprises Impact Upon Health and Wellbeing? Some Lessons From *CommonHealth*

Gillian Murray, Michael J. Roy, Rachel Baker, and Cam Donaldson

Introduction

Despite the existence of world-class health and social care provision in Scotland, health inequalities—the preventable and unfair differences in health status between social groups, populations, and individuals (Whitehead, 1992)—continue to widen and deepen. This challenge is by no means unique to Scotland but supports the premise that new thinking was required to address this longstanding issue from a different direction (Donaldson et al., 2011; Roy et al., 2013). This underpinned the geographical focus for a major five-year programme of research (2014–2019) undertaken to develop methods to evaluate the health and wellbeing impacts of social enterprises. Many of the factors that social enterprises aim to address are those that we know influence the health and wellbeing status of individuals and communities. These are otherwise known as the 'social determinants of health' (Wilkinson & Marmot, 2003): the conditions in which people are born, grow, live, work, and age, which are shaped by the distribution of money, power, and resources at global, national, and local levels. The project team was keen to establish whether social enterprises can be thought about (and thus studied as) a form of health and wellbeing 'intervention' through acting on these social determinants. The basic thinking was that even social enterprises that do not explicitly mention 'health' and/or 'wellbeing' in their mission statements or trade in health-related services with public funders, such as the National Health Service (NHS) (see e.g. Hall et al., 2015; Roy et al., 2013; Vickers et al., 2017), they are likely to have health and wellbeing impacts, irrespective of whether this is their primary intention. We use the term 'non-obvious' public health intervention in this context because social enterprises exist outside of what we normally think about as formal health systems such as the NHS—see Roy et al. (2017) in particular.

The programme of research 'Developing methods for evidencing social enterprise as a public health intervention,' which was quickly shortened to *CommonHealth*, was jointly funded by the UK's Medical Research

DOI: 10.4324/9781003125976-10

Council and the Economic and Social Research Council. It involved a partnership of five universities around Scotland: Glasgow Caledonian University, the University of Glasgow, Robert Gordon University, the University of the Highlands and Islands, and the University of Stirling. The Scottish social enterprise sector was involved in the research programme in a variety of ways. Thirty-seven social enterprises actively participated in the CommonHealth research projects, featuring as case studies or providing access to their staff, members of their board or other stakeholders, and/or beneficiaries (at times these roles overlapped) as interviewees. Advice on facilitating these relationships came from membership- and government-funded Scottish social enterprise support bodies such as SENScot, Social Firms Scotland, Social Enterprise Scotland. and CEiS.

The research programme drew in expertise from across a range of disciplines, including history, sociology, economics, geography, political science, and public health, and adopted a wide range of methodological approaches. The contexts in which the research was undertaken were also wide-ranging, not just geographically but in the variety of activities that the social enterprises were involved in: from women's self-reliant groups in inner-city communities to interventions focusing on addressing homelessness and from addressing the social exclusion of elderly people to working to address isolation in fragile rural communities. In this chapter, we outline the programme of research and provide a brief overview of the key findings of the CommonHealth projects. We will follow this with an outline of what the programme taught us about the effects that social enterprises have in relation to health and wellbeing and the implications for evaluation and measurement. We close the chapter with a brief discussion of where our research may be heading in future.

CommonHealth: An Overview

CommonHealth comprised eight distinct projects organised into three broad areas of research activity: conceptual, empirical, and evaluative in nature. There was also a transversal theme that ran throughout the project relating to knowledge exchange, with regular 'knowledge exchange forums' involving representatives from across the third and public sectors with an interest in the intersections between social enterprise, health, and wellbeing. In the last project—'Project 8'—we attempted to gather all of the findings and discussions together, highlight overarching themes and lessons, and lay the groundwork for synthesis across the programme post-project when all the projects had completed their research. Projects 1–7, the research projects relevant to this chapter, are outlined in turn.

Project 1: The 'History Project'

Project 1 set out to explore the modern history of social enterprise with a particular interest in the 'community business' movement, an important forerunner of social enterprise in Scotland. Forms of trading that prioritise social good have existed in many forms at a variety of often turbulent historical junctures (Roy, McHugh et al., 2015). The acceleration of deindustrialisation in Scotland from the late 1970s compounded economic and social challenges, providing a key impetus for the emergence of Scotland's community business movement (Murray, 2019). As well as charting the development of social enterprise in Scotland, the historical research also sought to consider the movement's relationship to the developments in thinking in public health that were happening in parallel.

This project was based on archival research, making use of regional and national archives and the Social Enterprise Collection (Scotland) held by the Glasgow Caledonian University Archive Centre. The Collection was created in 2011 when social enterprise pioneer John Pearce (see e.g. Pearce 1993, 2003) donated his personal archive of papers and literature to the Centre. The archival research also informed the development of an oral history project. Running in parallel to the archival research, 10 oral histories were recorded with community development workers and community business pioneers across Scotland. Thus, the project drew upon a rich range of documents and audio recordings for interpretive analysis.

The historical research found that the community development skills and values of community business pioneers were of great significance to the development of social enterprise in Scotland. Their legacy remains visible in the infrastructure of Scottish social enterprise today, where an asset lock on the redistribution of profits remains a central part of the Voluntary Code of Practice, to which a significant number of social enterprises in Scotland subscribe. However, the project found only scant evidence of community business pioneers working with public health practitioners in a formal capacity. Where their paths did overlap, it was through community health projects, often working at the 'radical edges' of public health that arose in response to the attempted suppression of the findings of the Black Report by the Thatcher Government in the early 1980s, which starkly revealed the extent to which such inequalities were socially determined (Townsend & Davidson, 1982). While the concerns of community business practitioners, and the skills and capacities they supported communities to develop, are highly comparable to those within community health projects, their learning remained in silos of knowledge, that is perhaps only now beginning to come together.

Since the 1970s, pluralism in health and welfare has frequently been associated with a reaction to the imposition of neoliberal policies from above and their effects on the structural composition of health systems. However, reflecting on the history of social enterprise in Scotland reveals how organisations in Scotland's developing social economy supported communities in comparable ways to community health projects. The acceptance of the discourse of socially determined health over the late 20th and early 21st century provides an example of the historical contingency in how we conceptualise 'health.' However, there has not been a comparable reconceptualisation of health actors who support the 'social determinants' arguments. Hence, the view that the contribution of civil society actors to health and wellbeing, from a systems perspective, has been limited to their role as organisations that have filled gaps caused by the rollback of state services. They have been characterised as service providers of last resort, rather than service innovators supporting a broad range of individual and community needs. Relating this historical insight to projects 2–7 on the *CommonHealth* programme, the resonance between the parallel development of the social economy and increasing acceptance of, and knowledge of, the social determinants of health opens up a new perspective on pluralism from below. It is this 'non-obvious' space that *CommonHealth* sought to research and articulate.

Project 2: The 'Contemporary' Project

Project 2 was focused on conceptual development, complementing Project 1 by studying contemporary social enterprise practice. The project had three aims to map and describe the activities of social enterprises; gather insight into how they report their social impact; and analyse the extent to which they considered their impact in health and wellbeing terms.

The project combined desk research with qualitative data collection to develop insight giving a 'macro' perspective on social enterprise in Scotland as well as producing detailed case studies. The desk-based research involved analysing social impact reports in the public domain that had utilised either of two popular forms of impact measurement method presently in use in Scotland: 'Social Return on Investment' and 'Social Accounting and Audit' (Arvidson et al., 2013; Pearce & Kay, 2008). Through analysing evaluative reports of the work of social enterprises in Scotland utilising a 'process coding' method, Macaulay et al. (2018b) describe both the self-reported impacts (measured or not) of the work of social enterprises and the mechanisms by which these are said to be derived. The method of coding allowed the identification of various processes and outcomes, which could be said to operate at the level of the individual, community, and/or the 'systems level.'

The case study phase, meanwhile, involved in-depth semi-structured interviews and a focus group with board members, staff, and beneficiaries from three social enterprises in different regions of Scotland.

Macaulay et al. (2018a) found that rather than social enterprise being a homogenous group of organisations with homogenous effects, different types of social enterprise, in different sectors, impact on dimensions of health in ways that are contextually and contingently dependent. They can engender a feeling of ownership and control, improve environmental conditions (both physical and social), and provide or facilitate meaningful employment. Crucially, the project also provided insights into how those who participated in the study understood the causal mechanisms through which their activities may impact health and wellbeing, even when these activities are not explicitly 'health focused.'

Project 3: Growth at the Edge

'Growth at the Edge,' the title of Project 3, explored the health and wellbeing effects of rural social enterprise activity on individuals and communities in the Highlands and Islands of Scotland. Over three years, 68 in-depth interviews were undertaken with stakeholders from a variety of roles, including rural social enterprise board members, staff, volunteers, and service users. These stakeholders were drawn from seven different organisations and, in addition to the interviews, were visited for extended periods to allow for ethnographic research on the rural communities and contexts in which they were operating.

Kelly et al. (2019) explain that social enterprises have a significant role in addressing social isolation and loneliness, which is a major public health concern because of the associated implications for both physical and mental health. Factors identified as contributing to social isolation, such as isolated people feeling like they have 'nothing to do,' and/or having poor social connections, can be compounded by living in a remote or rural area (Farmer et al., 2008). For example, access to transport can be challenging and being viewed as 'an incomer' can be difficult to socially navigate (Farmer et al., 2012).

The project also explored instances where social enterprises were addressing challenges created by the reduction in public budgets and withdrawal of public services. The organisations studied worked to counteract factors contributing to social isolation and loneliness, especially those exacerbated by rural contexts. The most significant among this range of activities involved providing spaces and opportunities for people to meet and interact with others, and the means to access these spaces. Over time, the increased sense of purpose that arose from interactions with the activities and spaces provided by social enterprises led to perceived improvements in health and wellbeing.

There were also cautionary findings from the project, particularly relating to the need to consider more widely the resources, capacity, and resilience of communities to be able to continue to respond to public health issues such as social isolation and loneliness. The study found that, in rural areas, the burden of maintaining social enterprise tends to fall on a relatively small number of community members. Feelings of stress or even 'burnout' were reported across all the social enterprises studied. There is often a small pool of rural volunteers to draw upon, especially people with skills such as business and accounting skills, and even holding driving licenses. These factors contributed to the social enterprises studied often seeming fragile and precarious, as has been noted in other rural studies (e.g. in rural Ireland—see O'Shaughnessy, 2008; O'Shaughnessy et al., 2011). This reinforces the idea that policy interventions supporting social enterprises in rural areas require to be tailored effectively to take into account specific contextual needs and requirements (Steiner & Teasdale, 2019; van Twuijver et al., 2020).

Project 4: 'Passage from India'

In January 2011, 13 women from seven different communities in Glasgow were supported by the Church of Scotland to travel to India to study women's self-help groups, a model that has been used there to address social and financial exclusion. Inspired by what they saw, the women returned to Scotland to explore how they could apply their learning to their own community contexts. The groups that were established as a result of the visit to India came to be known as 'Self-Reliant Groups' (SRGs), and Project 4 was based on five years of ethnographic research, where the researcher observed and participated in SRG activities and conducted in-depth interviews with SRG members.

SRGs are usually small groups of 5–10 people who come from a shared economic and social background and aim to meet regularly to support each other. At their meetings, they agree to start a collective savings fund; a typical contribution is £1 per person, per meeting. These savings, along with any other income generated by the group, can be lent to SRG members in times of need or crisis. The SRGs in this study were all supported by WEvolution, an independent organisation established in 2014 to act as a facilitator to emerging groups, provide key training opportunities, and offer loans. As the SRGs began to scale up, they often started small businesses to generate income (Hill O'Connor, 2013; Roy et al., 2014; Roy, Hill O'Connor et al., 2015), such as running a weekly lunch club, opening a laundrette, and making craft products for sale in the local church and craft markets.

Hill O'Connor et al. (2020) identify two key characteristics of the SRGs that made positive differences to the lives of the women involved. First, the savings they generated could provide members with control over their finances in times of acute financial stress. This not only gave them the ability to avoid high-interest weekly payment retailers or 'loan sharks' but also to direct savings towards people in the group who had a specific need; the opportunity to take a teenage son with developing behavioural issues on a short break to a caravan, for example. Within their groups, SRG members set the interest rates and repayment periods for the loans and rotated the role of treasurer, offering the women a sense of belonging, ownership, and trust that they did not necessarily experience in other areas of their lives.

Over time, their financial skills—which had often been a point of anxiety for members—accumulated to the point where they described a 'mastery experience,' which strengthened their self-efficacy. Second, the SRGs provided opportunities for productive activity: the activities associated with the small businesses the groups ran became a source of pride for the members who learned new skills and felt they were contributing to their communities. The SRG women also reported increased confidence as a result of participating in the group. This meant they were able to socialise more easily with people outside their immediate family and in a few cases even talk to large public audiences and the media about their SRG activities. Engaging with people in new and different ways had an impact on how the women engaged with figures of authority.

Connecting these findings to health and wellbeing, the external validation SRG members received through their engagement with the group, increased their sense of voice and ability to use it: an important precursor to agency and the ability to create change and pursue their own life choices (Hill O'Connor & Baker, 2017). The analysis identified how group members used the SRG activities to negotiate active citizenship, providing insight into how members could navigate the political economy of participating in the SRG. In liberal active citizenship terms, participation in the SRG allowed members to demonstrate (e.g. to the Jobcentre—the UK government-funded employment service) that they were 'responsible' and readying themselves for work. Membership in the SRG also provided space for negotiated 'active citizenship' (Jansen et al., 2006), where the women were able to make strategic decisions about balancing streams of income with their roles as carers (Hill O'Connor, 2016).

Project 5: Focus 50+

The aim of Project 5, Focus 50+, was to understand the impact of social enterprise activities on the health and wellbeing of participants aged 50 and over and how that impact was generated. Harnessing the European Union (EU) active aging policy definition that older age begins at 50 years (Davies, 2014), Scottish social enterprise networks and support agencies helped us to recruit three partner organisations that all delivered activities at least once a week to support older people in community spaces. The selection of organisations was based on the willingness of management/board to participate, their delivery of recurrent activities to study, and the availability and cognitive capacity of potential interviewees. Importantly, the study aimed to explore the health and wellbeing

impacts of involvement in social enterprise activities on all older participants regardless of their role. Therefore, staff, clients, carers, and volunteers were included in interviews. In total, 43 interviews were conducted
using an open-ended topic guide developed by the research team following a review of existing measures of subjective wellbeing, quality of life,
and sense of coherence. Data were collected over one year and included
social enterprise reports and observations.

Henderson et al. (2019) explain that all participants reported a greater
sense of purpose. Staff and volunteers valued the opportunity to support other people, while clients emphasised the importance of the social
enterprises providing 'somewhere to go' each week. By creating these
opportunities, the social enterprises united people who otherwise would
not have met and facilitated the formation of new social groups and connections. In this way, participating in the social enterprises directly ben-
efitted their health and wellbeing through a reduction in social isolation
and an increase in social connectedness, both of which are known to be
key determinants of health and wellbeing (Ottman et al., 2006).

The 'accessible informality' afforded by the social enterprise enabled
participants to shift roles and adopt strategies to enhance their own
self-perceptions of identity and capabilities, increasing self-worth and
self-confidence. Traits of what could be described as 'downward social
comparison' (Festinger, 1954) could be identified among the older people
participating in the study. This has been identified as a protective function
where older people distance themselves from others who are the same
chronological age (Chopik et al., 2018), hence reducing self-internalised
ageism which could threaten their wellbeing (Weiss & Freund, 2012).

The 'fluidity' and flexibility of the social enterprise activities enabled
multiple sub-activities to emerge simultaneously. For example, a language class that became an unintended support group for carers and a
Men's Group that helped with bereavement. Since such groups are often
difficult (and expensive) to target through traditional forms of 'intervention,' the findings from this project suggest that social enterprises could
play an important role in addressing health and wellbeing service provision challenges, particularly for older people (see Farmer et al., 2010).

Project 6: Aberdeen Foyer

Project 6 investigated the challenges that employees in social enterprises
encounter when engaging in social impact management tasks. Social
enterprises consistently report that providing evidence of their organisation's performance to funders is complex and challenging to plan and
implement. Creating organisational capacity to identify tools and train
staff to collect and record impact data is often difficult for small, often
overstretched organisations to manage. Given the *CommonHealth* programme's interest in elucidating the pathways and mechanisms between

social enterprise activities and health and wellbeing outcomes, insight into how social enterprises tackle the issue of 'social impact management' is significant. Social impact management can be defined as processes of measuring and monitoring the impact of social enterprises, such as for organisational and funder reporting. Understanding the impact measurement tools and processes that social enterprises use was also of interest, and this aspect was investigated from the perspective of managers considering the strategic future of organisations as well as staff and volunteers collecting and recording impact data.

A process that supported such organisations to identify robust outcomes and indicators was co-created with Aberdeen Foyer; a social enterprise based in Aberdeen in the northeast of Scotland that supports people towards independent living. The outcomes and indicators were then used to build an 'impact management process.' This was then tested with six further social enterprises engaged in delivering projects and interventions related to health and wellbeing. Their focus included housing, substance misuse, learning, employability, early intervention, and family support. Across these organisations, a total of 40 interviews were conducted with client-facing service delivery staff, focusing on the impact management activities in which they directly engaged. A further 20 interviews were conducted with operational and strategic-level management. The interviews were recorded, transcribed and coded, and then analysed thematically.

Fulford and Liddell (2018a, 2018b) found that social impact measurement activities needed to maintain both internal and external relevance, meaning that as well as satisfying the requirements of funders, the processes created should facilitate organisational learning. The ability of an organisation to undertake a systematic analysis of available social impact measurement resources and select the right tools for their requirements was crucial. Often, the researchers found there was a temptation for social enterprises to use tools that seem current or fashionable, even if they were a poor fit for the organisation's requirements. Making sure that all staff felt comfortable with their role in measuring social impact and the tools and language, they were expected to use was significant for successful social impact measurement. Finally, the researchers concluded that processes implemented should be meaningful within the daily workflow of staff, aligning closely with their working environment so that the process of social impact management does not become burdensome.

Project 7: Housing Through Social Enterprise

The research conducted through Project 7, 'Housing through social enterprise,' aimed to test the *CommonHealth* hypothesis that social enterprises may deliver health and wellbeing impacts, with a focus on the varied roles of social enterprise in parts of the housing sector. A longitudinal, mixed-methods study was completed over three phases. The research followed a cohort of new tenants from each organisation over the first year of their tenancy, interviewing them at the start of their tenancy, after 2–4 months, and after 9–12 months. At each of the interviews, tenants were asked questions relating to their health and wellbeing. This included measures of wellbeing and perceived impacts on wellbeing and quality of life from the property and the social enterprise housing service. The interviews covered a discussion relating to the property itself, how tenants were coping financially, and community and social supports they received.

Garnham and Rolfe (2019) found that many of the mechanisms linking housing to health and wellbeing operate through tenants' ability to establish a sense of 'home' in their new tenancy: recognising that housing is not just a physical shelter but a foundation for social, psychological, and cultural wellbeing. They found that tenants' health and wellbeing generally improved over the first year of their tenancy. A strong relationship with a named member of staff, who respected them and understood their particular needs, history, and situation, was found to be important to tenants. Furthermore, a good-quality property was one that was efficient and free from obvious physical defects but also well decorated, comfortable, and 'homely' with the condition on move-in day especially important. Although tenants had varying ideas about how much they wanted to improve or customise a property to their own tastes, their ability to influence this was dependent upon whether they had the capacity, permission, or resources to do so. Financial challenges were particularly acute at the start of a new tenancy, with some tenants struggling to recover from this because of ongoing high or unexpected expenses, many of which were related to their properties or tenancies. While tenants valued a sense of safety, friendliness, and amenities, and having social support networks in their local area, their neighbourhood priorities depended on their personal circumstances, characteristics, and prior experience. Ultimately, having a choice of where they would live was the most important issue for tenants.

Tenants of the 'hybrid' housing organisation (Rolfe et al., 2019) organised as a social enterprise showed relatively greater health and wellbeing improvements and satisfaction with their letting agency compared to the Housing Association and private landlord tenants. Considering the implications of these findings, therefore, social enterprises may have a significant role to play in relieving pressure on social housing and providing better outcomes for vulnerable tenants compared with the mainstream, for-profit sector. Moreover, the data suggested that it was precisely the blurring of the conventionally established boundaries between the social housing and private rental sector that led to improved tenant wellbeing and satisfaction since they were able to bring different principles (or 'logics'—see Pache & Santos, 2013) to bear: rather than simply focusing on extracting maximum profit, their activities were guided by the principle that 'vulnerable people get access to quality housing and are treated well' (Rolfe et al., 2019, p. 9).

Discussion

The groundwork for synthesising findings across the various *Common-Health* projects began during the final two years of the research programme. Through 'Project 8,' researchers ran a series of events that were designed to generate discussion between the project teams on their emerging findings as well as with policymakers and sector representatives. Further synthesis has taken place since the teams started to publish their individual project findings, and formal synthesis will continue for some time yet. As described earlier, the research conducted by various projects was generally exploratory and mostly utilised qualitative methods, albeit with tailored approaches per project. Although often beginning from different methodological foundations, the projects have permitted the development of rich descriptions based on lived accounts of people involved in and with social enterprises, whether as board members, staff, volunteers, or beneficiaries. The projects (generally speaking) did not seek to measure outcomes or impacts on large participant samples but sought to reveal the *plausible mechanisms* by which impacts on health and wellbeing were achieved, which can then serve as the basis for identifying some overarching findings about pathways between social enterprise, health, and wellbeing. Although articulated in slightly different terms in each project, taken together the qualitative findings point to a common set of intermediate determinants of longer-term health outcomes in relation to social inclusion, social capital, connectedness and sense of belonging, empowerment and control, confidence and self-worth, and sense of meaning or purpose in life. Figure 10.1 brings together some of the high-level insights from the qualitative studies on the impact of social enterprises on health and wellbeing across different geographical and demographic contexts.

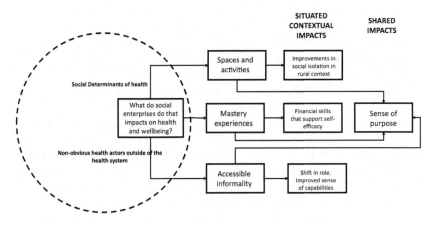

Figure 10.1 Pathways to impact—'sense of purpose' example

While the diagram shows how 'sense of purpose' can be described as a shared impact, this is just one example provided for the purposes of this chapter, and further synthesis will begin to illuminate further shared outcomes in future publications.

The diagram illustrates several of the experiences provided by social enterprises discussed, which we have identified as 'spaces and activities' (particularly project 3), 'mastery experiences' (project 4), and 'accessible informality' (project 5). The diagram also illustrates the observation that, whilst 'sense of purpose' or 'sense of worth' are very strong themes running throughout the separate analyses, across geographical context and different groups of beneficiaries, that other (intermediate) impacts are contextually dependent. This combination of context and shared impacts is key not only for drawing lessons from *CommonHealth* but also going forward, so addressing dual requirements for evidence of individual (often-small) social enterprises, as well as of the sector as a whole.

Historically, social enterprise in Scotland developed from a community base, with a patchwork of support from local authorities, government bodies, national regeneration funds, and, more recently, a tailored policy framework for a social enterprise which has culminated in a ten-year (2016–2026) social enterprise strategy co-produced between government and the sector. The most striking change over the longer term is how the professional dialogues that inform social enterprise and public health have gravitated towards each other over several decades; from the Ottawa Charter (WHO, 1986) and full recognition of the importance of the social determinants of health (Commission on Social Determinants of Health, 2008), to the more recent and emergent discourse around the 'wellbeing economy' (Coscieme et al., 2019; Costanza et al., 2018). There are structural forces at play that have undoubtedly informed the parameters of this convergence, particularly since the Great Financial Crisis of 2008, which precipitated a decade of austerity policies, the profound effects of which on health and wellbeing are just starting to be understood (Marmot, 2020). Gains, to this point, in life expectancy have stalled, or even fallen in places, for the first time in a century (Boseley, 2020). The immediate after-effects of the COVID-19 pandemic of 2020 in both health and economic terms have also barely begun to be understood. Project 1 revealed how a focus on how neoliberal policies has shifted health and welfare provision from a systems perspective, neglecting to reconfigure understandings of health actors from a community perspective. This alternative narrative around the 'service innovation' (Farmer et al., 2018; Osborne & Brown, 2011) that social enterprises provide in the spaces they create, which has been far more difficult to articulate and make heard, has been taken up by projects 2–7 exploring the ability of social enterprises to address a wide variety of needs.

Project 2 identified the diverse and complex relationship between social enterprise processes and intermediate health outcomes. The relationship between these processes and outcomes was examined in closer contextual detail in projects 3–5. What appears to be consistently important across the insights from these projects are the positive impacts that arise from the interaction between people, space, and activities that community-based social enterprises provide. Effectively, this means that social enterprises provide space for a 'dialogic' experience (Bakhtin, 1982) supporting opportunities for personal and collective growth and transformation, since 'every human being likes to resist, confront and make personal meaning out of social interactions' (Nesari, 2015, p. 643). This resonates with the idea of social enterprise as an 'alternative' economic space and an opportunity to 'reject the values and identities associated with the mainstream, instead choosing to operate differently and being concerned with different values' (McHugh et al., 2019, p. 81).

The project has also informed the impacts of social enterprises on intermediate outcomes that support longer term health outcomes. Projects 3–5 found situated contextual impacts that were specific to the geographical and social context of their operation. For example, project 3 found that rural transport initiatives were vital to addressing the social isolation and loneliness experienced in rural communities; project 4 demonstrated the impact that the financial skills gained by women in urban SRGs to their feelings of self-efficacy; and project 5 found that older people participating in social enterprise activities made downward social comparisons which provide a protective function to their wellbeing. Thus, in all three of these examples, community-based social enterprises provided activities that fulfilled the needs of people in their local areas and acted upon factors that can be connected to the social determinants of health. These findings are comparable to previous research which has depended on case studies to explore the impact of social enterprise in health and wellbeing. Indeed, the social enterprise research field, particularly in its early phase, was dominated by case studies generally. Where the *CommonHealth* research takes us further, though, is in the analysis of the shared impacts of community-based social enterprises, which appear to be consistent across contexts.

While projects 3–5 all identified and discussed the plausible mechanisms they observed differently—spaces and activities; mastery experiences; assessable informality—they all supported an increased 'sense of purpose' for those participating in the social enterprises studied. This suggests an element of consistency in the nature of social enterprise spaces in relation to people and activities that permit shared health and wellbeing outcomes (such as sense of purpose) to emerge. The comparative evaluation work completed in project 7 identified 'hybridity' (Doherty et al., 2014) as the potential element that amplified the health and wellbeing impacts of social enterprise housing associations in relation to both state and private sector housing providers. This insight provides a steer on directions for future research. The ability to identify some consistent findings is of crucial value to the social enterprise sector. Practitioners can describe in detail the complex impact that engaging with their organisation has on individuals and even their families, but the ability to begin to identify and articulate this impact beyond individual organisations and their clients is crucial to building knowledge on the connections between social enterprise, health, and wellbeing.

Relating this back to the voice of social enterprises, Project 2 looked at how social enterprises understood their impact and to what extent they expressed this in terms of health and wellbeing. This was examined in greater depth in project 6, which found that although social enterprises have a great deal of experienced-based knowledge about their activities and impacts, they can struggle to identify and make use of tools that allow them to express this impact for impact-reporting activities. Connecting with the sector's perspective on evaluating their impact was (and will remain) essential in the endeavour of shifting the collective knowledge of the sector from the 'non-obvious' to evidenced and knowable. It is crucial not to overlook the importance of partnership working between the sector and academia, such as we saw during *CommonHealth*, as a means of attracting resources to start to grapple with such issues. Comparing these experiences with the findings of project 6, our research suggests that social enterprises themselves have an important role in articulating their health impacts and should be supported to strengthen their voices in this area. Moreover, reflecting on the findings of project 7, it is suggested that future investigations should consider the nature and dimensions of 'hybridity' of social enterprise (i.e. their ability to draw on the logics of the state, market, *and* civil society/community—see Billis, 2010; Brandsen et al., 2005), and in what ways the nature of such hybridity supports the wellbeing impacts of community-based social enterprises.

Conclusion

There are several implications of the *CommonHealth* programme of research for understanding the impacts that social enterprises have in relation to health and wellbeing. This was (and still remains, in many ways) a previously understudied dimension of the contribution of civil society to individual and community health and wellbeing. The *CommonHealth* research projects have together illuminated and connected what social enterprises do to contribute to a variety of intermediate health outcomes that support improved health and wellbeing by acting on the social determinants of health: social inclusion, social capital, connectedness, and sense of belonging; empowerment and control; confidence and self-worth; and sense of meaning or purpose in life.

In relation to evaluation and measurement, in future research, it is imperative that approaches to researching social enterprise, health, and wellbeing do not 'flatten out' social enterprise into a series of stable component elements and outcomes but should look to employ methods that are able to capture the fluidity and plurality of social enterprise spaces and experiences. Although, as we have stated, the social enterprise experience is highly contingent and contextually specific—involving different places, spaces, beneficiary or target groups, and so on—this does not mean that some degree of consistency of outcome cannot be achieved. The level of consistency in the *nature* of the spaces in relation to people and activities and the interactions between them permits relatively common health and wellbeing outcomes to emerge.

The *CommonHealth* research has provided insights into health and wellbeing outcomes that map onto current understandings of the social determinants of health and has also supported the creation and development of new knowledge on the nature of social dynamics that support them across different community organisations and settings. There is a necessity to account for both context and commonality in order to evidence and articulate the potential pervasiveness of social enterprise as a driver of wellbeing.

Acknowledgements

This study was supported with the financial assistance of the Medical Research Council and Economic and Social Research Council, ref: MR/L0032827/1 for a project entitled *Developing Methods to evidence 'social enterprise as a public health intervention'*.

References

Arvidson, M., Lyon, F., McKay, S., & Moro, D. (2013). Valuing the Social? The Nature and Controversies of Measuring Social Return on Investment (SROI). *Voluntary Sector Review*, 4(1), 3–18.

Bakhtin, M. M. (1982). *The Dialogic Imagination: Four Essays* (M. Holquist, Ed. and C. Emerson, Trans.). University of Texas Press.

Billis, D. (Ed.). (2010). *Hybrid Organizations and the Third Sector: Challenges for Practice, Theory and Policy*. Palgrave Macmillan.

Boseley, S. (2020, February 25). Austerity Blamed for Life Expectancy Stalling for First Time in Century. *The Guardian*. www.theguardian.com/society/2020/feb/24/austerity-blamed-for-life-expectancy-stalling-for-first-time-in-century.

Brandsen, T., van de Donk, W., & Putters, K. (2005). Griffins or Chameleons? Hybridity as a Permanent and Inevitable Characteristic of the Third Sector. *International Journal of Public Administration*, 28(9–10), 749–765.

Chopik, W. J., Bremner, R. H., Johnson, D. J., & Giasson, H. L. (2018). Age Differences in Age Perceptions and Developmental Transitions. *Frontiers in Psychology*, 9. https://doi.org/10.3389/fpsyg.2018.00067.

Commission on Social Determinants of Health. (2008). *Closing the Gap in a Generation: Health Equity Through Action on the Social Determinants of Health*. World Health Organization.

Coscieme, L., Sutton, P., Mortensen, L. F., Kubiszewski, I., Costanza, R., Trebeck, K., Pulselli, F. M., Giannetti, B. F., & Fioramonti, L. (2019). Overcoming the Myths of Mainstream Economics to Enable a New Wellbeing Economy. *Sustainability*, *11*(16), 4374. https://doi.org/10.3390/su11164374.

Costanza, R., Caniglia, B., Fioramonti, L., Kubiszewski, I., Lewis, H., Lovins, L. H., McGlade, J., Mortensen, L. F., Philipsen, D., Ragnarsdóttir, K. V., Roberts, D., Sutton, P., Trebeck, K., Wallis, S., Ward, J., Weatherhead, M., & Wilkinson, R. (2018). Toward a Sustainable Wellbeing Economy. *The Solutions Journal*, *9*(2), 5.

Davies, R. (2014). *Older People in Europe*. European Parliament Research Service. www.europarl.europa.eu/RegData/bibliotheque/briefing/2014/140811/LDM_BRI(2014)140811_REV1_EN.pdf.

Doherty, B., Haugh, H., & Lyon, F. (2014). Social Enterprises as Hybrid Organizations: A Review and Research Agenda. *International Journal of Management Reviews*, *16*(4), 417–436. https://doi.org/10.1111/ijmr.12028.

Donaldson, C., Baker, R., Cheater, F., Gillespie, M., McHugh, N., & Sinclair, S. (2011). Social Business, Health and Well-Being. *Social Business*, *1*(1), 17–35.

Farmer, J., Carlisle, K., Dickson-Swift, V., Teasdale, S., Kenny, A., Taylor, J., Croker, F., Marini, K., & Gussy, M. (2018). Applying Social Innovation Theory to Examine How Community Co-Designed Health Services Develop: Using a Case Study Approach and Mixed Methods. *BMC Health Services Research*, *18*(1). https://doi.org/10.1186/s12913-018-2852-0.

Farmer, J., Hill, C., & Muñoz, S.-A. (2012). *Community Co-Production: Social Enterprise in Remote and Rural Communities*. Edward Elgar Publishing.

Farmer, J., Philip, L., King, G., Farrington, J., & MacLeod, M. (2010). Territorial Tensions: Misaligned Management and Community Perspectives on Health Services for Older People in Remote Rural Areas. *Health & Place*, *16*(2), 275–283. https://doi.org/10.1016/j.healthplace.2009.10.010.

Farmer, J., Steinerowski, A., & Jack, S. (2008). Starting Social Enterprises in Remote and Rural Scotland: Best or Worst of Circumstances? *International Journal of Entrepreneurship and Small Business*, *6*(3), 450–464.

Festinger, L. (1954). A Theory of Social Comparison Processes. *Human Relations*, *7*(2), 117–140. https://doi.org/10.1177/001872675400700202.

Fulford, H., & Liddell, M. (2018a). *Social Impact Management: Employee Perceptions and Experiences*. CommonHealth Briefing Paper Series: Paper Number 9. https://static1.squarespace.com/static/543e889fe4b0c26d0d7235e4/t/5bf41307032be48ae7ad3c38/1542722313562/Commonhealth_Paper9+_FINAL.pdf.

Fulford, H., & Liddell, M. (2018b). *Social Impact Management: Exploring Managers' Perspectives*. CommonHealth Briefing Paper Series: Paper Number 10. https://static1.squarespace.com/static/543e889fe4b0c26d0d7235e4/t/5bf41390032be48ae7ad42ff/1542722449499/Commonhealth_Paper10_FINAL.pdf.

Garnham, L., & Rolfe, S. (2019). *Housing as a Social Determinant of Health: Evidence from the Housing Through Social Enterprise Study*. Glasgow Centre for Population Health. www.gcph.co.uk/assets/0000/7295/Housing_through_social_enterprise_WEB.pdf.

Hall, K., Miller, R., & Millar, R. (2015). Public, Private or Neither? Analysing the Publicness of Health Care Social Enterprises. *Public Management Review*, 1–19. https://doi.org/10.1080/14719037.2015.1014398.

Henderson, F., Steiner, A., Mazzei, M., & Docherty, C. (2019). Social Enterprises' Impact on Older People's Health and Wellbeing: Exploring Scottish Experiences. *Health Promotion International, 102.* https://doi.org/10.1093/heapro/daz102.

Hill O'Connor, C. (2013, July). *The Role of Self Reliant Groups (SRGs) in Improving Individual Health and Wellbeing. If Not for Profit, for What? And How?* The 4th EMES International Research Conference on Social Enterprise, Liege, Belgium. www.iap-socent.be/sites/default/files/Hill%20O%27Connor%20ECSP-LG13-70.pdf.

Hill O'Connor, C. (2016). *The Emergence of Self Reliant Groups in Scotland: Illustrating a Continuum of Active Citizenship* [Ph.D.]. Glasgow Caledonian University.

Hill O'Connor, C., & Baker, R. (2017). Working with and for Social Enterprises: The Role of the Volunteer Ethnographer. *Social Enterprise Journal, 13*(2), 180–193. https://doi.org/10.1108/SEJ-07-2016-0033.

Hill O'Connor, C., Mazzei, M., & Baker, R. (2020). Self Reliant Groups from India to Scotland: Lessons from South to North. *Community Development Journal, 55*(2). https://doi.org/10.1093/cdj/bsy037.

Jansen, T., Chioncel, N., & Dekkers, H. (2006). Social Cohesion and Integration: Learning Active Citizenship. *British Journal of Sociology of Education, 27*(2), 189–205. https://doi.org/10.1080/01425690600556305.

Kelly, D., Steiner, A., Mazzei, M., & Baker, R. (2019). Filling a Void? The Role of Social Enterprise in Addressing Social Isolation and Loneliness in Rural Communities. *Journal of Rural Studies, 70,* 225–236. https://doi.org/10.1016/j.jrurstud.2019.01.024.

Macaulay, B., Mazzei, M., Roy, M. J., Teasdale, S., & Donaldson, C. (2018a). Differentiating the Effect of Social Enterprise Activities on Health. *Social Science & Medicine, 200,* 211–217. https://doi.org/10.1016/j.socscimed.2018.01.042.

Macaulay, B., Roy, M. J., Donaldson, C., Teasdale, S., & Kay, A. (2018b). Conceptualizing the Health and Well-Being Impacts of Social Enterprise: A UK-Based Study. *Health Promotion International, 33*(5), 748–759. https://doi.org/10.1093/heapro/dax009

Marmot, M. (2020). Health Equity in England: The Marmot Review 10 Years On. *BMJ, 368.* https://doi.org/10.1136/bmj.m693.

McHugh, N., Baker, R., & Donaldson, C. (2019). Microcredit for Enterprise in the UK as an 'Alternative' Economic Space. *Geoforum, 100,* 80–88. https://doi.org/10.1016/j.geoforum.2019.02.004.

Murray, G. (2019). Community Business in Scotland: An Alternative Vision of 'Enterprise Culture', 1979–97, *Twentieth Century British History, 30*(4), 585–606.

Nesari, A. J. (2015). Dialogism Versus Monologism: A Bakhtinian Approach to Teaching. *Procedia—Social and Behavioral Sciences, 205,* 642–647. https://doi.org/10.1016/j.sbspro.2015.09.101.

Osborne, S. P., & Brown, L. (2011). Innovation, Public Policy and Public Services Delivery in the UK. The Word That Would Be King? *Public Administration, 89*(4), 1335–1350. https://doi.org/10.1111/j.1467-9299.2011.01932.x.

O'Shaughnessy, M. (2008). Statutory Support and the Implications for the Employee Profile of Rural Based Irish Work Integration Social

Enterprises (WISEs). *Social Enterprise Journal,* 4(2), 126–135. https://doi.org/10.1108/17508610810902011.

O'Shaughnessy, M., Casey, E., & Enright, P. (2011). Rural Transport in Peripheral Rural Areas: The Role of Social Enterprises in Meeting the Needs of Rural Citizens. *Social Enterprise Journal,* 7(2), 183–190. https://doi.org/10.1108/17508611111156637.

Ottman, G., Dickson, J., & Wright, P. (2006). *Social Connectedness and Health: A Literature Review.* Cornell University ILR School. http://digitalcommons.ilr.cornell.edu/gladnetcollect/471.

Pache, A.-C., & Santos, F. (2013). Inside the Hybrid Organization: Selective Coupling as a Response to Competing Institutional Logics. *Academy of Management Journal,* 56(4), 972–1001. https://doi.org/10.5465/amj.2011.0405.

Pearce, J. (1993). *At the Heart of the Community Economy: Community Enterprise in a Changing World.* Calouste Gulbenkian Foundation.

Pearce, J. (2003). *Social Enterprise in Anytown.* Calouste Gulbenkian Foundation.

Pearce, J., & Kay, A. (2008). *Really Telling Accounts!* Social Audit Network.

Rolfe, S., Garnham, L., Anderson, I., Seaman, P., Godwin, J., & Donaldson, C. (2019). Hybridity in the Housing Sector: Examining Impacts on Social and Private Rented Sector Tenants in Scotland. *Housing Studies.* https://doi.org/10.1080/02673037.2019.1648770.

Roy, M. J., Baker, R., & Kerr, S. (2017). Conceptualising the Public Health Role of Actors Operating Outside of Formal Health Systems: The Case of Social Enterprise. *Social Science & Medicine, 172,* 144–152. https://doi.org/10.1016/j.socscimed.2016.11.009.

Roy, M. J., Donaldson, C., Baker, R., & Kay, A. (2013). Social Enterprise: New Pathways to Health and Well-being? *Journal of Public Health Policy,* 34(1), 55–68. https://doi.org/10.1057/jphp.2012.61.

Roy, M. J., Hill O'Connor, C., McHugh, N., Biosca, O., & Donaldson, C. (2015). The New Merger: Combining Third Sector and Market-Based Approaches to Tackling Inequalities. *Social Business,* 5(1), 47–60. https://doi.org/10.1362/204440815X14267607784848.

Roy, M. J., McHugh, N., & Hill O'Connor, C. (2014). Social Innovation: Worklessness, Welfare and Well-being. *Social Policy and Society,* 13(3), 457–467. https://doi.org/10.1017/S1474746414000104.

Roy, M. J., McHugh, N., Huckfield, L., Kay, A., & Donaldson, C. (2015). 'The Most Supportive Environment in the World'? Tracing the Development of an Institutional "Ecosystem" for Social Enterprise. *Voluntas: International Journal of Voluntary and Nonprofit Organizations,* 26(3), 777–800. https://doi.org/10.1007/s11266-014-9459-9.

Steiner, A., & Teasdale, S. (2019). Unlocking the Potential of Rural Social Enterprise. *Journal of Rural Studies,* 70, 144–154. https://doi.org/10.1016/j.jrurstud.2017.12.021.

Townsend, P., & Davidson, N. (1982). *Inequalities in Health: The Black Report.* Penguin.

van Twuijver, M. W., Olmedo, L., O'Shaughnessy, M., & Hennessy, T. (2020). Rural Social Enterprises in Europe: A Systematic Literature Review. *Local Economy.* https://doi.org/10.1177/0269094220907024.

Vickers, I., Lyon, F., Sepulveda, L., & McMullin, C. (2017). Public Service Innovation and Multiple Institutional Logics: The Case of Hybrid Social Enterprise

Providers of Health and Wellbeing. *Research Policy*, 46(10), 1755–1768. https://doi.org/10.1016/j.respol.2017.08.003.

Weiss, D., & Freund, A. M. (2012). Still Young at Heart: Negative Age-Related Information Motivates Distancing from Same-Aged People. *Psychology and Aging*, 27(1), 173–180. https://doi.org/10.1037/a0024819.

Whitehead, M. (1992). The Concepts and Principles of Equity and Health. *International Journal of Health Services*, 22(3), 429–445.

WHO. (1986, November 21). *The Ottawa Charter for Health Promotion*. First International Conference on Health Promotion, Ottawa. www.who.int/ healthpromotion/conferences/previous/ottawa/en/.

Wilkinson, R. G., & Marmot, M. G. (Eds.). (2003). *Social Determinants of Health: The Solid Facts* (2nd ed.). World Health Organization, Regional Office for Europe.

11 How Do Social Enterprises Influence Health Equities? A Comparative Case Analysis

Jo Barraket, Batool Moussa, Perri Campbell, and Roksolana Suchowerska

Introduction and Background

The systemic and social conditions that support health and wellbeing and the inequities that people experience in accessing these are a matter of growing emphasis in public health and health promotion. In light of improved understanding of the social determinants of health (Solar & Irwin, 2010), governments and societies are increasingly interested in the impacts of 'upstream' interventions that address these causes of health and wellbeing. In both practice and research, there has been growing interest in the role of social enterprise in general and work integration social enterprises or WISEs (Spear & Bidet, 2005) in particular, in supporting the conditions for improved health equity among people experiencing social and economic exclusion. While the literature on the effects of WISEs on the social determinants of health is growing (Elmes, 2019; Gordon et al., 2018; Macaulay et al., 2018; Roy et al., 2017), there is still relatively little comparative understanding of the organisational mechanisms through which WISEs produce these outcomes. With a particular focus on health equity of young people, this chapter seeks to respond to this gap in the literature, drawing on a comparative case study of four WISEs in the Australian states of Victoria and New South Wales (NSW).

Conceptual Approach

Guided by our interests in whether and how WISEs contribute to health equities among young people, our conceptual approach draws on the social determinants of health (Marmot, 2005; Solar & Irwin, 2010), combined with our earlier theorising (Suchowerska et al., 2019) about the organisational factors that inform social enterprise outcomes.

The social determinants of health provide a framework for articulating the principles of health equity. They refer to both the conditions in which people live and work and the structural mechanisms that distribute these conditions in society. Together, these factors shape and mediate individual and group-level health and wellbeing, giving rise to conditions

DOI: 10.4324/9781003125976-11

of health inequity (Marmot, 2005). Health inequities are systemic and unjust differences in health outcomes that develop between social, economic, demographic, or geographic groups. The social determinants of health inequities follow a 'social gradient,' whereby the more socioeconomically disadvantaged a person is, the greater their risk of ill health (Solar & Irwin, 2010). Mapping potential interventions for the social determinants of health inequities has been a primary focus of health promotion research, with conceptual frameworks offering a guide for implementation and practice.

We draw here upon the Victorian Health Promotion Foundation's 'Fair Foundations framework' to conceptualise and clarify the complex pathways of health inequities and identify how they are mitigated relative to our research findings. Adapted from the conceptual framework developed by the World Health Organisation (WHO), 'Fair Foundations' shows multiple entry points for tackling health inequities, which require more than just state action (Solar & Irwin, 2010). The social determinants of health are informed by three interacting layers: (a) the socio-economic, political, and cultural context; (b) daily living and material conditions; and (c) individual health-related factors (VicHealth, 2015). A combination of policies, societal norms, and economic arrangements interact to shape a society's socio-political context, stratifying populations and their access to health-promoting factors in daily life (VicHealth, 2015). These factors include education, income, social networks, quality employment, and housing. At the intermediary level, the resulting health inequities further undermine individual health by, for example, limiting opportunities to connect with others and engage in healthier behaviours, such as reducing or ceasing smoking and drug use.

Differential health outcomes are evident in the higher rates of morality, morbidity, and disability that cluster in disadvantaged populations (World Health Organisation, 2013). Crucially, the structural drivers of health inequities are socially produced and can be modified to promote better health. 'Fair Foundations' highlights the need for intersectoral action on the causal processes that underlie health inequities. Among other actors, social enterprises have gained attention for their role and capacity in improving health equities. While social enterprises have been recognised as a potential form of 'upstream' intervention (Roy et al., 2013) within this conceptual framework, there is limited evidence on the direct and indirect ways by which the organisational culture, systems, governance, and networks of social enterprises (Suchowerska et al., 2019) work to redress the causes of health inequities (Marmot, 2005).

Drawing on a systematic literature review, our first publication from the study presented here proposed a conceptual framework that identified key organisational factors through which social enterprise may realise health equity outcomes (see Figure 11.1). While not specifically focused on young people, this framework suggests that the outcomes of

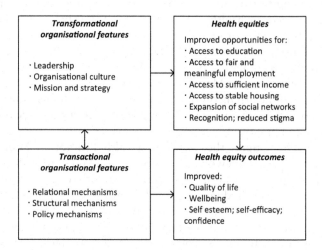

Figure 11.1 A theoretical model of how organisational features affect equities and health equity outcomes

social enterprise are informed by two types of organisational features: transformational features, which guide organisational responses to the institutional factors that shape health inequities; and transactional features, which shape day-to-day interaction among people within the enterprise and thus respond to the conditions for health inequities at the level of individuals within the organisation. Transformational and transactional features co-exist and may change through interplay between them (Suchowerska et al., 2019). With attention to both whether and how WISE, as one form of social enterprise, affect the SDOH equity among young people, we now turn to a review of the available evidence, before explaining our research context, methodology, and findings.

Health (in)Equities, WISEs, and Young People

Australia's young people enjoy world-leading health status. Yet, significant inequalities in health persist for Indigenous young people, refugees, and young people living in areas of relatively low socio-economic status (Australian Institute of Health and Welfare, 2011). Youth, or the transition from childhood to adulthood (typically, classified as 15–24 years), is also a period during which significant modifiable risk factors emerge and can have a substantial effect on future health and wellbeing (Australian Institute of Health and Welfare, 2014). As a group, young people in Australia also experience exclusion from the labour market, experiencing significantly higher than national average rates of unemployment and underemployment (Qian et al., 2019).

The current literature suggests that social enterprises address the SDOH inequities by generating pathways into education and employment for people who are socio-economically disadvantaged (Elmes, 2019; Ferguson & Xie, 2008); addressing sources of health inequity, such as food insecurity, for particular population groups (Farmer et al., 2016; Gibson-Graham & Cameron, 2007; Gordon et al., 2018); addressing intermediary factors by increasing social capital between people from diverse groups (Cheng, 2015; Evans & Syrett, 2007); revitalising local economies in locationally disadvantaged areas (Berkes & Adhikari, 2006; Eversole et al., 2013); and reconfiguring public and private spaces to improve participation of marginalised people (Barraket & Archer, 2010).

Building on earlier studies, an emerging body of empirical research on health, wellbeing, and social enterprise has been guided by SDOH equities frameworks. In a study of two community food social enterprises in Scotland, Gordon et al. (2018) concluded that social enterprises influenced all levels of the social determinants of health model but had a more notable impact on individual lifestyle factors and social and community networks than macro-level conditions. In relation to WISEs specifically, Elmes (2019), and in this book, finds that a WISE working with people living with mental illness who had experienced long-term unemployment had a positive influence on the structural determinants of health inequities by increasing social relationships and enabling target staff to improve their socioeconomic position, leading to reduced social stigma, through employment.

There is very limited research on the impacts of social enterprise on health inequities among young people, but what does exist suggests that social enterprise interventions have positive mediating effects on the mental health of disadvantaged young people (Ferguson & Xie, 2008). A study of the comparative efficacy of a social enterprise intervention and individually focused, supported on-the-job training found similar positive outcomes in mental health, housing and employment, suggesting that ongoing and integrated case management are critical factors in supporting disadvantaged young people (Ferguson, 2018a, 2018b). Recent research undertaken in Cambodia also found that social enterprises challenged traditional thinking within aid organisations regarding young people and thus helped to redress institutional drivers of inequities in that context (Cheng, 2015).

While the available research suggests that social enterprise has positive effects on health status, several recent papers have observed that available studies do little to explicate causal pathways or conditions for the effectiveness of social enterprise in general or WISEs in particular (Agafonow, 2018; Roy et al., 2014, 2018). As others have observed, much of the growing body of research evidence is also based on perspectives of social enterprise managers and funders, with relatively limited voice given to targeted beneficiaries in the literature to date (Chandra, 2018;

Cho et al., 2019; Macaulay et al., 2018). Informed by our conceptual framework and these gaps in the existing literature, our research questions were:

RQ1 What effects does participation in WISEs have on the social determinants of health equity for young people?

RQ2 What organisational features contribute to these effects?

Research Context

The research presented in this chapter was conducted with WISEs in the Australian states of Victoria and New South Wales (NSW). While there are an estimated 20,000 social enterprises in Australia, of which nearly one-third focus on employment creation for people experiencing disadvantage (Barraket et al., 2016), there is no national-level policy framework that supports social enterprise development. At the time of data collection (August 2018-November 2019), Victoria had an explicit policy framework to support social enterprise as part of a commitment to inclusive economy, while NSW did not. In the Australian context, employment services provision is predominantly the responsibility of the federal government. Australia has a residual welfare system (Esping-Andersen, 1990) and a quasi-market approach to employment services provision (Considine, 2001) with an emphasis on 'work first' rather than training and development to support labour market integration. WISEs are incidental rather than formally recognised as part of the employment services system. While there is growing interest in social enterprise in the context of health promotion in Australia, WISEs remain marginal in considerations of public health and health promotion.

Methodology

The research was based on a comparative case study design to investigate and analyse the ways in which social enterprises affect the SDOH equity for young people aged 15–24 from disadvantaged rural and metropolitan fringe areas. Prior to case selection, two preliminary engagement workshops were conducted with social entrepreneurs, young people, and public health professionals in Victoria and NSW to estimate and refine the research questions and methods with participants and identify paradigmatic cases for inclusion in the study.

Case study sample selection was based on a paradigmatic case sampling approach (Flyvbjerg, 2006), which seeks to include examples that demonstrate prototypical characteristics of the phenomena in question. The paradigm being explored was the interaction between social enterprise operations and SDOH equity for young people. We purposefully selected four well-established social enterprises—two in Victoria and two in NSW—with missions that explicitly seek to redress socio-economic disadvantage of young people and operate within or into disadvantaged areas as defined by the Australian Bureau of Statistics (ABS) SEIFA index. Case studies were undertaken in two states in order to provide institutional variance in terms of public policy. These states have been selected because they have the highest concentration of social enterprises in Australia (Barraket et al., 2016), while Victoria has explicit policy support for social enterprise and NSW does not. All WISEs approached agreed to participate in the study, giving us 100 per cent response rate at the level of case organisations. Table 11.1 presents summary information on the case WISEs.

Case-level data collection included theory of change or engagement workshops with staff and directors of each case organisation to elicit insights about the presumed outcomes and organisational processes through which outcomes were achieved in each case WISE; participant observation of up to two weeks within each WISE; semi-structured interviews with young people, WISEs' managers, WISEs' funding and supply chain partners, and customers; and collation of organisational documents relevant to case organisations' theories of change and social outcomes. Ninety-three interviews were conducted (see Table 11.2 for a summary of the interview participants).

Data were coded selectively against our research questions, using our conceptual framework to distinguish case study effects on individual, daily living, intermediary, and macro-conditions of health equity. Data were also reviewed for health equity outcomes self-reported by participating young people, case WISE managers, and ancillary service providers. Preliminary coding against the research questions was then reviewed across cases for dominant themes and differences in case study outcomes. With a focus on our questions of how particular effects are produced, we then worked backwards from key health equity findings to unpack—through interview and participant observation data—the specific organisational features that informed these outcomes.

Findings

Reflecting our research questions, our findings are organised to examine the effects of WISEs on social determinants of health equity for participating young people and the organisational features and conditions through which these are produced.

Effects of WISEs on SDOH Equity—Individual Health Factors

All young people who participated in the research reported an improvement in self-confidence as a result of WISE participation. These changes arose from positive recognition and being valued as a person and a worker; mastery of technical skills alongside workplace tolerance for

Table 11.1 Summary of case study WISEs

Sampling	Case A	Case B	Case C	Case D
Key social purposes	• Employment pathways for disadvantaged youth • Housing affordability • Environmental sustainability	• Youth engagement and employment pathways • Environmental sustainability • Support local community	• Training and employment pathways for disadvantaged young people • Social inclusion for young people	• Employment pathways for youth and refugees • Waste reduction and environmental sustainability • Local and fair food production
Geographic location	• Inner-Metropolitan Melbourne	• Inner-South Sydney	• Greater Melbourne	• South Coast New South Wales
Origins	• Established 2009	• Established 1979 (Evaluated program est. 2015)	• Established 2016	• Established 2011
Industry location	• Hospitality (Certificate II in Kitchen Operations)	• Information technology and electronics (Certificate III in Business, Business Sales or Certificate III in Information Technology)	• Construction (Certificate II in Building and Carpentry)	• Farming • Waste management (Certificate I in Access to Vocational Pathways or a Certificate II in Skills for Work and Vocational Pathways)

Table 11.2 Interviewees by case and participant type

Participant type	Case A	Case B	Case C	Case D	Total by type
Young people	5	6	9	7	27
Managers	1	3	4	4	12
Partners	3	0	0	4	7
Other Staff	5	6	6	2	19
External organisations and funders	4	5	2	4	15
Board members	2	2	0	3	7
Executive staff	4	1	1	0	6
Total	24	23	22	24	93

mistakes; and new opportunities for interaction with fellow workers, customers, and support staff. As one 19-year-old male experiencing homelessness described it:

> Before I came to [the WISE], I don't think I had a whole lot of relationships. I was just surrounded by a lot of drugs, a lot of alcohol just up the road here. I think for the most part, [the social enterprise was] pretty much my saving grace.
>
> (Young person, Case A)

Another young man with a history of unstable housing and drug use reflected that there was a flow on effect from the confidence they developed through mastering professional skills into other aspects of their life:

> I feel pretty confident in my coffee-making skills now . . . That, and just interacting with people—total strangers—was something that I was really uncomfortable with at first and I'd get really nervous approaching the table just to take an order and the more I familiarised myself with it, I was pretty all right eventually. Even now, outside of [the WISE] I find I have more confidence.
>
> (Young person, Case A)

Nearly all young people interviewed reported experiencing direct improvements in mental health, or the conditions for mental health, because of their participation in the WISE. Self-reported changes in mental health were generally attributed by participants to their increased confidence and sense of self-worth in work and learning settings that accommodated their needs:

> [The WISE] has been very lenient with my anxiety provoked mistakes. I do make pretty consistent mistakes. It's good to have a sort of practice run.
>
> (Young person, Case A)

Before I came to this course I was like pretty depressed . . . Because I just kept getting knocked back, I was sort of like giving up. I definitely feel like healthier mentally just coming here every day and being punctual, you know, having a routine, stuff like that . . . rather than just waking up and playing games every day.

(Young person, Case B)

Improvements in mental health appeared most pronounced among those young people who were experiencing relatively higher degrees of socio-economic disadvantage, such as homelessness, lack of family and social support, or experiences of abuse. For example, young people who had experienced abusive relationships described finding safe and rewarding relationships with WISE staff members, while staff at two of the case WISEs noted that young people from refugee backgrounds were offered trauma-informed support services as part of tailored responses to their needs. In addition to improved mental health, some improvements to physical health were also reported; these are detailed in relation to healthier behaviours and organisational features subsequently.

Effects of WISEs on SDOH Equity—Healthier Behaviours

A significant proportion of young people we interviewed reported improved sleep patterns and/or reduction or cessation of smoking and drug use as a result of participating in the WISEs. In one case WISE, however, young people noted that the transition from a school to a live-work setting which required a higher degree of self-responsibility actually stimulated some less healthy behaviours—particularly smoking—as young people 'found their feet' as emerging adult workers. The time structure required of regular work, combined with formal education about and modelling of healthier behaviours within the WISE, appeared to be the major contributors to positive effects. As one young woman described it:

Before the [WISE] course I wasn't doing anything . . . Like, I was at home for three years not doing anything because it was hard for anyone to find me somewhere.

(Young person, Case C)

It is notable that young people who reported increased smoking due to WISE participation linked this to lack of time structure, in the form of too many breaks on a work site (a pattern linked to the nature of the industry in which the WISE operated).

Improved awareness of nutrition and healthy eating was reported by young people at the two WISEs in our sample—a cafe and catering business and a farm providing local fresh food—that had some industry alignment with food. Notably, this awareness was more pronounced in interviews at the farm enterprise where food was produced, with both young people and other respondents describing examples of their becoming more interested in and confident about food preparation as a result of their involvement in the growing of food:

> Well I got to try a lot of new things that I had never tried before, so champagne fruit—that was a new one . . . I actually wanted to grow some at home because it tastes really nice.
>
> (Young person, Case D)

Conversely, young people at one of the enterprises in an outer metropolitan fringe area which did not have an industry connection to food production or consumption noted that access to decent affordable food near the enterprise premises was challenging:

> Yeah I feel good being here. I don't know about the food and being healthy here . . . The food truck's here, that's expensive though.
>
> (Young person, Case C)

A small number of respondents also reported positive changes to their health behaviours as a result of physical and social stimulation within the case WISEs. For example, one 23-year-old man described being inspired by his involvement with the WISE and wanting to 'keep the momentum going' immediately after his traineeship:

> I'm going to try take up gardening . . . so I might fix up the garden, grow some veggies. Spend some more time with my niece and nephew . . . You know, just try to get outdoors as much as I can.
>
> (Young person, Case B)

Effects of WISEs on SDOH Equity—Daily Living Conditions

While the WISEs varied in the accredited training that they offered, all were active in supporting young people to engage in vocational training and in empowering young people to explore further education. Both young people and ancillary service providers involved with all of our WISE case studies described the WISEs as providing valuable alternative pathways for education and training for young people not well-served by mainstream education. For several of the young people, the supported hands-on learning environment, and the real consequences of working in a live-work setting was both stimulating and challenging in ways they had not experienced in classroom environments:

> I'm more focused if I'm wanting to do something and I'm actually getting somewhere. Because in school I wasn't doing nothing, so I was getting in trouble.
>
> (Young person, Case C)

> At school it's just—it's waking up every day, and because I have anxiety and all that it's, like, it's too much of a hassle . . . I'd rather physical and hands on labour, so I work in a warehouse [at the WISE], that's why I do that.
>
> (Young person, Case B)

While access to secure housing was not a challenge for all young people involved in the study, all WISEs recognised the importance of secure housing to the wellbeing of the young people with whom they worked, and managers described reasonable adjustments they made in their program attendance requirements to accommodate issues for young people who were experiencing unstable housing. Three of the four case WISEs were proactive in helping find housing support where they identified it as a need of their young people. This ranged from formalised partnerships and referrals between the WISE and local housing providers, through to arranging informal emergency accommodation for young people in need.

Many of the young people we interviewed across the WISEs described challenges of transport access to support their participation in WISE programs and related work opportunities. In metropolitan areas, young people told us of travelling up to three hours per day, with up to six changes per round trip, to participate. For the young people involved in our regional and outer metropolitan case studies, public transport was either unreliable or non-existent, with some young people relying on a complicated network of support from family, friends, or fellow WISE participants in order to get to and from the WISE site(s). The metropolitan case WISEs were very aware of transport challenges and had purposefully located on major public transport routes. Staff at the regional case WISE also described being particularly attuned to lack of transport for some of their participants, and would at times become directly involved in ameliorating this problem:

> [A] [employment services] provider can fund [work safety equipment] but can't organise a car to pick someone up [like we do] and transport may be the barrier that's stopping that person getting to an interview or a work placement.
>
> (Manager, Case D)

Despite the purported focus of WISEs on creating pathways to employment, the large majority of young people who participated in the study had not secured ongoing employment as a result of WISE participation at the time of interview. Those who had, had done so either through formal connections with local employers brokered by the WISEs or through incidental relationships they had developed at the WISEs, which gave them access to new job opportunities. Several who had not yet secured work but wanted to identify their pre-existing social capital, in the form of family connections rather than the WISE, as the mechanism through which they were pursuing work possibilities.

The limited employment outcomes we observed in part reflected stage of life—with younger people in our study seeking developmental opportunities from their WISE participation rather than a job—and stage of personal development, with both young people and WISE managers reflecting that the function of the WISE was to move them along a trajectory towards employability, with outcomes differing for participants depending on their starting point. Nevertheless, those young people seeking employment at the time of interview largely attributed their difficulties in accessing work to the precarious labour market and high degree of exploitation of young people among mainstream employers.

Effects of WISEs on SDOH Equity—Intermediating Factors

Young people at every case enterprise reported developing new relationships with fellow participants and/or WISE managers and volunteers as a result of their participation. These relationships had an intermediating effect, in the sense that they helped young people to access new opportunities in education, income, quality employment, and housing. As described earlier, these relationships also supported young people's confidence and willingness to participate in the WISE workplace. Young people's confidence that these relationships would be sustained beyond their time at the enterprise was only strong in two of the case WISEs. In the first of these, young people were active online on social media and through online gaming, and largely expected their new friendships to be sustained through online interaction. In the second case where perceptions that new relationships would be ongoing, there were pre-existing school relationships between some of the young people, which then 'rippled out' to others in the cohort. Across all cases, young people were generally confident that they could maintain connections with WISE managers and continuing staff and volunteers should they need to but typically viewed this as unlikely due to physical distance and because they recognised that these relationships were professional rather than personal.

Effects of WISE on SDOH Equity—Socioeconomic, Political, and Cultural Conditions

All case WISEs took an assets-based approach to recognising the value of the young people with which they work, with some viewing this as a purposeful effort to change the systemic factors that underpin youth disadvantage:

> But we exist because that system is really broken, or it's really frag-mented or it's not functioning in a holistic way for a young person. So part of the challenge is interfacing with something that you don't think's functioning very well.
>
> (Executive Staff, Case A)

WISE partners from ancillary services and government funders observed that the WISE both responded to vital systems gaps and presented new ways of doing things that in some cases influenced their own practices. However, our interviews with WISE customers largely suggested that customers were positively predisposed to supporting the mission of the WISE and thus did not experience significant transformation of perspec-tives as a result of their consumer involvement.

Organisational Features Through Which Health Equity Outcomes Are Realised

Our cross-case analysis suggests that organisational culture—understood as the rules in use (Ostrom, 1999) or how things are done in an organisation—plays a significant role in subjective experience of health equity outcomes. Across all cases, young people described interperson-ally supportive organisational cultures that integrated a strong work ethic and enthusiasm for professionalism with unrelenting positive rein-forcement of young people and tolerance for workplace mistakes. These organisational characteristics were central to many young people's posi-tive experience of WISE and to which they attributed improvements in their mental health and employability:

> Just I think getting back into something, to be honest, after not being at school for so long. Having the courage and confidence to get back into something has been a very big change for me. Just coming to this course. I've got a lot more confidence now and everything. Talking to people and coming to this course and that. So, it's better.
>
> (Young Person, Case C)

> I'm usually a chatterbox but I've learnt to stop and listen a bit more instead of just rambling on. Focusing has been a big problem for

me . . . it helped that I had [Manager] just gently saying, 'Mate, you need to stop doing this, need to get back to doing this' . . . gentle reminders, which was good.

(Young Person, Case D)

Diversity of work activities also presented in our data as a significant factor in improved conditions for wellbeing, with young people reporting greater wellbeing in those social enterprises in our sample that exposed them either to multiple streams of work within an enterprise or rotated young people through multiple business sites. Access to diversity of work had three observable effects.

First, it allowed participants to develop a range of technical skills, which increase both their instrumental ability and their confidence to seek paid work:

I knew a bit, but not exactly what was required in cafes . . . I've [now] done work experience . . . so customer service, waiting tables, making coffees, interacting, clean downs of cafes and all that sort of stuff . . . I like working at [the café site], because it's floor work, so more interacting with customers, getting my hospitality skills up, this is how I carry a plate, this is how I greet customers. It's different to the kiosk that you have at the other two sites, because you greet the customer, you get their coffee order, sometimes they order food.

(Young person, Case A)

Second, the diversity of work activities gave participating young people the developmental space to explore their interests and skills, which some reported improved their sense of self and helped them identify personal or professional development goals. Third, the opportunity to work across business streams and/or business sites exposed young people to different groups of people—colleagues, customers, and suppliers—in different micro-organisational cultures, which they reported improved their social skills and their confidence to work in different types of workplaces.

Distinct but related to the importance of diverse work activities was the spatial design of the case WISEs. Among case WISEs that offered outdoor work and/or work that involved physical labour, young people were more likely to report effects (positive or negative) on physical health:

When I was at school I did not sleep hardly at all . . . Instead of just going home and sitting at home doing work I'd come here for a whole day and just do work for a whole day. And so that was good. And then . . . I'd go back to school more refreshed. I was able to sleep at night . . . yeah, because hard work . . . Which was good because

I didn't need to go to the gym as much. I actually cancelled my subscription, which was awesome.

(Young person, Case D)

Three of the case WISEs also included recreational spaces—such as ping pong tables and basketball courts—alongside work and learning spaces. Young people told us—and our participant observation confirmed—that these were important spaces for developing rapport with other young people with whom they were working, and for alleviating anxiety. One WISE also had a resident therapy animal, who participants described as providing calming energy and a source of support. Senior staff of this WISE noted that anxiety-related non-attendance had dropped substantially among its young people when the therapy animal was introduced to the WISE.

Beyond spatiality, a final organisational feature—or more accurately, function—of WISE that played a significant role in the realisation of health equity outcomes in terms of improved access to employment was the intermediating role that WISEs played in both the local services system and with local employers to support young people's ability to find and sustain work. With regard to local services intermediation, all case WISEs were active in systems of support for their young people, drawing together local educators, housing, and welfare support where needed in bespoke ways to meet the specific needs of individual young people:

we help to promote them a lot . . . their internship opportunities, or any jobs that they've got going, we will put that through our network . . . we have about 800 people in our network.

(WISE partner organisation, Case D)

With regard to local employment intermediation, two of the four WISEs were particularly active not just in connecting young people with employers but supporting their employment transition. In one case, the WISE went as far as attending staff induction of some of its participants, literally and figuratively playing a translation role for both the young people and the employer to ensure successful settlement into the workplace:

I've got constant phone calls with [WISE Manager], so that's been interesting and challenging and to be honest time consuming. But I think we've got a good working relationship . . . we can communicate and . . . tell each other . . . what's working well, what's not working so well.

(Local employer and WISE partner organisation, Case D)

Discussion and Conclusion

The findings from this study suggest that WISEs affect the social determinants of health equity among young people in multiple ways. We find similar to other studies that examine a variety of cohorts (Elmes, 2019; Gordon et al., 2018; Macaulay et al., 2018) that these effects are most pronounced in relation to individual factors, such as increased confidence and healthier behaviours, as well as intermediating factors such as improved relationships and networks. Drawing on our earlier conceptual propositions (see Figure 11.1), we find that organisational culture is a central organisational feature, which operates at both transformational and transactional levels (i.e. influencing both the institutional conditions that drive health inequities and the organisational conditions that drive health equity outcomes within the enterprise itself).

Overall, the WISEs in our study positively influence SDOH equity for their targeted beneficiaries, although some negative effects were identified in relation to behavioural factors where young people were experiencing developmental transitions and in relation to the physical proximity of WISEs to external goods and services—such as healthy food and reliable transport—that support healthier behaviours at work. Given the relatively common tendency of social enterprise to practise bricolage—or making do with the means at hand (Baker & Nelson, 2005)—in order to access resources to run their businesses (Di Domenico et al., 2010), the unintended negative consequences of physical location should be further considered in WISE design and roll-out.

While the case WISEs played a demonstrable role in plugging gaps in local service systems to support the health and wellbeing of their young people, they had limited control over systems deficiencies that have a significant effect on health equities. In particular, the structure and culture of the labour market is a major systemic barrier to improved health equities for young people. While there was some evidence in our research of WISEs having a positive mediating effect on local labour markets through their proactive partnership approaches with local employers, the scale of these effects was necessarily modest. Further, the 'wicked' interplay between housing affordability and transport access in metropolitan Australia, and the lack of availability of public transport in the regional area where we conducted research, are significant systemic constraints against which WISEs were only able to make minor inroads.

In terms of how WISEs improve the conditions for health equity of young people, our study largely confirms our earlier theorisation of the mechanisms through which WISEs realise outcomes (Suchowerska et al., 2019). In particular, our findings suggest that organisational culture that meets young people where they are at, recognises their unique assets, and integrates inclusion and tolerance for error with a strong commitment to professionalism, is critical to success. In addition, business design that offers participation in diverse activities fosters skills development, personal development, and social encounters with different types of people, which are important to building confidence and access to new opportunities for work and friendship. Finally, WISEs have a positive effect on the social determinants of health equity for young people by providing strong intermediation within local services systems and the local labour market.

This chapter makes two contributions to the literature. First, it provides further empirical evidence to inform the growing body of literature on social enterprise and the social determinants of health (Elmes, 2019; Gordon et al., 2018; Roy et al., 2017), with a particular focus on the under-researched cohort of young people experiencing disadvantage, and with a strong emphasis on presenting the perspectives of those the social enterprises seek to serve. Our cross-case analysis suggests that WISEs' responses to SDOH equity are highly context-specific, taking into account the local conditions for and barriers to the realisation of health equity, as well as the specific needs of the cohorts they seek to serve.

Second, our research delves much more deeply than past studies into questions of how—at the level of organisational structure and practice—WISEs produce health equity outcomes. In so doing, we respond to calls (Agafonow, 2018; Roy et al., 2017, 2018) for greater understanding of the organisational conditions and factors through which social enterprise generates particular kinds of social impact. This micro-analytic contribution builds on past research on social enterprise as spaces of wellbeing (Farmer et al., 2015, 2016) and demonstrates that the design and systems-integration of work and workplaces—not just the fact of work or training itself—can substantially influence the effectiveness of WISEs that seek to improve the social conditions for health and wellbeing among young people.

While the presumed promise of WISEs is greater employment, it is notable that at the time of this study, very few of the young people who participated in this study had realised new or ongoing employment as a result of their WISE participation. This in part reflects the life stage of many of our participants—with younger participants focused on further training or education, and highly disadvantaged participants grappling with improvements in mental health and living conditions as a precursor to employment—but also raises questions about the expected outcomes of WISEs as well as the limitations of snapshot research. In terms of the SDOH equity, the case WISEs in this study appeared to play a substantial role in improving the conditions for employability, rather than direct employment, of its participants. The health equity outcomes of WISEs that aim to provide a 'bridge' to employment in the mainstream labour market, rather than act as 'end employers' (Vidal, 2005), can only be truly understood through longitudinal research such as that presented (albeit in relation to a different demographic group) by Elmes in this collection and elsewhere (Elmes, 2019). While our study provides substantial new insights into how WISEs create wellbeing, the longer-term implications of wellbeing for economic and social participation warrant further longitudinal and comparative study.

Acknowledgements

This chapter is based on research supported by an Australian Research Council Linkage grant (LP160101793), co-supported by Victorian Health Promotion Foundation, Social Traders, and Foundation for Young Australians. The full research team includes the authors and Jane Farmer, Gemma Carey, Andrew Joyce, Chris Mason, and Joanne McNeill. We are grateful to the four case study organisations and 93 interviewees for their contributions.

References

Agafonow, A. (2018). Setting the bar of social enterprise research high. Learning from medical science. *Social Science & Medicine, 214*, 49–56. https://doi.org/10.1016/j.socscimed.2018.08.020.

Australian Institute of Health and Welfare. (2011). *Young Australians: Their health and wellbeing* (Cat. no. PHE 140). Australian Institute of Health and Welfare.

Australian Institute of Health and Welfare. (2014). *Australia's health 2014* (No. 14, Cat no. AUS178; Australia's Health Series). Australian Institute of Health and Welfare.

Baker, T., & Nelson, R. E. (2005). Creating something from nothing: Resource construction through entrepreneurial bricolage. *Administrative Science Quarterly, 50*(3), 329–366. https://doi.org/10.2189/asqu.2005.50.3.329.

Barraket, J., & Archer, V. (2010). Social inclusion through community enterprise? Examining the available evidence. *Third Sector Review, 16*(1), 13–28.

Barraket, J., Mason, C., & Blain, B. (2016). *Finding Australia's social enterprise sector 2016: Final report*. CSI Swinburne and Social Traders. http://apo.org.au/resource/finding-australias-social-enterprise-sector-2016-final-report.

Berkes, F., & Adhikari, T. (2006). Development and conservation: Indigenous businesses and the UNDP equator initiative. *International Journal of Entrepreneurship and Small Business, 3*(6), 671–690.

Chandra, Y. (2018). Social enterprise for the visually impaired: Voices from within. *International Journal of Disability and Human Development, 17*(1), 159–168.

Cheng, I.-H. (2015). Re-modelling and reconceptualising skills development in Cambodia: How are social enterprises preparing young people for successful transitions between learning and work? *International Journal of Educational Development, 43*, 134–141. https://doi.org/10.1016/j.ijedudev.2015.06.003.

Cho, S., Kim, M. A., & Kwon, S. I. (2019). Using the photovoice method to understand experiences of people with physical disabilities working in social enterprises. *Disability and Health Journal*, 12(4), 685–693. https://doi.org/10.1016/j.dhjo.2019.03.011.

Considine, M. (2001). *Enterprising states: The public management of welfare-to-work*. Cambridge University Press.

Di Domenico, M., Haugh, H., & Tracey, P. (2010). Social bricolage: Theorizing social value creation in social enterprises. *Entrepreneurship Theory and Practice*, 34(4), 681–703. https://doi.org/10.1111/j.1540-6520.2010.00370.x.

Elmes, A. I. (2019). Health impacts of a WISE: A longitudinal study. *Social Enterprise Journal*, 15(4), 457–474. https://doi.org/10.1108/SEJ-12-2018-0082.

Esping-Andersen, G. (1990). *The three worlds of welfare capitalism*. Princeton University Press.

Evans, M., & Syrett, S. (2007). Generating social capital? The social economy and local economic development. *European Urban and Regional Studies*, 14(1), 55–74. https://doi.org/10.1177/0969776407072664.

Eversole, R., Barraket, J., & Luke, B. (2013). Social enterprises in rural community development. *Community Development Journal*, bst030. https://doi.org/10.1093/cdj/bst030.

Farmer, J., Currie, M., Kenny, A., & Munoz, S.-A. (2015). An exploration of the longer-term impacts of community participation in rural health services design. *Social Science & Medicine (1982)*, 141, 64–71. https://doi.org/10.1016/j.socscimed.2015.07.021.

Farmer, J., De Cotta, T., McKinnon, K., Barraket, J., Munoz, S.-A., Douglas, H., & Roy, M. J. (2016). Social enterprise and wellbeing in community life. *Social Enterprise Journal*, 12(2), 235–254. https://doi.org/10.1108/SEJ-05-2016-0017.

Ferguson, K. M. (2018a). Employment outcomes from a randomized controlled trial of two employment interventions with homeless *Youth*. *Journal of the Society for Social Work and Research*, 9(1), 1–21. https://doi.org/10.1086/696372.

Ferguson, K. M. (2018b). Nonvocational outcomes from a randomized controlled trial of two employment interventions for homeless youth. *Research on Social Work Practice*, 28(5), 603–618. https://doi.org/10.1177/1049731517709076.

Ferguson, K. M., & Xie, B. (2008). Feasibility study of the social enterprise intervention with homeless youth. *Research on Social Work Practice*, 18(1), 5–19. https://doi.org/10.1177/1049731507303535.

Flyvbjerg, B. (2006). Five misunderstandings about case-study research. *Qualitative Inquiry*, 12(2), 219–245. https://doi.org/10.1177/1077800405284363.

Gibson-Graham, J. K., & Cameron, J. (2007). Community enterprises: Imagining and enacting alternatives to capitalism. *Social Alternatives*, 26(1), 20–25.

Gordon, K., Wilson, J., Tonner, A., & Shaw, E. (2018). How can social enterprises impact health and well-being? *International Journal of Entrepreneurial Behavior & Research*, 24(3), 697–713. https://doi.org/10.1108/IJEBR-01-2017-0022.

Macaulay, B., Mazzei, M., Roy, M. J., Teasdale, S., & Donaldson, C. (2018). Differentiating the effect of social enterprise activities on health. *Social Science & Medicine*, 200, 211–217. https://doi.org/10.1016/j.socscimed.2018.01.042.

Marmot, M. (2005). Social determinants of health inequalities. *The Lancet*, 365(9464), 1099–1104. https://doi.org/10.1016/S0140-6736(05)71146-6.

5 ok

Ostrom, E. (1999). Institutional rational choice: An assessment of the institutional analysis and development framework. In *Theories of the policy process*. Westview.

Qian, J., Riseley, E., & Barraket, J. (2019). *Do employment-focused social enterprises provide a pathway out of disadvantage? An evidence review*. The Centre for Social Impact, Swinburne. https://apo.org.au/sites/default/files/resource-files/2019/08/apo-nid251711-1377686.pdf.

Roy, M. J., Donaldson, C., Baker, R., & Kay, A. (2013). Social enterprise: New pathways to health and well-being? *Journal of Public Health Policy, 34*(1), 55–68.

Roy, M. J., Lysaght, R., & Krupa, T. M. (2017). Action on the social determinants of health through social enterprise. *Canadian Medical Association Journal, 189*(11), E440–E441. https://doi.org/10.1503/cmaj.160864.

Roy, M. J., Macaulay, B., Donaldson, C., Teasdale, S., Baker, R., Kerr, S., & Mazzei, M. (2018). Two false positives do not make a right: Setting the bar of social enterprise research even higher through avoiding the straw man fallacy. *Social Science & Medicine, 217*, 42–44. https://doi.org/10.1016/j.socscimed.2018.09.058.

Roy, M. J., McHugh, N., & Hill O'Connor, C. (2014). Social innovation: Worklessness, welfare and well-being. *Social Policy and Society, 13*(3), 457–467. https://doi.org/10.1017/S1474746414000104.

Solar, O., & Irwin, A. (2010). *A conceptual framework for action on the social determinants of health*. Social Determinants of Health Discussion Paper 2 (Policy and Practice). World Health Organization. http://apps.who.int/iris/bitstream/10665/44489/1/9789241500852_eng.pdf.

Spear, R., & Bidet, E. (2005). Social enterprise for work integration in 12 European countries: A descriptive analysis. *Annals of Public & Cooperative Economics, 76*(2), 195–231. https://doi.org/10.1111/j.1370-4788.2005.00276.x.

Suchowerska, R., Barraket, J., Qian, J., Mason, C., Farmer, J., Carey, G., Campbell, P., & Joyce, A. (2019). An organizational approach to understanding how social enterprises address health inequities: A scoping review. *Journal of Social Entrepreneurship*, 1–25. https://doi.org/10.1080/19420676.2019.1640771.

Victorian Health Promotion Foundation. ('VicHealth'). (2015). *Promoting health equity through addressing social determinants in healthy settings approaches: An evidence summary*. Victorian Health Promotion Foundation. www.vichealth.vic.gov.au/-/media/ResourceCentre/PublicationsandResources/Health-Inequalities/Fair-Foundations/Summary/Health-Equity_Summary-Report_Settings.pdf?la=en&hash=9D677EC17B8985BC9A40B58E18BBBF02438ECF23.

Vidal, I. (2005). Social enterprise and social inclusion: Social enterprises in the sphere of work integration. *International Journal of Public Administration, 28*(9–10), 807–825.

World Health Organisation. (2013). *The economics of social determinants of health and health inequalities: A resource book*. WHO. http://apps.who.int/iris/bitstream/handle/10665/84213/9789241548625_eng.pdf;jsessionid=7181D4EA0C6E5EBACED0176498AC54AD?sequence=1.

12 Working With Care

Work Integration Social Enterprise Practitioner Labour

Perri Campbell, Viktoria Adler, Jane Farmer, Jo Barraket, Roksolana Suchowerska, and Joanne McNeill

Introduction

Social enterprise practitioners enable their organisations to achieve social goals through commercial activity and are often required to provide support that draws on attributes such as emotional intelligence and empathy. Practitioners also have varying formally recognised and informal technical skills and experience in education, training, business operations, administration, and sector-specific skills like catering, woodwork, or gardening. There is currently a dearth of evidence about the ways that care, support, and technical skills come together to comprise the work done by practitioners in social enterprises. In this chapter, we focus on Work Integration Social Enterprises (WISEs), the main purpose of which is to 'allow individuals excluded from labour markets and from society at large to find a new role through economic activity and personalised social coaching' (Bucolo, 2006: 60). We explore the work done by social enterprise *practitioners*—that is, those who are paid to support, supervise, and train individuals employed to gain capability (here referred to as *participants*). We focus on those in 'contact roles' who engage directly with participants. Participants often experience a range of disadvantages, including socio-economic disadvantage, disability, illness, or a combination of these life challenges. Here we explore: What is the care work social enterprise practitioners are doing? How do they navigate their own personal and professional boundaries in this work? And, what does the nature of this work suggest about the practitioners' likely experiences of wellbeing or burnout and stress?

We use data from two Australian Research Council funded projects (2017–2020) exploring health, wellbeing, and work and involving seven case WISEs. In both projects, researchers observed, and social enterprise practitioners reported, undertaking complex and multidimensional roles to support participants' capability development, wellbeing, and engagement with their WISE. Here we understand capability as personal enabling resources that provide individuals the freedoms to convert opportunities into functionings (Sen, 1992); for example, the personal

DOI: 10.4324/9781003125976-12

resources to convert opportunities for employment into holding a job. We understand wellbeing as human flourishing or having the personal resources to lead a 'good life' (Atkinson, 2013). Taken together, the cases from these two studies provide insights into how social enterprise practitioner work bridges personal and professional boundaries to create supported learning and working environments. We apply ideas of 'emotional labour' to explore the dimensions of what practitioners do at work that requires care, mentoring, skills, experience, and personal emotional and time investments in WISE participants (Brotheridge and Grandey, 2002). We examine the potential implications of this work for the wellbeing of practitioners in the hybrid and dynamic social and commercial business spaces that social enterprises represent.

Background

While there is a substantial and growing body of literature that considers the benefits of WISE for participants (see e.g. Warner and Mandiberg, 2006; Roy et al., 2014), there has been a paucity of research on the experiences of practitioners in WISEs or social enterprises more broadly. The few studies that have focused primarily on social enterprise practitioners have been concerned with what is attractive about the sector (Olivier, 2018) and how organisations develop practitioner identification with social enterprise values at work (Hsieh et al., 2018; Truong and Barraket, 2018). Some studies have flagged social enterprise practitioner experiences of burnout and stress as a problem, but these experiences have not been examined in detail. There are few accounts of *how* WISE practitioners perform their roles to give shape to supported learning and working environments and how this work affects practitioner wellbeing.

Shaw and Carter (2007: 431) discuss the practices of *social entrepreneurs* in the United Kingdom. Social entrepreneurs can be, but are not necessarily, what we might term 'practitioners'—they are 'individuals who establish enterprises primarily to meet social objectives rather than to generate personal financial profit.' The authors identify personal risk to social entrepreneurs arising from 'the investment of personal local credibility and reputation' (see also Omrane et al., 2018). Kibler et al. (2018: 1) argue that such heightened social responsibility can lead to higher levels of stress among social entrepreneurs, particularly 'when trying to achieve commercial goals and give back to the community at the same time . . . entrepreneurs are likely to overload themselves with too many responsibilities and, consequently, deplete their personal resources' leading to reduced time with family and poor sleep quality. Kelly et al. (2019: 233) explore the negative impacts of 'delivering and sustaining social enterprise services' for paid practitioners and volunteers. Their study focuses on rural areas and identifies pressure points shaped by geographical location and social enterprise activity, which result in a limited workforce and access to funding. Practitioners and board members, in particular, reported a feeling of increased visibility within their community as an 'active member,' leading to a heightened sense of responsibility when things went wrong (Kelly et al., 2019: 234). Houtbeckers (in this book) explores the *responsibilisation* of entrepreneurs and practitioners in further detail. All of these studies suggest that the hybrid work of commerce and care that constitutes social enterprise labour creates particular pressures as well as rewards for social enterprise founders and workers.

The cost for some social enterprise practitioners, particularly leaders and managers, can relate to feelings of emotional, physical, and psychological fatigue or 'burnout' (Barraket et al., 2020; Kernot and McNeill, 2011: 239). The wider literature defines burnout as 'typified by three symptoms—emotional exhaustion, depersonalization, and reduced personal accomplishment' (Costa and Moss, 2018: 787). As Maslach (2003: xxiii) argues, burnout is not a problem of people but rather the environment and conditions in which they work. In addition to high levels of responsibility and stress, the environments that Maslach (2003: xxiii) writes about are both grounded in and stimulate care work and emotional labour which resonates with the environment typically found in WISEs.

Broadly speaking, the literature on emotional labour can be categorised into conceptualisations of what Brotheridge and Grandey (2002) describe as emotional labour that is 'job-focused' or 'employee-focused.' The first refers to workplace or industry requirements of emotion expression or simulation (e.g. being warm and friendly in customer service environments), while the latter relates to emotional self-regulation—such as employees minimising expressions of stress or pleasure—in order to cohere with workplace norms and (be seen to) operate successfully in their work environment. As Grayson and Shuster (2020: 69) suggest, 'it is not the performance of emotional management that is harmful. Rather, it is the expectation of having to manage emotions that is harmful in the workplace.' While much of the literature on emotional labour is concerned with its deleterious effects, some studies have also identified that emotional labour can be beneficial to health where there is genuine alignment between workers' emotions and values and the types of occupational activity required (Mann, 2005; Philipp and Schüpbach, 2010). Other studies have found that workplace emotional support (Karimi et al., 2014; Kinman et al., 2011) and individual emotional intelligence can play an important role in moderating the negative effects of emotional labour.

Alongside emotional labour, practitioner work in the WISE context is characterised by 'care work' which involves 'a face-to-face service that develops the human capability of the [participant],' that is, the 'physical and mental health, physical skills, cognitive skills, and emotional skills, such as self-discipline, empathy, and care' that are useful to oneself and others (England et al., 2002: 455). The development of participants' capability and ability (i.e. physical and cognitive skills) is a crucial part of WISE practitioners' everyday work. Evidence indicates, therefore, that social enterprise practitioner work will typically involve a high degree of care work and emotional labour and thus will impact—positively and negatively—upon practitioner wellbeing.

The demands, mobilisation, and experience of care work and emotional labour for practitioners working in hybrid WISE organisations are complex and, we argue, best understood through a combination of observation and interviews containing an element of reflection—data collection methods we used in both of our research projects. This is partly because while practitioners may be aware of and explicitly perform some aspects of their work, other aspects of their work may occur spontaneously, intuitively, tacitly, and involve activities with individuals and collectives. Practitioner labour influences, and is influenced by, elements including organisational culture, social and commercial goals of a WISE, and also the ways in which practitioners balance personal and professional boundaries. We argue that while much about the roles of WISE practitioners is prescribed by organisations, practitioners also have the discretion to build in elements that are distinctly personal or related to their culture as a work group. Practitioners have ways in which they identify with the WISE and connect with the WISE social goals. Some of this will relate to skills and experiences that they bring with them. Much of WISE work is done to impact on *individual* participants and growing their capability. WISE participants arrive with different skills and experience, and they have varying aptitudes so it is understood that practitioners will help to produce tailored experiences that enable each participant to develop. This can involve exposing participants to particular tasks in safe learning spaces with inputs of practitioner personal care and attention and drawing on practitioners' background work/life experience and skills. As well as flexing to address individual participant requirements, practitioner labour will flex in relation to the affordances of learning and work environments available in a WISE—both in terms of what they can do and what they can do for and with participants. As Farmer et al. (2019) argue, the geographical spaces and places of WISE organisations, along with the equipment, other workers, and organisational culture can all influence practitioner responses to participants, leading to assemblages of labour that help to provide support for participant self-actualisation or capability development (for more on this see Farmer et al. in this collection).

Methods

As noted earlier, data informing this chapter come from two research projects that examined supported work and learning across seven different WISE organisations.

The first project examined the impact of WISE on the social determinants of health equity, such as housing, education, and employment (see Barraket et al., 2020; Barraket et al. in this book). Four WISE, operating in different industry sectors, participated as case study organisations located in metropolitan and rural areas of the states of Victoria and New South Wales (NSW), Australia. The organisations shared the goal of supporting young people who have experienced social and economic disadvantage to gain work skills and experience. Data collection used in this chapter involved participant observation of up to two weeks within each WISE and semi-structured interviews with practitioners (for instance, trainers and managers). Stakeholder workshops; interviews with participants (young people), funding and supply chain partners, and customers; and collation of organisational documents were methods also used in the larger project.

The second project examined the role of WISE as spaces that help to realise wellbeing at individual and community levels (see Farmer et al., 2020; and Farmer et al. in this collection). This project had four case social enterprises, three of which were WISE and included in this chapter's analysis. The case social enterprises are located in regional cities in the states of Victoria and Tasmania. The organisations employ participants with combinations of experiences of physical and/or cognitive disabilities, restrictive health conditions, and socio-economic disadvantage. The study used mixed methods including participant observation, go-along interviews, and focus groups. For this chapter, observation and practitioner interview data are used.

The four case studies in project one aimed to support young people into employment, with each having a particular orientation: Case Study A: Hospitality; Case Study B: Electronics and IT; Case Study C: Building and Carpentry; and Case Study D: Waste Management and Farming. The three WISE case studies drawn from Project two all aimed to provide work integration for people aged between 17 and 60, living in regional cities (population around 100,000) and who experience various and often multiple forms of disadvantage (Barraket et al., 2017): Case Study E: Multiple services (including produce delivery, light manufacturing, assembly, and fleet car washing); Case Study F: Catering; and Case Study G: Multiple services (including timber product creation, clothing recycling, mail-outs, assembly, and data entry).

As different demographics of participants were targeted across the two projects, the types of support needed and how this was offered differed across the social enterprises. For example, participants of project one tended to require individually tailored help with housing, income, and mental health support. Some participants in project two, meanwhile, experienced intellectual disability requiring a practitioner to interface with the National Disability Insurance Scheme (NDIS) while also being drawn into aspects of helping participants with accommodation and life skills, in addition to building work capability.

In order to understand what is involved in social enterprise practitioners performing their work roles, we coded interviews with practitioners (total n = 62) across projects one and two and observation data. A coding framework was iteratively adjusted and developed to ensure alignment with the data (Saldaña, 2013: 194).

Data were coded for aspects that capture:

(a) *what practitioners do that involves care*: formal and informal procedures; advice and mentoring; selecting, matching, and triaging; planning; allocating tasks; providing help; supporting other practitioners; building relationships; and engaging with participants.
(b) *where and how practitioners navigate boundaries between personal and professional*: elements that go beyond formal tasks of work and mentoring and that might relate to life outside the social enterprise.

Coding from the two projects was compared and themes were identified across the two projects which are used to structure findings in the next section.

Findings

Across the case studies, practitioners described their formal roles and tasks at work. These included management and leadership roles, including involvement in administration and business operations. Several also reported deploying—to varying degrees—their technical skills from the industry sectors in which their social enterprises operate, including hospitality industry skills in being a barista, café manager or chef, building agricultural/ horticultural skills, and welding. Alongside this, practitioners often also had formal roles as all or part of their job as trainers, mentors, or social workers.

Here, we focus more on the informal care work that multiple practitioners described and that was also observed across the seven case study social enterprises in the two research projects. We first consider this care work and how it is intimately infused with the work of building capability. We then move on to examples of how practitioners must navigate the boundaries between professional and personal in their work.

Infusing Care Into Capability-Building

Ongoing and in their everyday work, practitioners must strike a balance between assisting participants in skills development and their mentoring, support, and care of them. Producing a job-ready person is the supposed role of the WISE, but practitioners exhibited care in driving this outcome as well as the knowledge that infusing care into work would help to realise the outcomes. A key element of this work is responding to the individual participant and their needs, not simply as a one-off, but considering their mood, needs, and capabilities in an ongoing and fluctuating flow. Simultaneously, the WISE has commercial imperatives so the ongoing and flexing care work must take up little time. In most cases, practitioners were seen to be observing, and then changing and evolving task-participant matches to build capabilities, requiring deft thinking 'on their feet.'

At the start of the participant journey to capability, practitioners may undertake background preparation to understand each participant's capabilities, experience and skills, and to consider whether and how these might change when the participant is working in a group dynamic. Various triaging tactics were observed and described by participants, as exemplified in these quotes where the practitioner at Case F (Catering) describes assessing where to place participants in a catering social enterprise in the first quote—initially, and in the second quote—ongoing:

> First—well I would get them to peel carrots and potatoes—for the simple reason is to see how they can work with their hands. You find . . . if they cannot peel, you don't really want them to touch a sharp knife . . . then we would try, we might do a recipe together where we're making something but they don't have to touch a knife—you would cut the things and they will make a quiche, say, and they can sprinkle the stuff in or they can mix an egg. Show them how to whisk properly . . . so they've got some input instead of just cleaning or dishes all the time.
>
> (Case F, Chef/Supervisor)

> Some you will find they mainly can only do repetitious stuff that they do week-in and week-out, then you might try and guide them to a little bit more, once they've got that to try and teach them something else.
>
> (Case F, Chef/Supervisor)

Practitioners also discuss strategies they employ to help people learn but also to help them make social connections. For example, a staff member from Case F discusses how she facilitates participants to help each other by teaming up more experienced with less experienced participants:

> some of the more experienced ones will sometimes come over and help one of the others . . . or you'll ask them—'how about you work together?'—and it gives that particular one that's more experienced, I think, a bit more confidence that they can do these things.
>
> (Case F, Chef/Supervisor)

Another practitioner at Case E discusses strategically placing people together within tight spaces so they will 'bump into each other' and chat, thereby making social interaction:

> If you had two people on a row [weeding], they'll end up both at different ends, not necessarily talking to each other. If you put three or four on, they all sit there together and they're all weeding along together. It's funny how it works.
>
> (Case E, Operations Manager)

Another balancing act is enabling autonomous work or the illusion of autonomy, to grow confidence and mastery, while still being around, as a supportive supervisor or practitioner, if things get stressful or go wrong. Participants could require very close and intense supervision, particularly during their initial training periods. In several instances, this intense type of supervision was essential to maintaining a safe workplace and to assure a certain level of product quality to customers. Assessing if regular and thorough supervision was needed or not, and its fluctuations, formed part of the job of practitioners in contact roles.

Staff at Catering (Case Study F) discussed having a fairly hands-off approach in the kitchen area, monitoring at a distance, but stepping in if they saw a problem. This does mean that they were constantly 'on' and rarely had an opportunity for time-out during the working day. As observed:

> They [participants] are largely working independently with supervision very much at a distance usually. [Participants] are working independently. Each worker takes their own bench—they will do their work and then double-check with Kay or Alison if it is ok—or they will be checked on by the supervisor.
>
> (Case F, Researcher's Observations)

Throughout the participants' time at the WISE, practitioners were alert to the need to grow participant capability. This required applying their experience and intuition as to what would work and again assessing this almost constantly to be alert for changing individual or group circumstances. In project one, practitioners were running two concurrent training programs for participants, with 'many different tasks involved in each staff role' in relation to these (Case C, Trainer). As well as teaching and assisting participants to implement tasks, practitioners explained that they applied intuitive responses, accrued through personal experience over time, in creating the right learning and working conditions.

Practitioners harnessed the different types of tasks and spaces in WISE settings to support individuals' development goals. Outdoor and garden spaces were discussed as some locations with potential for many different types of tasks, enabling practitioners to support participant progression, transitions to new levels of work mastery, and personal development. In these development contexts, practitioners were active in building rapport with participants while teaching hands-on skills. These personal and one-to-one or one-to-group moments provided intimate spaces where wider issues of capability could be tackled such as understanding health or gender role issues.

As well as passing on information, these situations can build capability through the novel types of personal relationship experiences that they open up for participants:

> So, you've got [participant] that you know could really do with some one-on-one time . . . So, I allow half an hour to work with [participant] and we have a bit of banter. And they have no real 'aha' moments really, but he's had a good experience for half an hour with a person, so an older male, who in their past experience, older males have been horrible. You've just designed this space for them to be, and maybe to help them realise that they've got choices, you know.
>
> (Case C, Trainer)

Over time, another issue can build—participant boredom with the work. Again, practitioners were able to describe some tactics, including work rotations that also enabled participants to gain experience across the different aspects of an organisation's work. As a practitioner at Case G discussed:

> so they have 3 months in the kitchen and then it rotates and I get another new lot of people . . . so basically they are . . . learning different skills . . . while I've got my people rostered for the kitchen there will be a group that are rostered on to do the washing . . . and the ironing . . . someone else to do the cleaning and then that rotates and sort of goes right round and then . . . so everyone sort of gets a turn at different things and they learn new skills.
>
> (Case G, Supervisor)

A rotating 'rostering' system could have its downsides and not suit everyone; and in these situations, the practitioner had to be alert to ensuring all participants experienced the same work flow while also supporting individuals to follow their preference or aptitude—as in the following quote where a practitioner reflects on the flexibility that must be open to individuals:

> she'll just go to the potatoes and put them in the sink and start peeling them . . . and then she'll . . . what other veggies we are having and she'll have them on the stove and then . . . right . . . what are

we doing for dessert?' . . . she's, I think, a bit disappointed that her time is running out and I said—look just because you're not on the roster, you know that doesn't mean that you won't be helping out with catering.

(Case G, Supervisor)

Practitioners, then, must remain alert to the journey of each participant and building their capability over time. They must consider how best each will learn and what their aptitudes are while also considering their mood, situation, and positioning in the group throughout days and over time. Where practitioners are working with larger number of participants and with larger groups, this element of tailoring for individuals inevitably must intensify workload and stress levels among practitioners due to their constantly assessing and reassessing participant capabilities and potential.

The Practitioner as Supporter, Mentor, and Coach

Along with incidental caring and support, there were times where participants required specific mentoring, coaching, or support type of inputs. This might be for reflections on personal development and setting goals or where a participant was experiencing a personal problem. Across the two projects, there were few formal mentors employed. Although their roles differ, trainers and supervisors often double as mentors as a result of the considerable contact time spent with participants. In smaller organisations, administrative and operational practitioners support participants when needed as well as taking care of the business side of the WISE. In this context, practitioner capabilities include a requirement to 'switch' between work/supervisor and personal developer/mentor roles, with related impacts on changing emotional practices and the need for practitioners to self-regulate both amount/extent of work and the degree of emotional involvement. While these mentoring sessions might be planned, they could occur spontaneously at junctures scattered throughout their working days. The informal mentoring work was observed to be individually tailored to participants and manifested for practitioners as detailed, person-oriented work that could be intense and time consuming, as discussed here:

Be it more sensitive things like sexual or drug and alcohol related and that sort of stuff. Yeah, and a tailored approach is really important and I think if we didn't it would be more risk involved and there would be less likelihood of positive outcomes from the young people because they will not of had the opportunity, given the limitations that might be in their lives already.

(Case D, Social Worker)

In addition to working with participants, practitioners work with external service providers, support networks, and family members to develop transition plans and goals. As one social worker explains this creates a unified approach, 'everybody gets an opportunity to be on the same page and working towards the same goal' (Case D).

The benefits of support are seen over the long term as relationships are built around a person, participants gain confidence, and personal development takes place. Practitioners shared stories of progression sometimes over longer timeframes. For example, one practitioner at Case Study E discussed supporting a young Aboriginal man to develop his talent for art, supporting and encouraging him in his early forays around selling his work and then providing mentoring support while the young man applied for a grant to start a printing and art business.

Despite the demands of their roles, practitioners often depicted these mentoring relationships with participants as an enjoyable and fulfilling part of working in a WISE. This is the work that practitioners often refer to as making their job 'worth it.' Other practitioners conveyed a mutual benefit from learning that happens as a result of accompanying participants in their work and training journey:

> So, the hospitality staff will be standing next to a young person and just being next to them, you can just feel an energy of support and you can feel an energy of presence and young people can feel that and they haven't had that before. So, teachers have never stood alongside them, the police don't stand alongside them, they stand over them, their parents have never stood alongside them. You know, not all young people obviously, I'm generalising, but many of the young people who come to us have had fractured or non-existent relationships or positive relationships with an adult.
>
> (Case A, Trainer)

Participants coming into WISE programs may be connected already with support services and while WISE practitioners seek to monitor the participants' wellbeing through interactions with these external connections, they can only do this when the participant is ready to disclose information.

> The external referrals will come out throughout the course when young people start opening up and sharing different things and you might have them disclosing a lot about their drug habits. And then just having those conversations of, 'Do you see it as an issue, as a problem, do you want support with it' . . . I think for a lot of them it's just about them regaining trust in adults again.
>
> (Case D, Social Worker)

In this context, some practitioners expressed awareness that after work hours and informal conversations play an important role in the relationship development that is crucial to their mentoring and support roles.

In project two, participants at all of the social enterprises associated the supervisor's office with support and security, suggesting their feeling that they could gain advice from these places and people when needed: 'I just go to Georgie [supervisor] . . . I just talk to her and that . . . just like anything . . . what I've been doing throughout the week' (Case E, Participant).

Bridging the Personal and Professional

WISE practitioners depicted their emotional investment in the success of their participants as they described going 'above and beyond' to ensure people feel supported and engaged. Practitioners described talking with and supporting participants outside business hours and providing resources like clothing, food, personal hygiene equipment, household equipment, and transport solutions. In providing this support, practitioners can experience feelings of concern, stress, and anxiety but also validation in that they often see it as part of their job and deeply aligned with their interests and motivations:

> Yes, so all the guys have my phone number, they contact me outside of work as well as inside of work which enables me to support them in that level as well. Sometimes it's hard in the kitchen for them to express how they're feeling and it can be a bit rough in there as well so this is a way that they might—instead of coming in here, that way they've got that option to actually contact me at home and talk to me about things that are going on as well. I have taken certain clients to the doctors and things like that, sort of helping out wherever you can really. But trying to also have that barrier in there as well where they're not also relying on you, which I think I have that balance with the guys a lot. Some of them don't have the support that they need.
>
> (Case F, Supervisor)

Practitioners also described having to be tuned in to where they could help with addressing non-work-related vulnerabilities and issues of participants—looking at how these could be addressed while at the workplace. Examples where practitioners instigated discussions and other interventions such as getting outside experts in to have conversations and give training were about issues including hygiene, medication, reproductive health, and other personal health issues. They discussed having conversations with participants about their personal lives, for example, helping participants with gaining safe and secure accommodation and facilitating support for mental health needs.

Practitioners at all of the sites expressed challenges with crossing boundaries between the professional and the personal in trying to support participants to gain capability or simply to live securely. However, some felt more able than others to set boundaries between the personal and professional, as one supervisor said:

> We try and maintain a professional supervisor support relationship, rather than being a friend. There are times we've had to say to people, say to employees, no I'm not your friend, I'm your supervisor, I'm your support person.
>
> (Case G, Supervisor)

Changing requirements and policies of external service providers in the wider environment could be a source of frustration. Practitioners gave examples of experiences where they thought these had hindered their flexibility and capacity to provide participants with practical support. Practitioners described supporting one participant's journey back into work at the WISE after the participant experienced an acute episode of mental illness:

> Although our funding rules say she's supposed to be here for eight hours a week, well that's the only basis on which we get paid. We actually came to an arrangement with her mum, so her mum came in for the first week, did a couple of hours for morning tea, that was it, then home, so two hours. Did that for a couple of weeks, then she came by herself without her mum, for a couple more weeks and then gradually went back up to essentially two days a week. For that long easing period, we didn't receive any funding, but it was part of getting her back to where she wanted to be and reconnecting her with work. It wasn't easy, for her or her mum, but we said to her . . . if your doctor, and you and she think that returning to work will aide with her recovery, then we will do what we need to do.
>
> (Case G, Manager)

This is an example of how practitioners need to build and use relationships beyond the immediate individual to help navigate rigid policies and to accommodate participants' diverse needs. As a final note in this findings section, practitioners sometimes recognised the stress that they were under in helping participants to realise social outcomes *while also helping to* meet the financial and business demands of a successful WISE business. This highlights another form of boundary that practitioners must navigate and one that is inherent in the hybrid social mission plus commercial business social enterprise model. As one practitioner noted:

'I think even when I first started here it was a lot more relaxed whereas now it's a lot more business orientated' (Case E).

Discussion and Conclusions

Across the seven case study WISEs in two projects, we have seen that social enterprise practitioners undertake a variety of formal roles around pursuing the commercial goals of the business (e.g. manager, supervisor) and in relation to the social purpose goals of training and development of social enterprise participants. We have also observed and been told by practitioners about work that directly involves care (e.g. mentoring, support, advice and practical help) and work that has care suffused within it (e.g. taking care about optimising participant opportunities to gain capabilities, security and social connection). In these ways, the WISE practitioners appear to be hybrid in their roles and flexible in their skills, which mirrors the hybrid business models that they work within. They are engaged in maintaining a viable commercial business while teaching an ongoing and changing stream of workers and caring for and about them. As has been exemplified in the findings section, the care work involves deployment of a considerable amount of experience, intuition and kindness, combined with a steely determination to 'get the best out of' the participants. While we should surely expect caring supervisors in all workplaces, the WISEs present special situations where there are large numbers of vulnerable people being trained as workers. This guarantees that care will always be needed as part of capability-building strategies, sometimes quite intensely, and not just occasionally or incidentally as might be expected in mainstream workplaces.

Our findings suggest that WISE practitioners in contact roles are involved in emotional labour. Aspects of the intense work involve both an interwoven kind of care (care applied while guiding the participants' capability development) and focused episodes specifically about care (such as sessions involving mentoring or help with a problem). The interwoven care involved being 'always on' to understand opportunities for capability development, while being attuned to the readiness of the participant and balancing between establishing a routine that provides a sense of security and taking those opportunities—sometimes risks— to build participants' capabilities. Practitioners often appeared to apply intuition learned on the job, with examples such as the use of small spaces to encourage people to interact and rotating participants through different physical environments to give them variety. In order to successfully negotiate participant development, practitioners were required to be highly attuned to the needs of participants *as individuals* whose needs are likely to change over time, involving quite short or longer time frames as individual participants learn at their own pace. Woven into the constant alertness to provide new development opportunities, practitioners also display empathy, agility, and creativity—in other words being *emotionally intelligent* while actually focused on developing participant work capability. At other times, practitioners were in care-focused situations where again their knowledge had to span considerable spaces of care, including helping with health problems, getting safe accommodation, and navigating form filling for grants as well as supporting participants to plan work-related goals.

This is all navigated at a fast pace of work and can involve a diverse and large number of participants. It can also involve navigating other relationships with participants' other services providers and families, and with business customers, other businesses, social enterprise executives, and board members. That is, while juggling care in capability development for participants, practitioners must also navigate and communicate across networks of people engaged in driving social purpose at the community level. Such extended interwoven environments of care could be unique to, or at least are likely associated with, the organisational hybridity of the WISE model, when considered alongside other organisational types. While this is not a comparative study, it seems likely that the complexity of care required to navigate WISE settings will be quite different to sites of explicitly market economic activity where the focus is primarily production for profit.

We saw that practitioners were also dealing with spanning boundaries between the care that they perceive individuals need and a notion of a defined scope of their technical work practice (Needham et al., 2017). While boundary spanning is generally considered to involve spanning organisational boundaries or boundaries between work and community 'spaces' (Needham et al., 2017: 289), here we consider the boundary spanning work of practitioners in some different ways. First, at the boundary between the practitioners' technical job and the practitioners' extended acts of care. Practitioners work in an embedded and difficult space in carrying out their work and it is potentially burdensome for them. Who is not going to provide their mobile phone number if they think that a person in their care might be vulnerable in their community life? From our study, it was unclear the extent to which practitioners had organisational validation or permission to assist participants outside worktime, but there were multiple instances of them doing this. A second aspect of boundary spanning we suggest relates to social life in the smaller regional cities where D, E, F, and G case studies were located. Here, the practitioners also crossed boundaries between their work in social enterprises and community life. They might encounter participants outside of work, in the community and will simultaneously be aware of the risks to which vulnerable participants could be exposed in everyday community life (Farmer et al., 2016: 250). Finally, as highlighted by Ungerson (2005), there is a difference between caring for and caring about someone that requires bridging work. The relationships involved in care work bridge formalised care as part of providing a service and informal 'care' feelings about supporting someone, including giving them emotional support. Little is known about the effects of such boundary spanning work on the health and wellbeing of practitioners.

In line with existing studies, we suggest that the emotional labour and boundary spanning we found, have both positive and negative implications for the wellbeing of practitioners (Brotheridge and Grandey, 2002). Negative effects of emotional labour are experienced when there is a lack of alignment between the expectations of the organisation and the capacity of the individual practitioner. Positive wellbeing occurs (even with burnout) where there is values alignment between practitioner and workplace goals (Maslach, 2003: xxiii). We found a strong degree of alignment between practitioners' expression of care (i.e. application of care, concern and support for participants) and organisations' social missions. Overall, practitioners expressed few problems with their roles and some spontaneously suggested they enjoyed aspects of their roles. Our findings might be interpreted as supporting existing studies that claim emotional intelligence, or the capability to span emotional boundaries and spaces, is both needed and contributes to the moderation of the negative effects of emotional labour.

Not necessarily depicted by staff interviewees in our study, but apparent from the wider literature of the social enterprise field, the negative effects of emotional labour (i.e. stress and burnout) in this sector emerge from the material precarity of the WISE model and the *pressure* this places on practitioners. (There were occasional validations of this from our results, for example where a practitioner commented on the increased commercial pressures over time.) Additionally, and implied in our findings, burnout could manifest from the *relational* pressures of WISE work (i.e. the work never stopping, the intensity of care work needed and its flowing into personal life). In this sense, 'negative emotional labour' arises from over-work rather than inauthentic work. Kelly et al. (2019) highlighted that WISE practitioners who feel a greater burden of personal responsibility are at risk of experiencing negative effects on their own health, in particular exhaustion and fatigue. Our findings do exhibit practitioners taking high personal responsibility which suggests potential for stress and burnout. In this respect, emotional labour may be experienced and play out similarly to other caring professions, such as nursing and teaching, rather than work in retail or service provision as could be implied by a simple focus on the commercial outputs (business side) of the WISE (Brotheridge and Grandey, 2002). At the same time, WISEs are often cash strapped and the material impacts of simply not having enough resources may add to the potential for burnout (Kelly et al., 2019: 233). This element is not widely acknowledged in the literature from other workplace settings.

We conclude that the social goals of WISE encourage and even necessitate practitioners to perform care work and emotional labour to support participants' skills development and transitions into work. Care work is not generally emphasised in position descriptions, and for many practitioners, including managers as well as trainers, it appears to be somehow viewed as inherent and perhaps unmentionable, yet it is essential. Where learning, work, and care happen together but elements are played down, there is potential for confusion, different practitioners taking different approaches and consequent stress, worry, fatigue, and even burnout. A practical implication is the need for WISE to consider practitioner values and care experience and approaches, alongside technical, objectively measurable skills in the recruitment process.

It is significant to highlight some limitations in our research. The studies that inform this chapter did not specifically set out to collect data about practitioner work. However, practitioner care emerged as a strong theme in both studies. We do not know objectively if practitioners experience stress or burnout as mental health conditions as they did not complete psychological health scales, nor were they asked about these issues. We did not gather information about practitioner retention or staff turnover, nor do we know about pay levels or training for their roles. We also do not know about practitioner motivations for entering social enterprise employment. We suggest these topics should be explored in future studies as relevant to ongoing recruitment, retention, and enjoyment of jobs, in the WISE sector.

This chapter emphasises the need for strong values alignment in practitioner recruitment. We suggest that there is value in future research that enables a systematic understanding and appreciation of the complexity of the roles that practitioners perform, particularly given the hybrid nature of WISEs, which demand a richer and more agile assemblage than is perhaps required by other organisational types that are explicitly commercial or explicitly for maximising public value. Further research is required to understand the impact of emotional labour and boundary-crossing on practitioner wellbeing, and the role that emotional support and emotional intelligence can play in moderating negative effects arising in WISE settings.

Acknowledgements

This chapter draws on two research projects. Project 1 was supported by an Australian Research Council Linkage grant (LP160101793), co-supported by Victorian Health Promotion Foundation, Social Traders, and Foundation for Young Australians. The full research team includes the authors and Gemma Carey; Andrew Joyce; Chris Mason; and Batool Moussa. We gratefully acknowledge the four case study organisations and 93 interviewees for participating and contributing.

Project 2 was supported by an Australian Research Council Discovery grant (DP170100388). The full research team includes the authors and Sue Kilpatrick; Michael Roy; Katharine McKinnon; Chris

Brennan-Horley; Sarah-Anne Munoz; Tracy De Cotta; Sherridan Emery; Peter Kamstra; and Melissa Kennedy. We would like to recognise the time and commitment of the employees, practitioners, volunteers, CEOs, and board members of the social enterprises who participated and thank them for their wonderful enthusiasm and support.

References

Atkinson, S. (2013) 'Beyond Components of Wellbeing: The Effects of Relational and Situated Assemblage', *Topoi*, 32: 137–144.

Barraket, J., Campbell, P., Moussa, B., Suchowerska, R., Farmer, J., Carey, G., Joyce, A., Mason, C., & McNeill, J. (2020) *Improving Health Equity for Young People? The Role of Social Enterprise. October 2020*, Centre for Social Impact, Swinburne University, Melbourne.

Barraket, J., Douglas, H., Eversole, R., Mason, C., McNeill J., & Morgan, M. (2017) 'Classifying social enterprise models in Australia', *Social Enterprise Journal*, 13(4): 345–361.

Brotheridge, C. M., & Grandey, A. A. (2002) 'Emotional labor and burnout: Comparing two perspectives of "people work"', *Journal of Vocational Behavior*, 60(1): 17–39.

Bucolo, E. (2006) 'French social enterprises: A common ethical framework to balance various objectives', in M. Nyssens, S. Adam, & T. Johnson (eds.) *Social Enterprise: At the Crossroads of Market, Public Policy and Civil Society*, Routledge, London.

Costa, D.K., & Moss, M. (2018) 'The cost of caring: Emotion, burnout, and psychological distress in critical care clinicians', *Annals of the American Thoracic Society*, 15(7): 787–790.

England, P., Budig, M., & Folbre, N. (2002) 'Wages of virtue: The relative pay of care work', *Social Problems*, 49(4): 455–473.

Farmer, J., De Cotta, T., McKinnon, K., Barraket, J., Munoz, S.-A., Douglas, H., & Roy, M.J. (2016) 'Social enterprise and wellbeing in community life', *Social Enterprise Journal*, 12(2): 235–254.

Farmer, J., De Cotta, J., Kilpatrick, S., Barraket, J., Roy, M.J., & Munoz, S.A. (2019) 'How work integration social enterprises help to realize capability: A comparison of three Australian settings', *Journal of Social Entrepreneurship*, DOI: 10.1080/19420676.2019.1671481.

Farmer, J., De Cotta, T., Kilpatrick, S., Barraket, J., Brennan-Horley, C., McKinnon, K., Adler, V., et al. (2020) *Mapping the impact of social enterprise on disadvantaged individuals and communities in Australia's regional cities*, Swinburne University of Technology, Melbourne, available at: https://apo.org.au/sites/default/files/resource-files/2020-08/apo-nid303490.pdf.

Grayson, B., & Shuster, S.M. (2020) 'Emotional labour, teaching and burnout: Investigating complex relationships', *Educational Research*, 62(1): 63–76.

Hsieh, Y.C., Weng, J., & Lin, T. (2018) 'How social enterprises manage their organizational identification: A theoretical framework of identity management approach through attraction, selection, and socialization', *The International Journal of Human Resource Management*, 29(20): 2880–2904.

Karimi, L., Leggat, S. G., Donohue, L., Farrell, G., & Couper, G. E. (2014) 'Emotional rescue: The role of emotional intelligence and emotional labour on well-being and job-stress among community nurses', *Journal of Advanced Nursing*, 70(1), 176–186.

Kelly, D., Steiner, A., Mazzei, M., & Baker, R. (2019) 'Filling a void? The role of social enterprise in addressing social isolation and loneliness in rural communities', *Journal of Rural Studies*, 70: 225–236.

Kernot, C., & McNeill, J. (2011) *Australian Stories of Social Enterprises: Stories of Challenge*, University of New South Wales, Sydney.

Kibler, E., Wincent, J., Kautonen, T., Cacciotti, G., & Obschonka, M. (2018) 'Why social entrepreneurs are so burned out', *Harvard Business Review*, December 6, 2018. Available from: https://hbr.org/2018/12/why-social-entrepreneurs-are-so-burned-out.

Kinman, G., Wray, S., & Strange, C. (2011) 'Emotional labour, burnout and job satisfaction in UK teachers: The role of workplace social support', *Educational Psychology*, 31(7), 843–856.

Mann, S. (2005) 'A health-care model of emotional labour: An evaluation of the literature and development of a model', *Journal of Health, Organisation and Management*, 19(4–5), 304–317.

Maslach, C. (2003) *Burnout: The Cost of Caring*, Malor Books, Cambridge, MA.

Needham, C., Mastracci, S., & Mangan, C. (2017) 'The emotional labour of boundary spanning', *Journal of Integrated Care*, 25(4): 288–300.

Olivier, B. (2018) 'Do social enterprises attract workers who are more pro-socially motivated than their counterparts in for-profit organizations to perform low-skilled jobs?' *The International Journal of Human Resource Management*, 29(20): 2861–2879.

Omrane, A., Kammoun, A., & Seaman, C. (2018) 'Entrepreneurial burnout: Causes, consequences and way out', *FIIB Business Review*, 7(1): 28–42.

Philipp, A., & Schüpbach, H. (2010) 'Longitudinal effects of emotional labour on emotional exhaustion and dedication of teachers', *Journal of Occupational Health Psychology*, 15(4): 494.

Roy, M.J., Donaldson, C., Baker, R., & Kerr, S. (2014) 'The Potential of Social Enterprise to Enhance Health and Well-Being: A Model and Systematic Review', *Social Science & Medicine*, 123: 182–193. https://doi.org/10.1016/j.socscimed.2014.07.031

Saldaña, J. (2013) *The Coding Manual for Qualitative Researchers*, Sage, London.

Sen, A.K. (1992) *Inequality Re-Examined*, Harvard University Press, Cambridge, MA.

Shaw, E., & Carter, S. (2007) 'Social entrepreneurship: Theoretical antecedents and empirical analysis of entrepreneurial processes and outcomes', *Journal of Small Business and Enterprise Development*, 14(3): 418–434.

Truong, A., & Barraket, J. (2018) 'Engaging workers in resource-poor environments: The case of social enterprise in Vietnam', *The International Journal of Human Resource Management*, 29(20): 2949–2970.

Ungerson, C. (2005) 'Care, work and feeling', *The Sociological Review*, 53(2): 188–203.

Warner, R., & Mandiberg, J. (2006) 'An update on affirmative businesses or social firms for people with mental illness', *Psychiatric Services* 57(10): 1488–1492.

13 Meeting People Where They're at

Building an Inclusive Workplace for Disabled People

Jillian Scott and Robert Wilton

Introduction

The social enterprise ethos of prioritising people over profits seems to align closely with disability-based organisations and their sister businesses created to provide vocational training and meaningful activity for disabled people. However, critics of social enterprises tailored to the needs and skills of specific disability groups argue that while the accessibility and accommodations provided in these settings may be superior to that of a mainstream workplace, participants are effectively segregated in these worksites (Bates-Harris, 2012). While questions of inclusion and belonging are complex (Hall, 2004; Lysaght et al., 2017), segregated or separate workplaces may limit opportunities to develop new capacities through relations with diverse others and to foster new forms of social encounter and exchange.

In this chapter, we use a case study of a non-profit café in Hamilton, Ontario, Canada, to examine a different approach to meaningful work for disabled people; one in which a broader focus on creating an inclusive workplace positions disabled people as one group within a broader community of paid employees and volunteers. Using an ethnographic case study incorporating participant observation in a volunteer role, and interviews with café staff and volunteers, we address two related research questions. First, how does this approach to meaningful work in a social enterprise setting shape the experience of inclusion for disabled people? Second, what implications does this approach hold for the wellbeing of those involved?

Through our analysis, we offer a detailed picture of the successes and limitations of this model to deliver on the café's mandate to 'welcome everyone around the table.' With respect to inclusion, the café's emphasis on immense flexibility and sustained social support in the workplace are key elements of an approach to value and embrace the varying capacities of both disabled and non-disabled workers. The recognition and valuing of these diverse capacities in the relational setting of the café, coupled with the powerful opportunity to help other community members, stokes

DOI: 10.4324/9781003125976-13

key aspects of wellbeing including positive self-regard, expanded capabilities, and new social connections. Ultimately, our analysis suggests that organising a business around the collective goal of placing people first and meeting them where they're at can create a working environment characterised by care, dignity, and authentic human connection that enhances workers' wellbeing. At the same time, such a space is itself fragile and difficult to sustain.

In what follows, we first review relevant literature on disability and employment in 'mainstream' and social economies. We then outline our conceptual framework, drawing from J. K. Gibson-Graham's diverse economies approach (Gibson-Graham, 2006). Next, we outline the details of our research context and methodology before turning to the substance of our analysis. Our concluding discussion focuses on how we imagine and enact inclusive workplaces and the implications for wellbeing. The definition of disability we use in this study draws from Ontario's Human Rights Code and encompasses a broad range and degree of conditions including physical, mobility, intellectual and psychiatric disabilities, hearing or vision loss, addiction, and chronic illness (Ontario Human Rights Commission, 2016). Throughout the chapter, we use the term 'disabled people' to foreground the collective experience of disablement faced by this population within society (McColl, 2019).

Background

Disabled People and Mainstream Employment

Recent data from the Canadian Survey on Disability indicate that 59 per cent of disabled people aged 25–64 were working, compared to 80 per cent of non-disabled adults in the same age bracket (Morris et al., 2018). Significantly, two-fifths of those disabled adults who were not employed (close to 650,000 people) were deemed to have 'potential to work.' Existing research has documented challenges in recruitment, interviewing, training, day-to-day work, promotion, and retention (Brewster et al., 2017; Krupa et al., 2016; Kuznetsova & Yalcin, 2017; Ruhindwa et al., 2016). Employment data in Canada and other countries reveal a persistent narrative of un- and underemployment facing disabled people (Kuznetsova & Yalcin, 2017; Morris et al., 2018; Ruhindwa et al., 2016).

Disabled people confront numerous barriers in their pursuit of meaningful work. Many of these barriers result from misinformation, lack of knowledge about the law and reasonable accommodation, as well as assumptions about disability on the part of management and co-workers (Darcy et al., 2016). For some mainstream employers, the notion of an inclusive workplace may be attractive in principle, but the perceived cost of accommodation is often assumed to be a stumbling block. Kuznetsova and Yalcin (2017) indicate employers overestimate the cost of accommodations due to a lack of experience and knowledge which results in prejudicial treatment of disabled job candidates as well as workers returning to work following serious injury. In some ways, it is understandable that employers are confused about the real cost of accommodations. As Padkapayeva et al. (2017) show through their analysis of published work on the cost-effectiveness of accommodation, there are no clear conclusions or best practices as of yet. Without empirical evidence or clear direction on how to provide useful accommodations, employers are reluctant to take on additional tasks to ensure inclusivity in the workplace. Smaller organisations in particular may have less experience and in-house expertise in developing inclusive environments and practices with little time to coordinate and connect with external expertise and advisors (Mandal & Ose, 2015). However, even large companies report low numbers of accommodations provided, which suggests a prejudicial avoidance in hiring and retaining workers with disabilities (Kuznetsova & Yalcin, 2017).

Although anti-discrimination/accessibility legislation has been passed in many contexts, the practical significance of such legislation is difficult to discern. In Ontario, Canada, Lysaght et al. (2018) note that provincial disability legislation (the 2005 *Accessibility for Ontarians with Disabilities Act* or AODA) prescribes inclusion but is light on details with few standards by which to measure progress or what shape it should take in work environments. As Darcy et al. (2016) suggest, a general understanding of accessible physical environments has yet to be reached, let alone recognition of the more nuanced and less visible needs of people with mental ill health, HIV/AIDS, or learning disabilities. Having laws in place to protect people from discrimination is not enough to change employers' conceptions of accommodations and the (in)capacity of disabled workers.

Enduring assumptions and prejudices about the needs and abilities of disabled workers—and a failure to create and enforce concrete employment standards—produce harms on a number of levels. These include a loss of opportunity to pursue leadership and promotion, lower incomes and ongoing economic dependence, further stigmatisation, social exclusion, damage to self-esteem, and a hindering of self-actualisation (Darcy et al., 2016; Kalef et al., 2014; Kim & Williams, 2012; Ruhindwa et al., 2016; Smith, 2021; Wilton, 2006). Confronting these enduring barriers creates stress for workers and job seekers, not least with respect to the question of when and if to disclose disabilities (Brewster et al., 2017; Kim & Williams, 2012; Krupa et al., 2016).

Alternative Employment Settings: Social Enterprises

As an alternative to the mainstream economy, social enterprises have been seen as a partial solution to unemployment and underemployment of disabled people (Evans & Wilton, 2019; Lysaght et al., 2018). Social enterprises represent one part of a broader social economy encompassing a diversity of organisations such as cooperatives and not-for-profit organisations; the commonality between them is that their creation and function serves a social mandate (Quarter et al., 2018). Various types of social enterprises in Canada are designed to welcome (paid or voluntary) workers with disabilities (Krupa et al., 2016; Lysaght et al., 2018). With a commitment to principles such as social responsibility, diversity, and community engagement, they may be uniquely positioned to redress disabled people's exclusion from the workplace. Such organisations may also be well positioned to adopt a 'holistic understanding' of the role of work in the life of disabled people (Lysaght et al., 1994).

Existing research suggests that individuals engaged in social enterprise employment take pride in their labour and the opportunity to contribute to the community and local economy (Evans & Wilton, 2019; Kalef et al., 2014; Lysaght et al., 2018; Smith, 2021). As Farmer, Roy, and Mandiberg (this book) note, social enterprises are valuable in the sense that they can provide meaningful work, some income, and valuable experience, but they also offer wider benefits that can be conceptualised in terms of wellbeing (e.g. feelings of improved self-worth and confidence, opportunities for social integration and connectedness, security, and support). More broadly, such enterprises demonstrate what anti-oppressive and inclusive workplaces can look like (Kalef et al., 2014).

At the same time, social enterprises confront several challenges. First, many social enterprises for disabled persons eschew a therapy-centred sheltered workshop model in favour of meaningful work opportunities (Lysaght et al., 2018; Smith, 2021). However, disability-specific enterprises might also be understood as separate or segregated work environments that do little to challenge broader exclusions from mainstream social and economic settings (Bates-Harris, 2012; Hemphill & Kulik, 2017). For this reason, it is important to think carefully about the kinds of social or relational settings that enterprises constitute, and the encounters that might be facilitated or constrained within these relational settings. Where enterprises make possible meaningful workplace interactions between disabled and non-disabled people (as co-workers, customers, etc.), there may be potential to disrupt the oppressive structure of attitudes and beliefs about disability (Wilton & Evans, 2016), and to enhance wellbeing through 'integration into a rich network of social associations' (Fleuret & Atkinson, 2007, p. 113).

Second, social enterprises are themselves often vulnerable to broader pressures from both the state and market economy. Organisations must often determine whether to risk dependency on donations and income from the goods and services produced or whether to rely partially on state funding. Financial independence allows for more flexibility around how work will be performed, who is eligible to work or volunteer, and what are expected levels of productivity (Smith, 2021). State funding may offer financial stability but can also lead to new challenges (such as timely reporting, statistics collection, and reapplication processes) that can take time away from the original social mission of the enterprise (Lysaght et al., 2018; Parr, 2000). Creeping professionalisation driven by state expectations may also be an unwelcome intrusion felt by participants in the enterprise and can create discomfort (Parr, 2000). Funder requirements could result in excluding those with severe disabilities who cannot perform according to the required pace, schedule, or intensity (Lysaght et al., 2018). How organisations navigate these tensions holds implications for the kinds of relational settings they can create and sustain.

Conceptual Framework

Diverse Economies

In this chapter, we use the work of feminist economic geographers J. K. Gibson-Graham to conceptualise the position of social enterprises in relation to the mainstream capitalist economy (Gibson-Graham, 2006). Gibson-Graham's work challenges the notion that the economy is a monolithic and homogeneously capitalist system. They advance this argument by highlighting the diverse non- and anti-capitalist economic activities that take place all around us. Examples include activities such as donating, bartering, 'free-cycling,' volunteerism, social enterprises, cooperatives, and resource sharing (Gibson-Graham et al., 2013).

Gibson-Graham et al. refer to these activities collectively as community-based alternative economies or diverse economies, showcasing valuable examples of dissent and a reimagining of the economic system. Gibson-Graham et al. argue that community-based economic endeavours can create empowering places for participants to address local issues and utilise ethical decision-making. Unlike conventional capitalism, diversifying economic activities can foster resilient people and environments with dividends potentially paid to future generations.

As part of this framework and of particular relevance to our analysis, Gibson-Graham directs attention to diverse forms of paid and unpaid work. They count people engaged in all types of productive activities as true participants in the economy (Gibson-Graham, 2006; Gibson-Graham et al., 2013). While not specifically concerned with disability, they recognise the inclusion of differences reflective of the community as essential to place-based community development (Gibson-Graham, 2006; Gibson-Graham et al., 2013). Moreover, they understand communities as heterogeneous and requiring a diversity of economic forms and participants to create sustainable, resilient, and productive economies. This emphasis on tailoring diverse productive activities to the unique capacities and qualities of a given community resonates with a focus on inclusive and accommodating workplaces for disabled persons. It fore-grounds place-based strategies that invite all members of a community to contribute their talents and time in flexible ways, embracing varying needs and ways of working. In this chapter, we are interested in how one site within the diverse economies—541 Eatery and Exchange—works to challenge the devaluing of disabled people's capacity for productive work, while at the same time fostering social inclusion and wellbeing.

Methodology

Research Context

Established in 2014, the 541 Eatery and Exchange is a social enterprise café located at 541 Barton Street East in the Barton Village neighbour-hood of Hamilton, Ontario. Housed in what was originally the Bank of British North America, the original façade and 'authentic' interior features of the building, coupled with its high-quality menu items, give the café a feeling akin to the pricey hipster coffee shops found in more affluent parts of the city. Inside, the space is divided into front of the house for customers facing out onto Barton and back of house containing the main kitchen space, break room, and small office. Like many social enterprises, 541 relies on funding from multiple sources. Currently, the café is a program of, and receives partial funding from, a large church in a neighbouring city. The church's financial commitment effectively cov-ers the monthly lease and three staff positions (executive director, youth outreach worker, and volunteer coordinator). The remaining operational costs, including the paid staff positions, are covered through food and beverage sales, periodic grants, fundraising events, and donations.

The founders of the 541 enterprise were deliberate in their choice of location. They were reacting to a citywide analysis of social inequality and neighbourhood health that identified Barton Village as one of Ham-ilton's most economically and socially disadvantaged areas with some of the city's worst health outcomes (Buist et al., 2013). Providing access to affordable healthy food was the priority for the organisation, with explicit emphasis on partnering with their neighbours rather than one-way service delivery. This aim is achieved in part by catering to a socially and economically diverse clientele, with those paying full price helping to subsidise others who cannot. The café uses a 'button jar system' where patrons who cannot afford the full price of a meal can take the cor-responding number of buttons (each button is worth the equivalent to $1.00) to cover the cost of their meal up to $5.00 per day per person. The optional pay-it-forward system creates three ways customers make purchases—to make a donation to the button system while paying full price for their meal, to make use of the button system to cover all or part of the price of their meal, or to neither contribute nor use the button system when paying for their meal.

On a daily basis, there are patrons from Barton Village as well as those who travel a greater distance. Most of the patrons using the button system towards the cost of their meals come from the immediate area either as permanent residents or temporary residents of the homeless shelter a few blocks away. The long queue that forms every morning outside the front doors before the 8 AM opening is largely composed of these two groups. The social atmosphere of the café reflects the diversity of its patrons and staff. For much of the time, the lively atmosphere is sustained by the cheerful banter of workers, conversation amongst patrons, and friendly interaction between workers and customers. Occasionally, loud voices or unusual behaviours draw the attention of customers and workers but are, to borrow from Hester Parr's work (2000), quickly deemed part of the 'unusual norm' characteristic of the café's diverse community of customers and workers. 'Deviant' disruptions to the sense of safety in the café (e.g. violent or aggressive behaviours) are not tolerated, however, resulting in staff asking the patrons involved to either adjust their behaviour or leave.

The café also explicitly aims to welcome a diverse body of paid and voluntary workers from within and beyond the Barton Village neighbourhood. As a result, some volunteers are welcomed that would likely experience exclusion from other workplaces or volunteer opportunities such as teens without work experience, seniors, people with disabilities, people with criminal records, and people without secondary or post-secondary education. On any given shift, there is typically a combination of local volunteers and those from outside the community coming from a range of social and economic realities from marginalisation and homelessness to upper-middle-class privilege. All volunteers are offered a meal in exchange for working a shift regardless of the amount of work completed. Many of the 150 volunteers who help run the café over the course of a year also make use of the button system as café patrons. Within this broad focus on inclusion and diversity, there is an attentiveness to the needs and capacities of disabled people, but this is typically framed in terms of making the café work for everyone rather than as an issue of disability-specific workplace accommodation. As such, the café offers a useful case study to explore the strategies used to create an inclusive work environment for paid and volunteer workers.

Data Collection

The study employed two qualitative research methods—participant observation and in-depth semi-structured interviews to gather data on 541 as a workplace for the period between July 2019 and December 2019. In total, 115 hours were spent conducting participant observation on-site by the first author in the 'front of house' environment, primarily in a serving capacity behind the counter (91 hours over 24 shifts) as well as in the 'back of house' or kitchen area as a dishwasher (24 hours over 8 shifts). Volunteering in both halves of the café allowed for interactions with a variety of workers and customers while attaining a deeper understanding of the demands on the worker that exceeded what an interview alone could provide. Anonymised field notes recorded immediately following the end of each work shift outlined how the day-to-day interactions and operations of 541 foster inclusion in their workplace. To ensure transparency, introductions with each co-worker included explanation of the first author's dual roles (researcher and volunteer). Signage was also displayed with a photo and brief description of the researcher's purpose during their shifts.

Interviews were conducted over the research period including with two paid administrators (the executive director and the volunteer coordinator), four paid managers, and five volunteers. All interviews were audio-recorded with permission of the interviewees, and the audio files were deleted upon the completion of the anonymised transcripts. The purpose of the interviews was to tease out and articulate the reasoning behind observed interactions and behaviours with questions tailored to the interviewee's role and duties. After working alongside paid staff and volunteers, the researcher selected interviewees in an attempt to represent a spectrum of experiences within a manageable sample size (e.g. differences in the amount of history with 541, kinds of abilities and roles, personal background).

Method of Analysis

Analysis began with both authors conducting a preliminary read through of transcripts to determine macro-level codes relating to the character of the workplace and the motivations and experiences of paid staff and volunteers. Once the authors reached consensus, the first author undertook a more detailed coding of transcripts. In what follows, we look first at the strategies used by staff to craft an inclusive workplace. We then turn to consider how this space is experienced by volunteers and with what implications for their wellbeing. Finally, we consider the challenges of sustaining the enterprise.

Analysis

Building an Inclusive Relational Space

In this section, we look specifically at the strategies employed within the café to create an inclusive space for a diverse population of paid and volunteer staff. Staff often described these strategies as simply 'spending time with people' and 'meeting them where they're at.' However, from observations during the research period, there appeared to be three key components to fostering and maintaining inclusion within the café.

Expecting, Welcoming, and Respecting Difference

The first of these entailed an explicit openness to difference, both in terms of identity and in terms of capacity for work. Accommodation of work preferences and abilities was the norm as staff looked for opportunities for new and long-term volunteers. One manager shared the thinking behind this as:

> Any way that people can enter in, we try and make that possible. We try to keep an eye out for those tasks and work where people can participate. We have plenty of room for folks who are not tradition-ally thought of and we want to make spaces for and are inclusive to them. [They] are my joy. Bring those folks in because they're often very capable. You just need to find the right task.

While inclusion of marginalised people was frequently mentioned dur-ing interviews, staff typically did not talk explicitly in terms of disability accommodations. Indeed, paid staff and volunteers often struggled to identify their co-workers using the lens of disability. One of the manag-ers explained:

> There's not a big difference in my mind about working with a volun-teer with a disability and one without because it's always 'do what you feel capable doing' and then have them do that. In my mind it's just kind of all the same. Just what you're comfortable doing is fine.

Only when pushed did respondents describe tasks that a disabled co-worker might struggle with but then would quickly and enthusiastically outline how they worked around this and in what ways the individual contributed as an integral part of the team. The consistent reluctance to identify co-workers by disability speaks to a culture of respect for indi-vidual workers in which disability is incorporated into a broader under-standing of diverse capacities that all people bring to the café.

Worker-Centred Supervision and Support

Closely connected to an openness to difference was a second strategy concerned with supporting people at work. Volunteers are invited to contribute according to their interests, abilities, and preferred sched-ule whenever possible. The volunteer coordinator matches tasks to the person rather than the opposite, which is then fine-tuned with input from staff. This process of volunteer placement and support occurs uniformly for everyone regardless of perceived or stated dis/ability. A manager describes establishing volunteer work expectations the following way:

> You figure out what they're comfortable doing and then work with them that way. It's not like you say, 'This is what is expected of you as a volunteer'. You just meet them where they're at and that's fine.

Staff also recognised the dynamic nature of people's social-emotional states, cognitive load management, and physical abilities. For this reason, expectations about capacity for work and the kinds of support needed could change from week to week or even over the course of a day. During shifts, managers were attuned to volunteers' social-emotional states deciding in the moment when to step in to assist and when to foster independence. Staff described continual adjustments to accommodate their work crew as an expected part of any shift. This was made possible by the use of 'planned redundancy' (having more workers assigned to a shift than was necessary). As one staff member explained:

> We found that a lot of people who struggle with anxiety or depression—we started being more careful about when we schedule those people. So trying to avoid like the lunch rush, or telling them like, 'Hey, like if you start feeling overwhelmed you can just come have your break during the lunch rush and that's okay.' I've found that mood disorder accommodations are fairly simple for us at least. Because we do have other staff and other volunteers, it's okay for someone to take a break whenever they need one.

As tasks arose volunteers were asked if they would like to do said task or perhaps learn how if it was new to them. A conversation-based, democratic approach to the division of labour was used as one manager highlights:

> When bossing people around at the front of house [laughs], I try to phrase everything like a question instead of, 'Hey, this needs to be done.' I'll usually say, 'Would anyone like to do this thing?' Often it's a job that I'm happy to do myself if no one feels up to it. We let volunteers lead because some days, with certain people, we do know that they have health problems or whatever. Some days they're not feeling up to doing much and that's fine.

Caring for Each Other

In addition to specific supports on the job, staff members worked to sustain 541 as a space of care. While staff were particularly alert to local customers in need of support, this concern extended to volunteers and fellow staff members as well. The characteristic of the culture created at 541 is checking in with others. Sharing personal struggles and requests for help were regular occurrences amongst staff and volunteers. Staff reported they are 'very real' with each other which allowed for mutual problem solving like taking on additional shifts to give a staff mate a needed reprieve from the demanding work environment. This openness was also exhibited by volunteers. For example, one volunteer described an allegiance developed over the hours worked together and the comfortable atmosphere in the kitchen workspace where authentic discussion of 'what ails you' can naturally occur. They continued to describe their evolving relationships in this manner:

> I feel like 541 has a very unique space where we do have a lot of downtime and there's a lot of different people here. You meet a lot of different people and you sort of want to keep up with like how's so-and-so doing. Just seeing everyone every single week and this is part of your family, part of your team. So you just go in and see how's this person doing. Are they still doing okay?

When someone needed time off, the response was always an encouragement to take care of oneself. This was described by a volunteer this way:

> You call in and they're like, 'No big deal. Take care of you.' I don't think I've ever called in and they were like, 'Oh man, we really needed you. That sort of sucks.'

If volunteers were repeatedly absent without contacting the café, staff would try to connect to inquire how they were doing and then discuss their level of interest in continuing or adjusting their hours.

This openness to, and acceptance of, the changing needs of the staff and volunteers allowed those capable in the moment to offer support and assistance. Staff reduced the risk of being honest and vulnerable with co-workers by modelling it as common practice. In so doing, they decreased the stigma and judgement individuals may feel in seeking help, replacing this with a humane and collaborative approach to work. This was perhaps the most used and most effective strategy demonstrated to handle the dynamic demands of operating the café while simultaneously ensuring the wellbeing of its workers.

Volunteer Experiences: Inclusion and Wellbeing

In this section, we turn to consider volunteers' experiences of work at 541 and their implications for wellbeing. In approaching the analysis, we are mindful of Fleuret and Atkinson's (2007) contention that spaces conducive to health and wellbeing can be understood in relation to four 'forms of spatial construction' that shape the material, social and affective character of a given site. These include *capability* (opportunities to achieve valued forms of being and doing), *integration* (linked to diverse forms of social connection), *security* (linked to supports and protections from harm), and the *therapeutic* character of a site. These elements surface in many people's accounts of their experiences at 541.

Feeling Seen and Valued

As we demonstrated earlier, 541 explicitly aims to provide meaningful work for a diversity of volunteers with varied needs and capacities. Staff also emphasised the importance of recognising workers' contributions, making people feel seen and known as valued members of the café's community. Volunteers often recalled this individualised attention and recognition. One such recollection was:

> When I started to volunteer I was really blown away by how I was received into it because the managers that were working here really cared for me and what I brought to it, which I thought was something that was so cool.

The importance of being recognised was echoed by a number of volunteers. Many remembered being complimented by a manager for their distinct aptitudes such as conversational ease with customers and speed with kitchen tasks. Volunteers frequently identified their skills and defined their unique role within the team through reference to such feedback. Some described with pride the details of their work and accumulated skills. A disabled volunteer stated, 'It made me feel good that day helping someone out,' as they described assisting a new volunteer that was feeling overwhelmed. Incidences such as this challenge the notion of disabled people being passive recipients of care or services when the same individuals are relied upon and eagerly perform as responsible and supportive co-workers.

In some cases, managers' efforts to value workers' skills led to new capabilities, with confident volunteers stepping up to guide and help new recruits. For example, a speedy dishwasher who mentioned, 'I like when they tell me that I'm the best,' later revealed how confidence in their ability had led them to offer advice to their co-workers. They proudly explained:

> I notice that when I come volunteer I help show other people how to do it. Because I see how they do it and it's like, 'You're doing a great

job but let me show you a couple tips that'll help you get it through quicker.'

During orientations, managers also pointed out which volunteers had a lot of experience and/or expertise with certain jobs at the café and encouraged the newer volunteers to ask experienced volunteers for help. This was another way volunteers were seen and valued as they were openly identified as recommended 'go to' workers for their knowledge and abilities.

A Space of Social Connection

Besides the interaction that took place working side by side, volunteers casually engaged with one another during breaks. Every volunteer was offered a meal in return for working their shift which drew a variety of volunteers to a common area (the break room). The social mix of people interacting throughout the workday in this space was quite diverse resulting in conversations and connections unlikely to spontaneously occur outside the café context. Engaged conversation mates in the break room, including both non-disabled volunteers and those with a wide range of disabilities, chatted as they arrived or left shifts, or during breaks on nearly every shift observed. This casual social engagement over a coffee or meal was an equalising activity, providing the potential for expanded social networks. Due to diversity amongst shift mates, previously unknown resources and experiences were offered to support co-workers who could tap into multiple social networks and bolster resiliency. Over the course of the fieldwork, the first author witnessed some of these interactions build into relationships beyond the café context, with some volunteers reporting that they felt more at home in their community as a result.

A Therapeutic Setting

Many volunteers linked their work at the café directly to benefits for their own physical and mental health. Retirees enjoyed the regular social interaction and chance to productively participate in charitable work. A number of volunteers saw the work they engaged in as addressing inequities in the city, which was reported as fulfilling and aligned with their own sense of moral duty. More broadly, volunteers enjoyed a number of intangibles received in return for their work including social connection, expression of values, new confidence in emerging and mastered skills, and positive self-regard based on their abilities.

Additionally, some volunteers incorporated their volunteer schedule into recovery and treatment plans relating to physical injury, mental ill health, and/or substance misuse. One volunteer related just how difficult days with little to occupy your mind could be while coping with an addiction stating they prefer to come to the café to work:

> to help me stay away from my extracurricular activities, AKA drugs. So I'm hoping that after I do my rehab stint I can come back in more often too, ya know? And that'll help keep me out of trouble and stuff too, right?

Another volunteer outlined the benefit of committing to shifts in order to avoid isolation during periods of acute mental ill health. They added:

> that's why I'm choosing to volunteer because I'm trying to get out there, trying to stay productive, trying to maintain a normal life. . . . Right now it's a lifeline for me.

Sustainability of the Model

While our analysis highlighted the many positives associated with 541's approach, it also drew attention to the challenges of sustaining this social enterprise model at both individual and organisational levels. At an individual level, staff in management positions face challenges in balancing what are effectively two separate jobs. They must manage the café as well as perform a social work role as they care for customers, volunteers, and each other. They perform these tasks in a particularly dynamic environment. One moment they can be engaged in light-hearted banter with customers and then quickly realise their attention is urgently needed by someone in crisis or must intervene in a verbal or physical altercation, or respond to an overdose in the customer bathroom. While much of the time the café is peaceful, the staff are well aware this can—and does—change without warning. One manager recalled being faced with this reality of their new job.

> That was probably the most daunting thing realizing, 'Oh, there are emergency situations that sometimes happen in here and it is on the front of house manager to address that at first.'

Staff members mentioned the need for a professional social worker to join the café's team to relieve some of this burden, but the thin margins and budget constraints made this impossible. Instead, staff cope by relying on each other for support and cultivating relational bonds as one respondent noted:

> I think 541 holds together, albeit beaten up at times, like we're in a season right now of just getting the shit kicked out of us. Burnout.

Fatigue. What I hope for 541 is that the staff continually come back to each other and even deeper into our relationships together because I think that's the strength of it.

Despite the demands on staff, the work performed was deeply meaningful at a personal level. One manager explained:

> Being here and seeing so many different things, like death, and addiction and also being here for good things like recovery and families, it just feels like my community and also my home. I'm not in the place where I would ever think of leaving now.

In terms of 541's ability to retain its workers, it is clear staff are selected partially due to this personal investment in the idea of supporting the café's community members. This fundamental agreement among staff provided some stability in the functioning of the café in a highly unpredictable social environment.

At an organisational level, efforts to maintain the café's social mission guide a number of operational decisions. For example, using a volunteer model, while initially proposed as a cost-cutting measure is not truly efficient from a business perspective. The executive director explained:

> It saves us money, but when we don't get volunteers and we just do things with staff, we're more efficient. But it teaches us to value slowness. It allows us to provide a place for people who wouldn't have employment anywhere.

As with many social enterprises, trade-offs between mandate and economic reality come with financial implications which can also threaten an organisation's long-term sustainability. The choice of inclusion over efficiency was described by one staff member in the following way:

> we're very good at making room for people because being a restaurant is not our first, even primary goal. We're good at it because we're willing to sacrifice things. Like in a bad rush, things like efficiency, or pumping through orders. You know, maybe that will be the death of us really . . . People saying 'You weren't fast enough when I was here at lunch'. That's why I think maybe we're just a signpost for a time and then it may have to end.

It is the fundamental dedication to inclusion and serving its community that makes 541 uniquely able to attract and rally support in the form of donations and volunteers. Conversely, this dedication also threatens its long-term sustainability by its reliance on the funding relationship with its partner church, paying customers, and other donors, which could conceivably change in times of economic uncertainty or recession.

Discussion and Conclusion

As one element of diverse, community-based economies, social enterprises can serve as empowering places, valuing varied forms of work and providing critical social supports. In this chapter, we have been concerned with the ways in which one social enterprise, 541 Eatery and Exchange, has interpreted its social mandate of equity and inclusion to create an enabling work environment for paid staff and volunteer workers. Through our analysis, we have captured the café's material setting and social atmosphere, and we have highlighted the strategies used by staff to build a relational space that is explicitly welcoming to, and valorising of, varying capacities for work. While we recognise the limitations of a single case study, we believe that commonalities between 541 and similar social enterprises mean that our findings about the creation of this relational space, the benefits that accrue to its users, and the challenges involved in sustaining the enterprise will resonate with other like-minded organisations.

In conclusion, we return to the research questions identified at the outset of the chapter concerning disabled people's inclusion and wellbeing in social enterprise settings. With respect to inclusion, we were responding to concerns that while disability-specific social enterprises can serve as important sites of work for disabled people, they may also work against broader objectives of social inclusion and community participation. Our case study offers an interesting alternative in that 541's mission and the day-to-day practices of its staff are not focused on disability *per se*; rather the focus is on creating a space in which all workers are welcomed and in which all contributions to the café are valued. While the café's workforce comprised a significant number of disabled people, the decision to think in terms of the varied capacities and shifting vulnerabilities of all workers (both paid and unpaid) challenges the taken-for-granted boundary between non-disabled and disabled workers—a boundary that underpins the enduring barriers to employment outlined at the outset of this chapter. In this way, 541 offers an important example of how to move beyond a narrow focus on the 'problem' of disability accommodations to engender a caring, and inclusive workplace that honours the contribution each worker brings.

A second and related point concerns the way in which 541 operates as a space of meaningful encounter and relationships among a diverse group of volunteers and paid staff. We are mindful of existing work highlighting the superficial nature of some encounters and the limits of 'tolerance' exhibited by those in positions of privilege (Valentine, 2008; Wiesel et al., 2013; Wilton & Evans, 2016). At the same time, our longitudinal qualitative data did show evidence of sustained interactions and friend-ships, both within and beyond the café. This was connected in important ways to the atmosphere of the enterprise itself. The emphasis on finding work for all allowed diverse volunteers to work together with a common purpose, over time engendering the potential for shared identification across lines of disability and other social difference.

This approach to inclusion has important implications for wellbeing. People's lived experiences of work at 541 demonstrate the ways in which improved wellbeing emerges through multiple 'forms of spatial construc-tion' (Fleuret & Atkinson, 2007, p. 113). In particular, these relate to the recognition and development of workers' capabilities, the opportunities for social integration across lines of difference, and therapeutic effects of meaningful work. Our analysis also provides an effective illustration of Atkinson's (2013, p. 142) contention that wellbeing emerges 'through situated and relational effects that are dependent on the mobilization of resources within different social and spatial contexts.' At 541, these effects rely heavily on the work of paid staff to cultivate a space that supports and enhances subjective wellbeing (see Farmer and Roy, this book). The day-to-day work of building and sustaining such a relational space can be exhausting but personally rewarding for the staff while also requiring continuous and honest communication to ask for and offer the requisite support for such an effort. More broadly, sustaining these well-being effects requires ongoing efforts to negotiate what Gibson-Graham (2006, p. 67) describe as the 'inherited circumstances of difficulty and uncertainty' that confront organisations within the diverse economy.

References

541 Eatery and Exchange, 2015. *541 Eatery and exchange.* [Online] Available at: http://fivefortyone.ca/about-us/ [Accessed 24 June 2020].

Atkinson, S., 2013. Beyond components of wellbeing: The effects of relational and situated assemblage. *Topoi*, 32(2), pp. 137–144.

Bates-Harris, C., 2012. Segregated and exploited: The failure of the disability service system to provide quality work. *Journal of Vocational Rehabilitation*, 36(1), pp. 39–64.

Brewster, S., Duncan, N., Emira, M. & Clifford, A., 2017. Personal sacrifice and corporate cultures: Career progression for disabled staff in higher education. *Disability and Society*, 32(7), pp. 1027–1042.

Buist, S., Johnston, N. & DeLuca, P., 2013. *Code red.* [Online] Available at: https://codered.thespec.io [Accessed 15 April 2020].

Darcy, S., Taylor, T. & Green, J., 2016. 'But I can do the job': Examining dis-ability employment practice through human rights complaint cases. *Disability and Society*, 31(9), pp. 1242–1274.

Evans, J. & Wilton, R., 2019. Well enough to work? Social enterprise employ-ment and the geographies of mental health recovery. *Annals of the American Association of Geographers*, 109(1), pp. 87–103.

Fleuret, S. & Atkinson, S., 2007. Wellbeing, health and geography: A critical review and research agenda. *New Zealand Geographer*, 63(2), pp. 106–118.

Gibson-Graham, J. K., 2006. *A Postcapitalist Politics*. Minneapolis, MN: University of Minnesota Press.

Gibson-Graham, J. K., Cameron, J. & Healy, S., 2013. *Take Back the Economy: An Ethical Guide for Transforming Our Communities*. Minneapolis, MN: University of Minnesota Press.

Hall, E., 2004. Social geographies of learning disability: Narratives of exclusion and inclusion. *Area*, 36(3), pp. 298–306.

Hemphill, E. & Kulik, C. T., 2017. The tyranny of fit: Yet another barrier to mainstream employment for disabled people in sheltered employment. *Social Policy & Administration*, 51(7), pp. 1119–1134.

Kalef, L., Barrera, M. & Heymann, J., 2014. Developing inclusive employment: Lessons from telnor open mind. *Work*, 48, pp. 423–434.

Kim, M. M. & Williams, B. C., 2012. Lived employment experiences of college students and graduates with physical disabilities in the United States. *Disability and Society*, 27(6), pp. 837–852.

Krupa, T., Howell-Moneta, A., Lysaght, R. & Kirsh, B., 2016. Employer perceptions of the employability of workers in a social business. *Psychiatric Rehabilitation Journal*, 39(2), pp. 120–128.

Kuznetsova, Y. & Yalcin, B., 2017. Inclusion of persons with disabilities in mainstream employment: Is it really all about the money? A case study of four large companies in Norway and Sweden. *Disability and Society*, 32(2), pp. 233–253.

Lysaght, R., Krupa, T. & Bouchard, M., 2018. The role of social enterprise in creating work options for people with intellectual and developmental disabilities. *Journal on Developmental Disabilities*, 23(3), pp. 18–30.

Lysaght, R., Petner-Arrey, J., Howell-Moneta, A. & Cobigo, V., 2017. Inclusion through work and productivity for persons with intellectual and developmental disabilities. *Journal of Applied Research in Intellectual Disabilities*, 30(5), pp. 922–935.

Lysaght, R., Townsend, E. & Orser, C. L., 1994. The use of work schedule modification to enhance employment outcomes for persons with severe disability. *The Journal of Rehabilitation*, 60(4), pp. 26–33.

Mandal, R. & Ose, S. O., 2015. Social responsibility at company level and inclusion of disabled persons: The case of norway. *Scandinavian Journal of Disability Research*, 17(2), pp. 167–187.

McColl, M. A., 2019. *Should I say 'disabled person' or 'person with a disability'?* [Online] Available at: https://theconversation.com/should-i-say-disabled-person-or-person-with-a-disability-113618 [Accessed 29 July 2020].

Morris, S., Fawcett, G., Brisebois, L. & Hughes, J., 2018. *Canadian Survey on Disability: A Demographic, Employment and Income Profile of Canadians with Disabilities Aged 15 Years and Over, 2017*. s.l.: Statistics Canada.

Ontario Human Rights Commission, 2016. *Code grounds: Disability*. [Online] Available at: www.ohrc.on.ca/en/code_grounds/disability [Accessed 25 July 2020].

Padkapayeva, K., et al., 2017. Workplace accommodations for persons with physical disabilities: Evidence synthesis of peer-reviewed literature. *Disability and Rehabilitation*, 39(21), pp. 2134–2147.

Parr, H., 2000. Interpreting the 'hidden social geographies' of mental health: Ethnographies of inclusion and exclusion in semi-institutional places. *Health and Place*, 6, pp. 225–237.

Quarter, J., Mook, L. & Armstrong, A., 2018. *Understanding the Social Economy: A Canadian Perspective*. 2nd Edition. Toronto: University of Toronto Press.

Ruhindwa, A., Randall, C. & Cartmel, J., 2016. Exploring the challenges experienced by people with disabilities in the employment sector in Australia: Advocating for inclusive practice—a review of literature. *Journal of Social Inclusion*, 7(1).

Smith, T. S. J., 2021. Therapeutic taskscapes and craft geography: Cultivating well-being and atmospheres of recovery in the workshop. *Social and Cultural Geography*, 22(2), pp. 151–169.

Valentine, G., 2008. Living with difference: Reflections on geographies of encounter. *Progress in Human Geography*, 32(3), pp. 323–337.

Wiesel, I., Bigby, C. & Carling-Jenkins, R., 2013. 'Do you think I'm stupid?': Urban encounters between people with and without intellectual disability. *Urban Studies*, 50(12), pp. 2391–2406.

Wilton, R., 2006. Working at the margins: Disabled people and the growth of precarious employment. In: D. Pothier & R. Devlin, eds. *Critical Disability Theory: Essays in Philosophy, Politics, Policy, and Law*. Vancouver, BC: UBC Press.

Wilton, R. & Evans, J., 2016. Social enterprises as spaces of encounter for mental health consumers. *Area*, 48(2), pp. 236–243.

14 Beyond the State of the Art

Where Do We Go Next on the Topic of Social Enterprise, Health, and Wellbeing?

Michael J. Roy and Jane Farmer

Introduction

In his new novel, published to wide acclaim in the midst of the global COVID-19 pandemic of 2020, the prominent science fiction author Kim Stanley Robinson imagines the work of a new international climate crisis agency dubbed *The Ministry for the Future*. Set in the near future, the agency is established in the immediate aftermath of a catastrophic heatwave in which tens of millions die and is charged with 'defending all living creatures present and future who cannot speak for themselves.' Although clearly a work of speculative fiction, it is notable that he makes a case for organisations in the social economy to play their role in the new world that must emerge, working on the principles of:

> open admission, democratic organization, the sovereignty of labor, the instrumental and subordinate nature of capital, participatory management, payment solidarity, inter-cooperation, social transformation, universality, and education . . . Taken together, if these principles were to be applied seriously everywhere, they would form a political economy entirely different from capitalism as generally practiced. They make a coherent set of axioms that would lead to a new set of laws, practices, goals and results.
>
> (Robinson, 2020: 287–288)

Throughout the book, Robinson taps into a strong tradition of utopian thinking, a tradition that stretches back to the very earliest pioneers of the social enterprise movement, such as the early UK industrialist Robert Owen who is regularly identified as a 'founding father' of co-operation (Banks, 2019). This tradition is carried on today in the work of the social economy community, working to build and maintain a vision and prospect of a better world for people, families, communities, and society, including—most recently—during the COVID-19 pandemic. The sociologist Erik Olin Wright (2012: 1) exhorts us to employ utopian thinking to explore 'emancipatory alternatives to dominant institutions

DOI: 10.4324/9781003125976-14

and social structures' on the basis that 'Many forms of human suffering and many deficits in human flourishing are the result of existing institutions and social structures' and that 'Transforming existing institutions and social structures in the right way has the potential to substantially reduce human suffering and expand the possibilities for human flourishing.' Over the course of this book, we have examined *actually existing* emancipatory alternatives in the form of social enterprises. While we do not claim they are the *only* organisational form that exists specifically designed to improve health and wellbeing, we have seen how social enterprises attempt to do so in a myriad of different, everyday 'extraordinarily ordinary' (Amin, 2009) ways. In this closing chapter, we seek to bring the connections and themes developed across the chapters together to ask: *what have we learned* about social enterprise, health, and wellbeing that we did not know before? And as we close this particular chapter in the development of the field, we reflect on some of the limitations of what we have covered herein, and look towards the future, asking: *where do we go from here?*

What Have We Learned? Connections and Themes Across the Chapters

Theory of Social Enterprise, Wellbeing, and Health

Our first conclusion is that the chapters in this book do tie together in cross-validating a conceptual framework that links social enterprise with wellbeing realisation. Beyond this involves 'going out on a limb' and by extrapolation of what is stated about links between wellbeing and health (Cross et al., 2018); to link social enterprise to health outcomes—while acknowledging there are multiple understandings of health and wellbeing as concepts. The evidence across chapters in this book provides a level of verification as to the processes that unfold to help realise wellbeing, and the evidence is also consistent with previous literature (e.g. Roy et al., 2014). Given this, we draw across the chapters to propose a new, potentially clearer, theory of how social enterprise generates health and wellbeing. To do this, we extend and adapt the previous figure provided by Roy et al. (2014), a version of which was presented in Chapter 1. Further, drawing on Kilpatrick and Emery, Chapter 4 in this book, and evidence from elsewhere (such as Farmer, De Cotta et al., 2020; Kilpatrick et al., 2021), we also suggest a conceptual framework showing how social enterprise and wellbeing operates at interlinked individual and community levels. Figures 14.1 and 14.2 show this.

First, considering individuals and extending on the conceptual model initially developed by Roy et al. (2014), we propose that wellbeing realised is contingent on multiple factors at the *Social Enterprise* level (A)—including various internal organisational characteristics and issues

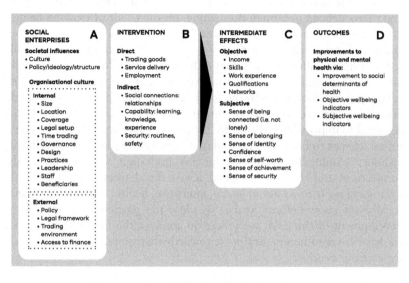

Figure 14.1 Social enterprise, individual wellbeing, and health

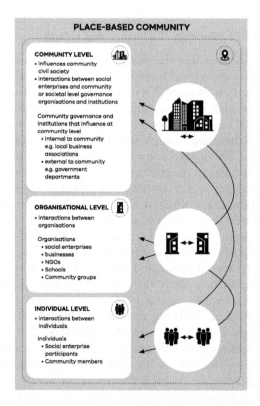

Figure 14.2 Social enterprises and community-level wellbeing

dictated by the external environment. Together, these factors and others (for we do not wish to imply this is a definitive listing) influence an organisational culture for each social enterprise. Some cultural aspects are likely shared across the sector, but others will vary between social enterprises. In Figure 14.1, we depict the culture of the social enterprise as having porous boundaries: the culture will influence its own (re-) production as well as being influenced by changes to social enterprise features. External to the social enterprise is the prevailing societal culture which, we propose, is re-produced via influences including from policy, ideology, tradition, and local structures (an example is how social enterprise 'beneficiaries' perceive benefits from engaging in work—a key attribute valued in late capitalism, which we reflect more upon later in this chapter). Again, we depict societal culture as having porous borders, in recognition of the dialectic that social enterprise as a sector and individually can influence and shape society, as well as society influencing and shaping social enterprise.

Again, following Roy and colleagues' previous work (Roy et al., 2014), the next column (see Figure 14.1) envisages social enterprise as a potential (wellbeing and health) *Intervention* (B). Here, we suggest that *direct* positive effects for individuals come from the provision of useful goods and services and the provision of employment. *Indirect*, and interconnected, positive effects have been shown by studies featuring in multiple chapters of this book (e.g. De Cotta et al., Chapter 2), while these are variously termed, here we broadly categorise them into: Social connection, Capability, and Security, with influence in dimensions relating to both *work* (e.g. development of networks and skills enabling improved access to jobs) and *life* (e.g. development of friends and life skills like gardening, and cooking) (Farmer et al., 2019). These indirect effects are interesting because arguably until recently they have remained largely unacknowledged, at least not explicitly. Perhaps this is because they are challenging to objectively evidence, or because the social enterprise is regularly applied specifically for the outcome of providing jobs, rather than these indirect benefits.

Regarding *Intermediate effects* (C), the advance here is to portray these as more consistent and less fuzzy than previous studies. Certainly, social enterprise beneficiaries gaining income influences a key social determinant of health (albeit we acknowledge the quantity of this income could be problematical). While evidence in this book suggests gains of work experience and skills, there was varying evidence of being able to use these to attain 'mainstream' jobs. Thus, as suggested by findings of Elmes (Chapter 7), positive effects were accrued from these *while a person was working in a social enterprise* to gain or generate them. Effects could alter if the person could not attain a mainstream job or even continued in the same social enterprise role in the longer term as this could simply lead to boredom or frustration. Related to Social connection, Capability and Security (at Column B), intermediate effects of feelings of belonging, identity, and self-worth have long been associated with social connection (Baumeister and Leary, 1995), while capability (life and job capability) is associated with feelings of achievement, self-worth, and competence (Fleuret and Atkinson, 2007). Social connection, Capability, and Security are interconnected and associated with improved self-confidence. Again, though, drawing on Elmes' longitudinal study (Chapter 7), all of these impacts appear contingent on ongoing 'meaningful' (Sayer, 2009) social enterprise work. The idea that wellbeing is not a stable outcome that stays once attained, but rather is processual and fluctuating, aligns with thinking about the relationality of wellbeing (Atkinson, 2013). Findings in this book did not establish whether there are some ongoing residual wellbeing effects—like benefits from life skills attained—that remain even when people stop working at a social enterprise.

The chapters in the book offer little direct evidence of social enterprise having positive effects on what would be commonly accepted as health indicators over the long term. Elmes (Chapter 7) showed positive effects on indicators including the use of health services, but this could be via increases to intermediate effects variables (i.e. Column C in Figure 14.1). That is: health indicators could be subject to the influence of changes to objective wellbeing such as employment, income, and education and/or subjective wellbeing such as feelings of identity and belonging gained via newfound Social connection, Capability, and Security.

We conclude that if social enterprise is to be applied in anticipation of producing wellbeing or health effects (i.e. as a public health 'intervention'), there is evidence to support benefits, but the nature and 'extent' of this is likely contingent on factors in Column A and sustained engagement in social enterprise (or other activity giving similar effects). Figure 14.1 does not take account that there may also be negative impacts of social enterprise and that social enterprise may not benefit everyone; this potential for positivity bias is reflected on later in this chapter.

The work of Kilpatrick and Emery (Chapter 4) can be drawn on to conceptualise how social enterprise can also impact wellbeing at the place-based community level (see Figure 14.2). For the purposes of their study, Kilpatrick and Emery harness social capital theory to show how social enterprises influence community wellbeing via individuals, other organisations, and governance-level institutions. Figure 14.2 can be coupled with Figure 14.1 as a way to conceptualise individual wellbeing plus how social enterprises might influence wellbeing at the community level.

At the level of individual people, Figure 14.2 suggests those engaged in a social enterprise (e.g. staff, beneficiaries, volunteers) contribute to realising wellbeing for themselves and their fellow community members through their interactions with those community members (e.g. individual consumers or employees of organisations with which the social enterprise contracts). This aligns with findings detailed in a previous paper from the same study where Farmer, De Cotta et al. (2020) showed 'spaces of integration' within communities where social enterprise employees interact with other community members.

At the organisational level, social enterprises are part of the 'socio-economic engine' or network of organisations in the community. In relation to wellbeing, they provide opportunities in the community for building social connection, capability, and security. Other organisations will also contribute to these aspects of wellbeing such that social enterprises are organisations that contribute to, for example, the sum of community learning (capability-building) resources and places. Social enterprises help to realise wellbeing at this level by interacting with other organisations to provide products and services that both benefit the community directly and also 'communicate' the value of a social purpose organisational model that harnesses the capabilities of marginalised workers. The result is to help infuse the philosophy that all members of the community have worth into the culture of the community.

Finally, at the community / civil society level, social enterprises interact with community governance organisations such as business associations as well as those beyond the immediate community such as government departments. These interactions are characterised by their capacity to influence the local community milieu via policy or collective decision-making. At this level, again, social enterprises can have influence on community wellbeing through participating in local forums either as individual organisations or as a group. By showing that they can successfully apply funding from government grants to include marginalised people in community life, social enterprises may encourage more government funding to flow into local communities and/or the social enterprise sector, thus influencing how the sector is seen and valued, and its growth. In this way:

> Wellbeing benefits are not automatically generated by having a social enterprise located in a community: it is through the interactions between the social enterprise and the community that the wellbeing benefits arise.
>
> (Kilpatrick and Emery, chapter 4, in this book)

Building from the social capital work of Falk and Kilpatrick (2000) to show how community wellbeing is influenced, as Kilpatrick and Emery do in Chapter 4, emphasises the social connection/ network-building as well as the capability/ skills development elements associated with multiple wellbeing theories. Figure 14.2 suggests that to understand their impact on community wellbeing, social enterprises need to examine the extent to which they create, facilitate, and maintain connections and networks both between and across the different 'levels'.

Of course, the updated frameworks we offer for conceptualising social enterprise, wellbeing, and health are provided for comment, testing, and refinement. We do not suggest these are definitive: rather they are an extension of previously available conceptualisations. We believe that being more definitive provides greater opportunities for understanding and consistently capturing social enterprise impacts, which should be useful for practice. It also facilitates opportunities to promote social enterprise as having the potential to make key social impacts, beyond employment. We note, however, that there are different ways of thinking about wellbeing in chapters in this book, and there are multiple different approaches that can be taken to understanding impacts from social enterprises. The Scottish *CommonHealth* project (see Chapter 10) asked if social enterprise is a form of public health intervention and findings across this book suggest the answer is 'yes, but. . .'

While the conceptualisations presented in the figures could be interpreted as supporting the idea of work as *the* pathway to wellbeing for people experiencing disadvantage, from another perspective, there is a suggestion that it is the activity that provides income, connection, capability, and security (in relation to a place and community) that generates positive wellbeing effects. That is: it is *not necessarily work* (and not remunerative employment) but *meaningful activity* that matters in terms of wellbeing (see Sayer, 2011). Thus, the conceptualisations presented herein potentially open the door to ideas such as Universal Basic Income, enabling people the freedom to participate in creative, artistic, civic, or environmental activity rather than work: that is; different pathways to wellbeing. In a similar fashion, while there is an emphasis in late capitalism that wellbeing is something that individuals should strive to achieve, to build for themselves through their self-directed actions, findings across this book support the idea that wellbeing is realised in composite assemblages that involve *other people*, access to appropriate material structures, and institutions, places, and values (White, 2017). The findings in this book therefore support the commentary of Atkinson (2020): that too much contemporary emphasis is placed on self-acquisition of wellbeing, given it is so strongly affected by interactions between people, community, and structural factors.

Just before we leave these ideas about how wellbeing comes about, it is significant to foreground some key things about social enterprises that appear to make them particularly useful: (1) there is potential to design for wellbeing in social enterprises, including designing materiality and practices; (2) the flexibility of activity(/work) in social enterprises is very significant—people do not have to do one job with the same tasks always, they can grow in and out of tasks or stay with the same ones; (3) timely and plentiful amounts of support in social enterprises is significant—beneficiaries even drew upon support for finding a home and when they were feeling down (see Campbell et al., Chapter 12 and Murray et al., Chapter 10). Linked to this, an emergent recurring theme across the book was the pivotal role of the experiences of social enterprise staff—with questions raised about *their* wellbeing as an issue perhaps insufficiently considered in research and policy. Time and again, chapters emphasised staff as 'good people' who were giving a lot in resource-constrained settings (i.e. the chapters by Munoz, Houtbeckers, Campbell, and colleagues, and Scott & Wilton). Although unexplored in the book, many social enterprise staff are relatively poorly paid and not necessarily collectively organised. These are issues significant to a culture of wellbeing across the social enterprise sector.

New Approaches to Capturing Benefits

A significant theme raised by chapters in this book is that applying novel methodologies, thinking, and techniques has helped to make breakthroughs in knowledge, opening up new possibilities to understand relationships between social enterprise, wellbeing, and health. Principally, this has involved harnessing ideas of relationality and employing data visualisation.

First of all, drawing on spaces of wellbeing theory (Fleuret and Atkinson, 2007) which is premised on relational thinking, and employing qualitative geographical information system (GIS) mapping techniques, De Cotta et al. (Chapter 2 in this book) have been able to show *where* (and *where not*) wellbeing realises in spaces and physical places in social enterprises. By probing into the data underlying their visualisations of social enterprises as spaces of wellbeing, their study enables analysis of *how* social enterprises help to realise wellbeing. The 'making wellbeing tangible' that arises from their study addresses a major challenge around conceptualising wellbeing as an outcome that can be convincingly communicated and compared across situations. The significance of making qualitative concepts tangible has previously been highlighted by Brennan-Horley et al. (2010) in their study of creativity in a city. As we have seen, wellbeing is a notoriously fuzzy concept, and multiple, descriptive depictions using inconsistent terminology have arguably not helped practice or policy to focus on what is most significant to wellbeing. While the work of De Cotta et al. in Chapter 2 helps to explain where and how wellbeing realises, this still does not help social enterprises to measure the 'amounts' of wellbeing they generate. Nonetheless, for the first time, it offers practitioners a way to understand and to literally *show* wellbeing realisation and thus to consider actions that can be taken to optimise opportunities for wellbeing. This approach opens up opportunities for new ways to evaluate social enterprises that take account of the physical spaces and objects, behaviours, and practices that come together (relationally) to influence wellbeing. The work builds on and verifies studies that emphasise the significance of various features of social enterprises that influence their impact such as modes of organisation and governance (Suchowerska et al., 2019).

Beyond helping to analyse the micro-level impacts of social enterprises on individual wellbeing, the application of data visualisation also helps in understanding and conveying the impacts of social enterprise on wellbeing at community and region levels as shown in Kilpatrick and Emery (Chapter 4). Mapping of data can be used to show the geographical reach of social enterprises thus highlighting the scale of social network-building and trading they can stimulate. Such mapping can be used to make visual a role for social enterprises as community spaces significant to social inclusion and cohesion (described by Scott and Wilton in Chapter 13) that can enable marginalised people and those not marginalised to meet in spaces where people experiencing disabilities or social disadvantages are shown as capable and providing worthy, sometimes uniquely valuable, goods and services.

Highlighting relationships between social enterprise and place identity, in Chapter 9, Munoz discusses how a rural environment influences the nature of the social enterprises that form there. Drawing on the idea of an enterprise as a space where 'emotional place attachment' (Kibler et al., 2015) can be encouraged leads us to the idea that the social enterprise can be conceptualised (and thus studied) as a form of place-based 'therapeutic assemblage' (Foley, 2011) in which social relationships are foregrounded. Related to this theme, the chapter by Munoz responds clearly to the challenge she laid down a decade ago regarding bringing geographical approaches to bear on social enterprise scholarship (Muñoz, 2010). Her chapter raises implications about the importance of place (Farmer, Kamstra et al., 2020): of identity, and closeness to, or relationship with, place as a factor of wellbeing (viz. Wiseman and Brasher, 2008). Through employing spatial thinking, she suggests that rural social enterprises generate kinds of wellbeing that occur not only within the specific spaces of service provision but have important 'spillover effects' that are able to be carried over into the homes and 'everyday' public spaces to which they are connected. Until now, this is a phenomenon that has rarely been empirically observed or explored.

Societal Wellbeing and Social Enterprise: Transformation or Incremental Change?

Given the radical interdisciplinarity both within and across chapters in this book, it is no surprise that we see different paradigmatic approaches being brought to bear. Very simplistically, these approaches can be divided into two distinct categories: one that foregrounds 'diverse economies' thinking with *transformational* aspirations for society and a holistic approach to wellbeing either explicitly or implicitly (the chapters by Houtbeckers, McKinnon, and Kennedy, and Scott and Wilton, for example); and another that adopts a more *incremental* and transactional approach that foregrounds wellbeing components and levels, potentially to satisfy the desire for measurement within neoliberal systems (the chapters by Farmer et al. and Krupa et al., for instance). It could be said that these approaches reflect the different approaches to social enterprise that we are familiar with in the broader literature too, which is often shaped along disciplinary lines. There is a broad divide between an approach that seeks to be transformational: critical, implicitly or explicitly antagonistic, and seeks to *challenge* neoliberal capitalism, often represented by sociologists and anthropologists; and a second approach that appears to *accept* and try to 'make the best of' how social enterprise is harnessed within neoliberalism. Within this latter approach, adherents appear to either believe that neoliberalism's harsh effects for certain individuals or groups can readily be mitigated, or that the system itself can be amended, perhaps around the edges and by increments, to become a kinder, 'more acceptable' form of capitalism. This latter perspective seems to be that most regularly adopted by mainstream business management scholars and economists, albeit notable exceptions to this observation can be found all over the place.

Our first example of the transformational approach is the chapter by Houtbeckers (Chapter 3), who attempts to explore the current 'frontiers' of social enterprise thinking and transcend extant understandings of social enterprise, with a view to enabling a transformation to postgrowth societies. She argues that a postgrowth transformation is needed to reverse the commodification of land and nature that is symptomatic of our shift towards a 'market society' (Polanyi, 1947)—or 'a way of life in which market values seep into every aspect of human endeavor . . . a place where social relations are made over in the image of the market' (Sandel, 2012: 1). This shift has proven to be catastrophic to human and non-human life, and Houtbeckers argues that such a context means that we need to consider how interspecies solidarity can be enhanced, including the practice of empathy with non-human species. This is not a marginal issue, she contends, but central to guiding policy aimed at shaping socially- and ecologically-just societies. Houtbeckers suggests that social enterprises have the potential to act as organisations that can help to shape a future economy focused on the maximisation of wellbeing rather than economic growth.

In what might be considered a fringe pursuit until the turn of the millennium, in recent times, we have seen prominent examples of moves in such a direction. Countries such as Ecuador and Bolivia (Tanasescu, 2017) have both reorganised their constitutions guided by a principle that is familiar to scholars and commentators of decolonial emancipatory alternatives to capitalism: *Buen Vivir* (Williford, 2018). Reminiscent of the Aristotelian notion of *Eudaimonia*, *Buen Vivir* roughly translates as 'living well' or 'good living' (Villalba, 2013) and 'describes a way of doing things that is community-centric, ecologically-balanced and culturally-sensitive. A far cry from the market-is-king model of capitalism'

(Balch, 2013: 1). The popular social and solidarity economy movement guided by the principle of *Buen Vivir* is a subject that deserves to be far better known in the global north (although see Eynaud et al., 2019; Giovannini, 2015). Similarly, the idea of living well *together* is a driving premise of McKinnon and Kennedy in Chapter 5, in which they show how social enterprises contribute to a 'community economy of wellbeing.' Drawing on scholarship on community economies (see Community Economies Collective, 2019), particularly the work of Gibson-Graham et al. (2013), both McKinnon and Kennedy and Scott and Wilton (Chapter 13) focus on the diverse forms of enterprise, exchange, and labour that, the argument goes, are key to sustaining communities. Both the chapters argue in different ways about the attention that needs to be focused on forms of economic activity that have the potential not just to enable people to survive but to survive *well*. McKinnon and Kennedy close their chapter with suggesting that wellbeing could potentially be given a more prominent place in the 'ethical coordinates' that inform community economies praxis. We admire the work of critical feminist geographers such as Gibson-Graham (2006, 2008) and the influence that their diverse economies framework has had on social enterprise praxis and postcapitalist thinking. We need to continue to remind ourselves about what sustainable community economies are *for*. The necessity of imagining postgrowth futures, convincingly argued in the chapter by Houtbeckers, would suggest that maximising the wellbeing of people and the planet is an imperative: the end in itself. Viable and sustainable community economies have to be one of the most fundamental building blocks to building such a future.

Turning to the chapters in this book that focus most on identifying and showing wellbeing 'components' and levels of impacts, perhaps these can be viewed as attempting to mitigate the worst effects of neoliberal capitalism by helping policy and practice to find ways to measure the transactional value of social enterprises. Arguably, the stance of 'incrementalists' is that, in order to be sustainable, social enterprises require to: a) be generally popular and acceptable to governments and society; b) access funding from governments, philanthropy, and the public as investors, and as consumers; and so c) in ways, be able to show their role and value as a specific form of beneficial 'intervention.' Researchers from the incrementalist paradigm might argue they seek to change society from the inside out, harnessing policy and terminology favoured by the prevailing policy and practice fields. While they still seek to flip the social order in the direction of structural societal wellbeing over relentless economic growth, they seek to do this *with* policy and practice.

Given the state of public health and environmental damage that we find ourselves in as a global society, it could well be that the transformationalists are 'right': there simply is not the time to take an incremental approach (Vatn, 2020). However, the incrementalists might argue they are providing evidence about practical ways for change to occur. Intellectually, this tension shows a healthy field; practically, however, time may be running out! As noted, utopian versus pragmatist perspectives are strongly mirrored in current discussions about how to mitigate climate damage, with some commentators suggesting that Green New Deal and green recovery plans that work with current economic structures are feasible for pursuing and achieving necessary change, while others state that the stage is now set for disaster and only radical upheaval can save us (Bloomfield and Steward, 2020; Mastini et al., 2021; Stilwell, 2020; Vatn, 2020).

Limitations and Gaps

There are limitations and gaps in what we have covered—either at all or in sufficient depth—which deserve to be foregrounded and acknowledged. Drawing attention to these then suggests scope, encouragement, and inspiration for where work might head in the future. We set out first limitations, then gaps, subsequently.

Positive bias: First of all, the evidence in this book is generally positive about social enterprise impacts. A regular criticism of the social enterprise literature generally, particularly that of the early 'pre-paradigmatic' (Nicholls, 2010) phase, is that too often we see work that is overly focused on the positive aspects of social enterprise, while downplaying or ignoring altogether the negative aspects. On the micro-scale, there are still few studies that probe the downsides of being involved with or working within a social enterprise, particularly in wellbeing terms (although see Elmes, 2019; Kelly et al., 2019). There is similarly little coverage of associations between funding and contractual processes and constraints placed on what social enterprises can do (Diochon and Anderson, 2009; Sunley and Pinch, 2012). Since governments now have a major role in promoting and funding social enterprise start-up and activity, it is likely that social enterprises are constrained to delivering what governments want. Perhaps this is to the detriment of realising greater wellbeing? Part of the issue of positive bias is that much research depends on access to, and partnership with, social enterprises; and second, research requires funding, and this is often from government funders or from the social enterprise sector itself. This tends to make it more challenging to examine or raise negative impacts—although note the work of Elmes, Chapter 7 in this book, who raised negative and neutral effects of social enterprise on wellbeing over time. The point being: it is sometimes difficult to highlight more problematical aspects of social enterprise, so suitable methodology has to be experimented with (such as the mapping, comparative and longitudinal methodologies as used in various chapters in this book). Another issue is the concept of wellbeing itself: as Atkinson (2020) highlights, there is no (generally accepted) opposite of wellbeing or 'unwellbeing' and so going in search of wellbeing is, arguably, inherently a seeking-out of the positive.

WISE and work: We fully acknowledge too that we have focused a *lot* of attention on the Work Integration Social Enterprise (WISE) form, despite making our case from the outset that health and wellbeing realisation could, and likely does, happen in most or even *all* forms of social enterprise. Again, in our defence, this is simply down to the fact that health and wellbeing impacts are easier to study in organisations that have a specific remit to improve social or wellbeing outcomes of specific groups. Given the emergence of WISEs in the transformation of mental health and disability services provision, particularly over the second half of the last century as noted in our opening chapter, it is no surprise that WISEs maintain such prominence. However, we fully acknowledge that more empirical research remains to be undertaken focused on different forms of social enterprise, and particularly in underexplored contexts.

A related limitation concerns the emphasis on work itself, and how multiple chapters in this book reflect how work is viewed and shaped within late capitalism (and also in full recognition that the whole notion of 'wellbeing' is not exactly politically neutral either—see Bache and Reardon, 2016). When everyday political and economic life is shaped and dominated by ideas of individual freedom and self-interest (the 'market society' mentioned previously) it is perhaps no surprise that a 'new political economy of moral worth' (Somers, 2017) has emerged, raising spectres of 'deserving' and 'undeserving' poor, narratives of 'skivers' and 'strivers' (Scott and Masselot, 2018; Shildrick and MacDonald, 2013), and constructions of what citizenship has come to mean and entail (Evans and Wilton, 2019). Indeed, it is in such a context that critics have taken aim at social enterprise itself, dismissing the work they do as merely the embodiment of the neoliberal transformation of welfare (Garrow and Hasenfeld, 2014) or even a 'neoliberal social movement' (Spicer et al., 2019).

Problematically for this argument, there is evidence that work confers multiple benefits (Ivanov et al., 2020); however, as noted earlier, it is some of the peculiarities of work in social enterprises that appear to make it particularly beneficial to *marginalised* people. We are not talking here about 'mainstream work' conferring wellbeing for people experiencing disadvantages, but rather—flexible work that is embedded in holistic support structures. Much of the work of social enterprises is socially and community-focused, underpinned by a moral and social ethos and with a collective nature of the endeavour (see Montgomery et al., 2012). Ultimately, perhaps social enterprise can be understood as a space where—in neoliberalism—it is acceptable to 'be good to people' because it presents a solution for how differently abled people can be supported but that still aligns with the mores of a market society.

Some chapters do invite critique on work as wellbeing. De Cotta et al. (Chapter 2) encourage debates on the wider symbolic understanding of social enterprises in contemporary society, noting that social enterprises are associated with allowing people to claim or reclaim their identity as a worker. Elmes (Chapter 7) highlights that work benefits may be limited to work situations that remain supportive and engaging and where work is experienced as a pathway to development. Overall, as highlighted by Roy and Hackett (2017), we should be wary of critique that conveniently and simplistically overlooks the role and potential of social enterprise to *combat* neoliberal encroachment and its potential to transform society for the better, albeit that much of the current emphasis is on the benefits of work.

Temporality: Another limitation concerns the 'what happens next?' question. The nature of a considerable amount of 'intervention'-type research is that we rarely get to find out if the positive (and/or negative) impacts are sustained over time and what happens to people afterwards. This is a practical question that exposes linked theoretical and methodological issues. Atkinson (2013) and others who take a relational view of wellbeing (e.g. Conradson, 2012) suggest that it is a process and, in quality, dependent on circumstances—which raises challenges for those seeking to measure it (Fleuret and Atkinson, 2007). A gap in longitudinal research is filled by Elmes' chapter in this book (e.g. Elmes, 2019; Chapter 7). The mapping of wellbeing work of De Cotta et al. (Chapter 2) and relational thinking of Munoz (Chapter 9) also highlight the contingent nature of wellbeing—varying by multiple influential features (as highlighted in the figures). However, there are considerable difficulties in undertaking research over time, including remaining in contact with people after they have left a social enterprise, particularly given the precarity experienced by some of the populations with whom social enterprises work. Strategies need to continue to be explored to maximise opportunities to understand what happens with wellbeing over time, and what influences this; for example, incentives to maintain the interest of research subjects, more inclusive research methods and deliberately over-sampling to take account of high attrition (one of the challenges faced by Calò et al., 2019, for example).

Social enterprise and wellbeing in diverse belief systems: Moving to gaps in this book, perhaps most significant is our neglect of Indigenous social enterprise and the global South. We fully recognise that the language of social enterprise used in this book—and the problems the sector exists to address—have been framed, shaped, and dominated by scholarship undertaken using understanding from the global north. Our brief mention of *Buen Vivir* here reminds us that social enterprise models and understandings from the global South and of Indigenous peoples globally are critical to conversations (Eynaud et al., 2019; Peredo and McLean, 2010), not least because these perspectives expose different ways to survive and thrive sustainably, that is without unrelenting economic growth, which regularly happens at the expense of the global south—see Hickel (2021), that can be juxtaposed with capitalism to show it is *not the only way*.

For example, Indigenous understandings of wellbeing offer a quite different lens to those located in the literature from the global north. Australian Aboriginal Peoples consider wellbeing as a social and emotional phenomenon, concerning individuals as part of communities and strongly rooted in relationships with place: 'a multidimensional concept . . . that includes mental health, but which also encompasses domains such as connection to land or "country", culture, spirituality, ancestry, family, and community' (Gee et al., 2014: 57). Wellbeing is described as coming about through guiding principles that appear to strongly resonate with the ethos that drives social enterprise globally (see also Henry et al., 2017; Newth and Woods, 2014; Peredo and McLean, 2010; Tapsell and Woods, 2010; Vazquez-Maguirre and Portales, 2018). Although there is a dearth of research generally about Indigenous social enterprise, there are significant emergent perspectives, for example, around the impact of social enterprise at a community level (e.g. Spencer et al., 2017).

More broadly with respect to diverse perspectives, there is seemingly infinite capacity of people to innovate in contexts where deep necessity really is the mother of invention. In such situations, innovation often occurs despite, or even because of responses to, structural or institutional voids (e.g. in Sub-Saharan Africa—see Littlewood and Holt, 2018; Rivera-Santos et al., 2014) where the state is largely absent. We fully recognise that new avenues for change emerge from fruitful and respectful dialogues between global north and south (dos Santos and Banerjee, 2019; Laville and Eynaud, 2019), and there is a need to create and maintain meaningful spaces for marginalised voices to be heard *on their own terms*. Work that adopts a critical black feminist lens (for example), encourages us to understand how, and whether, social enterprises are *actually* addressing long-standing and deep-seated inequalities:

> For social enterprises to work for racialized people, these socially inclined businesses must be purposefully embedded in the community; otherwise they are only masquerading as agents of social change.
>
> (Hossein, 2020: 2)

In recognising the specific gap around diverse perspectives in this book, we highlight too that these limitations extend more widely to the social enterprise research field, its international leadership, and the funding available in this space. In recognising these gaps, we want to set up the case for future work that could be undertaken in the next generation of scholarship on this topic.

Social enterprise impacts on systems: Although we have given over a fair amount of space in this book to studies that employ novel (to the field) spatial methodologies, there has been little recognition of social enterprises operating as part of a complex adaptive community system with different configurations of actors. That is, although Kilpatrick and Emery (Chapter 4) are able to show the wellbeing impacts of social enterprise within a community, they stop short of showing whether social enterprises impact upon the organisations they contract with or partner with—the extent to which social enterprises 'spread wellbeing' within a community. A social enterprise 'ecosystem' (Hazenberg et al., 2016; Roy and Hazenberg, 2019) comprises micro-, meso-, and macro-level factors and a range of dialectical relationships between the social enterprise and the context in which it exists. They include distinct legal, cultural, socio-economic, policy, political environments, and so on (see Defourny et al., 2020) which are all factors that are highly likely to exert constraints or enable the success of social enterprises in health and wellbeing terms. They are therefore deserving of far closer attention in the future, perhaps through work that utilises some of the innovative spatial modelling techniques we have presented herein.

Social Enterprise, Wellbeing, and Health: What Next?

Boldly, with the caveats of limitations and gaps discussed here, we state that there is now a considerable amount of evidence established about the relationship between social enterprise and wellbeing realisation and, by extension, health. Certainly, there are still considerable challenges to measurement, if that is what is desired or needed (see Chandra et al., 2021), but the book shows that there are multiple novel options for capturing wellbeing impacts. Advancements in data science could present further potential in this respect in the future (Allin and Hand, 2020).

Through multiple chapters in this book, it has been shown that social enterprise can influence individuals' wellbeing and potentially, health; and it can influence community wellbeing. Is the next step, then, societal and planetary wellbeing?

All dials point to the scale and need for immediate attention to an existential crisis: a crisis that involves radical biodiversity loss, climate change with catastrophic impacts and damaging pollution (Vatn, 2020). As a wide range of scholars continue to point out (e.g. Hickel, 2019; Mastini et al., 2021; Vatn, 2020), this crisis arises due to our obsession with economic growth, which is closely linked with social inequality, where inequality is itself a cause of environmental destruction (Hickel, 2017; Raworth, 2017). The current situation of the richest 20 per cent of the world's population receiving 83 per cent of global income, while the poorest 20 per cent get 1 per cent is simply not sustainable (Vatn, 2020). Clearly, to preserve our planet for future generations, we need to create an economic system that thrives without growing, taking us back full circle to where we began this chapter, with calls for bold responses to an existential crisis (albeit from a work of speculative fiction).

Post-pandemic, governments around the world (even centrist and conservative governments) are turning to action plans like the Green New Deal to tackle what has, until recently, appeared as a huge, insurmountably complex problem (Bloomfield and Steward, 2020). Stilwell (2020) highlights that although the conditions for social and economic change are promising right now (i.e. cheap money, high unemployment, and a new accepted role for the state), allowing governments to be innovative, some countries still face barriers. Australia, for example, has long been a resource-dependent, strongly neoliberal nation and so will likely be a laggard when it comes to green recovery. So, as Stilwell (2020) highlights, green social and economic change must be a social movement, albeit one that has organised and strategic political alliances alongside.

There are great opportunities for social enterprise in this space. Not only have we seen that it helps to realise wellbeing, works innovatively in tricky spaces and has inspiring, clever practitioners, and leaders, but it also reaches out into communities with its beneficial activities and social and community orientation. Further, like it or not, social enterprise is an 'adopted child' of neoliberalism: respected as a vehicle for change that is acceptable across the political spectrum, in social and commercial domains and rural and urban locations.

Some social enterprises are already active as environmental businesses, for example, in recycling and environmental rehabilitation, such as the *Remade Network* based in Glasgow, focusing on repair and reuse of IT equipment. Other social enterprises incorporate environmentalism and climate justice into their day-to-day activities. For example, *Streat*, a hospitality WISE working with homeless youth in Melbourne emphasises recycling and sustainability practices in business and communicates to make consumers more informed about green choices (Stewart, 2020). Such work supports the idea of a 'circular economy': environmentally friendly products and practices while maintaining a clear social mission.

The social impacts aside, arguably the biggest national security gaps highlighted by the COVID-19 pandemic have been in the energy and food sectors (see Lindberg et al., 2019), while manufacturing, buildings, and mobility and have been highlighted as key areas central to green change (Bloomfield and Steward, 2020). Can social enterprises move more into these business spaces: helping green recovery to occur, and influencing planetary wellbeing? If directly, this will require moving from traditional easy entry spaces like gardening, cooking, and charity shops; or it might happen through partnerships with corporates to move into new green business endeavours. Collectively as a movement, can social enterprise scale up the kinds of innovation exemplified by *Streat* or the

Remade Network and a raft of others, to embrace and promote green recovery, climate justice, and healing climate damage?

As we pointed out when considering the paradigms in social enterprise and wellbeing research in this book, there is currently an apparent gap between the incremental and the transformational approach to achieving 'more wellbeing.' Clearly, though, both approaches seek a better future. Social enterprise seems to be ideally placed in the moral and practical space necessary to be a prime mover for generating a new green 'wellbeing economy' (Coscieme et al., 2019; Roy, 2021) thus helping a rehabilitated planet to flourish.

In this book, from multiple approaches and perspectives and drawing on novel methodologies and techniques, we have seen how social enterprise helps to realise (health and) wellbeing. In this chapter, we have drawn on this knowledge to present a new model of how social enterprise can impact on individual and community wellbeing, shown how new methodologies and techniques have informed the first wave of thinking and highlighted ways in which different approaches to wellbeing have been brought to bear in social enterprise research. We have called out limitations and gaps—noting there is particular room for a new companion book on diverse perspectives on wellbeing and social enterprise that accounts for global, Indigenous scholarship, postcolonial scholarship, critical perspectives on race, gender, class, and their intersectionality. Finally, we have thrown down the gauntlet to where social enterprise could go next to influence wellbeing at a much bigger, grander, and visionary scale.

References

Allin P and Hand DJ (2020) *From GDP to Sustainable Wellbeing: Changing Statistics Or Changing Lives?* London: Palgrave Macmillan.

Amin A (2009) Extraordinarily Ordinary: Working in the Social Economy. *Social Enterprise Journal* 5(1): 30–49. DOI: 10.1108/17508610910956390.

Atkinson S (2013) Beyond Components of Wellbeing: The Effects of Relational and Situated Assemblage. *Topoi* 32(2): 137–144. DOI: 10.1007/s11245-013-9164-0.

Atkinson S (2020) The Toxic Effects of Subjective Wellbeing and Potential Tonics. *Social Science & Medicine*: 113098. DOI: 10.1016/j.socscimed.2020.113098.

Bache I and Reardon L (2016) *The Politics and Policy of Wellbeing: Understanding the Rise and Significance of a New Agenda*. Cheltenham: Edward Elgar Publishing.

Balch O (2013) Buen Vivir: The Social Philosophy Inspiring Movements in South America. *The Guardian*, 4 February. Available at: www.theguardian.com/sustainable-business/blog/buen-vivir-philosophy-south-america-eduardo-gudynas.

Banks J (2019) Robert Owen Statue Returns to Co-Op Bank HQ. *Co-operative News*, 2 January. Available at: www.thenews.coop/134849/topic/history/robert-owen-statue-returns-co-op-bank-hq/.

Baumeister RF and Leary MR (1995) The Need to Belong: Desire for Interpersonal Attachments as a Fundamental Human Motivation. *Psychological Bulletin* 117(3): 497.

Bloomfield J and Steward F (2020) The Politics of the Green New Deal. *The Political Quarterly* 91(4): 770–779.

Brennan-Horley C, Luckman S, Gibson C, et al. (2010) GIS, Ethnography, and Cultural Research: Putting Maps Back into Ethnographic Mapping. *The Information Society* 26(2): 92–103.

Calò F, Roy MJ, Donaldson C, et al. (2019) Exploring the Contribution of Social Enterprise to Health and Social Care: A Realist Evaluation. *Social Science & Medicine* 222: 154–161. DOI: 10.1016/j.socscimed.2019.01.007.

Chandra Y, Shang L, Roy MJ (2021) Understanding Healthcare Social Enterprises: A New Public Governance Perspective. *Journal of Social Policy*. DOI: https://doi.org/10.1017/S0047279421000222.

Community Economies Collective (2019) Community Economy. In: Antipode Editorial Collective (ed) *Keywords in Radical Geography: Antipode at 50*. John Wiley & Sons, Ltd, pp. 56–63. DOI: 10.1002/9781119558071.ch10.

Conradson D (2012) Wellbeing: Reflections on Geographical Engagements. In: Atkinson S, Fuller S and Painter J (eds) *Wellbeing and Place*. London; New York: Routledge, pp. 15–34.

Coscieme L, Sutton P, Mortensen LF, et al. (2019) Overcoming the Myths of Mainstream Economics to Enable a New Wellbeing Economy. *Sustainability* 11(16): 4374. DOI: 10.3390/su11164374.

Cross MP, Hofschneider L, Grimm M, et al. (2018) Subjective Well-Being and Physical Health. In: Diener ED, Oishi S and Tay L (eds). *Handbook of Wellbeing*. Salt Lake City, Utah: DEF Publishers, pp. 1–19.

Defourny J, Nyssens M and Brolis O (2020) Testing Social Enterprise Models Across the World: Evidence From the "International Comparative Social Enterprise Models (ICSEM) Project". *Nonprofit and Voluntary Sector Quarterly*. DOI: 10.1177/0899764020959470.

Diochon M and Anderson AR (2009) Social Enterprise and Effectiveness: A Process Typology. *Social Enterprise Journal* 5(1): 7–29. DOI: 10.1108/175 08610910956381.

dos Santos LL and Banerjee S (2019) Social Enterprise: Is It Possible to Decolonise This Concept? In: Eynaud P, Laville J-L, dos Santos LL, et al. (eds) *Theory of Social Enterprise and Pluralism: Social Movements, Solidarity Economy, and Global South*. New York; Abingdon: Routledge, pp. 3–17.

Elmes AI (2019) Health Impacts of a WISE: A Longitudinal Study. *Social Enterprise Journal* 15(4): 457–474. DOI: 10.1108/SEJ-12-2018-0082.

Evans J and Wilton R (2019) Well Enough to Work? Social Enterprise Employment and the Geographies of Mental Health Recovery. *Annals of the American Association of Geographers* 109(1): 87–103. DOI: 10.1080/2469 4452.2018.1473753.

Eynaud P, Laville J-L, dos Santos LL, et al. (eds) (2019) *Theory of Social Enterprise and Pluralism: Social Movements, Solidarity Economy, and Global South*. New York; Abingdon: Routledge.

Falk I and Kilpatrick S (2000) What Is Social Capital? A Study of Interaction in a Rural Community. *Sociologia Ruralis* 40(1): 87–110.

Farmer J, De Cotta T, Kamstra P, et al. (2020) Integration and Segregation for Social Enterprise Employees: A Relational Micro-Geography. *Area* 52(1): 176–186.
Farmer J, De Cotta T, Kilpatrick S, et al. (2019) How Work Integration Social Enterprises Help to Realize Capability: A Comparison of Three Australian Settings. *Journal of Social Entrepreneurship.* DOI: 10.1080/19420676.2019.1671481.
Farmer J, Kamstra P, Brennan-Horley C, et al. (2020) Using Micro-Geography to Understand the Realisation of Wellbeing: A Qualitative GIS Study of Three Social Enterprises. *Health & Place.* DOI: 10.1016/j.healthplace.2020.102293.
Fleuret S and Atkinson S (2007) Wellbeing, Health and Geography: A Critical Review and Research Agenda. *New Zealand Geographer* 63(2): 106–118.
Foley R (2011) Performing Health in Place: The Holy Well as a Therapeutic Assemblage. *Health & Place* 17(2). Geographies of Care: 470–479. DOI: 10.1016/j.healthplace.2010.11.014.
Garrow EE and Hasenfeld Y (2014) Social Enterprises as an Embodiment of a Neoliberal Welfare Logic. *American Behavioral Scientist* 58(11): 1475–1493. DOI: 10.1177/0002764214534674.
Gee G, Dudgeon P, Schultz C, et al. (2014) Aboriginal and Torres Strait Islander Social and Emotional Wellbeing. In: Dudgeon P, Milroy H and Walker R (eds) *Working Together: Aboriginal and Torres Strait Islander Mental Health and Wellbeing.* 2nd ed. Canberra: Australian Government, pp. 55–68.
Gibson-Graham JK (2006) *A Postcapitalist Politics.* Minneapolis: University of Minnesota Press.
Gibson-Graham JK (2008) Diverse Economies: Performative Practices for 'Other Worlds'. *Progress in Human Geography* 32(5): 613–632. DOI: 10.1177/0309132508090821.
Gibson-Graham JK, Cameron J and Healy S (2013) *Take Back the Economy: An Ethical Guide for Transforming Our Communities.* Minneapolis, MN: University of Minnesota Press.
Giovannini M (2015) Indigenous Community Enterprises in Chiapas: A Vehicle for Buen Vivir? *Community Development Journal* 50(1). Oxford Academic: 71–87. DOI: 10.1093/cdj/bsu019.
Hazenberg R, Bajwa-Patel M, Mazzei M, et al. (2016) The Role of Institutional and Stakeholder Networks in Shaping Social Enterprise Ecosystems in Europe. *Social Enterprise Journal* 12(3): 302–321. DOI: 10.1108/SEJ-10-2016-0044.
Henry E, Newth J and Spiller C (2017) Emancipatory Indigenous Social Innovation: Shifting Power Through Culture and Technology. *Journal of Management & Organization* 23(6). Cambridge University Press: 786–802. DOI: 10.1017/jmo.2017.64.
Hickel J (2017) *The Divide: A Brief Guide to Global Inequality and Its Solutions.* London: Penguin Random House.
Hickel J (2019) The Contradiction of the Sustainable Development Goals: Growth Versus Ecology on a Finite Planet. *Sustainable Development* 27(5): 873–884. DOI: 10.1002/sd.1947.
Hickel J (2021) The Anti-Colonial Politics of Degrowth. *Political Geography.* DOI: https://doi.org/10.1016/j.polgeo.2021.102404.
Hossein CS (2020) Racialized People, Women, and Social Enterprises: Politicized Economic Solidarity in Toronto. *Feminist Economics.* DOI: https://doi.org/10.1080/13545701.2020.1821078.

Ivanov B, Pfeiffer F and Pohlan L (2020) Do Job Creation Schemes Improve the Social Integration and Well-Being of the Long-Term Unemployed? *Labour Economics.* DOI: https://doi.org/10.1016/j.labeco.2020.101836.

Kelly D, Steiner A, Mazzei M, et al. (2019) Filling a Void? The Role of Social Enterprise in Addressing Social Isolation and Loneliness in Rural Communities. *Journal of Rural Studies* 70: 225–236. DOI: 10.1016/j.jrurstud.2019.01.024.

Kibler E, Fink M, Lang R, et al. (2015) Place Attachment and Social Legitimacy: Revisiting the Sustainable Entrepreneurship Journey. *Journal of Business Venturing Insights* 3: 24–29. DOI: 10.1016/j.jbvi.2015.04.001.

Kilpatrick S, Farmer J, Emery S, De Cotta, T. (2021) Social Enterprises and Regional Cities: Working Together for Mutual Benefit. *Entrepreneurship & Regional Development.*

Laville J-L and Eynaud P (2019) A Cross-Disciplinary and International Perspective About Social Enterprise. In: Eynaud P, Laville J-L, dos Santos LL, et al. (eds) *Theory of Social Enterprise and Pluralism: Social Movements, Solidarity Economy, and Global South.* New York; Abingdon: Routledge, pp. 44–66.

Lindberg R, McCartan J, Stone A, et al. (2019) The Impact of Social Enterprise on Food Insecurity—an Australian Case Study. *Health & Social Care in the Community* 27(4): e355–e366.

Littlewood D and Holt D (2018) Social Entrepreneurship in South Africa Exploring the Influence of Environment. *Business & Society* 57(3): 525–561. DOI: 10.1177/0007650315613293.

Mastini R, Kallis G and Hickel J (2021) A Green New Deal Without Growth? *Ecological Economics* 179: 106832.

Montgomery AW, Dacin PA and Dacin MT (2012) Collective Social Entrepreneurship: Collaboratively Shaping Social Good. *Journal of Business Ethics* 111: 375–388.

Muñoz S-A (2010) Towards a Geographical Research Agenda for Social Enterprise. *Area* 42(3): 302–312. DOI: 10.1111/j.1475-4762.2009.00926.x.

Newth J and Woods C (2014) Resistance to Social Entrepreneurship: How Context Shapes Innovation. *Journal of Social Entrepreneurship* 5(2). Routledge: 192–213. DOI: 10.1080/19420676.2014.889739.

Nicholls A (2010) The Legitimacy of Social Entrepreneurship: Reflexive Isomorphism in a Pre-Paradigmatic Field. *Entrepreneurship Theory and Practice* 34(4): 611–633.

Peredo AM and McLean M (2010) Indigenous Development and the Cultural Captivity of Entrepreneurship. *Business & Society* 52(4): 592–620. DOI: 10.1177/0007650309356201.

Polanyi K (1947) Our Obsolete Market Mentality: Civilization Must Find a New Thought Pattern. *Commentary* 3: 109–117.

Raworth K (2017) *Doughnut Economics: Seven Ways to Think Like a 21st-Century Economist.* London: Chelsea Green Publishing.

Rivera-Santos M, Holt D, Littlewood D, et al. (2014) Social Entrepreneurship in Sub-Saharan Africa. *Academy of Management Perspectives* 29(1). Academy of Management: 72–91. DOI: 10.5465/amp.2013.0128.

Robinson KS (2020) *The Ministry for the Future.* London: Orbit.

Roy MJ (2021) Towards a 'Wellbeing Economy': What Can We Learn from Social Enterprise? In: Gidron B and Domaradzka A (eds) *The New Social and*

Impact Economy: An International Perspective. Nonprofit and Civil Society Studies. Cham: Springer International Publishing, pp. 269–284.

Roy MJ, Donaldson C, Baker R, et al. (2014) The Potential of Social Enterprise to Enhance Health and Well-Being: A Model and Systematic Review. *Social Science & Medicine* 123: 182–193. DOI: 10.1016/j.socscimed.2014.07.031.

Roy MJ and Hackett MT (2017) Polanyi's 'Substantive Approach' to the Economy in Action? Conceptualising Social Enterprise as a Public Health 'Intervention'. *Review of Social Economy* 75(2): 89–111. DOI: 10.1080/0 0346764.2016.1171383.

Roy MJ and Hazenberg R (2019) An Evolutionary Perspective on Social Entrepreneurship 'Ecosystems'. In: De Bruin A and Teasdale S (eds) *A Research Agenda for Social Entrepreneurship*. Cheltenham: Edward Elgar Publishing Ltd, pp. 13–22.

Sandel MJ (2012) What Isn't for Sale? Available at: www.theatlantic.com/ magazine/archive/2012/04/what-isnt-for-sale/308902/.

Sayer A (2009) Contributive Justice and Meaningful Work. *Res Publica* 15(1): 1–16. DOI: 10.1007/s11158-008-9077-8.

Sayer A (2011) *Why Things Matter to People: Social Science, Values and Ethical Life*. Cambridge: Cambridge University Press.

Scott K and Masselot A (2018) Skivers, Strivers and Thrivers: The Shift from Welfare to Wellbeing in New Zealand and the United Kingdom. In: Bache I and Scott K (eds) *The Politics of Wellbeing: Theory, Policy and Practice*. Wellbeing in Politics and Policy. Cham: Springer International Publishing, pp. 253–277.

Shildrick T and MacDonald R (2013) Poverty Talk: How People Experiencing Poverty Deny Their Poverty and Why They Blame 'The Poor'. *The Sociological Review* 61(2): 285–303. DOI: 10.1111/1467-954X.12018.

Somers MR (2017) How Grandpa Became a Welfare Queen: Social Insurance, the Economisation of Citizenship and a New Political Economy of Moral Worth. In: Mackert J and Turner BS (eds) *The Transformation of Citizenship, Volume 1: Political Economy*. Abingdon, Oxon: Taylor & Francis, pp. 76–98.

Spencer R, Brueckner M, Wise G, et al. (2017) Capacity Development and Indigenous Social Enterprise: The Case of the Rirratjingu Clan in Northeast Arnhem Land. *Journal of Management & Organization* 23(6): 839–856. DOI: 10.1017/jmo.2017.74.

Spicer J, Kay T and Ganz M (2019) Social Entrepreneurship as Field Encroachment: How a Neoliberal Social Movement Constructed a New Field. *Socio-Economic Review* 17(1): 195–227. DOI: 10.1093/ser/mwz014.

Stewart C (2020) Remade Network from Govanhill Delivers First Batch of Free Computers to Springburn Groups. *Evening Times*, 11 December. Glasgow. Available at: www.glasgowtimes.co.uk/news/18936505.remade-network-govanhill-delivers-first-batch-free-computers-springburn-groups/.

Stilwell F (2020) 'Snap Back' or 'Press on': From the Current Crisis to a Green New Deal? *Journal of Australian Political Economy, The* (85): 219.

Suchowerska R, Barraket J, Qian J, et al. (2019) An Organizational Approach to Understanding How Social Enterprises Address Health Inequities: A Scoping Review. *Journal of Social Entrepreneurship*: 1–25. DOI: 10.1080/194 20676.2019.1640771.

Sunley P and Pinch S (2012) Financing Social Enterprise: Social Bricolage or Evolutionary Entrepreneurialism? *Social Enterprise Journal* 8(2): 108–122.

Tanasescu M (2017) When a River Is a Person: From Ecuador to New Zealand, Nature Gets Its Day in Court. *The Conversation*, 19 June. Available at: http://theconversation.com/when-a-river-is-a-person-from-ecuador-to-new-zealand-nature-gets-its-day-in-court-79278.

Tapsell P and Woods C (2010) Social Entrepreneurship and Innovation: Self-Organization in an Indigenous Context. *Entrepreneurship & Regional Development* 22(6): 535–556. DOI: 10.1080/08985626.2010.488403.

Vatn A (2020) Institutions for Sustainability—Towards an Expanded Research Program for Ecological Economics. *Ecological Economics* 168. DOI: https://doi.org/10.1016/j.ecolecon.2019.106507.

Vazquez-Maguirre M and Portales L (2018) Profits and Purpose: Organizational Tensions in Indigenous Social Enterprises. *Intangible Capital* 14(4): 604–618. DOI: 10.3926/ic.1208.

Villalba U (2013) Buen Vivir vs Development: A Paradigm Shift in the Andes? *Third World Quarterly* 34(8): 1427–1442. DOI: 10.1080/01436597.2013.831594.

White SC (2017) Relational Wellbeing: Re-Centring the Politics of Happiness, Policy and the Self. *Policy & Politics* 45(2): 121–136.

Williford B (2018) Buen Vivir as Policy: Challenging Neoliberalism or Consolidating State Power in Ecuador. *Journal of World-Systems Research* 24(1): 96–122.

Wiseman J and Brasher K (2008) Community Wellbeing in an Unwell World: Trends, Challenges, and Possibilities. *Journal of Public Health Policy* 29(3): 353–366. DOI: 10.1057/jphp.2008.16.

Wright EO (2012) Transforming Capitalism through Real Utopias. *American Sociological Review* XX(X): 1–25.

Index

Note: Page numbers in *italics* indicate figures; page numbers in **bold** indicate tables.

Aberdeen Foyer project 198–199
Accessibility for Ontarians with
    Disabilities Act (AODA) 251
accessible informality, social
    enterprise 198
Aristotle 11, 277
AssistAll social enterprise 69, 70, 90;
    3D wellbeing topographies *114,
    115*; aspects helping wellbeing 30,
    32; celebration 78; city identity,
    reputation and social inclusion
    78–80; community wellbeing
    96–97; interactions amongst
    diverse populations 75; material
    wellbeing 93; mental mapping 110;
    occupational wellbeing 93; physical
    wellbeing 98–99; social capital map
    72, 73; social wellbeing 95; spider
    map of bridging networks *124*
Atkinson, Sarah: aspects of wellbeing
    111, 259–260, 265; community
    wellbeing 68, 274; concept of
    wellbeing 279; relational view of
    wellbeing 281; spaces of wellbeing
    framework 12, 107; understanding
    wellbeing 11–12, 28; wellbeing as
    components 44; wellbeing theory 29
Australia: *Improving Health Equity
    of Young People* program 15;
    *Mapping the impact of social
    enterprise on regional city
    disadvantage* 15, 67; opportunity
    shop (op-shop) 5; social enterprise
    differing between states 3; Victoria
    and New South Wales (NSW) 210,
    234; *see also* health equities

Australian Disability Discrimination
    Act 137
Australian Research Council 15, 230

Barraket, Jo 15
Better Life Index 10
Black Report, Thatcher Government
    193
Blair, Tony 3
Brennan-Horley, Chris 15
Buen Vivir 277–278, 281
Bureau of Labor Statistics 146
burnout: definition 232; emotional
    labour and 245

café '541 Eatery and Exchange':
    caring for each other 258–259;
    experiences at 265; founders of
    254; goal of 255, 264; model of
    262–264; social enterprise café
    254; supervision and support
    of 257–258; volunteering at
    256, 259–262; *see also* inclusive
    workplace for disabled people
Cambodia, social enterprises 213
Cameron, Jenny 85, 88
Canada: café '541 Eatery and
    Exchange' 254–255; Cleaning
    Business and consumer-survivor
    movement 162–164; Mental Health
    Commission of Canada 147;
    social enterprise differing between
    provinces 3; Umbrella Organisation
    of 161–162; *see also* inclusive
    workplace for disabled people
Canadian Survey on Disability 250

care work: benefits of WISE (work
integration social enterprise) for
participants 231–233; boundary
spanning in 244–246; bridging
personal and professional
241–243; case studies 234;
changing requirements and
policies of providers 242–243;
coding framework 235; demands,
mobilisation and experience of 233;
emotional labour 231, 232–233;
enabling autonomous work 237;
infusing care into capability-
building 235–239; methods of
233–235; outdoor and garden
spaces 237–238; participant
boredom with 238; personal
relationship experiences 238;
practitioner as support, mentor
and coach 239–241; practitioners
230; research projects 234; rotating
rostering system in 238–239;
supporting participants 241–242
Catering social enterprise 30, 69, 90;
3D wellbeing topographies *114*,
115; aspects helping wellbeing
30, **32**; community wellbeing
96–97; incidental spaces 43;
material wellbeing 92; mental
mapping 110; occupational
wellbeing 94; physical wellbeing
98–99; psychological and spiritual
wellbeing 99; social wellbeing
94–95; spaces of support 42
CEiS 192
Centre for Social Impact, Swinburne
University of Technology 15
charity shop, Salvation Army 5
Church of Scotland 196
Cleaning Business, consumer-survivor
movement 162–164
Commission on the Measurement of
Economic Performance and Social
Progress 10
CommonHealth program 205,
274; Aberdeen Foyer project
198–199; Contemporary Project
194–195; Focus 50+ project
197–198; 'Growth at the Edge'
project 195–196; 'History Project'
193–194; 'Housing through Social
Enterprise' project 199–200;
implications of 204–205; overview

of 192; partnership in attracting
resources 204; 'Passage from India'
project 196–197; pathways to
impact *201*; plausible mechanisms
201, 203–204; Scotland 15,
191–192; sense of purpose *201*,
202; sense of worth 202; spaces and
activities 202
Community Centre social enterprise
69, 90, 97; catering business 90;
employment opportunities 81;
identity, reputation and social
inclusion 78–80; interactions
amongst diverse populations 74–75
community economic development
(CED), serious mental illnesses
151, 156
community economies: community
wellbeing 96–98; interdependence
and reciprocity in 85; material
wellbeing 91–93; methodology
89–91; occupational wellbeing
93–94; physical wellbeing 98–99;
psychological and spiritual
wellbeing 99–100; social enterprise
case studies 86–87; social wellbeing
94–96; sustaining 278; theorising
wellbeing in 87–89; wellbeing at
foundations of 100–102
Community Economies Collective 101
community engagement spaces,
contribution to wellbeing 39, 41
community integration, serious mental
illnesses 156
community sustainability, rural social
enterprise 174
community wellbeing 96–98, 101;
definition of 68
consumer-survivor movement,
Cleaning Business in 162–164
cooperation, Owen as founding father
of 268
COVID-19 1, 61; pandemic 202, 268,
284
Cultivate Christchurch 88–89

degrowth 51; postgrowth
transformation 55
disability-based organisations,
prioritising people over profits 249
disabled people: alternative
employment settings 251–253;
diverse economies 253–254;

mainstream employment and 250–251; social enterprises for 252–253; *see also* inclusive workplace for disabled people

diversity spaces: community wellbeing 80–81; contribution to wellbeing 39, 40–41; generating interactions of diverse populations in 74–76

Dombroski, Kelly 88

Donaldson, Cam 15

Duke University 2

Easterlin Paradox 11

Economic and Social Research Council 192

economic growth, gross domestic product (GDP) 54–55

'*economie sociale*' (social economy) 2

'*economie solidaire*' (solidarity economy) 2

EMES (*EMergence d'Enterprise Sociale en Europe*) 2

emotional labour: boundary spanning and 244–245; care work and 246; contact roles in 243–244; demands, mobilisation and experience of 233; literature on 232; negative effects of 245; practitioner work in 232–233; *see also* care work

employment: disabled people and mainstream 250–251; diverse economies 253–254; health and wellbeing 133–135, 136–137, 141–142; income 133, 135; Individual Placement and Support Model (IPS) 148; influencing people's health 129–131; jobs 133; serious mental illnesses and work integration 146–147; social capital 135–136; social enterprises as alternative 251–253; Vanguard Laundry Services methodology 131–132; *see also* inclusive workplace for disabled people; Vanguard Laundry Services; work integration social enterprises (WISEs)

Employment Assistance Plans (EAPs) 92

empowerment, serious mental illnesses 156

entrepreneurs: responsibilisation of 232; *see also* social entrepreneurs

Eudaimonia 277

Fair Foundations 211

Farmer, Jane 15

Farm social enterprise 69, 90; capability 33, 34–35; community wellbeing 96–98; employment and economic opportunities 76–77; food growing hub 79; gardening as mobile business arm of 120; integration and segregation 116–118; integration vs. segregation at *117*; interactions amongst diverse populations 75–76; Market Garden 116, *117*; material wellbeing 91–92; mental mapping 110, *111*; occupational wellbeing 93–94; physical wellbeing 99; psychological and spiritual wellbeing 99–100; security 33, 36–37; sketch of workplace activities *111*; skill development spaces 41; social capital map for 71, 73; social inclusion in 81; social integration 33, 35–36; space of diversity 40; spaces of repetition 42; spider map of bonding networks *123*; therapy 33, 38; three-dimensional map of 31, *33*; 3D wellbeing topographies *114*, 115

Finnish Degrowth Movement 52

Fitoussi, Jean-Paul 10

Fleuret, Sebastian 12

flexibility, social enterprise 198

fluidity, social enterprise 198

Focus 50+ project 197–198

Fuqua School of Business, Duke University 2

geographical information systems (GIS) method 27, 29, 108; ArcGIS 115; mapping 108–110; qualitative 109, 125; qualitative mapping techniques 275; training 126

Gibson-Graham, J. K. 85, 87–88, 250, 253

Glasgow Caledonian University 15, 192; Archive Centre 193

Global North 170, 176

global positioning system (GPS) 177

Global South 176

Google Maps 113

Google Maps API 112, 119

Great Financial Crisis of 2008 202

Green New Deal 279

green spaces, contribution to
wellbeing **39**, 40
Gross Domestic Product (GDP)
10–11; maximising wellbeing and
56; social policy changes 54–55

Harvard Business School 2
health: biomedical understandings
of 8–9; capturing benefits of
275–276; definition 8; employment
influencing 129–131; inequities in
210; social determinants of 9, 13,
191, 210–211; social enterprise,
wellbeing and 8–12, 283–285;
social enterprise and 9–10, *10*;
state of the evidence 13–14; work
integration social enterprises
(WISEs) and connection to
147–148; *see also CommonHealth*
program
health equities: case study WISEs
215, **216**; conceptual approach
to 210–212; cultural conditions
of 222; daily living conditions
219–224; diversity of work
activities 223–224; effects of WISEs
on social determinants of health
(SDOH) 215–219; employment
outcomes 221; healthier behaviours
218–219; individual health factors
215, 217–218; intermediating
factors 221; interviewees by case
and participant type 215, **217**; local
employers and 224; methodology of
research 214–215; organisational
features and outcomes 222–224;
political conditions 222; principles
of 210–211; research context 214;
SDOH equity for young people 212,
214–215, 225–227; SDOH equity
frameworks 213; secure housing
220; socioeconomic conditions 222;
theoretical model of organisational
features and *212*; transport access
220; WISE (work integration social
enterprises) 210, 212–214; young
people and 212–214
Healy, Stephen 85, 87–88
Highlands and Islands of Scotland
195; *see also CommonHealth*
program
home care services, rural social
enterprise 174–175

'Housing through social enterprise',
CommonHealth 199–200

*Improving Health Equity of Young
People* (Australian Research
Council and VicHealth) 15
incidental spaces, contribution to
wellbeing **39**, 43
inclusive workplace for disabled people:
building inclusive relational space
256–259, 264; café '541 Eatery and
Exchange' 254–255, 264–265; caring
for others 258–259; data collection
255–256; feeling seen and valued
260–261; method of analysis 256;
methodology 254–256; prioritising
people over profits 249–250; research
context 254–255; space of social
connection 261; sustainability of
model 262–264; therapeutic setting
261–262; volunteer experiences at
259–262; welcoming and respecting
differences 257; wellbeing and 250,
259–262, 265; worker-centred
supervision and support 257–258
income, rural social enterprise
175–176
India, 'Passage from India' project
196–197
Individual Placement and Support
Model (IPS) 148
Industrial Revolution 2
inequities *see* health equities
intervention(s): developing 157–158;
health and wellbeing 191;
implementation and adoption
planning 158–159; public health
145, 164; selection of theories,
methods and strategies 151,
156–157
intervention mapping 164–165;
design 151, 156–157; evaluation
plan 159–160; WISE (work
integration social enterprise)
145–146; WISE applications of
148–160; *see also* serious mental
illnesses (SMIs)

Kilpatrick, Sue 15

learning disabilities: inclusive
workplace for 251; *see also* disabled
people

leverage points: design 53, 54; feedbacks 53, 54; intent 53, 54; parameters 53, 53; social enterprises and 52–54; system characteristics 53, 53–54
livelihoods, social enterprise ensuring 59–61

McKinnon, Katharine 15
Majority World, postgrowth societies 54–55
Mapping the Impact of Social Enterprise on Regional City Disadvantage (Australia) 15, 67; city identity, reputation and social inclusion 78–80; creating economic opportunities 76–78; data collection 69–70; interactions amongst diverse populations 74–76; interviews 73–74; methodology 69–70, 89–91; social capital map for AssistAll 72, 73; social capital map for Farm 71, 73
material wellbeing 91–93
Meadows, Donella 52
Mental Component Summary (MCS) 134
mental health: employment and mental illness 129–131; inclusive workplace for 251; questionnaires for 132; *see also* serious mental illnesses (SMIs)
Mental Health Commission of Canada 147
micro-entrepreneurs, ensuring livelihoods 59–61
Ministry for the Future, The (Robinson) 268
Minnesota Diversified Industries 6
Munoz, Sarah-Anne 15

National Disability Insurance Scheme (NDIS) 95, 234; *see also* care work
National Health Service (NHS) 191
NVivo 90, 111

occupational wellbeing 93–94, 101
Ontario's Human Rights Code 250
opportunity shop (op-shop), Australia 5
Ottawa Charter 202
Owen, Robert 268
Oxford University 2

paid labour, ensuring livelihoods 59–61
Parr, Hester 255
participant(s) 230; benefits of support 239–241; benefits of WISE (work integration social enterprise) for 231–233; boredom with work 238; bridging personal and professional 241–243; disadvantages of 230; making social connections 236–237; personal relationship experiences 238; practitioner as supporter, mentor and coach to 239–241; skills development of 235–238, 246; *see also* care work
'Passage from India' project 196–197
Personal Wellbeing Index (PWI) 135
Personal Wellbeing Index–Adult (PWI-A) 132
Physical Component Summary (PCS) 133–134
physical wellbeing 98–99, 101
Plants as Persons (Hall) 62
positive psychology, movement 11
postgrowth 51
Postgrowth and wellbeing (Büchs and Koch) 55
postgrowth transformation: economic growth and material use 54–55; maximizing wellbeing 50
practitioner(s): assisting participants in skills development 235–238, 246; dealing with participant boredom 238; enabling autonomous work 237; responsibilisation of 232; rotating rostering system for participants 238–239; as supporter, mentor and coach 239–241; supporting and engaging 241–243; supporting development goals 237–238; term 231; *see also* care work
psychological wellbeing 99–100, 101

Queensland Health 134, **134**

RAND SF-36 Health Survey 1.0 132, 133
recovery concept, serious mental illnesses 157
Related-Samples McNemar Change Test 133
Related-Samples Wilcoxon Signed Rank 134

Remade Network 284, 285
repetition spaces, contribution to
wellbeing **39**, 42
Robinson, Kim Stanley 268
Roy, Michael J. 15, 59
rural social enterprise 174–176;
everyday and leisure spaces
179, 182–183; geo-coding 177,
182–183; person-centred approach
178–179; Scotland 170–171;
social entrepreneurship and 184;
as space of wellbeing 176–184;
spaces of wellbeing theory *179*,
181; transport space *179*, 180–182;
type of wellbeing facilitated by *179*,
180–183, 185

Salvation Army, charity shops 5
San Giovanni Hospital, cooperative
business 6
Scotland: Aberdeen Foyer 198–199;
CommonHealth program
15, 191–192; community
business tradition 3; rural social
entrepreneurship as everyday life
171–174; social economy 194;
social enterprise in 7–8, 202; social
enterprise in rural 170–171; *see
also CommonHealth* program
self-employment, social enterprise
ensuring livelihoods 59–60
Self-Reliant Groups (SRGs), 'Passage
from India' project 196–197
self-sufficiency 51
Sen, Amartya 10
SENScot 192
serious mental illnesses (SMIs):
case studies 160–164; Cleaning
Business 162–164; community
economic development (CED) 151,
156; developing the intervention
157–158; empowerment and
community integration 156;
evaluation plan 159–160;
exploitation of people with 150;
implementation and adoption
planning 158–159; intervention
design 151, 156–157; limited
potential for growth and
competence 149; needs assessment/
problem analysis 148–150; patient
identities 149; performance
objectives **152–155**; recovery

concept 157; segregation of people
with 149; specifying objectives for
desired health outcomes 150–151;
Umbrella Organisation 161–162;
work integration and 146–147; *see
also* mental health
skill development spaces, contribution
to wellbeing **39**, 41–42
Skoll Centre, Oxford University 2
SMIs *see* serious mental illnesses
(SMIs)
Snowchange Cooperative, Finnish 62
social business 2
social capital: bonding 70, 71, 72,
81; bridging 70, 71, 72, 73–74, 74,
81–82; definitions of 68; health and
wellbeing concept 68–69; linking 70,
71, 72, 74, 81–82; map for AssistAll
72, 73; map for Farm 71, 73
social economy, principles of
organisations in new world 268
social engineering 54
social enterprise(s) 1; alternative
employment settings 251–253;
ambiguous 58–59; applying
for impact 6–8; aspects helping
wellbeing 29, 30, **32**; AssistAll 30,
32; capturing benefits of 275–276;
collective benefits of 14; community/
civil society level *270*, 273;
conceptual framework of wellbeing
and 269, *270*, 271; in ensuring
livelihoods 59–61; Farm and
Catering 30, **32**; health and 9–10,
10; health and wellbeing 8–12,
283–285; as health treatment 9;
impacting on systems 283; individual
level *270*, 272–273; inequities
in health and education 210;
intermediate effects *270*, 271–272;
intervention *270*, 271; leverage
points analysis 52–54, **53**; as more-
than-capitalist 86; organisational
level *270*, 273; place-based
community *270*, 272–273; positive
bias 279–280; as postgrowth
organisations 50; prioritising people
over profits 249; realising wellbeing
43–45; rise of 1–4; rural 174–176;
societal wellbeing and 276–279;
state of the evidence 13–14; term
3; transcending understanding
of, to maximise wellbeing 59–63;

wellbeing benefits of 67–68; and
wellbeing in diverse belief systems
281–282; *see also* rural social
enterprise
Social Enterprise Scotland 192
social entrepreneurs, practices of
231–232
social entrepreneurship: opportunities
for 170–171; rural, in everyday life
171–174; rural social enterprise
and 184
Social Firms Scotland 192
social inclusion: community events
78–80; community wellbeing
80–82; in economic opportunities
76–78; interactions among diverse
populations 74–76
Social Innovation Research Institute,
Swinburne University of
Technology 15
social procurement 6
social value 16
social wellbeing 94–96, 101
society, wellbeing and social
enterprise 276–279
spaces, fostering wellbeing 27
spaces of wellbeing: across three social
enterprises 38–39; capability 38;
data analysis 31; data collection
30–31; gathering data 110–113;
ideas/themes for 29, 32; identifying
with map of WISE *112*; methods
of 29–30; sampling of 30; sketch
of activities at Farm *111*; social
enterprises 275; social integration
38–39; theory 12, 13, 28, 45, 86;
typology of spaces contributing to
wellbeing 39, 39–43
spatial narrative 116
spiritual wellbeing 99–100, 101
State Government of Victoria
(Australia) Social Enterprise
Strategy 6–7
state of the evidence, social enterprise,
health, and wellbeing 13–14
Stiglitz, Joseph 10
Streat (hospitality WISE) 284
support spaces, contribution to
wellbeing 39, 42

temporality, wellbeing and 281
Thatcher Government, Black Report
by 193

thrift shop, United States 5
transformation, societal wellbeing and
social enterprise 276–279

UK's Medical Research Council
191–192
Umbrella Organisation, negotiating
with mental health agency 161–162
U.S. Postal Service 6

Vanguard Laundry Services:
attrition rates **131**; barriers and
enablers in work environment
137–138; bullying from peers 138;
dissatisfaction of treatment at 138;
evaluation of participants **131**;
health and wellbeing 133–135,
134, 136–137; income and jobs
133; longitudinal case study of
WISE 129; methodology of study
131–132; Personal Wellbeing Index
(PWI) 135; questionnaires for 132
VicHealth 15
Victorian Health Promotion
Foundation, Fair Foundations
framework 211
Voluntary Code of Practice,
Scotland 193

waged labour, ensuring livelihoods
59–61
wellbeing: Australian Aboriginal
Peoples 282; capturing benefits
of 275–276; community 96–98;
concept of 28; conceptual
framework of social enterprise
and 269, *270*, 271; ethnographies
of initiatives maximizing 51–52;
green spaces **39**, 40; incidental
spaces **39**, 43; inclusive workplace
for disabled people 250, 259–262,
265; inequities in 210; interspecies
solidarity in understanding 61–63;
material 91–93; occupational
93–94; at organisational level 102;
physical 98–99; politics of 12;
postgrowth societies maximizing
49–51, 55–57; psychological
99–100; realising social enterprises
43–45; redefinition of 56; rural
social enterprise as space of
176–184; scaling the peaks of
113–115; skill development

spaces **39**, 41–42; social 94–96;
social enterprise, health and 8–12,
283–285; social enterprise and, in
diverse belief systems 281–282;
societal, and social enterprise
276–279; spaces for community
engagement **39**, 41; spaces of 12,
28–29, 275; spaces of diversity
39, 40–41; spaces of repetition
39 42; spaces of support **39**, 42;
spiritual 99–100; state of the
evidence 13–14; term 16; theorising
in community economies 87–89;
transcending understanding of
social enterprise and maximising
59–63; transformation towards
postgrowth societies 54–55; types
facilitated by rural community
transport *179*, 180–183; typology
of spaces contributing to **39**, 39–43;
understanding of 11, 50–51;
work integration social enterprises
(WISEs) and connection to
147–148; *see also CommonHealth*
program; employment; rural social
enterprise; work integration social
enterprises (WISEs)
WEvolution 196
work integration social enterprises
(WISEs): AssistAll 30, **32**; barriers
and enablers in work environment
of 137–138; cartographic stylings
for mapping within 113–118;
Community Centre 90; connection
to health and wellbeing 147–148;
contextual factors influencing effects
of 138–139; delivery journeys *119*;
development of 5; effects over time
140–141; elements of **152–155**;
employment and 129–131;
environmental-level changes
154–155; evaluation of participants
and attrition rates **131**; exploring
work in 6–7; Farm and Catering
30, **32**; Geographic Information
Systems (GIS) 108; growth of 4–6;
health and wellbeing 133–135,
134, 136–137, 141–142; health
equity and young people 212–214;

identifying spaces of wellbeing with
simplified map of *112*; income in
133, 135; individual behavioral
changes **152–153**; integration and
segregation 116–118; intervention
mapping 145–146; jobs in 133;
mapping 125–126; mechanisms
of 139–140; method at Vanguard
Laundry Services 131–132;
off-site work locations *120*;
purpose of mapping in 108–110;
qualitative findings of 135–138;
quantitative findings of 132–135;
sampling of 30; scaling the peaks
of wellbeing 113–115; serious
mental illnesses and 146–147;
social capital of 135–136; social
inclusion in employment 130;
sparking connections in community
119–122; spider maps as social
capital web 122–124, *123*, *124*;
unbounding 118–124; wellbeing at
107; wellbeing benefits of 67; work
and 280–281; *see also* care work;
health equities
workspaces, producing wellbeing 44
World Health Organisation (WHO)
8, 211
Wright, Erik Olin 268

young people: case study WISEs **216**,
234; daily living conditions of
219–224; health (in)equities, WISEs
and 212–214; healthier behaviours
for 218–219; interviewees by
case and participant type **217**;
labour market and health equities
221, 225–227; mental health
improvements 218; secure housing
for 220; social determinants of
health (SDOH) equity for 210,
214–215; transport access 220;
WISE effects on SDOH equity 215,
217–224; *see also* care work; health
equities
Yunus, Muhammad 2
Yunus Centre for Social Business
and Health, Glasgow Caledonian
University 15

Printed in the United States
by Baker & Taylor Publisher Services